ENGLISH LITERATURE

A Critical Survey

BY

THOMAS G. WILLIAMS

Essay Index Reprint Series

BOOKS FOR LIBRARIES PRESS
FREEPORT, NEW YORK

First published in Great Britain in 1951.

Copyright. All rights reserved.

Reprinted 1971 by arrangement with Pitman Publishing.

INTERNATIONAL STANDARD BOOK NUMBER:
0-8369-2034-1

LIBRARY OF CONGRESS CATALOG CARD NUMBER:
74-134160

PRINTED IN THE UNITED STATES OF AMERICA

PREFACE

THE purpose of this book is to outline some of the salient features in the growth of our English literary tradition. As much of literary theory has been included as will furnish one who sets out on a systematic course of reading and criticism with the bare essentials of a technical equipment. The discipline of literature, like every other organized body of knowledge, requires the use of a critical apparatus—a method and a terminology—and an endeavour has been made to supply this.

Every work of literature stands somewhere in a perspective of history. Every writer has exercised his skill in a given historical situation. Consequently, much attention has been paid to the background of authors and their works—to the social, intellectual and moral climate which has influenced creative literary activity. This is not at all to forget that literature exists primarily to be read, and being read, to be loved and cherished for the delight of its unfailing companionship. Yet books are not accidents or "sports" all outside the run of nature; they do not just happen. One can believe this without accepting a determinist view of literary evolution. No amount of abstract generalization about movements, periods, influences and reactions can wholly explain the coming into existence of a work of art. Nevertheless it is equally true that every writer belongs to his age; he is born into a social inheritance and it is in terms of a contemporary culture that he has to express himself. That culture includes language, the raw material of literature, which shapes our thoughts and is shaped by them. It includes also the structural forms, the rhythms, the imagery, which past writers have established as traditional; these constitute the unity which gives meaning to the diversity which every new writer manifests. While, therefore, it is of the first importance that a work of art should become a part of the living experience of the reader, that experience can but be enriched by the placing of the work within a "frame of reference." For the purposes of this book, the frame of reference has been widened to include literary movements in other countries which have had a clear bearing on our own literature.

As to the arrangement of the material: the plan adopted has been to trace out a number of separate lines of development rather than to advance chronologically along the whole front. This has involved a certain amount of repetition, but in a book of this kind it may even be considered to be a merit to deal with—to take an example—the poetry, the drama and the prose of Dryden, in different contexts.

It will be found that numerous authors of note and works which have an assured place among the classics of our literature are unmentioned. This could hardly have been otherwise if room was to be found in a short book for some treatment of literary theory and backgrounds. Moreover the inclusion of too much detail would have been at the risk of obscuring the main course of development which it is part of the aim of the book to make clear.

The writer has kept equally in mind the interests of the general reader who is an amateur of letters and of the young professed student of literature. In our days these interests are not widely different. Thanks to such agencies as the B.B.C. programmes and the organs of Adult Education, an acquaintance with the English classics is becoming as much a part of popular culture as their study is an academic pursuit which has to a considerable extent displaced the discipline of the ancient classics. It is hoped that the book will be useful for advanced groups in the Secondary Schools, for young undergraduates, for trainees in Teachers' Training Colleges, and for those who are working for diplomas at the Schools and Colleges of Speech, Drama and Music. In addition there are the many students in Literary Institutes, in University Tutorial, Diploma and Extension classes, and the readers of the numerous cheap reprints of the classics, who may find here some help in bringing their special studies into relation with the broad movements of our literature.

I have to acknowledge with gratitude the substantial help and advice given to me by Miss H. M. McCrae. My thanks are also due to my wife for typing the manuscript.

For permission to quote from copyright works, I express my indebtedness to the following: Messrs.Wm. Blackwood & Sons, Ltd. —Saintsbury's *History of Criticism*; Messrs. Gerald Duckworth & Co., Ltd.—G. K. Chesterton's *William Blake*; Mr. T. S. Eliot and Messrs. Faber & Faber, Ltd.—*Portrait of a Lady, Ash Wednesday*, and *Tradition and the Individual Talent*; Mr. Philip Gosse—Sir Edmund Gosse's *Modern English Literature*; the trustees of the Hardy Estate and Messrs. Macmillan & Co., Ltd.—Hardy's *The Dynasts*; Professor Gilbert Murray—*Classical Tradition in Poetry*; Messrs. Routledge and Kegan Paul & Co., Ltd.—Edward Dowden's *Shakespeare, His Mind and Art*.

T. G. W.

CONTENTS

CHAPTER I

LITERATURE AS AN ART

WHENEVER anyone in speech or writing is concerned not only to say a thing, but to say it well and memorably, he is engaged in a literary enterprise. He is, to a greater or lesser extent, exercising an art, the art of letters. Rarely, in effect, does a writer succeed in achieving so memorable an utterance that the world will not willingly let it be forgotten; but when this is achieved, the words belong to literature: the record of "the best that is known and thought in the world," as Matthew Arnold defined it in his *Essays in Criticism*.

It is by no means true that all our literature has come to us because writers have applied themselves of set purpose to create it. Much of it has come into existence, unbidden and unsuspected, because men and women of natural refinement and quick sensibility have wished to record their thoughts and experiences. They have enjoyed writing for its own sake; they have found pleasure in communicating ideas, in expressing emotions and situations, whether real or imaginary, and in recalling the things that have come into their lives and shaped their personalities. A writer is often more intent on interpreting himself to himself than on revealing himself to others. Pepys' *Diary* was so private in intention that it was written in a cypher of his own invention, with the consequence that the world remained ignorant of the existence of a unique treasure until the manuscript was deciphered more than a century later. A further example out of very many that could be cited is the poetry of Gerard Manley Hopkins, none of whose poems was published in his lifetime. Writing may thus be an activity of genius, carried on with no idea of a possible future reader sharing the author's private thoughts and feelings. It may well be a mode of self-discovery and an avenue to self-fulfilment.

While there are these modest, fastidious writers and thinkers who look inwards for their satisfactions, there is no gainsaying the fact that for the most part writing, as much as speech, implies a public which is to be entertained, instructed or persuaded. It is a primary function of the writer, therefore, to make himself understood. Communication is of the essence of the matter. The speaker who talks inaudibly, the writer whose words carry no coherent meaning to another mind, might as well have remained silent or not taken up his pen. It may indeed be said that until there has resulted some reaction between the mind and mood of the creator of a work of art and those of another person, it is impossible to say whether in fact a work of art is in question at all, for it is precisely in this quality of being able to kindle the thought and emotion of the beholder with a portion of the divine fire which inspired the creator that the essence of the work consists. "The meaning of any beautiful created thing," said Oscar Wilde, "is as much in the soul of him who looks at it, as it was in his soul who wrought it. Nay, it is rather the beholder who lends to the beautiful thing its myriad meanings and makes it marvellous for us."

So it is with literature. The hearer or the reader has something of his own to contribute. As with every other art there has to be a two-way transaction, converging from the artist and the art lover upon the work of art. This must be capable of stimulating creative activity in the observer, just as it itself arose out of the creative activity of the artist. Unless we go half-way to meet the author's mood and intention, we shall not derive the fullest value out of literature.

Literature and Language

The raw material of language consists of words—their meanings, their sounds, their associations and their power of entering into syntactical relationships, whereby developed thought is made possible. When this raw material has been worked into patterns of sound and meaning, capable of providing us with aesthetic enjoyment, then we have literature. The art of literature consists therefore in the use of language to communicate from one mind to another experiences which to the originating mind are significant. The significance may be in the experience itself, that is, in the details of the actual happening, or in the effects which it produced in the mind of him to whom it happened. These two things we usually distinguish as the objective and the subjective, the matter and the manner, or the "what" and the "how."

Language can do no more than represent experience symbolically. In the sequence of sound-waves set up by the spoken utterance of a word such as "rain," or in the pattern of the light-waves set up by the making of black marks on white paper to represent these sounds, there is nothing even remotely resembling either the physical fact of a downpour, or any of the emotional states of mind to which this may give rise. Yet language may act upon thought and feeling in such a way that the mind is made more perceptive by the imaginative experience than it would be by one that was real. This is because language contains within itself certain powers of stimulating the imagination. The individual word is thus endowed with potency, but there is a still higher potency in words organized in syntactical and rhythmical patterns to serve the purposes of our daily intercourse. Even this is not the highest expression of the symbolical quality of language, for above it again there is the more massive unity and depth given to experience by such literary forms as the epic, the drama and the novel which provide imaginative reconstructions of experience of the greatest complexity.

Since language is supreme among the faculties with which humanity is endowed, not only answering the necessities of mere survival but also serving the delights and consolations of "divine philosophy," it could perhaps be argued that literature, or the art of using language to apprehend experience imaginatively, and to give pleasure by communicating it, is supreme among the arts. The study of literature embracing

> All thoughts, all passions, all delights,
> Whatever stirs this mortal frame,

is as wide and as complex as the study of life itself, and nothing which life offers lies outside its scope. As men value life variously, some asking of it one thing, some another, so literature may be approached from many angles and used for many ends.

Literature as the Vehicle of Tradition

In its traditional forms, literature has brought down to us the thoughts and emotions which animated the souls of our ancestors. These are the influences which have more than all else contributed to create the mental climate in which we have been nurtured. We cannot escape their influence even if we would. The very language we use in our daily intercourse is impregnated with the associations which words and phrases acquired when they became the symbols of the imaginative experience of the great writers. Our very opinions take colour from the words we use to express them. Literature is the most vital element in our social heritage.

Literature as an Aid to Living

Furthermore, literature is a vast treasury from which we can obtain the materials we require for the building up of our intellectual and moral knowledge. It supplies us with standards of comparison in all matters that are concerned with the art of living. We learn therein what countless men of wisdom and genius have made of life. Their writings provide us with both an enlargement of experience and an interpretation of life. In this respect literature helps us in the business of living much as history does. Both are "great storehouses of ends," that is to say, of speculations regarding the ultimate purposes of human existence. "A good book," wrote Milton in a noble passage, "is the precious life-blood of a master-spirit, embalmed and treasured up on purpose to a life beyond life." Literature is therefore a great dynamic, supplying us with the knowledge, the stimulus and the energy for the individual adventure of living. At the same time, it is the supreme compensator, whereby, in the words of Emerson, "man indemnifies himself for the wrongs of his condition."

Literature Among the Arts

Above all, literature is supreme among the arts which add grace to human existence. Traditionally, the description "Fine Arts" applied only to Architecture, Sculpture, and Painting, all three alike in being plastic and visual. But it is impossible in modern times to relegate literature and music, or even drama and dancing, all of which use symbolic material, to the category of lesser arts, since these are in fact the principal supports of our contemporary culture. Among them literature occupies a central place and is the art which reflects most directly the features of the age, while also reacting upon it most powerfully.

But the fundamental difference between the three arts of Architecture, Sculpture, and Painting on the one hand, and the symbolic arts on the other, is that the exercise of the former results in the production of objects which exist permanently and externally in space, and can be touched and handled and scrutinized from any angle of vision; whereas literature, music, drama and dancing can be understood only in terms of time and sequence, and then only with the assistance of an interpreter, whose personality becomes an element of considerable importance, necessarily interposing itself between the original creative mind and ourselves as listeners or observers. The consideration of such matters as these is the province of Aesthetics; it concerns us here only so far as it suggests the standing of literature among the arts.

We must keep in mind the fact that literature is basically a *speaking* art. It existed as the spoken word long before it was written down.

Many primitive tribes in the world to-day possess literatures, though they have as yet no alphabets and no art of writing. They intone and recite heroic songs and legends which have come down to them by oral tradition. And as oral literature precedes written literature, so poetry precedes prose. The earliest literary productions have always embodied deep feeling, particularly religious feeling, and the emotions evoked by war and by tribal achievements and disasters. The characteristic form of the rhapsody is a rhythmical chant, which in time develops into a metrical arrangement of sounds. This association of early poetry with music is confirmed by the way in which the ancient Greek writers on prosody treated of it as a branch of the art of musical composition.

Literature has in our own day become for the most part a matter of silent reading with the eyes, rather than of utterance requiring the use of the organs of speech. Not a hundredth part of what is now written as literature is ever spoken aloud. It may be that the development of the new techniques of radio transmission and the cinema will bring about important changes in this respect, by calling into existence a literature which, being intended for oral communication, will have a rhythm and structure different from those which are intended for soundless reading.

The Vagaries of Literary Taste

An old Latin proverb runs: *De gustibus non est disputandum* (There can be no arguing about tastes). The same thought is expressed by Browning—

> Now who shall arbitrate?
> Ten men love what I hate,
> Shun what I follow, slight what I receive.
>
> *Rabbi Ben Ezra*

Taste, that is to say, is subjective; good taste is no more than the fashion of the time. As we shall see later, many have arisen to protest against a conception of art which offers so precarious a hold for judgment. If there are no fixed canons and accepted traditions, if every literary opinion is in effect reducible to the bald statement of a personal preference: "I like this," or "I do not like that," or, again, "I prefer this to that," then it becomes clear that no final judgments are possible. The difficulty, moreover, is that no sooner have those who have tried to establish universal standards formulated their objective criteria of excellence on the basis of existing work, than a writer appears who, caring little or nothing for such dogmas, produces something original and wayward which is immediately recognized as having the stamp of genius upon it. Whereupon a reconsideration and a new formulation are called for, albeit with no greater likelihood of survival. "What happens when a new work of art is created," says T. S. Eliot, "is something that happens simultaneously co all works of art which preceded it." The poet Keats, on first looking into Chapman's *Homer*, felt

> like some watcher of the skies
> When a new planet swims into his ken,

and, like the astronomer, was compelled thereby to adjust his values.

The history of the vagaries of literary taste in England is a fascinating study, but it must be sufficient for our present purpose to note that such vagaries do take place and to suggest that speculation as to their causes will often throw a vivid light on the basic principles of artistic expression. It will be found in general that there is in all ages a close relation between the prevailing modes of literature and those of social behaviour, and between both of these and the trends of philosophic thought. It is not difficult to understand why an art which is as closely integrated with life as literature should in its main features body forth the pulse and swing of the social mind. Strong currents of human thought and feeling tend always to give rise to counter-currents. The systole and diastole of the human spirit produce now a respect for order and now a passion for freedom. In one phase the reason is dominant, in the other the emotions. Reverence for tradition, and the expression of corporate life, give way in due course to the appetite for experiment, and the expression of the individual life.

The student of the history of art cannot therefore fail to notice that artistic creative energy expresses itself not like science and technology along a continuous line of development, but in a movement of ebb and flow. He observes that the fluctuations of taste are regulated by two principal forces, the one being, as Walter Pater put it, the principle of liberty, the other the principle of authority. In one epoch the artist is disposed to pay his homage to established modes, and the typical art of the time shows qualities of ordered discipline. At another, the artist is in a mood to question the unknown, to make new trial of his art and to assert his uniqueness as a sentient being. It never happens that either the principle of control or the principle of free-ranging initiative is dominant to the total exclusion of the other; the forces exist side by side, and art is in a permanent state of disequilibrium.

Classicism and Romanticism

"The Classical Tradition," says Professor Gilbert Murray, "implies
. . . that . . . there have been ages and individuals with greater
powers than others. There are works of beauty that stand out above
the ordinary changes of taste and fashion and have approved themselves to be of permanent value. For us the Tradition has flowed
through a fairly clear channel: from Greece through Rome, with a
confluent stream from Israel, through Christianity, with some bright
torrents from the Pagan North, and then, broken into many languages
and local variants, down to modern Europe and America. And on the
whole, in the long history certain achievements stand out as greatest,
and certain characteristics mark the central stream."[1] The classicist is
one who is prepared to give the fullest recognition to these achievements
and to apply their standards of taste to his own work.

The romanticist, on the other hand, while not denying the genius
of the great masters, does not recognize the validity of their standards;
his creative activity obeys a law of its own being. Looking out on the
world of experience the romantic artist directs his gaze not straight
upon the central focus, but obliquely towards the penumbral parts.
Searching into the recesses of his own mind, he finds inchoate sentiments and desires, vague imaginings, incoherent thoughts and transient
glimpses of reality dimly illumined by

> The-light that never was on sea or land.

It is out of such materials that the romanticist fashions his universe.
His intuitions come unbidden, and the process of artistic creation is for
him not one which can be reduced to a formal adherence to rules and
principles. Much of our study of literature resolves itself into an inquiry
into the ways in which these complementary modes of truth come to
expression in poetry and prose.

The Creative Impulse

Writers have always been profoundly interested in all that concerns
the process whereby a poem, a novel, a play or other literary work
comes into existence, and many have given us details of their creative
methods. Though these differ as widely as human beings do, we can
nevertheless discern two principal procedures: the one is the way of
organization and control, with the intellect presiding, when the end is
present in the beginning, and every part falls into its predetermined

[1] *The Classical Tradition in Poetry*, p. 261.

2

place; the other is the way of inspiration, when there is in the writing
an element of automatism. Mary Shelley tells us how the idea of her
novel *Frankenstein* shaped itself in her mind: the process went on
below the level of consciousness, until finally the conception of the
monster, already complete in form and feature, forced itself through
to the surface. Her husband, the poet, in his *Defence of Poetry* describes
as follows his notion of the process of creative activity—

> The mind in creation is as a fading coal, which some invisible influence,
> like an inconstant wind, awakens to transitory brightness; this power
> arises from within, like the colour of a flower which fades and changes
> as it is developed, and the conscious portions of our nature are unprophetic
> either of its approach or its departure. Could this influence be durable in
> its original purity and force, it is impossible to predict the greatness of its
> results; but when composition begins, inspiration is already on the
> decline, and the most glorious poetry that has ever been communicated
> to the world is probably a feeble shadow of the original conception of
> the poet.

Contrast with this the way of the fully conscious artist as described
by Ben Jonson in the following passage from *Timber*—

> To this perfection of nature in our poet we require exercise of those
> parts, *exercitatio*, and frequent. If his wit will not arrive suddenly at the
> dignity of the ancients, let him not yet fall out with it, quarrel, or be over
> hastily angry, offer to turn it away from study in a humour; but come
> to it again upon better cogitation, try another time with labour. If then
> it succeed not, cast not away the quills yet, nor scratch the wainscot, beat
> not the poor desk, but bring all to the forge and file again. . . . There
> is no statute law of the kingdom bids you be a poet against your will
> . . .; if it comes in a year or two, it is well. The common rimers pour
> forth verses, such as they are, *ex tempore*, but there never comes from
> them one sense worth the life of a day. A rimer and a poet are two things.
> It is said of the incomparable Virgil that he brought forth his verses like
> a bear, and after formed them with licking. Scaliger the father writes
> it of him, that he made a quantity of verses in the morning, which afore
> night he reduced to a less number.

Literature as Moral and Spiritual Elevation

Much of the criticism of literature has been concerned with values
which are not strictly literary at all. Literary values rightly considered
are aesthetic values: they arise out of judgments relating to a piece of
writing as a work of art, the materials of the art being words and their
meanings, associated with their sounds in isolation and in relation to
each other, and with the vague overtones and undertones which they
have acquired. When we judge literature on grounds not connected

with the skill with which these materials have been handled, but with questions of ethics, politics or sociology, we are in fact not exercising literary criticism at all, but are making moral or philosophical or other judgments. The following passage, taken from Shelley's *Defence of Poetry*, illustrates this concern with literature as a means of "improvement"—

> The exertions of Locke, Hume, Gibbon, Voltaire, Rousseau, and their disciples, in favour of oppressed and deluded humanity, are entitled to the gratitude of mankind. Yet it is not easy to calculate the degree of moral and intellectual improvement which the world would have exhibited, had they never lived. A little more nonsense would have been talked for a century or two; and perhaps a few more men, women and children burnt as heretics. We might not at this moment have been congratulating ourselves on the abolition of the Inquisition in Spain. But it exceeds all imagination to conceive what would have been the moral condition of the world if neither Dante, Petrarch, Boccaccio, Chaucer, Shakespeare, Calderon, Lord Bacon, nor Milton had ever existed; if Raphael and Michelangelo had never been born; if the Hebrew poetry had never been translated; if a revival of the study of Greek literature had never taken place; if no monuments of ancient sculpture had been handed down to us; and if the poetry of the religion of the ancient world had been extinguished together with its belief.

The Historical Sense

The student of literature has to keep in mind constantly the dual aspect of every historical epoch. There is the life of the time expressed in outward action, the manifest comings and goings, the triumphs and catastrophies, the daily round of domestic and public affairs. This is pre-eminently the province of the man of action, the reformer and the statesman. There is also beneath the surface the flux of feeling, imagination and thought, expressing itself in literature, art, philosophy, and religion. This is the domain of the poet, "hidden in the light of thought." But between these two kinds of human activity there is a necessary relation, and no understanding of either is possible without due consideration of the other.

Literary study involves therefore not only the reading of books and the consideration of them on abstract aesthetic grounds, but also a study of the outward manifestations of the spirit of the age. This is the "frame of reference" within which a writer must keep if he is to have any significance at all for his readers. All writing involves selection and selection implies preference, but the preference must be exercised within limits which are based on a socially accepted set of values. For that reason, the student of literature must cultivate the historical sense. He must regard the appearance of a book—of poetry, fiction, drama, essays or whatever else it be made up of—as a social *fact*, to be understood only when it is placed in relation to the whole movement of the age.

SUGGESTIONS FOR FURTHER READING

HERBERT READ: *The Meaning of Art* (Penguin).

A. MELVILLE CLARK: *Studies in Literary Modes* (Oliver & Boyd).

SIR WALTER RALEIGH: *Style; On the Art of Reading; On Writing and Writers* (Edward Arnold).

C. E. MONTAGUE: *A Writer's Notes on his Trade* (Chatto & Windus).

T. S. ELIOT: *What is a Classic?* (Faber & Faber).

J. MIDDLETON MURRY: *The Problem of Style* (Oxford University Press).

HOLBROOK JACKSON: *The Reading of Books* (Faber & Faber).

R. A. SCOTT JAMES: *The Making of Literature* (Secker & Warburg).

D. DAICHES: *A Study of Literature for Readers and Critics* (Oxford University Press).

H. J. GRIERSON: *Criticism and Creation* (Chatto & Windus).

Ed. WALTER ALLEN: *Writers on Writing* (Phoenix House).

E. M. W. TILLYARD: *Poetry Direct and Oblique* (Chatto & Windus).

CHAPTER II

THE ENGLISH LANGUAGE

A̲ʟʟ language, in so far as it is living speech, manifests the characteristics of an organism in that it undergoes continuous growth
and adaptation. Dead languages, their forms embalmed in
dictionaries, remain forever unaffected by the processes of change and
decay. English, in daily use as a mother-tongue by some two hundred
million people, is continually discarding words and idioms which,
having done good service in their day, no longer serve a useful purpose.
Meanwhile it acquires other words which help us to think and to talk,
to build up for ourselves a coherent mental picture of our relations
with our surroundings and to communicate our conceptions to others.
At every level of consciousness the human mind is ceaselessly at work
on this task. Much of the creative activity involved in keeping a
language fit for the work it has to do in the world goes on in the depths
of the sub-conscious mind. But much of it also demands the utmost
concentration, whether this be the effort of the scientist inventing
terms to match some fresh advance of his knowledge, or that of the
poet seeking to find a more sensitive utterance for feelings that are as
old as man himself.

A language is a social product, and reflects closely the mental and
moral features of the cultural community which has created it. But
these features are modified as the generations succeed each other, and
the symbols of the language, that is, its words and structural forms,
gather associations and become impregnated with the stuff of which
history is made. Many of the words in which Shakespeare's thought
has come down to us have, since he used them three hundred and
fifty years ago, become encrusted with new meanings; they have in
them to-day not only something of the culture of the sixteenth century,
but of every succeeding epoch. That is one of the many obstacles to a
full understanding of an early writer. It was remarked by Robert
Bridges[1] that a complete life spent in the study of the writings of St.
Paul or Plato would not enable one to think as he did, or to understand
precisely the original meaning of a single sentence that he wrote. This

---

[1] *Collected Essays: XIV Word Books.*

has an application to all literature which belongs to a civilization which is past.

Without a well-developed instrument of language and a literature, no cultural advance beyond the most rudimentary is possible for any people. Writing, by storing up experience and knowledge, enables the present to build upon the past. With its aid mental effort becomes cumulative in its effects. To study a people's language and literature is therefore to study its mind in the making. Language as the medium of communication, and literature as the sum-total of what has been deemed most worthy of communication, provide together the most significant index of cultural growth and achievement.

The Origins of English

English is derived from a branch of the Teutonic family of languages, namely the Low German branch, which comprises also Frisian, Dutch and Flemish. The other principal branches of the family are High German (represented to-day by modern German) and Scandinavian (comprising Icelandic, Norwegian, Danish and Swedish).

The Teutonic family is itself a member of a still greater family of Indo-European or Aryan languages, of which the other divisions are Celtic, Slavonic, Romance, and Sanskrit. They point to a common origin three or four thousand years ago. Celtic, the tongue spoken by the original dwellers in Britain, is still extant in the Welsh of Wales, the Gaelic of the Scottish Highlands, the Erse of Ireland and the Manx of the Isle of Man. The Cornish language was a variant which became extinct in the eighteenth century. Closely associated with it is Bas-Breton which is still used in Brittany.

The settlers who introduced Teutonic speech into Britain spoke a number of well-defined dialects, of which some of the variant features have survived into our own day. A few Celtic words were incorporated into the speech of the invaders (e.g. *basket, cairn, shamrock, clan*), but the number is so small as to suggest the almost total extinction or displacement of the Celtic population, at any rate in the Eastern parts of Britain.

The division of the country into separate kingdoms (the Heptarchy) emphasized the distinction of the dialects, of which the principal were Northumbrian, Mercian (or Midland), East Anglian, Kentish, and West Saxon. These were not sharply distinguished, and as we shall see later, it was a hybrid form, known as East Midland, containing Anglian elements, which ultimately gave us standard English. The dialects differed (i) in respect of some word-usages: e.g. the West Saxons talked of *beer* (*beor*) while the East Anglians used the word *ale* (*alu*); (ii) in inflections: e.g. the present tense ending *eth*, as in *maketh*, was a Kentish and East Anglian form, while the ending *s*, as in *makes*, was Northumbrian; (iii) and in vowel-values: e.g. Northern and Western England tended to use the short *a* in such words as *castle*, *master*, while Southern England used the long *a*, as at present.

All these dialects were highly inflected. The noun, pronoun, article and adjective were declined in five cases, singular and plural, and (as in modern German) there were three genders. The verb also had numerous inflections, the commonest being the *en* ending of the infinitive and of the plural of the present tense.

It seemed at one time probable that the Northumbrian dialect was destined to become the standard form of English because it was in the monasteries of the North that scholarship under the leadership of the Celtic missionaries from Ireland progressed most rapidly. At Jarrow there arose a school of religious poetry which had a deep influence on our pre-conquest literature. The Danish raids disturbed this peaceful development, and it was the impact of the Danish language that hastened the simplification of the structural forms of the Anglo-Saxon dialects. If we compare the speech of England north of Watling Street (roughly the part occupied by the Danes) with that of the South, in the forms used in the eleventh century, it will be found that the process of shedding inflexions had gone very much further in the North. Supremacy among the Anglo-Saxon peoples was won finally by the West Saxons, and that is doubtless the reason why most of the writings of the ninth and tenth centuries have come down to us in the dialect of Wessex.

Influence of Norman-French

The Norman-French conquest of England in 1066 gave England a new aristocracy, the members of which, since as a rule they held estates on both sides of the Channel, for a time maintained their contacts with the Continent and brought thence new cultural influences. Had it been otherwise, the process of assimilation of the Normans into the life of England might have been even more rapid than it was, and the impress of the French language on English might have been less pronounced. But it happened that literary developments in France had, by the eleventh and twelfth centuries, gone much further than in neighbouring countries. The *trouvères* of the North and the *troubadours* of the South had worked into literary forms a wealth of epic themes relative to the exploits of Charlemagne's paladins (the "matter of France"), to classical history, such as the story of Troy (the "matter of Rome"), and to the legendary lore of King Arthur (the "matter of Britain"). To these were added the extravagant oriental tales associated with the far-flung campaigns of Alexander the Great, which were brought back by travellers and Crusaders. The whole of this narrative poetry was contained in the *Chansons de Geste*.

At about the same time there occurred among the troubadours a profuse blossoming of lyrical verse of astonishing range of mood and expression. It would be difficult to match from the literature of any other country, in any age, such variety in the use of structural forms and such elaboration of style. Poetry in the hands of these lyrists leapt beyond the traditional limits set to it by the Church, and took on a new aspect. Hitherto the dominant theme had been the adoration of the Virgin Mother; now the lore of courtly love began to occupy an equal place. The fashion set by the troubadours spread over the whole of western Europe, and produced the conventional love lyric whose development can be traced through the Middle Ages and into the Renaissance. The Elizabethan song-writers and sonneteers and the Cavalier love-poets show an affinity in spirit to these early lyric writers.

The effect of the impact of these highly developed French literary modes on England was to lower the prestige of the vernacular. English continued to be the language of popular use, but for religious offices, law and administration, educated correspondence, scholarship and the like, as well as literature, the accepted medium was Latin or Norman-French.

Three principal features mark the evolution of English during the twelfth and thirteenth centuries: (1) the loss or "levelling" of most of the grammatical inflections, (2) the enrichment of the vocabulary by the adoption of words from the Romance languages, and (3) the gradual rise of East Midland speech to predominance as a literary medium.

The Levelling of Inflections

We have already seen how, under the impact of Danish, the reduction of the inflections had begun. Gradually the language in all its dialect forms changed, until the relation of words in a sentence was determined by their position rather than by their termination. In the following passage from *Beowulf*:

> ne wæs þæt gewrixle til
> þæt hie on bā healfa   bicgan scoldon
> frēonda feorum,

the last two words get their meaning from the case endings, genitive and dative plural respectively. In a modern English rendering: "it was not a good exchange which on both sides had to be paid for with the lives of friends," there are no case-endings and the meaning is conveyed by the word-order, helped by prepositions.

A few survivals of Anglo-Saxon case-endings may be mentioned: the possessive pronouns, *his, whose, mine, our, their,* still show the mark of their genitive-case origin (*his, hwaes, min, ure, þara*). The existence of the parallel words *two* and *twain* is explained as a distinction of gender: *twa* is the neuter and also the feminine form of the word in the nominative case, while *twegen* is the corresponding masculine form. Such plurals as *stones, oxen, geese, childer* (dialect form of *children*), indicate that nouns were variously declined, but the survival of the -*s* plural was helped by the circumstance that in French the levelling of plurals to a universal -*s*, representing the commonest Latin accusative plural ending, had already been accomplished. Numerous English plurals were assimilated to this pattern; for example, the plural *scipu* (ships) from *scip* (ship) became *ships*, while *strœta* (streets) from *strœt* (street) became *streets*. In Chaucer's English this -*s* plural had the form -*es*, which was generally spoken as a distinct syllable, as, for example, in the decasyllabic line:

> And smalè fowlès maken melodie.

Accretions to the Vocabulary

The principal accretions to the stock of accepted words related, as we should expect, to the concerns of the Court, the Church, the law, warfare, and sport. A few examples of borrowings from French of the Norman period are *duke, homage, altar, penance, estate, sue, falcon*.

The East Midland dialect was the most advantageously placed of all from the point of view of the chances of survival and supremacy. It was spoken in London and in the Universities of Oxford and Cambridge. It was the dialect of the wealthiest commoners, the great wool merchants of East Anglia. Since it occupied a middle position between

Northern and Southern dialects, it was the most easily understood by all. East Midland speech was gradually employed by the educated classes everywhere, and awaited only its adoption by Chaucer for his prose and verse before it became the standard for literary purposes. There was as yet no fixed spelling; standardization followed naturally, if only gradually, from the dissemination of printed books after Caxton's introduction of the printing press into England in 1476.

In the sixteenth century the expressiveness and plenitude of the English language were enormously increased by the new accessions of words, idioms and constructions which resulted from the attention paid by scholars to the elegant classical literatures of Greece and Rome. In contrast to the earlier borrowings from Latin, which are called "popular" because they came *via* the French vernacular, these new acquisitions are called "learned" because they were book-words, "ink-horn terms," which at best entered only slowly into the currency of spoken English. Many of the innovations failed to find a permanent place in the living English vocabulary, and survive only as museum pieces in our literature, as in this sentence from Bacon's *Advancement of Learning:* "Fire is no constant cause either of induration or of colliquation"; or this from Prynne's *Histriomastix*: "Obscene and filthy jests which inquinate the minds of men." Other words have maintained themselves but precariously, e.g. *pulchritude, concinnity*. But the great majority of scholarly terms soon found a place for themselves in normal speech and writing. We have only to consider how useful to us are such words as *operate, reduce,* and *commit,* with their numerous derivatives, to realize the debt we owe to the humanists of the age of the Renaissance who first introduced them.

It may be that we should attribute the power of absorption, assimilation and adaptation which is characteristic of modern English to the success of these early experiments in word-borrowing. The far-flung interests of England since she entered upon her career as a world-civilizer in the sixteenth century have brought into the language thousands of new words to match new things and new ideas. Foreign trade has brought us *tomato* (Mexico), *bamboo* (Malaya), and *dollar* (Holland); navigation has added *yacht, deck, frigate*. The imitations of cultural modes which originated in Italy has supplied us with many terms of art: *pianoforte, opera, quarto, studio, madrigal, chiaroscuro, sonnet*; to French etiquette and manners we owe such words as *badinage, ridicule, parterre, prestige, memoir, parcle* and *levee*. War is an activity which alters its character and methods so rapidly that every new outbreak leads to the formation of new words.

Unquestionably the largest group of modern additions to our stock is the highly specialized vocabulary of science and technology consisting almost entirely of words deliberately assembled from Greek and Latin roots and affixes. With the growth of the sphere of government and administration, there is a further need for new words to match new conceptions, though here much is accomplished by using old words in figurative or metonymic senses: for example such modern terms as *ration, point, coupon, basic, ceiling, target, trust,* and *shop* (as in "closed shop"). We have become adept too at devising such conglomerates as *Benelux, P.A.Y.E.* and *Unrra,* often to serve ephemeral purposes. Numerous words have entered our language as "legitimates" after having for a period enjoyed a less respectable status as slang and jargon, just as others have descended in social scale and no longer hold a place in educated speech or writing.

Semantics

The application of the historical method to the meaning of words has given us a new science, known as Semantics. This seeks to discover the general laws governing shifts of meaning, including the movements of expansion and contraction. It is obvious that such a study requires as a necessary preliminary a long effort of research into the succession of meanings which words have carried in recorded speech and writing since they entered the language. To record the usages of words and to classify them is the work of lexicographers.

Dr. Johnson's *Dictionary* was a pioneer endeavour of this kind. Though in relation to the level of scholarship in his day he is to be considered a learned man, he was deficient in many important respects, e.g. in his knowledge of etymology, and of Teutonic languages other than English. But with the aid of his remarkable memory and his very extensive reading, he was able to adduce quotations to support his definitions from a wide field of literature. Since the eighteenth century, dictionary and concordance makers have accumulated further vast quantities of material, and to-day even newspapers are scanned daily for new words, or words used with new meanings. The greatest work of lexicography in English is the Oxford English Dictionary the preparation of which occupied more than half a century.

On the foundation of observed usages thus collated and classified, the semantist gets to work, codifying changes in meaning and searching to discover uniform tendencies.

General Characteristics of English

The general characteristics of English as a language may be summed up as: (1) its receptiveness, or capacity to assimilate rapidly elements from the most diverse sources; (2) its opulence and prodigality, resulting from extensive borrowings over a period of a thousand years and more; (3) its audacity in invention and adaptation; (4) its servicability both for practical uses and for yielding aesthetic pleasure; (5) its grammatical simplicity, consequent on the predominance of the positional, as contrasted with the inflectional, element in its structure; (6) the variety of its cadences, produced by the union of a strong monosyllabic Anglo-Saxon fundament with an accretion of poly-syllabic words of Romance origin; (7) its progressive character, evident from a comparison with German, which has moved much more slowly towards the abandonment of grammatical inflections.

Specimens of English: Twelfth to Sixteenth Century

The following passages provide material for the study of the development of the language during the formative period. They illustrate the progress made at intervals of about half a century—

1137. Anglo-Saxon Chronicle

I ne canne ne I ne mai tellen alle þe wunder, ne alle þe pines þæt hi diden wrecce men on þis land; and þæt lastede þa XIX wintre wile Stephne was King; and œure it was uuerse and uuerse.

1300. The Proverbs of Hendyng

Drawe thyn hond sone ageyn,
Gef men the doth a wycke theyn,
    Ther thyn ahte ys lend:
So that child with-draweth is hond
From the fur ant the brond
    That hath byfore bue brend.
'Brend child fur dredeth'
    Quoth Hendyng.

1356. The Voyage and Travaile of Sir John Mandeville

And there groweth a maner of fruyt, as though it weren Gowrdes; and when thei ben rype, men kutten hem a-to, and men fynden with-inne a lytylle best, in flesch, in bon and blode, as thogh it were a lytille lomb, with-outen wolle.

1420. *London Lack penny* (John Lydgate)

> Then to the Chepe I gan me drawne
> Where much people I saw for to stand;
> One offred me velvet, sylke and lawne,
> An other he taketh me by the hande,
> 'Here is Parys thred, the fynest in the land';
> I never was used to such thynges in dede,
> And, wantyng mony, I myght not spede.

1490. *Prologue to Virgil's Eneydos* (Caxton)

And certaynly, our language now used varyeth ferre from that whiche was used and spoken when I was borne. For we englysshemen ben borne under the domynacyon of the mone, which is never stedfaste, but ever waverynge, wexynge one season, and waneth and dycreaseth another season. And that comyn englysshe that is spoken in one shyre varyeth from a nother. In so much that in my days happened that certyn marchanntes were in a shipe in tamyse, for to have sayled over the sea to Zelande, and for lacke of wynde thei taryed atte forlond, and wente to lande for to refreshe them. And one of them named sheffelde, a mercer, came to an hows and axed for mete, and specyalle he axed after eggys. And the goode wyf answerde, that she coude speke no frenche. And the marchaunt was angry, for he also coude speke no frenshe but wolde have hadde eggys; and she understode him not. And thenne at laste a nother sayd that he wolde have eyren; then the good wyf sayd that she understod hym wel. Loo! what sholde a man in these days now wryte, egges or eyren?

1550. *The Ploughers:* Sermon by Hugh Latimer

For howe many unlearned prelates have we now at this day? And no mervel. For if the plough-men that now be were made lordes, they woulde cleane gyve over ploughinge, they woulde leave of theyr labour & fall to lordyng outright & let the plough stand. And then bothe ploughes not walkyng, nothing shoulde be in the common weale but honger.

Examples of English of later date will be found in the following sections.

SUGGESTIONS FOR FURTHER READING

OTTO JESPERSON: *Growth and Structure of the English Language* (Blackwell).
H. WYLD: *The Growth of English* (Murray).
P. B. BALLARD: *Thought and Language* (Univ. of London Press).
R. C. TRENCH: *On the Study of Words; English Past and Present* (Dent).
H. W. FOWLER: *A Dictionary of Modern English Usage; The King's English* (Oxford Univ. Press).

CHAPTER III

DESIGN IN POETRY

THE difficulty of defining poetry is similar in its nature to the difficulty of defining beauty. To say that poetry is beautiful thought beautifully expressed does not carry us very far, even if it helps us at all, because it still leaves us to decide what qualities of thought and utterance entitle them to be called beautiful. There is in fact no word associated with the appreciation of the fine arts which leads to more confusion in our thinking than the word "beauty." An object in nature which is generally considered ugly and even repulsive may yet inspire a work which is universally acclaimed as great art because it has a power of giving aesthetic satisfaction. Shakespeare and others have written great and memorable poetry about actions which are evil and sordid, and about people who are gross and immoral. Perhaps if we substitute the word "true" for "beautiful," we should come a little nearer to understanding the essence of poetry.

The Nature of Poetry

At the same time, notwithstanding many critics who have addressed themselves to the question "What is Poetry?" and found the answer rather in the quality of the thought of the poet than in the forms in which he expresses his thought, we cannot admit that the verbal attributes of poetry are unimportant. Poetry is a particular way of communicating ideas. A chemical equation, a railway time-table, an Act of Parliament are other ways of conveying information, each using a form or method of its own which experience has proved to be adapted for the end in view. What then is the characteristic form of poetry, in the absence of which we should call it not poetry but some other means of expressing a thought or feeling and of conveying it from one mind to another?

While it is true to say that poetry serves not only a useful end but also an aesthetic one, this is not a definition. For good oratory does as much, and so does a well-written novel or essay. They may all give rise to intellectual and emotional excitement. This stimulation is, however, particularly marked when we read or hear significant truths cast in a mould which perfectly matches the meaning. The effect is produced not by the thing said (the content), nor by the verbal arrangement (the form) alone, but by the union of the two in a way that seems inevitable and unalterable. The meaning and the expression cannot in fact be divorced, because the quality of each is transfused by the other. Each of the following verses deals in a special way with the topic of death, but each particular perfection arises from the absolute congruity of the verbal pattern and the mood—

Full fathom five thy father lies;
Of his bones are coral made
Those are pearls that were his eyes;
Nothing of him that doth fade
But doth suffer a sea-change
Into something rich and strange.
Sea-nymphs hourly ring his knell:
Hark! now I hear them,—Ding-dong, bell.

SHAKESPEARE: *The Tempest*

Beneath those rugged elms, that yew-tree's shade,
Where heaves the turf in many a mould'ring heap,
Each in his narrow cell for ever laid,
The rude forefathers of the hamlet sleep.

GRAY: *Elegy Written in a Country Churchyard*

He has outsoared the shadow of our night;
Envy and calumny and hate and pain,
And that unrest which men mis-call delight,
Can touch him not and torture not again;
From the contagion of the world's slow stain
He is secure, and now can never mourn
A heart grown cold, a head grown gray in vain;
Nor, when the spirit's self has ceased to burn,
With sparkless ashes load an unlamented urn.

SHELLEY: *Adonais*

In the first, we have death imagined and presented in the colours and contours of a dream-world and the language is as positive as dream-pictures are apt to be. In the second, Gray's rhythm is slow and ponderous as befits the unhurrying tempo of rural existence. In the third, we are carried along by Shelley's imaginative force to a conception of death triumphing over life. Each of the passages demands of the reader an exercise of creative imagination, akin to that which was originally inspired in the poet by some upsurge of emotion impelling

him to write. The thought of the poet and the quality of his feeling
becomes clear to himself only as he finds the words and images to
utter it. Similarly for the reader, there are not two things to be
apprehended, first the thought and then the form of words in which it
is embodied, but one thing only, namely the poetry which is a co-
existence or condominium of meaning and expression.

Pattern in Poetry

As long as we never lose sight of the fact that a pattern of words,
metrically arranged, however regular and melodious the flow, is not
necessarily to be accounted poetry, there is no harm, and there may be
some value, in examining the pattern closely. We may thus discover
something of why and when words arranged in patterns tend to
please us.

The appeal which the nursery rhyme makes to the child comes from
the strong rhythm which goes well with the physical movements of
swaying or jogging in time with the falling of the stressed syllables.
Why rhythmic movement and sound should be pleasurable to us
has not yet been explained by the psychologists, but the fact may be
connected with a race-memory of manual tasks made easier by being
reduced to a regular beat accompanied by chanting. Sailors pulling at
a rope, women pounding rice in a churn, children rocked in a cradle,
are familiar examples, and even the repetition work of the modern
factory is made somewhat more bearable by "music while you work."
In the visual arts, the pleasure which is derived from contemplating
the pattern in things is no less pronounced. The creative skill of the
architect, the painter, the sculptor and the decorator is directed to the
organization of masses, forms, colours, and contours in ways which
promise to give the artist release from the emotional tension which
possesses him. It is a peculiar attribute of the artist's bodily and mental
activity that it tends to express itself in a repetitive, rhythmical order of
sounds, lines, shapes or masses.

The Discipline of Form

Poetry, like all the arts, attains its values by submission to a discipline
of form. It achieves its results not in spite of but by virtue of the
necessities of a formal structure. The sonnet writer regards the
rigorous demands of the pattern as being not rules to be obeyed or
obstacles to be surmounted, but rather as opportunities to be seized.
It is through the form that the organic design of a poem is unfolded

and its balance and unity revealed. Consider for example how the changes of form in Coleridge's *Kubla Khan* match the discontinuities of the dream-sequence. Starting with the quiet octosyllabic iambic rhythm of—

> In Xanadu did Kubla Khan
> A stately pleasure-dome decree,

the description mounts in breathless and laboured pentameters towards the dire enchantment of the "romantic chasm"—

> And from this chasm, with ceaseless turmoil seething,
> As if this earth in fast thick pants were breathing.

Then, when the sacred river has sunk in tumult to the ocean, the "dome of pleasure" again rises in the dream-vision, but now as shadow only. The octosyllabic lines are resumed, but the slow iambs have now become dancing trochees according with the "mingled measure"—

> The shadow of the dome of pleasure
> Floated midway on the waves;
> Where was heard the mingled measure
> From the fountain and the caves.

Further changes of rhythm mark succeeding moods: the recollection of the "damsel with a dulcimer," the ecstatic shout of the creative artist—

> That with music loud and long
> I would build that dome in air,
> That sunny dome! those caves of ice!

and finally the awed whisper of the lines—

> And close your eyes with holy dread,
> For he on honey-dew hath fed
> And drunk the milk of paradise.

It is not to be supposed that Coleridge wrought consciously to achieve these effects. He was guided rather by his intuitive feeling for the value of the words themselves and for the pattern they made in association.

The imaginative stress which possesses the artist has to find release in some externalizing process; his tension of thought or feeling must issue in expression. The poet's mind is so constituted that the natural vent for his creative urge is through language symbols, deployed so as to take on an added strength and significance. This deployment results in design or form.

The design of a poem is to be studied not in individual lines or stanzas, though these are elements of importance in it. The counting of syllables, the marking of stresses, the noting of rhyme schemes and other such methods of analysing the spacial qualities of verse are only

3

incidental to the study of the structure of the poem as a whole. The full study requires consideration of the arrangement of its parts, of the movement of feeling, of the correspondence of the imagery with the development of the theme, and finally of the manner in which the poet has imposed an organic unity in terms of language upon the experience which moved him to write.

It is worth noting here that the adjective "poetic" or "poetical" is used with a much wider connotation than the corresponding noun "poetry." A sweep of natural landscape, a Tarantella, the Taj Mahal, a piece of Dresden china, are often called "poetic" in virtue of their power at times to produce in us as we view them a pleasurable emotion which bears comparison in intensity with that which we feel on reading, say, Collins' *Ode to Evening*. A painter or a choreographer may thus sometimes be said to possess a "poetic vision." But though a cricket enthusiast has been heard to speak of "the poetry of the game," we feel that this is stretching language beyond its due limit, and in practice we keep the word "poetry" to its association with words and the pattern of their sounds.

There have been critics, and many of the highest eminence, such as Aristotle, Sir Philip Sidney, Coleridge, Shelley and Matthew Arnold, who have urged that the soul of poetry lies not in the imposition of a formal pattern on words or syllables, but in the projection of truth by the creative imagination. Nevertheless, in rejecting metre, they did not necessarily reject rhythm, and it is very important to distinguish between these two qualities. Many poets have used a rhythmical language, the pattern being based on stresses, not on the metrical foot. Gerard Manley Hopkins and T. S. Eliot are notable examples. There exist also works of prose and works of verse whose quality is such that each might have taken a different form without risk of detriment or even with advantage. Pope's *Essay on Man* would have lost little by discarding its metrical dress, while the impassioned prose of De Quincey's *Suspiria de Profundis* has a vowel-music which provides at least some of the delight which arises from mellifluous verse.

It is surely a most significant thing that human beings should from time immemorial have been moved to embody the record of their highest imaginings and deepest emotions in a repetitive pattern of language. Such patterns, so far from acting as fetters on the freedom of thought and the range of spirit, have rather proved themselves to be of positive assistance in releasing the poet from the pressure of the actual, and liberating him for the pursuit of the ideal.

Levels of Poetry

Poetry can exist at different levels and still deserve the name of poetry. No long poem ever written is sustained throughout at the same level, for if such a poem rises in some passages to great heights, it must also descend in others to the level of pedestrian verse. That this should be so follows from the nature of inspiration which is fitful and subject to no control.

> *Glendower.* I can call spirits from the vasty deep.
> *Hotspur.*   Why, so can I, or so can any man;
>   But will they come when you do call for them?
>   SHAKESPEARE: *Henry IV, Part I* (III. 1)

The magic lines even in great poetry are sparsely distributed, and we should be happy if the connecting tissue is of a high average quality.

But it is also true that intensely imaginative poetry is to be found less often in some kinds of verse than in others. Satirical, polemical and didactic verse is usually reckoned to be of a lower order, and this for obvious reasons. The poet's intellect is engaged far more than his imagination; the pleasure of the reader is similarly of an intellectual rather than of an emotional kind. This is far from saying that poetry has no concern with ideas. The greatest poetry is compact of ideas, but the ideas have been transmuted by feeling and imagination into "something rich and strange." Verse which has a conscious aim, e.g. to maintain or explain a thesis, to advocate a kind of conduct, to castigate evil, or even to narrate an episode, may soar to great heights, but is far oftener liable to "fly an ordinary pitch." The ascent when it occurs is in the nature of a miracle; the descent is a commonplace. The gravitational pull of the world of material things and everyday concerns is strong enough to explain why the great flights must be both rare and brief. Even Milton, addressing himself to his "great argument," to—

> assert Eternal Providence
> And justify the ways of God to man,

sinks in long passages to a prosaic level, as in the lines—

> Tyranny must be,
> Though to the tyrant thereby no excuse.
> Yet sometimes nations will decline so low
> From virtue, which is reason, that no wrong,
> But justice and some fatal curse annexed,
> Deprives them of their outward liberty.
>   *Paradise Lost, Book XII*

Wordsworth, too, wrote many banal passages; for example, these lines from *The Sailor's Mother*—

> One morning (raw it was and wet . . .
> A foggy day in winter time)
> A woman on the road I met
> Not old, though something past her prime.

and these from *The Thorn* referring to "a little muddy pond"—

> I measured it from side to side
> 'Twas three feet long and four feet wide.

Basic Patterns

Though poetry is all one, being a method of communicating intensely lived experience and intensely apprehended thought in language which is not only representational, but is also rich in emotive suggestion and musical quality, it is possible to distinguish certain basic patterns or modes of poetical expression. These correspond to the varying standpoints from which the poet looks upon his experience. He can look at events objectively and, without being concerned overmuch with their effect on himself, render an impersonal account of what he sees. He cannot wholly cancel himself out because his selection of detail and his method of treatment are personal and can never be identical with those of another who might observe the self-same events. Nevertheless the aim will be to record and describe as from the outside. The individual emotion set up by the events is put on one side.

The result will be what the Greeks called epic poetry, which can be subdivided into narrative and dramatic. This distinction arises from the form adopted: viz. whether the matter is recorded and described by the poet as to a distant audience or presented in speech and action to a present audience. For example, in *Sohrab and Rustum*, Matthew Arnold stands aside and the narrative proceeds from beginning to end without our being conscious of the poet's own reactions to the events which take place. In a great dramatic work, such as *Macbeth*, the withdrawal of the poet is even more complete.

The other principal division of poetry is personal and subjective. What the poet has observed and experienced has set up in his mind trains of thought and waves of feeling, and it is these which occupy his attention. It is through the poet's testimony to the effect of the external world upon himself that we get to know the nature of his experience. His record is of a private and unique vision which has possessed his soul and set up an inner tension which can only be released by some process of externalizing it—

A timely utterance gave that thought relief.

A painter would find his relief in the painting of a picture. The externalization of a poet's feelings would result in a lyrical poem.

The lyrical utterance is usually brief. The original association of the lyric with song is understandable, since song, whether of gladness or lament, is an instinctive mode of expression. We have grounds for supposing that the art of music and poetry were not at first differentiated, and lyrical poetry has preserved much of the spontaneity and immediacy of song.

Since poets do not work by rule, and states of human consciousness are hardly ever "pure," being compounded of many elements, it is natural that poetry should often manifest itself in forms which are not easy to classify. Though by far the largest proportion of our poetic literature is lyrical in spirit, it is comparatively unusual to find a lyric in which the personal feeling is not related to a general reflection.. In the stanzas of Burns' *To a Mouse* (quoted on page 120), the first is an expression of the poet's deep personal sympathy with the sufferings of an innocent creature, and the second stanza is a broad reflection on life and destiny. From the particular instance the poet has passed to the universal application.

Furthermore, the lyrical poet often focuses in himself some feeling which has a social reference, belonging to the experience of humanity, a nation, or a group. Church hymns (e.g. *Lead Kindly Light*), patriotic or nostalgic songs, (e.g. *On the Bonnie Bonnie Banks of Loch Lomond*), dedicatory odes (e.g. *Ring Out Wild Bells*), calls to action (e.g. *Scots wha' hae*) and the like, give expression to communal rather than to personal thoughts and feelings. Lyrical writing is frequently found in association with narrative, as in Wordsworth's *Lucy* poems. The name *Lyrical Ballads* given by Wordsworth and Coleridge to their joint venture in 1798 suggests the introduction of a lyrical note into narrative poems, and Coleridge's *Christabel* and *Kubla Khan* are consummate examples of this union. The absolute categories to which some critics cling, because they help their thinking, may mean little to the poet. The form of a poem should be considered as inseparable from its content; it is the source of the aesthetic experience which we seek when we read poetry.

Each of the basic divisions of poetry, the objective and the subjective has been crystallized in a number of forms, and in the following pages some of the outstanding ones are enumerated and described.

The Epic

Narrative poetry occasionally, though rarely, rises to a level of dignity, elaboration and significance which place it in a class apart, and entitle it to the description "epic." Often the epic consists of the history of a whole civilization, related to some heroic figure or action in which the pride of a race or nation is centred. The canvas is a large one, and the figures and the incidents are rather bigger than life-size. There are no limits to the introduction of fully worked-out descriptions of people and scenes even though they be subsidiary to the main theme. Yet the principal interest is in the action to which unity is given by the consistent presentation of the principal protagonists, as moving towards some "far-off divine event." While the method is narrative, the epic makes considerable use of dialogue, which might perhaps be better called declamation.

We can distinguish between the natural epic, or the epic of growth, and the imitative or synthetic epic, the epic of art. The material for an epic poem of the former kind may have grown by a process of aggregation and consolidation, that is to say, by the assembly of a number of heroic narratives of separate origin and the gradual organization of them by nameless poets and minstrels into a progressive narrative having a soul of unity. Such are the epics of the ancient world, the *Iliad* and the *Odyssey* of ancient Greece, the *Niebelungenlied* of Scandinavia, the Icelandic *Edda*, the *Beowulf* fragment of the Anglo-Saxons, and the *Roman de Roland* of early medieval France.

The epic of art is, as its name implies, a more conscious and deliberate contrivance, the product of a developed literary technique. The model for this type of epic poem was the *Æneid* of Virgil, and it exercised a potent influence on Dante's *Divina Commedia*, Tasso's *Gerusalemme Liberata*, Milton's *Paradise Lost* and others.

These two kinds of epic show certain superficial resemblances, e.g. the division into twelve books, the invocation to the Muses, the conventional "he spoke" or "thus saying" to introduce the set dialogue, the use of extended similes, the elevated style and the seeking after sonorous effects by the use of high-sounding names. But these resemblances conceal many differences. The natural epic was impersonal, while the imitative epic has clearly imprinted on it the mark of the poet's temperament. The ancient epics came into existence in a world which was assured of its values; its virtues and vices were of the rudimentary kind, lacking the nice distinctions of a later age. Of crude courage and fortitude there was plenty, while revenge and rapine stalked abroad without concealment. Love and hatred were starkly opposed. In the conduct of primitive men there are few half-tones or shades. Further, there are no divided loyalties. The true epic is thus the heroic expression in literature of the whole nation, not merely of a section of it. In that respect Milton's *Paradise Lost*, for example, falls short. It was, notwithstanding its debt to pagan classicism, the outcome of an intensely Puritan spirit. Though he takes the universal story of mankind as its theme, this is handled in a way which makes it in effect the revelation of a personal standpoint. *Paradise Lost* and *Paradise Regained* nevertheless come nearest to true epic quality of any English writings.

The title of epic has sometimes been claimed for Tennyson's *Idylls of the King*, which aimed at the depicting of the exploits of Arthur and his Knights of the Round Table on a broad scale. But there are many obvious deficiencies. Firstly, though Arthur himself is always in the background, the poem remains a compilation of stories, rather than one coherent narrative. Secondly, the work is a vehicle for Tennyson's moralizing, and the didactic mood is foreign to the epic. Thirdly, the high polish of the verse, its conscious artistry, the literary embellishments, while they add to our aesthetic pleasure in reading the poem, are far removed from the artlessness of the true epic. Lastly, the character of Arthur himself is not conceived in the epic spirit; he does not carry conviction. In his attitudes he is too close to the Victorian ideal of the gentleman to stand out as an authentic heroic figure: the manners which are depicted are based on those of the respectable Victorian household rather than those which belong to the early centuries of our era.

Ballad Literature

Every nation in Europe treasures a form of artless and anonymous native literature representing the earliest stages in the development of its poetry. Known as ballad literature, its form was spoken narrative in rough rhymed verse, agreeable to unsophisticated popular taste and, since it was unwritten, capable of endless improvisation in detail of incident and expression. It is in consequence of this oral tradition that there exist so many versions of all the well-known ballads.

The themes are drawn from incidents of the common lot, love, and longing and death, with dreams and portents, journeyings and adventures, fighting and feasting. These are directly told as tales of action, with no conscious ornament of style, no abstract moralizing, no refinement of characterization and motivation. Though the treatment is naïve, many ballads show great dramatic force and a wonderful feeling for rhythm. We have Sir Philip Sidney's confession that the hearing of *Chevy Chase*, recited by a "blind crowder" (fiddler), stirred his blood like the sound of a trumpet.

The style of the ballad shows clear marks of its unlettered origin. There is the same use of a repetitive pattern as is found in so many nursery rhymes and folk-tales. Refrains, consisting of complete lines or exclamatory phrases are common. A lame rhythm is often helped along by means of some word-jingle to eke out the line. Speech is given in a direct rather than in a reported form. Rhyme, as we might expect, often gives place to assonance, as in—

> She stept to him, as red as any rose,
>   And took him by the bridle-*ring*:
> "I pray you, Kind Sir, give me one penny,
>   To ease my weary *limb*."
>   *The Bailiff's Daughter of Islington*

The commonest verse form of the ballad is the four-lined stanza, made up of lines of iambic rhythm containing four stresses, or alternating four-stressed and three-stressed lines rhyming in couplets. In all these matters, the ballads show stylistic characteristics which are common to the people of all European countries.

The names and incidents also bear a resemblance to a considerable extent. The magic numbers, three and seven, are constantly used. The commonest objects are made of, or decorated with, silver or gold; often horses are shod with gold. When the ballads are not historical, there is generally a sexual element, with death as a frequent consequence of love's betrayal.

Narrative Poetry

The Epic and the Ballad are far from exhausting the varieties of narrative poetry. Its wide range can be illustrated by reference to such a collection as Chaucer's *Canterbury Tales*, where many kinds exist side by side. Among them are the romantic tale of chivalry (*The Knight's Tale*), the tale of magic (*The Squire's Tale*), the moralizing tale (*The Clerk's Tale*), the tragic life-story (*The Monk's Tale*), the fable (*The Nun's Priest's Tale*), the fabliau (*The Reeve's Tale*), the burlesque (*Chaucer's Tale of Sir Thopas*) and the story from life (*The*

Canon's Yeoman's Tale). Numerous examples of most of these types of narrative are to be found in medieval literature. The fabliaux, for example, formed a considerable part of the popular literature of France from the twelfth to the fourteenth century. They were written and recited by professional *jongleurs* in eight-syllabled rhymed verse, their subjects being mostly merry jests, often at the expense of the priesthood. The anti-feminine tone of the fabliaux is perhaps to be explained as a reaction against the more cultivated literature of Mariolatry and the love-cult of chivalry. In contrast, there was the vogue of the "moral example" and the miracle story, equally widespread in the Middle Ages and forming a considerable part of the popular literature favoured by the Church.

In the Elizabethan age in England most of the narrative poetry was of the conventionally moralizing kind, as Sackville's *Mirror for Magistrates* and Samuel Daniel's *The Complaint of Rosamond*, or else was interpenetrated with lyrical feeling, as, for example, Marlowe's *Hero and Leander* and Shakespeare's *Venus and Adonis* and *The Rape of Lucrece*.

The romantic tale has had a very numerous progeny, and in the early nineteenth century, when the romantic spirit in literature was dominant, it was much in evidence. Coleridge's *Christabel* and *The Ancient Mariner* were outstanding products of a new method in narrative poetry. There were also the Lays of Sir Walter Scott, e.g. *The Lady of the Lake* and *Marmion*, based on legendary or historical themes drawn from the Scottish Border, Byron's more exciting and voluptuous tales of Oriental crime (e.g. *The Giaour, The Corsair, Lara*), and Shelley's *Revolt of Islam*, which was inspired by revolutionary ardour as well as a longing for ideal beauty. Keats's greatness in narrative poetry is seen in such different masterpieces as *La Belle Dame sans Merci*, which derives its magical power from what is not said but only suggested, and *St Agnes' Eve*, with its rich and colourful accessories of romance. Later we have Tennyson's *Lady of Shalott, Enoch Arden*, and the *Idylls*; Browning's *Pied Piper of Hamelin*, Mrs. Browning's *Aurora Leigh*, Arnold's *Sohrab and Rustum*, William Morris's renderings of the Icelandic Sagas, Swinburne's *Tristram of Lyonesse* and (to jump to the twentieth century) John Masefield's *Dauber*, each illustrating some new aspect of narration in verse. Narrative poetry may be of the utmost brevity and simplicity, as in Wordsworth's *Lucy* poems, or may become a full-bodied novel in verse, such as Coventry Patmore's *The Angel in the House*.

Poetic Drama and Dramatic Poetry

The use of poetry in Drama is to raise a mood or situation to a higher intensity by giving to the language in which it is expressed the added beauty of a formal, rhythmical utterance. Thereby the delineation of passion is endowed with a lyrical quality, grief is ennobled, satire arms itself with a more pointed barb, and comedy is touched with delicate wit or wayward fancy. Subject to the condition that it is intended to be heard spoken from a stage rather than read from a book, and also that it stands not in its own right but in service to the requirements of character and situation in the play, poetic drama can exist in a wide variety of forms. It will not use a pattern such as, for example, the Sonnet or the Spenserian stanza, whose rigid structure disqualifies it from service to the ever-changing circumstance of a play. But, as an examination of any Shakespearian play will show, the verse ranges from narrative and descriptive to lyrical, and from heroic to satirical. It can in an instant turn from bantering repartee to the heights and depths of passion, and from foolery to philosophy. Drama has therefore not claimed a province of poetry as territory held in sovereignty; rather it is a way of making poetry serve ends which are not primarily poetic at all, but which, with the aid of language used in special ways, can be raised to the level of the ideal.

A distinction may usefully be drawn between poetic drama and dramatic poetry. Drama is none the less drama for being poetic, since it remains subject to all the conditions which apply to drama as an art. It has still to observe the conventional limitations and obey the necessities imposed by the physical conditions of stage representation in the presence of a public audience. But dramatic poetry is poetry in which the poet speaks not in his own person but, merging himself in the character which he has created out of his imagination, or which he is bringing to life from the pages of history, speaks vicariously. Many of Browning's *Dramatic Romances and Lyrics* are of this kind, including such poems as *How They Brought The Good News from Ghent to Aix* and *The Bishop Orders his Tomb at St. Praxted's Church*.

The Pastoral Convention

The pastoral is a species of literary composition of which the origins are to be sought in early Greek poetry. Its traditions, handed down by Rome, were first assimilated by the humanists of Renaissance Italy, and thence transmitted to France and England. The earliest form assumed by the pastoral was the bucolic idyll, reminiscent of the work of Theocritus, who depicted for the sophisticated Alexandrians of the fourth century B.C. the manners and loves of the Sicilian rustics, and the charm of the island scenes. While there were doubtless realistic details in these idylls, much was idealized, and a fashion was set of presenting romance with a background of shepherd life and nature, and of using an artificial poetic diction. This convention was adopted by Virgil in his *Eclogues* (the word means short selected pieces), in many of which he gives expression to a delight in the labours of the field and the beauties of nature, and to the quiet serenity and happiness of life lived in close contact with elemental things. Virgil's love of the countryside was genuine, notwithstanding the fact that the literary form he adopted was a convention.

The pastoral achieved a wide popularity in Italy and France in the early sixteenth century. The *Arcadia* of Sannazaro (*c.* 1500) in alternating verse and prose is said to have passed through nearly sixty editions within a period of as many years. In England, Spenser in *The Shepherd's Calendar* (1579) gave us the first pastoral in the Theocritan manner. It contained twelve eclogues, one for each month of the year, all except the first and last being in dialogue form. But he used the dialect and idiom of the English peasant, and the countryside he described is that which he knew. Although Spenser's rustics seem to be well acquainted with the gods and heroes of antiquity, they have themselves very English names, e.g. Willie, Cuddie, and Colin.

The following stanza is taken from the January Eclogue. The shepherd's boy complains that his love is unrequited—

> I love thilke lasse, (alas why doe I love?)
> And am forlorne, (alas why am I lorne?)
> Shee deignes not my good will, but doth reprove,
> And of my rurall musick holdeth scorne.
> Shepheards devise[1] she hateth as the snake
> And laughes the songs, that *Colin Clout* doth make.

The *Arcadia* of Sir Philip Sidney was written in imitation of Sannazaro, and established the vogue of the pastoral in English. Cast in a mould of poetical prose, the moralizing romance found numerous imitators in the Elizabethan age, and has supplied suggestions to poets, playwrights, and romancers in every period of our literature since. It directed the attention of Greene and Lodge to the possibilities of the

---

[1] i.e. *skill.*

pastoral for drama. Peele's *Arraignment of Paris* (1584) is a pastoral play written for the Queen's Court, and containing a shepherd-interlude reminiscent of *The Shepherd's Calendar*. Through such works Shakespeare was influenced in the direction of pastoral romance, as is shown in such plays as *As You Like It* and *The Winter's Tale*, with their open-air setting and their chivalric idealization of the women characters. Fletcher's *Faithful Shepherdess* (1610) stands along with Ben Jonson's *Sad Shepherd* as the greatest of our pastoral plays. Milton, notwithstanding that he condemned Sidney's *Arcadia* as "vain and amatorious," himself used the pastoral convention in much of his early poetry, e.g. *Arcades*, *Lycidas*, and *Comus*. Herrick was a pastoral lyrist whose descriptions belonged not to an ideal world but to the actual rusticity he knew.

Almost eclipsed by the sophistication of the fashionable society of the Restoration age, the pastoral form was for a time neglected, but Pope revived it in his *Pastorals*, written at the age of sixteen. His prefatory *Discourse* contains the following description—

> A pastoral is an imitation of the action of a shepherd, or one considered under that character. The form of this imitation is dramatic, or narrative, or mixed or both; the fable simple, the manners not too polite nor too rustic: the thoughts are plain, yet admit a little quickness and passion, but that short and flowing; the expression humble, yet as pure as the language will afford; neat, but not florid; easy, and yet lively. In short, the fable, manners, thoughts, and expressions are full of the greatest simplicity in nature.

The last important work which is fully in the pastoral tradition in English is Allan Ramsay's play *Gentle Shepherd* (1725). The nature poetry of Burns, Wordsworth and Tennyson has nothing in common with the idyllic strain of the true pastoral. With them the countryside and the folk who dwelt in it were a part of living experience and not a poetic formula. We approach again the traditional pastoral convention in Matthew Arnold's *The Scholar Gipsy*.

The Elegy

The Elegy in English has no conventional form such as it had in classical literature. In Greek and Latin all emotional or reflective poems written in alternate dactylic hexameters and pentameters were called elegiac. Lamentation for the dead was not even their usual subject, and most of them dealt with patriotic and erotic themes. When during the Renaissance, the elegy found its way into English literature, the term was narrowed down to describe a song of lamentation for the dead, usually, though not necessarily, addressed to the memory of a particular person.

The most perfect elegies in English are Milton's *Lycidas*, Shelley's *Adonais*, Matthew Arnold's *Thyrsis*, and Swinburne's *Ave atque Vale*. Gray's *Elegy written in a Country Churchyard*, having no individual application, is not strictly an elegy in the modern sense, notwithstanding its title. Tennyson's *In Memoriam* can best be described as a collection of elegies. When the expression of sorrow is brief and ejaculatory rather than meditative it is more properly called a dirge, lament, monody or threnody, e.g. Jane Elliot's *A Lament for Flodden*, Wordsworth's *Three Years She Grew*, and Peacock's *Margaret Love Peacock*. Other examples of English elegiac verse are Chaucer's *Book of the Duchess*, Dunbar's *Lament for the Makaris*, Donne's *A Funeral Elegy*, Dryden's *Ode on the Death of Mrs Anne Killigrew*, and Bridges' *Elegy on a Lady*.

It is natural that the elegiac poet, writing out of deep emotion, should allow his thoughts to range over the great problems of human existence and the meaning of mortality. Thus to the expression of personal grief there is often added an effort of speculative philosophy.

The Ode

The word ode, derived from a Greek root, meaning "to sing," implies a relation with the lyric, and like the lyric it has taken a number of forms, the musical character being eventually lost altogether. But the term still retains the sense of a poem written for a special occasion, or an invocation which aims at a high elevation of thought and feeling.

We may distinguish between the choric ode, associated in origin with the Greek poet, Pindar, and the heroic ode, associated with the Greek poetess, Sappho, and the much later Latin poet Horace. Both of these kinds have been imitated by English poets. There is also the ode so-called which is no more than a piece of sustained lyric utterance without reference to any classical model.

The Pindaric ode is represented in English by Thomas Gray's two great examples, *The Progress of Poesy* and *The Bard*. Each is constructed on a system of strophe, antistrophe and epode, thrice repeated. On the supposition of a divided chorus, the antistrophe answers to the strophe in identical metrical form, while the epode stands as a kind of after-song or refrain, and follows a different pattern. William Collins varies this arrangement in imitation of a different type of classical choric ode, e.g. in his *Ode to Liberty*, which consists of strophe, epode, antistrophe and second epode. Both Gray and Collins wrote also a number of odes in uniform stanzas on the Sapphic model. Examples are Gray's *Ode on a Distant Prospect of Eton College*, and Collins' *Ode to Simplicity*.

The third kind of ode, irregular in form, is frequently found in the work of the romantic poets. Shelley's *Ode to the West Wind*, Wordsworth's *Ode on the Intimations of Immortality* and Tennyson's *Ode on the Death of the Duke of Wellington* are so markedly different in conception that it will be seen that precise definition of the term "ode" is no longer possible.

Satiric Poetry

Satire is a particular kind of expression of humorous dispraise in literary garb. It passes easily into invective, when the element of humour is deficient, and into caricature when it is too prominent. It has a didactic purpose, whether this be openly confessed, or left to be inferred. Satire is not itself a literary mode with a structural form of its own, but is rather an attitude towards a subject and to be found in almost every kind of writing. Thus satire may be an element in narrative or dramatic poetry, though not in lyric or elegy. It may constitute the undercurrent of thought in a novel. In some literary forms, e.g. the parody and the burlesque, it is indispensable, and in epigram it is usually prominent.

Among the Greeks, Aristophanes created the comedy of satire, ridiculing the affectations and opinions prominent in his day in *The Frogs, The Wasps*, and many other plays. In the literature of Rome, satire formed so important an element that it was associated with particular metrical structures and it may be spoken of as a distinct branch of literature. Among its greatest exponents were Horace, Juvenal and Martial, who were imitated by the English neo-classicists, Dryden and Pope. Out of the animal fables of Æsop, a Greek writer of the sixth century B.C., the Middle Ages developed the "bestiaries," or beast-epics, in which *Reynard the Fox* plays a large part. In these, human foibles and vices were held up for ridicule and censure. Chaucer's *Nun's Priest's Tale*, telling of Chanticleer the Cock and Dame Pertlot the Hen, is an excellent example.

Satire in the Renaissance age took a new form as the mock-heroic poem or comedy. Butler's *Hudibras* and Dryden's *MacFlecknoe* carried on the tradition in England into the seventeenth century, and in the eighteenth century this was strongly developed by Addison, Swift, Pope, and Johnson. Swift invented a new and powerful vehicle of prose satire in *Gulliver's Travels*. As the scope of literature expanded, Fielding and Smollett discovered new opportunities for the exposure of folly in the novel. Byron was a master of the satiric method which has irony as a main ingredient. It is a form of speech or writing in which the meaning intended to be conveyed is hidden beneath or is even contradicted by the literal sense of the words used.

Drama, depicting character in action, has been in all ages the subtlest means of parading oddity or perversion or downright wickedness in its own features. For here the author's point of view is eliminated, while actions not only speak for themselves, but also call forth reactions in others so that the angles of reference are multiplied. Jonson's *Comedy of Humours* and the eighteenth-century *Comedy of Manners* represent in English literature the flowering of satiric drama.

In the poetry of the Romantic Age, satire became a less prominent element, by reason of the fact that its spirit consorted ill with the dominance of the imagination. In occasional poems such as Byron's *English Bards and Scotch Reviewers*, satire still found its way into verse, but it used increasingly the vehicle of prose and was widely diffused in the novel and the essay. There are indications, however, of a rehabilitation of poetic satire in contemporary writing, and much of the poetry of T. S. Eliot has a satiric flavour.

It would require far more space than is available in this volume to enumerate the lesser kinds of verse-forms, which are as varied as the manifestations of human thought and feeling. It is necessary to mention only the epigram, the epitaph in verse, the hymn, the parody, and nonsense verse, whether irregular in form or written to a pattern like the "Limerick." Such verse forms may minister to the highest purposes of human existence or may serve only for our amusement in an idle hour. But the delicacy or triviality of the theme may still be matched with verbal music. As an example of such a union, the form known as Anacreontic may be mentioned.

Anacreontics

Anacreontics are light-hearted and graceful poems dealing with the topics of Love and Wine, after the manner of the Greek poet, Anacreon, of the sixth century B.C. Many were translated by Abraham Cowley.

The two following poems of Robert Herrick are excellent examples of the style—

Upon a Maid

Here she lies (in bed of spice)
Fair as Eve in Paradise:
For her beauty it was such
Poets could not praise too much.
Virgins come, and in a ring
Her supremest requiem sing;
Then depart, but see ye tread
Lightly, lightly o'er the dead.

Anacreontic

Born I was to be old,
    And for to die here:
After that, in the mould
    Long for to lie here.
But before that day comes,
    Still I be bousing;
For I know, in the tombs
    There's no carousing.

A later writer of anacreontic trifles in English was Thomas Moore, who published a collection of them in 1800.

Poetic Diction

The problem of providing poetry with the aptest language was notably discussed by Wordsworth in the preface to the Second Edition of the *Lyrical Ballads*; but it is one which had long before engaged the attention of poets and critics. Aristotle in his *Poetics* laid it down as a principle that the language of poetry should be distinctive. Poetry, being in his view concerned with ideal, rather than actual, truth, must be lifted above the associations of mundane life and saved from commonness. Its dignity could be preserved and its beauty protected only by the use of a diction which had the sanction of a tradition and admitted no words and expressions which were contaminated, as Dr. Johnson said, with "the grossness of domestic use."

Though this canon of poetic diction to a large degree governed the attitude of writers particularly during the period of the Renaissance and the following centuries when classical influences were strong, another aspect of the true function of poetry is to be found not so much in formal statement of principle as in the actual practice of poets. The verse of Chaucer is relatively free from conventional epithets, superimposed ornament of style, inversions, periphrases and other conscious contrivances, whose object is to avoid the necessity of calling a spade a spade. He was able to use for verse a simple and direct style employing the words of everyday speech and combining them in the familiar idiom of the people—

> Whoso shall tell a tale after a man,
> He moste reherse, as neighe as ever he can,
> Everich word, if it be in his charge,
> Al speke he never so rudely and so large;
> Or elles he moste tellen his tale untrewe,
> Or feinen thinges, or finden wordes newe.
>
> *Prologue: Canterbury Tales*

This tradition of a natural, forthright style, was never forgotten in England. Much of Shakespeare's greatest poetry is couched in language which is an echo of the vernacular. Milton, on the other hand, sought for an elevated diction fit to express—

> Things unattempted yet in prose or rhyme

and achieved his end by the adoption of a Latinized idiom and vocabulary. The unit of utterance with him became the period, a rhetorical device for holding the weight of the sentence until the close. Qualifications of the main statement are fitted into the body of it, so that the sense is not completed until all or nearly all of these have been placed in due subordination, and the way made open for the predicate to complete the meaning—

> Into this wild Abyss,
> The womb of Nature, and perhaps her grave,
> Of neither Sea, nor Shore, nor Air, nor Fire,
> But all these in their pregnant causes mixed
> Confusedly, and which thus must ever fight,
> Unless the Almighty Maker them ordain
> His dark materials to create more worlds—
> Into this wild Abyss the wary fiend
> Stood on the brink of Hell and looked awhile,
> Pondering his voyage; for no narrow frith
> He had to cross.
>
> MILTON: *Paradise Lost*

Compare this with the so-called loose style, more characteristic of English common-speech, with a repetitive pattern of subject, predicate and object placed in that order, with qualifying phrases and clauses closely attached—

> I'll have these players
> Play something like the murder of my father
> Before mine uncle: I'll observe his looks;
> I'll taunt him to the quick: if he but blench,
> I know my course. The spirit that I have seen
> May be the devil; and the devil hath power
> T'assume a pleasing shape.
>
> SHAKESPEARE: *Hamlet*

Other features of classical diction include the use of the conventional or stock epithets, often involving tautology. Milton's epics afford many examples: *winged* speed, *impetuous* fury, *sovran* throne, *aetherial* fires, *pearly* shells, *dolorous* groan, *hostile* frown. There is an avoidance of direct statement: a lake is a "liquid plain," gunpowder is "smutty grain," fragrance is "balmy spoils." Objects acquire in this way a kind of literary label, the use of which is presumed to lift the description from the level of the commonplace to one which has the associations of poetry.

Milton may be said to have invented the poetic diction which disfigured so much minor eighteenth-century verse. When used not in passages transfused with emotional significance, where it was tolerable, but in verse which was merely imitative, it became a stale jargon, a stereotyped trick of speech devoid of all power to give us any aesthetic satisfaction. The following lines from Thomson's *Seasons* will serve as an example—

> When with his lively ray the potent sun
> Has pierced the streams, and roused the finny race,
> Then, issuing cheerful, to thy sport repair;
> Chief should the western breezes curling play,
> And light o'er ether bear the shadowy clouds.

The Reaction against Poetic Diction

It was against the employment of this pseudo-poetic diction that Wordsworth argued. He advocated the use in poetry of "a selection of the language really used by men," and claimed that there could not be "any difference between the language of prose and metrical composition." In giving his opinion that "the first poets of all nations wrote from passion excited by real events" and that poetic diction was of later growth, Wordsworth was certainly wrong, for even in the diction of Homer and Hesiod there is to be found a strong traditional element. Nor could he in practice always rid himself of the impulse to conform to an accepted pattern of poetic speech. Notwithstanding some superb achievements in the pursuit of his "experiment," Wordsworth was in constant danger of echoing the artificial phraseology of the poets whom he criticizes—

> Nor less, to feed voluptuous thought,
> The beauteous forms of Nature wrought,
> Fair trees and lovely flowers;
> The breezes their own languor lent;
> The stars had feelings, which they sent
> Into those magic bowers.

In this stanza, the words *beauteous, languor* and *bowers* are typical of the depreciated verbal coinage which drove out of eighteenth-century poetry the sound currency of living speech.

The controversy is still far from being resolved. But the issue is perhaps not now considered so important as it seemed when Words-worth and Coleridge based on it whole theories of the nature of poetry. The verse of their immediate predecessors dealt very largely with nature, and it will be observed that the hackneyed forms which are complained of arose principally in descriptions of the external world. It was the lack of a genuine love and a direct observation of natural objects which led some writers to the use of an artificial diction. The range of modern poetry is vastly enlarged, and the temptation to borrow is correspondingly less strong. Tradition in our life counts for much less than it formerly did because of the changes in the fundamental pattern of society which compel us to adopt fresh patterns of behaviour in every generation. It could hardly be that language, including the language of poetry, should escape the infection of change. It is to-day accepted that a poet is to be esteemed not because of his conformity to rules or standards prescribed by the authority of the past, but rather because of a quality that is in himself and his writing; in short, his own personality.

Wordsworth's discussion of the proper relation between language and poetry was vitiated by a false aesthetic theory, which suggested that the poetic vision could exist independently of language, as though it were possible to conceive "a mute, inglorious Milton," a poet in fact,

> Yet lacking the accomplishment of verse.

This would be to suppose that the language of poetry is nothing more than a dress, an added ornament, and to assume that the vision could exist without it. Rather should it be said that without language there could be no vision, and that the poetic impulse is limited and conditioned by the extent to which the poet is able to give verbal expression to his thought and feeling. It is, in truth, through the use of the appropriate art-medium (language, form, colour, or sound) that the artist becomes fully aware of what it is that possesses his soul. The poet's true function is the discovery of himself.

SUGGESTIONS FOR FURTHER READING

OWEN BARFIELD: *Poetic Diction: A Study in Meaning* (Faber & Faber).
A. E. HOUSMAN: *The Name and Nature of Poetry* (Cambridge Univ. Press).
C. DAY LEWIS: *The Poetic Image* (Cape).
W. M. DIXON: *English Epic and Heroic Poetry* (Dent).

CHAPTER IV

PROSODIC FORMS

PROSODY treats of the architecture of verse. It is the science which is concerned with the structural systems embodied in all metrical compositions. When we speak of the *laws* of prosody, it is important to remember that these laws are in no way to be regarded as forming a code of rules binding on writers of verse. They are rather statements of certain uniformities formulated after observation and comparison of the practice of versifiers. The laws of prosody therefore have the character of all scientific laws. They tell us how particular metrical effects are produced, without in any way suggesting that these effects are necessary, or are most to be commended, or are only thus to be achieved. Just as the poet relying upon his intuitive sense of word-music, may be ignorant of prosody as a science, so also the lover of poetry can achieve a high degree of aesthetic satisfaction from his reading, without understanding the technicalities of prosodic structure. Notwithstanding this, the study of prosody is an interesting and profitable aspect of literary appreciation.

The word "metre" is derived from a Greek root signifying to measure, and when used in connexion with verse, it implies the existence of units of measurement. There is, however, considerable contention among prosodists as to the real nature of these units, the employment of which in rhythmical patterns constitutes the structural principle of verse. The convention of printing verse in "lines," which are not the normal unit lines of prose-print on a page, renders the pattern to some extent visible, but within the line the rhythmical principle or pulse is discernible only by the ear or by the ear-memory involved in silent reading.

English is a language of strong accents. It is a characteristic of English words and phrases that the stresses fall unevenly on the syllables. In French the stresses are distributed much more evenly, or to put it another way, there are no marked stresses. The English word *extra-ordinary* has a minor stress on the first syllable, a major stress on the third, while on the second, fourth, fifth and sixth syllables there is no stress at all. The French word *extraordinaire* is spoken evenly, with almost equal value given to each of its five syllables.

The accentuation of English words affects their meaning. *Absent*, with the stress on the first syllable, is an adjective, but with the stress on the second it is a verb. *Gallant* and *present* are other examples of words having two quite different meanings according to the position of the stress. The "Good Afternoon" with which we greet a roomful of people when we enter and the "Good Afternoon" with which we take our leave are spoken with different inflections.

In English verse the fullest use is made of this accentual characteristic of words and phrases, in order to produce a cadence or parallelism of sound which is called metre. Just as a pattern of colours involves the juxtaposition of two or more colours or shades, so the pattern of metre is made by a rhythmical sequence of strongly and weakly accented syllables organized in feet and lines. Such a sequence, if uniform over a long passage, gives a crude sing-song effect, appropriate enough for cradle songs and nursery rhymes, which are often accompanied by rhythmical movement. But the higher music of verse is achieved through counterpoint or antithesis, whereby, without the abandonment of the fundamental rhythm, there are divergencies from the norm.

The Quantitative Principle of Metre

Classical metres were based on quantity, the unit length of speech-time being that of the syllable containing a short vowel. The syllable having a long vowel was assumed to require double the time for utterance. A long vowel was such either by nature or by virtue of its position (e.g. before two consonants). An iambic foot consisted of a one-unit syllable followed by a two-unit syllable; a dactyl consisted of a two-unit syllable followed by two one-unit syllables. A dactylic line often contained as a variant a spondee, that is, two two-unit syllables in succession. More rarely, a pyrrhic was used, that is two one-unit syllables in succession.

English verse-rhythm may contain an element of quantity, in so far as a stressed syllable frequently has a long vowel, and occupies a longer time in utterance than an unstressed or weakly stressed syllable. This is seen to be the case in the lines—

Tóll for the bráve

The bráve that áre no móre.

The marks of length (-) coincide with the marks of stress (').

But it will be seen from the two following lines that this correspondence is by no means to be considered as a fundamental principle—

All súnk beneath the wáve

Fást by their nátive shóre.

The vowels on "sunk" and "fast" support major stresses yet are
short.

Attempts have been made by some English poets to reproduce the
effect of Greek or Latin quantitative rhythms. "It was actually a moot
question in the year 1579," say the authors of *The Age of Shakespeare*,[1]
"whether . . . English poetry should not be written for the future
in metres consecrated by Greek or Latin usage." About that time
many experiments were made, especially in the writing of hexameters,[2]
e.g. by Gabriel Harvey, Sir Philip Sidney, and Edmund Spenser,
but the force and fixity of the syllabic accent in English words condemned to failure such attempts to ignore it in favour of a quantitative
principle.

Notwithstanding these failures, and others which lie at the door
of some of our Augustan poets, the attempts were resumed by certain
of the Romantics. Southey wrote his *Vision of Judgement* as laureate
task-work in hexameters. Better known to-day are Longfellow's
Evangeline and Arthur Hugh Clough's *Bothie of Tobernavuolich*. From
the latter the following lines are quoted—

> You are shut in, left alone with yourself and perfection of water,
> Hid on all sides, left alone with yourself and the goddess of bathing,
> Here, the pride of the plunger, you stride the fall and clear it,
> Here the delight of the bather, you roll in beaded sparklings,
> Here into pure green depth drop down from lofty ridges.

It will be seen from this example that Clough, while seeking to
reproduce hexametric rhythm, departed from the classical rule by
sometimes using stressed vowels (even if short) in the place that should
be occupied by long vowels (e.g. "hid" in the second line). Tennyson
attempted something more ambitious, composing verses in which
every stressed syllable should be long and every long syllable stressed.
He came near to accomplishing this in his "Alcaics" on Milton.

---

[1] Seccombe and Allen: *The Age of Shakespeare*, Vol. I (G. Bell & Son).
[2] The normal hexameter line in Greek and Latin verse consisted of five dactyls (varied
by an occasional spondee) with a trochee or spondee to end the line.

Alcaic metre, invented by Alcaeus, a lyric poet who lived in Lesbos about 600 B.C., runs as follows—

> O mighty-mouthed inventor of harmonies,
> O skilled to sing of Time and Eternity,
> God-gifted organ voice of England,
> Milton a name to resound for ages.

Swinburne and Browning both succeeded tolerably in producing the effect of choriambics, which are feet of four syllables, the first and fourth being long, the others short (— ‿ ‿ —).

The Accentual Principle of Metre

While Greek and Latin verse was thus based entirely on quantity, English verse is based on tonal accent, with speech-rhythm superimposed. It is unfortunate that the nomenclature of prosody has been borrowed from the classical writers on the subject, since we have to adapt the meanings of their prosodic terms to suit a versification constructed upon totally different principles. In Greek and Latin verse accent and speech-rhythm were disregarded. But when we use the term "iambic" to describe the metrical form of the lines—

> But she is in her grave, and oh,
> The difference to me!

we are using it with reference to the way in which a relatively weakly stressed syllable is followed by one which is more powerfully stressed, this sequence being subject to the overriding necessity of not sacrificing sense by ignoring speech-rhythm. Moreover there is no suggestion of metrical feet (here consisting normally of two syllables) being equivalent in time value.

If we analyse more closely the rhythm of English verse, we shall find that it is extremely complex in character. First of all, we shall notice that some of the syllables have imposed on them a heavy tonal accent, while others are but lightly intoned—

> Tomorrow∧and tomorrow∧and tomorrow∧
>
> Creeps∧in this petty pace∧from day to day∧
>
> To the last syllable∧of recorded time.

These heavy tonal accents are produced by a relatively forcible emission of voice, resulting in loudness. Next there is a succession of irregular pauses or retardations, shown above by the sign ∧ breaking up the lines into phrases or words corresponding to units of thought, e.g. "from day to day." These pauses are related to speech-rhythms, and are a function of grammar since they assist in establishing meaning. It will be observed that there is no uniform relation between these slackenings of speed and the incidence of the stresses.

Metrical Forms

We may now proceed to the analysis of the metrical forms which are common in English verse. To help us in this analysis we require a notation. To begin with, the irreducible unit of metre is called the foot, consisting usually of a stressed syllable associated with one or two unstressed or weakly stressed syllables. A foot of two syllables (duple metre) may be one of rising (iambic) or falling (trochaic) cadence; that is, the accentual force may surge from the first to the second syllable, or on the other hand it may sink down from a stronger to a weaker stress, e.g.

Duple metre rising—

> Whenas in silks my Julia goes.
> > HERRICK: *To Julia*

Duple metre falling—

> Werther had a love for Charlotte
>
> Such as words could never utter.
> > THACKERAY: *The Sorrows of Werther*

Triple metre, consisting of feet of three syllables, may similarly manifest a rising or a falling cadence. In the passage—

> And the beasts, and the birds and the insects were drowned
>
> In an ocean of dreams. . . .
> > SHELLEY: *The Sensitive Plant*

the stress falls on the third syllable of each foot, called an anapaest.

Compare this with the line of falling cadence called a dactyl—

> Just for a riband to stick in his coat . . .
> > BROWNING: *The Lost Leader*

Although a foot of triple metre with the stress on the middle syllables (known as the amphibrach) is sometimes distinguished from the anapaest and the dactyl, there is little purpose served in so doing, because it is more natural to read a so-called amphibrachic line as one of the above with an incomplete foot to begin or to end the line, or both. Thus the line—

Most friendship is feigning, most loving mere folly.

SHAKESPEARE: *As You Like It*

is best considered as triple rising (anapaestic), with an iambic (duple rising) start, and a loose or hypermetric syllable at the close. It would of course have been equally possible to consider the line as one of falling (or dactylic) cadence, with an unattached syllable at the beginning and an incomplete dactylic foot at the end.

It is seldom that the metrical pattern is rigidly followed for many lines in succession. Variations are admitted, and indeed it is often through departures from the norm that the most delightful sound-effects are produced. An inversion of stresses will give an iamb in a trochaic line or a trochee in an iambic line. The rhythm of duple metre is frequently varied by a change to triple metre, or *vice versa*. Feet are left unfinished, producing effects of pause which may be of considerable significance in conveying sense or mood. Sometimes the smooth flow of iambics or trochees is broken by the interposition of one or more feet in which both syllables have either an equally heavy stress (the spondee) or have equally weak stresses (the pyrrhic): as in the italicized parts of the following—

Here where the proud their long-*drawn pomps* display

GOLDSMITH: *The Deserted Village*

'Twas mus*ical*, but sadly sweet

BYRON: *Siege of Corinth*

Swift, swift, you dragons of the night, that dawning
May bare the raven's eye . . .

SHAKESPEARE: *Cymbeline*

. . . let that be left
Which leaves itself: *to the sea-side straightway*

SHAKESPEARE: *Antony and Cleopatra*

Blank Verse

Certain prosodic forms have played so outstanding a part in our literary history that they must receive fuller treatment.

The term "blank verse" connotes "without rhyme" but, as commonly used, it refers to unrhymed iambic pentameter, a measure introduced by the Earl of Surrey (see page 88) in his translation of the *Aeneid*. This subsequently became the principal medium for epic and narrative poetry and poetic drama.

As first used in English, blank verse was a stiff, pedestrian measure, lacking grace. The stresses were nearly all of equal force, rigidly spaced on the iambic model; the thought usually breaks off with the lines—

> By the calm seas came fleeting adders twain,
> Which plied towards the shore (I loathe to tell)
> With reared breast lift up above the seas:
> Whose bloody crests aloft the waves were seen.
> The hinder part swam hidden in the flood.
> Their grisly backs were linked manifold.
>
> EARL OF SURREY: *Translation of the Aeneid*

If we compare these lines with the following, written thirty years later, it will be seen how greatly the line had developed within such a short space of time—

> And had she lived before the siege of Troy,
> Helen (whose beauty summoned Greece to arms,
> And drew a thousand ships to Tenedos)
> Had not been named in Homer's Iliad;
> *Her* name had been in every line he writ.
> Or had those wanton poets, for whose birth
> Old Rome was proud, but gazed a while on her
> Nor Lesbia nor Corinna had been named;
> Zenocrate had been the argument
> Of every epigram or elegy.
>
> MARLOWE: *Tamburlaine II. iv*

Here we have blank verse made flexible, the "mighty line" forged to a fine temper, capable of an infinite variety of cadence. Marlowe's music found a still richer echo in the verse of Shakespeare and Milton—

> Be not afraid. The isle is full of noises,
> Sounds and sweet airs, that give delight and hurt not.
> Sometimes a thousand twanging instruments
> Will hum about mine ears, and sometimes voices
> That, if I then had waked after long sleep,
> Will make me sleep again.
>
> SHAKESPEARE: *The Tempest III. 2*

> Down thither prone in flight
> He speeds, and through the vast ethereal sky
> Sails between worlds and worlds, with steady wing
> Now on the polar winds; then with quick fan
> Winnows the buxom air, till, within soar
> Of towering eagles, to all the fowls he seems
> A phoenix, gaz'd by all.
>
> MILTON: *Paradise Lost V*

One further example of the immense range of blank verse may be quoted from the nineteenth century—

> And I have felt
> A presence that disturbs me with the joy
> Of elevated thoughts; a sense sublime
> Of something far more deeply interfused,
> Whose dwelling is the light of setting suns,
> And the round ocean and the living air,
> And the blue sky, and in the mind of man;
> A motion and a spirit, that impels
> All thinking things, all objects of all thoughts,
> And rolls through all things.
>
> WORDSWORTH: *Tintern Abbey*

If we examine these passages, it will be seen how the hard regular beat of the earliest blank verse has given place to a complex harmony.

The lines of Surrey are all decasyllabic, containing five equal stresses, and they invariably end on a strong stress completing the grammatical sentence or phrase. The more developed forms of blank verse are marked by—

(1) *Enjambement*, or the carrying of the sense over from one line to the next.

(2) Lines lengthened by the addition of weak (i.e. unstressed) end-syllables, sometimes called feminine endings (e.g. *noises*).

(3) Inversions of rhythm.

(4) The use of caesura or rhetorical pause in varying positions in line. In the passage quoted from Shakespeare, the caesura appears in successive lines after the 4th (twice), 2nd, 6th, 1st, and 6th syllables. The effect of this variation is to produce a speech-unit of constantly changing length. The delicate balance between the metrical pattern and the natural speech rhythm issues in the characteristically ordered freedom of blank verse, neither unduly fettered by the iron demands of the rhythmical scheme, nor on the other hand liable to collapse entirely into plain prose, though disintegration may go far.

The following passage from Beaumont and Fletcher: *A King and No King* represents blank verse in an advanced stage of disintegration—

> First Swordsman
>> We have examined, from your lordship's foot there
>> To this man's head, the nature of the beatings;
>> And we do find his honour is come off
>> Clean and sufficient: this, as our swords shall help us!
>
> Bacurius
>> You are much bound to your bilbo-men;
>> I am glad you are straight again, Captain. 'Twere good
>> You would think on way to gratify them.

and the next, from Webster's *Duchess of Malfi*, further illustrates the progression of Jacobean dramatic verse in the direction of prose—

> Why, now 'tis most apparent; this precise fellow
> Is the duchess' bawd: I have it to my wish!
> This is a parcel of intelligency
> Our courtiers were cas'd up for: it needs must follow
> That I must be committed on pretence
> Of poisoning her; which I'll endure, and laugh at.
> If one could find the father now! but that
> Time will discover. Old Castruccio
> I' the morning posts to Rome: by him I'll send
> A letter that shall make her brothers' galls
> O'erflow their livers. This was a thrifty way.

The basic pattern is even here not completely obliterated by the stronger speech-rhythms which have been superimposed on it.

The Heroic Couplet

The heroic couplet[1] has a longer ancestry than blank verse, since it was introduced into English literature by Chaucer. It has been used

---

[1] The heroic metre of classical literature was the dactylic hexameter, as used for the *Iliad* and *Odyssey* and the *Aeneid*. In French literature the heroic metre is the alexandrine, an iambic line of six feet, the name being possibly derived from its use in early poems recounting the exploits of Alexander the Great.

The term *heroic* as used in literary phraseology is derived from the "heroic age" of Greece, the exploits of whose demi-gods and legendary figures furnished the themes for Greek poetry and drama. The interest in classical literature, which was an important feature of the Renaissance, led to imitations of the grandiose style, which was applied to romantic themes without any regard for naturalness or probability, and carried off by bombastic declamation concerning "impossible valour devoted to a pursuit of impossible beauty." Such heroic romances became popular first in France, in the early seventeenth century, then the mode passed to England and we have heroic tragedies such as Dryden's *Tyrannic Love*, a play marred by ranting absurdities. It was considered by Dryden that the rhyming or heroic couplet was the only appropriate vehicle for this kind of historical oratorio, which was chanted rather than spoken. The term "heroic poetry" is sometimes used in the sense of "epic," and heroic verse in English may imply no more than the use of the iambic pentameter, as in the title *Heroic Stanzas*, given by Dryden to his elegiac poem on Oliver Cromwell.

for a great variety of purposes: in particular, for narrative, drama, satire, polemics and exposition. But it is not a medium adapted for lyrical utterance, since its qualities spring rather from intellectual than from emotional states of consciousness. Heroic verse, it must be noted, is constituted by the rhyming distich or couplet, not by the single line. Occasionally a grouping of three rhyming lines is permitted. Chaucer's use of the heroic couplet in *The Canterbury Tales* demonstrated once for all its value for narrative—

> I wol my-selven gladly with you ryde,
> Right at myn owne cost, and be your gyde.
> And who-so wol my jugément withseye
> Shal paye al that we spenden by the weye.
> And if ye vouchesauf that it be so
> Tel me anon, with-outen wordes mo,
> And I wol erly shapé me therfore.

The tradition was passed on to the Elizabethans by the Scottish poet Blind Harry in his *Wallace*. Marlowe used it to excellent effect in his *Hero and Leander*, and Ben Jonson in his panegyric on Shakespeare—

> Soul of the age!
> The applause! delight! the wonder of our Stage!
> My Shakespeare rise, I will not judge thee by
> Chaucer, or Spenser or bid Beaumont lye
> A little further, to make thee a room:
> Thou art a monument, without a tomb,
> And art alive still, while thy book doth live,
> And we have wits to read and praise to give.

Shakespeare himself often used the rhymed couplet, particularly to round off an argument or close a scene—

> The time is out of joint:—O cursed spite,
> That ever I was born to set it right!
> *Hamlet I. 5*

The apogee of the heroic couplet was reached in the Augustan Age of English poetry, which corresponded closely to the life of Alexander Pope, when it became the principal medium used in poetry of the serious sort. In the hands of Pope and his imitators it was a polished weapon of controversy, barbed with wit and sharpened with antithesis.

The heroic couplet and the artificial diction which was associated with it were rejected by the Lake poets in favour of a style which came nearer to natural speech, though some of the Romantics, e.g. Shelley, Byron, and Keats, still had a use for it. The later Romantics, such as Swinburne, used it extensively, but allowed themselves a freedom which was quite foreign to the ideal of correctness pursued by the Augustans. The following examples point the contrast—

> Behold the child, by Nature's kindly law,
> Pleased with a rattle, tickled with a straw:
> Some livelier play-thing gives his youth delight,
> A little louder, but as empty quite:
> Scarfs, garters, gold, amuse his riper stage,
> And beads and pray'r-books are the toys of age:
> Pleas'd with this bauble still, as that before:
> 'Till tir'd he sleeps, and Life's poor play is o'er.
>
> POPE: *Essay on Man. Epistle II*

With this compare the following passage—

> A thing of beauty is a joy for ever:
> Its loveliness increases; it will never
> Pass into nothingness; but still will keep
> A bower quiet for us, and a sleep
> Full of sweet dreams, and health and quiet breathing.
>
> KEATS: *Endymion*

In the latter we have the heroic couplet using the same freedoms as characterize mature blank verse; namely, a diversified rhythm, enjambement, feminine endings, a varied caesura. Three of the lines contain eleven syllables. There is nothing left of the antithetical polish of Pope's couplets; a subtle music has taken its place.

Stanza Forms

The term *stanza* has an affinity of meaning with the classical term *strophe*, both implying a recurrence of a structural form within a poem to the extent of two lines or more. English poets have invented innumerable forms of stanza, and some of them have become so firmly established in our literary tradition as to require detailed reference.

The earliest well-marked stanza is that known as the Chaucerian stanza of seven five-foot iambic lines, rhyming, *a b a b b c c*, which was his first departure from the octosyllabic couplet. It was used for *Troilus and Criseyde*, the *Legend of Good Women*, the *Parliament of Foules* and other poems—

> And for ther is so greet diversitee
> In English and in wryting of our tonge,
> So preye I God that noon miswryte thee,
> Ne thee mismetre for defaute of tonge.
> And red wher-so thou be or elles songe,
> That thou be understoode I God beseche!
> But yet to purpos of my rather speche.
>
> *Troilus and Criseyde: The Envoy*

This stanza was an adaptation from the famous *ottava rima*, an Italian form of eight lines of eleven syllables, rhyming *a b a b a b c c*, used by the epic poets Tasso and Ariosto. By the curtailment of the line to the English "heroic" type of ten syllables, and the omission of the fifth line, we get the Chaucerian stanza. Byron in *Don Juan* followed the Italian eight-lined model except that he too used a ten-syllabled line. The Chaucerian Stanza is sometimes called *Rime Royal*, an allusion to its use by James I of Scotland in *The King's Quair*.[1]

The nine-lined Spenserian stanza was a development from the Chaucerian, and is achieved by the addition of two lines, making the rhyming scheme *a b a b b c b c c*, and by the transformation of the final pentameter into an Alexandrine. By this means there was created a poetic instrument of consummate melody, yet apt for rapid narrative. The interlacing rhymes, the central couplet (4th and 5th lines), the prolongation of the rhythm in the "linked sweetness long drawn out" of the Alexandrine rolling over like every ninth breaker on the beach, all help to produce the richly suffused harmony of which the stanza is capable in the hands of a master poet. In the words of Lowell, "the melody of one stanza seems for ever longing and feeling forward after that which is to follow."

The following example is from the description of Mammon's cave in Book II of *The Faerie Queene*—

> Both roofe, and floore, and walls were all of gold
> But overgrowne with dust and old decay,
> And hid in darknesse, that none could behold
> The hew thereof: for vew of chearefull day
> Did neuer in that house it selfe display,
> But a fainte shadow of vncertain light;
> Such as a lamp, whose life does fade away:
> Or as the Moone, cloathèd with clowdy night,
> Does shew to him, that walkes in feare and sad affright.

Among those who have used the stanza with complete success are: James Thomson (*Castle of Indolence*), Burns (*Cottar's Saturday Night*), Byron (*Childe Harold*), Keats (*Eve of St. Agnes*), Shelley (*Adonais*), and Tennyson (*Lotus Eaters*).

The Sonnet

The Sonnet is not strictly speaking a stanza, because it is a complete poem and not a recurring pattern within a poem. This is so, notwithstanding the fact that Sonnets have often been written in sequences

---

[1] Quair = quire or book.

such as Sir Philip Sidney's *Astrophel and Stella* and E. B. Browning's *Sonnets from the Portuguese*. Even when the sonnet sequences are variations on a single theme, each sonnet has an independent existence.

The true sonnet has always fourteen lines, but in the Italian variety the lines have eleven syllables (cf. *ottava rima* above), in the French twelve, and in the English ten. The rhymes in the classical model of Petrarch (14th century) were arranged *a b b a a b b a* in the octave (or opening section) and *c d e c d e, c d c e d e, c d c e e d, c d c d c d*, or other arrangement of two or three rhymes, in the sestet (or conclusion), provided always that the sonnet did not *end* in a couplet. This form of the sonnet has been often imitated, e.g. by Milton, Wordsworth, Arnold, and Rossetti, but the relative paucity of rhymes in our language compared with Italian may have given rise in English to a rhyme scheme presenting less difficulty. The sonnets of Shakespeare are built up of three quatrains, with separate pairs of rhymes (*a b a b*, *c d c d, e f e f*) and a couplet (*g g,*) to conclude. This example has also been widely followed—

> That time of year thou mayst in me behold,
> When yellow leaves, or none, or few do hang
> Upon those boughs which shake against the cold,
> Bare, ruin'd choirs, where late the sweet birds sang.
> In me thou see'st the twilight of such day,
> As after sunset fadeth in the west,
> And by and by black night doth take away,
> Death's second self, that seals up all in rest.
> In me thou see'st the glowing of such fire,
> That on the ashes of his youth doth lie,
> As the death-bed, whereon it must expire,
> Consum'd with that which it was nourished by.
>   This thou perceiv'st, which makes thy love more strong,
>   To love that well, which thou must leave ere long.
>   SHAKESPEARE: *Sonnets* No. 73

The Petrarchan and the Shakespearian models may be further compared in the following examples from Milton and Keats respectively, written on a similar theme—

Petrarchan Model

> How soon hath time, the subtle thief of youth
> Stolen on his wing my three-and-twentieth year!
> My hasting days fly on with full career,
> But my late spring no bud or blossom shew'th.

Perhaps my semblance might deceive the truth
That I to manhood am arrived so near;
And inward ripeness doth much less appear,
That some more timely-happy spirits endu'th.
Yet be it less or more, or soon or slow,
It shall be still in strictest measure even
To that same lot, however mean or high,
Toward which Time leads me, and the will of Heaven.
All is, if I have grace to use it so,
As ever in my great Task-Master's eye.

JOHN MILTON

Shakespearian Model

When I have fears that I may cease to be
Before my pen has glean'd my teeming brain,
Before high piled books, in charact'ry,
Hold like rich garners the full-ripen'd grain;
When I behold upon the night's starr'd face,
Huge cloudy symbols of a high romance,
And think that I may never live to trace
Their shadows, with the magic hand of chance;
And when I feel, fair creature of an hour!
That I shall never look upon thee more,
Never have relish in the faery power
Of unreflecting love! then on the shore
Of the wide world I stand alone, and think
Till Love and Fame to nothingness do sink.

JOHN KEATS

It will be noticed that in Milton's sonnet the *volta*, or turning point between the octave and the sestet, is well marked, whereas in Keats' sonnet it is less so. On the other hand the latter falls into a pattern of quatrains, beginning "When I have fears," "When I behold", and "And when I feel." The final couplet has an effect of climax or resolution, which is quite foreign to the Italian type.

Lesser Metrical Forms

It has been found possible in English poetry to accommodate a large number of metrical forms which have been first used in other languages, as well as to achieve a great variety of verbal music with new arrangements. Among the borrowed forms which have been successfully employed are *Terza Rima, Ballade, Sestina, Rondeau, Triolet,* and *Villanelle.*

Terza Rima is a structural scheme originating in early Provençal and Italian folk-rhymes, which has since been elevated to the highest literary uses. It is a system of stanzas of three lines the first and third of which rhyme, the end syllable of the second line being linked in rhyme with the first and third of the next stanza and so throughout the poem (*a b a, b c b, c d c, d e d,* etc.). Every rhyming sound except the first and last is thus used three times. *Terza rima* was the measure of Dante's *Divina Commedia*, and Boccaccio also used it. Its difficulty has prevented its frequent use in English, but Shelley adopted it for his *Ode to the West Wind*—

O wild West Wind, thou breath of Autumn's being	*a*
Thou from whose unseen presence the leaves dead	*b*
Are driven, like ghosts from an enchanter fleeing,	*a*
Yellow, and black, and pale, and hectic red,	*b*
Pestilence-stricken multitudes: O thou,	*c*
Who chariotest to their dark wintry bed.	*b*
The winged seeds, where they lie cold and low, . . .	*c*

Another notable example of the use of *terza rima* in English is the poem *Casa Guidi Windows* by E. B. Browning.

The *Ballade*, which has no relation to the Ballad, is of French derivation. Its true form consists of three stanzas of eight lines each, concluding with an *envoi* of four lines, all lines being of equal length. Three rhymes only are permitted, and these are repeated throughout in a fixed order: *a b a b b c b c,* followed by *b c b c* in the *envoi*. Each stanza and the *envoi* should end with an unchanged refrain of one or two lines. An early example is Chaucer's *Compleynt of Venus* (without an *envoi*). Examples from mid-Victorian times, when interest in the Ballade was revived after a long interval, are to be found in the poems of Swinburne, Austin Dobson, Andrew Lang, W. E. Henley, and Edmund Gosse, most of whom experimented successfully also with the forms described below.

The *Sestina* was an Italian form used by Dante and Petrarch. It is a poem of thirty-nine lines, arranged in six stanzas of six lines each, with an *envoi* of three lines. There are two rhymes only, and the rhyming words are repeated in a different order in the successive stanzas. Swinburne's famous example, "I saw my soul at rest upon a day," uses in the opening stanzas the rhymes day, night, way, light, may delight; these are varied in the second as follows: delight, day, light, way, night, may, and so on throughout. In the *envoi*, all six words are used.

The *Rondeau* is another literary plaything involving a rigid pattern. There are three stanzas of five, three and five octo- or decasyllabic lines containing only two rhymes. The opening phrase is used as a refrain at the end of the second and third stanzas. The *Roundel* is a variant of this, consisting of three three-lined stanzas linked by two rhymes.

The following example of the *Rondeau* is by Sir Thomas Wyatt—

Complaint for True Love Unrequited

What 'vaileth truth, or by it to take pain?
To strive by steadfastness for to attain
How to be just, and free from doubleness?
Since all alike where ruleth craftiness,
Rewarded is both crafty, false and plain.

Soonest he speeds that most can lie and feign;
True meaning heart is had in high disdain;
Against deceit and cloakèd doubleness
    What 'vaileth truth?

Deceived is he by false and crafty train,
That means no guile, and faithful doth remain
Within the trap, without help or redress:
But for to love, lo, such a stern mistress,
Where cruelty dwells, alas, it were in vain.
    What 'vaileth truth?

The *Triolet* is a poem consisting of a single eight-lined stanza with two rhymes, arranged *a b a a a b a b*. The first line is repeated as the fourth and seventh, while the second occurs again as the eighth. The neatness and delicacy of the form owes much to its origin in the Troubadour poetry of France.

The following is a Triolet written by Patrick Carey (*c.* 1651)—

Worldly designs, fears, hopes, farewell!
  Farewell all earthly joys and cares!
On nobler thoughts my soul shall dwell;
Worldly designs, fears, hopes, farewell!
All quiet in my peaceful cell,
  I'll think on God, free from your snares;
Worldly designs, fears, hopes, farewell!
  Farewell all earthly joys and cares!

The Villanelle. Originally a pastoral form, appropriate for use in dancing, the villanelle has been known since the sixteenth century. Like all these artificial prosodic constructions, it acquired in due course a standard form, the features of which are five three-lined stanzas (or tercets), followed by a four-lined stanza (or quatrain).

The rhyme scheme in each tercet is *a b a*, and in the quatrain *a b a a*. The villanelle lends itself to light irony, humour and pleasant recollections.

Rhyme

According to one view of the matter, rhyme or rime is a needless obstacle to the free expression of the poet's thought; according to another, it is just one of the limitations he deliberately places upon himself, in order that he may create a formal order which perfectly synthesizes thought, feeling, and verbal music, much as a sculptor, according to the conception he wishes to embody in his materials, may choose either a hard or a soft stone to work upon. Milton, though he had used rhyme with the happiest results in his early poems, discarded it in his epic works. In the Prefatory Note on the Verse of *Paradise Lost*, he declared that rhyme is "no necessary adjunct or true ornament of poem or good verse, in longer works especially, but the invention of a barbarous age, to set-off wretched matter and lame metre." "Poets," he went on to say, have been compelled by the "vexation, hindrance and constraint of rhyme to express many things otherwise and for the most part worse, than else they would have expressed them." He rejected therefore "the jingling sound of like endings" as having "no true musical delight." Dryden had a similar thought, when in the prologue to his play *Aureng-Zebe* he declared himself "weary of his long-loved mistress, Rhyme" and gave for his reason—

Passion's too fierce to be in fetters bound.

Notwithstanding the high authority of Milton and Dryden we may well prefer to think that their decrying of rhyme although expressed in such general terms had reference to the particular tasks they had in hand. Moreover, devices such as metrical sequence, stanza construction and the like, could with equal force be decried as "fetters."

The almost universal experience of lovers of poetry is that rhyme is one among many of the structural devices whereby the poet succeeds in enhancing the emotive quality of language. If we need any justification for the use of rhyme, we need but point to the delight it gives us. The detection or recognition of similarities is an intuitive act. Even to the youngest child repetitive patterns in line or colour, sound or movement are sources of pleasure. The universality of rhyme in the nursery jingles is a strong pointer to the aesthetic value of rhyme in mature poetry.

Rhyme has an important function to perform in emphasizing the rhythm of a line. By marking off the units of sound pattern with echoes, it assists the hearing mind to keep in conscious touch with the metrical flow. It is one of the difficulties of speaking blank verse well that, in the attempt to preserve the speech rhythm which runs on from line to line, the structural principle of the verse may be insufficiently brought out.

Rhyme consists in a correspondence of sound in the final syllables of two or more words. The correspondence can be analysed into (a) an identity of vowel sounds, (b) an identity of end-consonantal sounds, if any, and (c) an identity of accentual stress. This three-fold identity must follow a difference in the consonantal sounds which precede the vowels.[1]

The correspondence of sound may stretch over two or even three syllables, but if so, the requirement that it should follow a difference applies only to the first syllable: e.g. the true rhyme of *tenderly* and *slenderly* is only in *ten* and *slen*; the words *dictionary* and *missionary* are not rhymes at all, notwithstanding the identity of the second and third syllables, because *dict* and *miss* do not obey the principle of rhyme. Single rhymes such as *find* and *kind* are known as "masculine," double or treble rhymes are called "feminine." In feminine rhymes the final syllables must be unaccented.

Some of the pleasure which we get from rhyme may result from correspondence of sound which are not true identities, but only close approximations thereto. These may be described as off-rhymes, near enough to satisfy our ears, and yet leaving something, not fully resolved, to cheat us into listening more closely. They give us the satisfaction of recognizing variety even in resemblance or resemblance in variety. The following is an example from William Blake's *The Tiger*—

> What immortal hand or eye
> Could frame thy fearful symmetry?

and Walter de la Mare in *Haunted* uses the same combination of sounds in rhyming "cry" and "taciturnity."

The real test of a rhyme is not in the seeing, but in the hearing. Eye-rhymes, such as *heard, beard; give, hive;* are not, strictly speaking, rhymes at all. It generally happens that a rhyme is both ear-rhyme and

---

[1] Such a rhyme as *fled, bled* may be admitted on the ground that the "fl" and "bl" consonantal combinations are virtually single sounds, and essentially different from each other.

eye-rhyme at the same time as in *confess, repress*, but it may happen that
an ear-rhyme is not apparent to the eye, as in *whale* and *sail*.

Rhyme is often used with great effect internally—

> We were the *first* that ever *burst*
> Into that silent sea.
> COLERIDGE: *The Ancient Mariner*

It would have been equally possible, however, to write these lines
not as eight-six measure, but as four-four-six, so that the rhymes
would then become normal end-rhymes.

Like every other poetical device, rhyme can easily show a declension
from its true nature of contributing to the satisfaction of a natural
love of recurrent sound. There are rhymes which are mean and feeble,
as *is* and *his*; there are imperfect rhymes which may offend the sensitive ear, as *tease* and *piece*; there are rhymes whose purpose is to be
quaintly humorous rather than accessory to verbal music—

> Quarrel with minc'd pies, and disparage
> Their best and truest friend, plum-porridge.
> BUTLER: *Hudibras*

> There was a young lady of Portugal,
> Whose ideas were excessively nautical.
> EDWARD LEAR: *Limerick*

Many rhymes occur so often that they do not any longer afford
the delight of surprise—

> Where-e'er you find the cooling Western breeze
> In the next line it whispers through the trees.
> POPE: *Essay on Criticism* (1711)

Although Pope was here ridiculing the use of hackneyed rhymes,
we find him elsewhere using the very same pair, apparently forgetful
of his earlier scorn—

> Warms in the sun, refreshes in the breeze,
> Glows in the stars, and blossoms in the trees.
> POPE: *Essay on Man I* (1732)

It is obvious that association of meaning may account for the
frequent occurrence of certain rhyme-pairs, such as *name-fame
rest-blest*.

Assonance

Assonance falls short of rhyme by requiring a correspondence only
in the vowel sounds of the final syllables. The consonants which follow

them are not identical, e.g. *house, loud; tall, fought*. Assonance may result from a failure to achieve rhyme, when rhyme is intended, or on the other hand, it may be sought for its own sake. In French and Spanish poetry assonance has been used at various periods as a literary artifice, but in English its deliberate use is rare. It is found more often in prose, and some of the beauty of the language of the Bible results from assonantal harmony intuitively achieved, as in such phrases as "the wings of the wind," "their bows shall be broken," "the earth is the Lord's and the fulness thereof." Assonance is frequently used in our proverbs: "A stitch in time saves nine," and "Strike when the iron is hot."

An examination of the vowel sounds in Wilfred Owen's *Anthem for Doomed Youth* will reveal how subtly assonance enters into the verbal harmony of the lines.

Alliteration

Alliteration is a literary artifice which consists in the use of the same initial consonantal or vowel sound in words used in close association. Through such repetition a certain emphasis is achieved, and the universality of its appeal is shown by the frequent use of it in proverbial speech: as "Look before you leap" and "Much wants more," and in such phrases as "pots and pans," "sweet seventeen."

It is necessary to distinguish between alliteration used as a principle of metrical structure, e.g. in Anglo-Saxon and early English poetry, and as an ornament of style. With the revolution in prosodic practice associated with Chaucer, the structural use of alliteration was abandoned in favour of the new principles of syllabic stress and rhyme. Thereafter it served only an aesthetic purpose imparting, when used with discretion, now a delicate charm and now a forcefulness, to verse.

When alliteration is used in excess, it produces a ludicrous effect of bombast—

> Whereat with blade, with bloody baleful blade,
> He bravely broached his boiling bloody breast.
>> Bottom in *Midsummer Night's Dream*

This may be contrasted with the verbal felicity of—

> Now air is hushed, save where the weak-eyed bat
> With short, shrill shriek, flits by on leathern wing;
> Or where the beetle winds
> His small but sullen horn.
>> COLLINS: *Ode to Evening*

where the alliteration compensates for the absence of rhyme. It will be noticed that to the effect of the initial sounds is added that of internal sounds (in *shrill, beetle, small, sullen*) echoing the·*l* of *leathern*. A similar effect is produced in the lines from Shakespeare's sonnet—

> When to the sessions of sweet silent thought
> I summon up remembrance of things past

where the effect of the true alliteratives is reinforced by the final sounds in the words *sweet, silent thought*, and *remembrance, things, past*. This is by no means all, for there is also an intricate weft of *n* and *m* sounds interlaced in the pattern.

Free Verse (*Vers libre*)

In the years which followed the First World War, the revolt against what were called the outworn conventions of poetry took the form of advocacy of Free Verse, or verse which while retaining a distinguishable rhythmical flow, was yet unrelated to a metrical pattern or norm. It was not an altogether unknown verse form, since the American poet, Walt Whitman, in the middle years of the nineteenth century, had used it for his *Leaves of Grass* and other poems. The following lines will afford an example of his style—

> You may read in many languages, yet read nothing about it,
> You may read the President's message and read nothing about it there;
> Nothing in the reports from the State department, or Treasury department,
>   or in the daily papers or weekly papers
> Or in the census or revenue returns, prices current, or any accounts of stock.
> WHITMAN: *A Song for Occupations*

Critics of free verse have urged that it should rather be classified as a species of prose, since prose also may have its cadences and its modulated flow. It would be possible to select passages of prose which pass gradually from the completely irregular rhythm of normal speech to a style of writing in which there is an embryonic metrical quality, and from this again to passages which, though still written as prose, are so regular as to induce the pleasurable expectancy of stress which patterned verse provides—

> Then I returned and saw all the oppressions that are done under the sun: and behold, the tears of such as were oppressed, and they had no comforter; and on the side of their oppressors there was power, but they had no comforter. Wherefore I praised the dead which are already dead more than the living which are yet alive; yea better than them both did I esteem him which hath not yet been, who hath not seen the evil work which is done under the sun.   *Ecclesiastes:* IV

The following passage from *Isaiah* is capable of being scanned as perfectly regular dactyls—

> How art thou/ fallen from/ Heaven, O/ Lucifer/ son of the/ morning.

In modern literature, examples are not difficult to find in such writers as Dickens, Ruskin, and Blackmore. The following, from Blackmore's novel, *Lorna Doone*, is printed here as though it were a passage of unrhymed verse. It will be felt to have a distinctly trochaic rhythm, and strongly recalls Longfellow's *Hiawatha*—

> In the great white desolation,
> distance was a mocking vision:
> hills looked nigh and valleys far;
> when hills were far and valleys nigh.
> And the misty breath of frost,
> piercing through the ribs of rock,
> striking to the pith of trees,
> creeping to the heart of man,
> lay along the hollow places,
> like a serpent sloughing.
>
> *Lorna Doone*, Chapter XLIV

It is possible to take the view that as Blackmore is in this passage false to the nature of prose, so *vers libristes* are false to the nature of verse, when they repudiate all that ministers to the aesthetic delight of waiting and recognizing the recurrent stress when it comes, or even, at other times, of matching the aberrant stresses against the ground pattern. If, on the other hand, free verse is defended on the ground that it does in fact use a consistent metrical pattern, it should no longer be called free verse, because it then becomes merely one more added to the vast number of prosodical forms which are always being devised. The question is really whether free verse is a technique whereby a rhythmical balance is created which is different in kind from that which arises from the use of recognizable metre.

Sprung Rhythm

Gerard Manley Hopkins, in his rejection of the values of Victorian poetry of the Tennyson school, included in his protest the prosodic principles which had been followed for so long in English poetry. The conventional form of rhythm, which he called Running Rhythm, is based on an equivalence of syllable-content in the metrical foot—so many stressed and so many accompanying unstressed syllables providing a recurrent pattern or pulse within the line. Hopkins claimed that this syllabic method was not native to the genius of the language, and he experimented with an alternative technique to which he gave the name Sprung Rhythm. This, he said, came nearer to the natural stress rhythm of our speech, and consequently was a more effective poetic medium than the forced and artificial metrical structure of Running Rhythms. In Sprung Rhythms the stresses are not spaced out evenly: they can either dispense with the escort of light syllables altogether, or be attended by from one to four of them. The stresses are often given additional emphasis by the use of alliteration. Hopkins insisted that Sprung Rhythm made no appeal to the eye; it was rhetorical, intended to be spoken.

Sprung Rhythms were not an invention of Hopkins. They are common in nursery jingles: "This little pig had roast beef," and in folk names, "Will-o'-the-Wisp." Something like them is found in the early English alliterative measures of Langland and others, and in Shakespeare's songs and sonnets, e.g.—

> Cóme unto these yéllow sánds
>
> And thén take hánds
>
> Cúrt'sied when you háve and kíss'd
>
> The wíld wavés whíst.
>
> *The Tempest* I. 2

and

> Was it the próud fúll sáil of his gréat vérse
>
> *Sonnet* 86

But above all, in the irregular metre of the choruses in Milton's *Samson Agonistes* Hopkins recognized not only occasional sprung-rhythms, but a deliberate, conscious experiment in the use of natural speech-stress·instead of a syllabic notation—

> See how he lies at random, carelessly diffused,
> With languished head unpropt,
> As one past hope abandoned,
> And by himself given over,
> In slavish habit, ill-fitted weeds
> O'er-worn and soiled.
> Or do my eyes misrepresent? Can this be he
> That heroic, that renowned
> Irresistible Samson? whom, unarmed,
> No strength of man, or fiercest wild beast could withstand;
> Who tore the lion as the lion tears the kid.

The relation between this kind of verse and free verse is clear. In the passage quoted, Milton is no longer curbed or coerced by a system of numbered syllables. Losing sonority and sacrificing the incantatory effect of blank verse, he has acquired instead an unwonted freedom of expression.

The distinction, for there is one, between Sprung Rhythm and free verse is in the use of the "slack," that is to say, the light syllables which separate the stresses. Though Sprung Rhythm rejects "numbers," or the regular measured beat of metre, it retains nevertheless its own time-values, while free verse adheres to no definite pattern in the grouping of the unstressed syllables.

Sprung Rhythm has had a considerable influence on contemporary poets who have tried, often with great success, to substitute a rhythmical pattern determined by the thought and emotion for a pattern which has been die-stamped upon it.

SUGGESTIONS FOR FURTHER READING

G. SAINTSBURY: *History of English Prosody* (3 vols) (Macmillan).
S. GREW: *A Book of English Prosody* (Grant Richards).
EGERTON SMITH: *Principles of English Metre* (Oxford Univ. Press).
T. S. OSMOND: *English Metrists* (Clarendon Press).
S. HAMER: *The Metres of English Poetry* (Methuen).

CHAPTER V

PRE-RENAISSANCE POETRY

IN the middle of the fourteenth century, when we begin our review of the development of English poetry, it was by no means certain which direction this development would take. It was an open question whether the poets would carry on in the native tradition of non-metrical alliterative verse or adopt the new measures of metrical rhymed verse which were already in use in the countries with which England had close cultural links. The countries from which England borrowed most were France—because of her geographical nearness and the long political association of the two countries—and Italy—because of the common allegiance to the Roman Church and the persistence of the prestige of ancient Rome in all lands which had once been comprised in her empire.

Alliterative Verse

The native tradition of verse was most powerful among those who wrote in the West-Midland dialect. They used material principally from the medieval romances based on the Arthurian legends, and tales from the French compilation known as the *Roman de la Rose*. Among these was the narrative poem, *Sir Gawayne and the Grene Knight*, the finest flower of English chivalric romance before Chaucer. The unidentified author may possibly have written also the three poems *Pearl*, *Cleanness*, and *Patience*. The story, which is set at the court of King Arthur, is told in about 2500 alliterative lines, varied occasionally by short rhymed lyrics. The following is a passage (descriptive of a battle-axe) with modernized spelling—

> The grain all of green steel, and of gold hewn,
> The bit burnished bright, with a broad edge,
> As well shapen to shear as sharp razors.

In this poem old English alliterative measure reached its highest level, but at the same time in its acceptance of occasional rhyme it points to the future. Langland's *Piers Plowman* is more uncompromisingly antiquarian in its language and style. He shows a preference for archaic words, though he cannot forgo the use of the borrowings from French which had already become acclimatized in the vernacular of the fourteenth century. The poem was a bitter satire on social sins, clerical abuses and hypocrisy, and a glorification of simple piety. It is conveyed, according to a medieval convention, in the guise of a vision seen in a dream. Like *Sir Gawayne* it was written in the West-Midland dialect and exists in three versions of differing lengths. *Piers Plowman* provides us with a picture of medieval society and manners, and in its range of interest is second only to Chaucer's *Canterbury Tales*. The structural arrangement of the verse consists of lines divided by a medial pause, unequally placed by reckoning of syllables, with the alliterative stresses falling, as a rule, two in the first part and one or two in the second, for example—

> In somer seson   when soft was the sonne
> I shope me in shroudes   as I a shepe were,
> In habite as an heremite   unholy of werkes,
> Went wyde in this world   wonders to here.

The reaction against foreign influences on our poetry was not destined to succeed. The tide which was flowing so strongly in Western Europe towards the Renaissance could not be withstood, and English culture was carried along on the current.

Chaucer

Geoffrey Chaucer was a few years younger than Langland, and died in the same year (1400). His training fitted him admirably to bring English and Romance culture into a fruitful relation. His travels in France and Italy, his readings of the poets of other countries, his first-hand acquaintance no less with court life and chivalric manners than with the common lot of the citizens of London, his knowledge of Latin literature and his interest in contemporary science and philosophy, all contributed to make him a man of catholic tastes, receptive to the influences of the age and withal one who was intensely human in his sympathies. He accepted the world as he saw it with a humorous tolerance for its weaknesses and its follies.

Chaucer was a born story-teller, but to his narrative he added a lyrical gift. He had an effortless facility in the writing of verse which, though his prose is not unimportant, was his natural mode of expression. His early writing was an imitation of the "courtly makers" of France, and consisted mostly of elegant exercises on erotic themes, conventional in method, subject and spirit.

When we call Chaucer "the father of English poetry," we should think not only of his contribution to our permanent literature but also of his influence on our prosody. For example, he introduced the iambic decasyllabic or heroic metre, a measure which has served the generations of English poets down to our own day so variously and so well. This metre he adapted from the eleven-syllabled line of the Italian poets, but instead of following their rigid rule for the placing of the caesura, he varied its position freely. For example—

> But atte laste | with muchel care and wo,
> We fille accorded, | by us selven two.
> He yaf me al the brydel | in myn hond
> To han the gouernance | of hous and lond,
> And of his tonge | and of his hond also
> And made him brenne his book | anon right tho.
> *Wife of Bath's Prologue*

Chaucer thus enabled heroic verse to be used with a close approximation to normal speech-rhythm, without losing the metrical pattern. The importance of his device will become apparent later when we have to consider the use of blank verse for drama in Elizabethan times, since it was through a similar freedom in the use of his medium that Shakespeare was able to achieve his miracles of verbal beauty.

It has not to be forgotten that Chaucer lived in the Middle Ages and that his mind was formed on the medieval pattern. He knew nothing of the world beyond the narrow seas which enclosed Europe and the near East; he measured time by observing the heavens, and accepted without question the subjection of human life to planetary influences; he was a true son of the universal Church. His world might have been a limited one, but at any rate Chaucer had unusual opportunities for observing it. At the age of 16 or so, he became a page in the household of the Duke of Clarence, one of the sons of King Edward III. He served in the French wars, was taken prisoner and ransomed. By the age of 20 he had already seen much of court life and the pageantry of war and chivalry. After further service about the king at his court, he went abroad on diplomatic missions, including one to Genoa and Florence, where we have reason to believe he met Petrarch and Boccaccio, and became acquainted with the poetry of Dante. This experience must have been of great spiritual significance to him, and his writings provide abundant evidence of it. At the age of 34, Chaucer, now married, was appointed to the post of collector of customs at the Port of London and set up house at Aldgate. Here his experience of men broadened out to include the merchants and craftsmen, and doubtless also the underworld of the City. In 1386 he was Knight of the Shire for Kent, but soon after fell on dark days with the loss of a pension, which was not restored until the last year of his life.

Phases of Chaucer's Poetry

Chaucer's poetical work falls into three successive phases, in each of which his writing bears the stamp of a predominant influence or tendency. The first phase is that in which his models were French. He knew well the *Roman de la Rose*, that great French fountain of romance admired in court circles, and he probably translated it. From it he borrowed the octosyllabic measure in which he wrote the elegy: *The Book of Blanche the Duchess*[1] (1369), and also the romantic convention of the allegorical dream-vision, which he was to use so often in later works. Another poem of this period was *The Compleynte to Pite* (1370), in which for the first time Rime Royal was used (see page 54). This shows that Chaucer was already experimenting with verse, and improving on his models. Nevertheless his work during this early phase was mainly imitative.

The second phase is marked by Italian influences. On his visits to Italy in the 1370's the artist in him was awakened by the colourful life, the antiquities, and the stimulus of the great contemporary writers. From Dante he got the idea of the *House of Fame*; from Boccaccio he learned the stories of *Troylus and Criseyde* and of *Palamon and Arcite* (used in the *Knight's Tale*); while the idea of a story-sequence, on which *The Legend of Good Women* and *The Canterbury Tales* are based, may well have occurred to him while reading the *Decameron*. But all these suggestions he used with complete independence of the originals, enriching them from his quick imagination and enlivening them from his quenchless fount of humour. In *The Parliament of Foules*, an allegory, he employed once again the device of the dream-vision, but now with complete mastery, incorporating in his work elements drawn from the widest literary sources, and using them in a spirit of lively satire.

In the third phase of Chaucer's work, the foreign influences are less evident and the native genius of the poet expresses itself with still more freedom. He could not of course discard his scholarship; his knowledge of the Latin poets, especially Ovid and Virgil was profound, and to this learning there was added the further acquaintance he made with French and Italian authors on his later diplomatic missions to the

---

[1] Blanche was Duchess of Lancaster, wife of John of Gaunt, who was a patron of Chaucer.

Continent. But the use he made of characters and situations which he found in his reading became less basic and more incidental. He turned away from the conventional figures of medieval romance to the panorama of London life, as he watched it pass beneath the windows of his house at Aldgate, or saw it in the rough and tumble of the London inns.

So he conceived the plan of the *Canterbury Tales* which occupied him during the last thirteen years of his life. It was based on the idea of a pilgrimage to the Tomb of St. Thomas à Becket at Canterbury. Each of the pilgrims gathered for the start at the Tabard Inn in Southwark undertook to help beguile the journey along the Kentish roads by telling two stories on the way out and two on the way back. The best story-teller was to be fêted by the rest at a parting supper. The general organization was left to the Host of the Tabard, who himself joined the cavalcade, and acted during the intervals between the stories as a kind of umpire, question-master and conciliator rolled into one. The *Prologue* described the pilgrims one by one with exquisite understanding and humour, and they are the first characters in English literature who truly become alive for us. The picture is an invaluable record of the English social scene in the fourteenth century.

The plan was not carried to completion, for only twenty-three tales in all are told and the poem ends with Canterbury not in fact reached. Many of the stories, notably those for which he used the decasyllabic couplet, were specially written for inclusion in the *Tales*, while others consisted of earlier work adapted for the purpose. They are of astonishing variety, but a rough division of them corresponds to the distinctions of social standing in the tellers. The Knight tells a romance of love and chivalry, the Prioress a sad, old legend of Christian boy-martyrdom; the Monk's tale is a collection of moral tragedies ("nat worth a boter-flye" was the Host's verdict); the Shipman, a rascally pirate, shocked some of the company with a spicy yarn; Chaucer himself in a bantering mood answered the Host's invitation to play his part by burlesquing the popular romances of knight-errantry. When interrupted, he revenged himself by switching over to a tedious tale in prose.

In the *Canterbury Tales* Chaucer was no longer content to use a mould which had become traditional, and to pour into it an alloy formed of the conventional ingredients. Looking into the life about him for the material on which his creative imagination might play, he showed that there was poetry and romance, humour and sentiment,

6

in workaday lives, and it was his supreme merit that he seized upon this and turned it to the purposes of great art.

John Gower

A century after his death, Chaucer's name was usually linked with those of John Gower and John Lydgate to form a trinity of pre-eminent fourteenth-century poets. John Gower (1330–1408) was a literary scholar and craftsman of distinction, yet far inferior to Chaucer as a poet. Lacking imagination and humour, he brought nothing original into our literature. His reputation rests on his *Confessio Amantis* (Confession of a Lover), consisting of a sequence of moral tales purporting to be told to Genius, the priest of Venus. Gower had a talent for story-telling, but he used it for didactic rather than for artistic purposes. He set greater store by his Latin and French poems and appears to have written the *Confessio Amantis* in English only in deference to a royal request. Nevertheless his prestige, added to that of Chaucer, helped to establish a literary standard for English.

John Lydgate

John Lydgate (1370–1447) belonged to a later generation, and confessed himself a disciple of Chaucer. At first a monk, he afterwards devoted himself entirely to literature and produced an enormous quantity of mediocre verse, below the best of which he was capable. His writing falls into the fifteenth century, a particularly barren period in our literary history, and the reputation he acquired may to some extent be explained by the sheer quantity of verse he produced at a time when there were so few others to challenge him. Caxton at the end of the century ranked him above Chaucer, an estimate which may be due to the fact that the secret of Chaucer's versification had by then been lost. "Certaynly the englyshe was so rude and brood," he said, "that I coude not wele vnderstand it." The forms of the language had become so modified in the interval between Chaucer and Lydgate that the style of the latter presented no difficulties to Caxton, who described it as "clere in sentence, in longage excellent."

Lydgate, despite the half-century which divided him from Chaucer, was the more typically medieval of the two. This was shown in his undiscriminating use of all the trappings of medieval romance, such as the astrological and mythological apparatus, and the prologues and invocations. His prolixity and pedantry betray a want of artistry.

In *The Story of Thebes*, Lydgate supplies a sequel to Chaucer's *Knight's Tale*, and in the *Troy Book* amplifies the background of *Troylus and Criseyde*. *The Fall of Princes* is one of the longest poems in English, consisting of 7000 stanzas each of seven lines. It took ten years to write and is a dismal catalogue of the fates suffered by illustrious men of history since the time of Adam.

The English Chaucerians

The disciples of Chaucer may be classified as the English Chaucerians and the Scottish Chaucerians. Of the former John Lydgate was the most outstanding. Another was Thomas Occleve (1370–1450), whose principal work (in rime royal), entitled *The Regiment of Princes*, is an imitation of a Latin original, and was written for the moral instruction of Prince Hal. Occleve was a Londoner, and he gives us in the introduction to the poem some realistic scenes of the low life of the City, depicted with some humour.

Stephen Hawes (1475–1523), the third of the English Chaucerians and a disciple of Lydgate, was drearily scholastic and didactic. The interest he has for the student of literature lies in his development of allegorical romance in a direction which leads towards Edmund Spenser. This is shown in *The Pastime of Pleasure*, a poem of seven-lined stanzas dealing with the education of the Knight, Grande Amour, his instruction in the Seven Sciences, his marriage to La Belle Pucelle, his falling from grace in old age and his repentance.

The last of this group was John Skelton (1460–1529), poet laureate of Henry VIII, who won a reputation as an eccentric buffoon, and occasionally got into scrapes because of his railing at Cardinal Wolsey and the leaders of the Church in *Colyn Cloute*, *Phylype Sparowe*, *Why Come Ye Not to Courte?* and other poems. He had the greatest respect for Chaucer—

> In Chaucer I am sped,
> His tales haue I red:
> His mater is delectable,
> Solacious and commendable; . . .
> Chaucer, that famus clerke
> His termes were not darke,
> But pleasant, easy and playne;
> No worde he wrote in vayne.

It is easy to recognize in this kind of doggerel, which has been called Skeltonian verse, the Hudibrastic manner of Samuel Butler.

Skelton recognized his own deficiencies as a poet in his famous lines—

> For though my ryme be ragged,
> Tattered and jagged,
> Rudely rayne beaten,
> Rusty and moughte eaten;
> If you take well therewith,
> It hath in it some pyth.

The Scottish Chaucerians

The Scottish Chaucerians include King James I (1394–1437), Robert Henryson (1425–1506), William Dunbar (1463–1530) and Gavin Douglas (1475–1522). King James's knowledge of Chaucer was acquired during the twenty years of his honourable captivity in England, and when, after ransom, he returned to Scotland, he introduced the poet to his subjects. The King himself was remarkable among medieval princes for his cultured taste, and he gave evidence of this in *The King's Quair*, an allegorical love-romance for which the Chaucerian stanza was used. Based on the story of the King's own wooing of Lady Jane Beaufort, whom he married, the sincere feeling of the poem, notwithstanding the big part played in it by allegory, may be attributed to the autobiographical source of the incidents.

It is a curious fact that Chaucer was held in greater repute in Scotland than in England. Perhaps the explanation is that the changes in the structure of the language went on more slowly in the north than in the south, and consequently the versification of Chaucer was better understood and appreciated. While in England he was read for delight in his vigorous narrative, in Scotland he could be enjoyed also for the artistry of his style. The Scottish poets of the fifteenth century employed not only Chaucer's verse and stanza forms, but also made use of his themes and shared his spirit.

In *The Testament of Cresseid*, Henryson carries on the Chaucerian story by bringing tragedy on the heroine as a punishment for the breaking of her vows to Troilus. His book of thirteen animal fables, *Morall Fabillis of Esope*, though but a retelling of familiar tales, is the outstanding Scottish work in this department of literature. Henryson uses the Chaucerian stanza and resembles his literary master in his oblique humour, his frank realism and his sense of drama.

William Dunbar (the Rhymer of Scotland) was the foremost literary artist of the group we are considering, and he has claims to be considered the greatest of all Scottish poets with the exception of

Robert Burns. Though he followed many of the medieval conventions of courtly poetry, he used them with greater restraint. The *Thrissil and the Rois* was written to celebrate the marriage of James IV and Margaret Tudor, and in it the device of the beast-parliament was used (compare Chaucer's *Parliament of Foules*). The *Twa Maryit Women and the Wedo* is in the old alliterative tradition. In *The Dance of the Sevin Deidle Synnis* Dunbar is no longer derivative; the poem, consisting of eleven stanzas of twelve lines each in "eight and six" metre, shows a macabre imagination at work on a theme which is reminiscent of a Burns poem of diablerie. The *Flyting of Dunbar and Kennedie* is a supreme example of the literature of scurrilous abuse, using a vocabulary largely invented for the occasion. In such ways Dunbar reveals himself as a poet of original genius.

Finally, among Scottish Chaucerians, there stands Gavin Douglas (1475–1522). His work almost bridges the gap between the medieval and the humanistic in literary modes. In *The Palice of Honour* he was a complete medievalist using all the time-honoured devices of the courtly love poetry inspired by the *Roman de la Rose*, such as the dream-allegory and the Court of Venus, while in his translations from Ovid and especially Virgil he approaches his task in a spirit of humane scholarship even though he is not fully equipped for it.

The Ballads

Whether ballad poetry existed before the fourteenth century we do not certainly know, but from that time until the seventeenth century, ballad poetry was produced in vast quantities. Most of what we know of the popular ballads come from collections made in the seventeenth century or later, when they were given a literary form which belongs to a period considerably later than that in which they came into existence. It is probable that the great age of ballad-origin was the fifteenth and early sixteenth centuries. One of the most typical of the true ballads and among the earliest known to us, *Chevy Chase*, must have been composed by its anonymous author after the Battle of Otterburn (1388).

The principal compilations of ballad literature in English are those of Allan Ramsay, Bishop Percy, Ritson, and Child. In 1724 Allan Ramsay began in Edinburgh the publication of *The Evergreen* and *Tea Table Miscellany*; in 1765 Bishop Percy published his *Reliques of Ancient English Poetry*; and in 1790 Ritson issued his *Ancient Songs and Ballads*. There have been many later compilations, such as that of

Professor Child of Harvard University whose *English and Scottish Popular Ballads* was published towards the end of the nineteenth century. He gave numerous versions of some of the ballads, many of which he discovered as oral tradition among the descendants of those who had emigrated to New England in the seventeenth century.

A classification of the ballads recorded in such publications shows the following separate kinds—

(1) The group of Robin Hood ballads, of which an edition was printed by Wynkyn de Worde in 1500.

(2) The Arthurian group, including *The Grene Knight, Merlin, The Marriage of Sir Gawain, King Arthur* and *The King of Cornwall.*

(3) The historical ballads, such as *Chevy Chase, Sir Patrick Spens, The Rose of England, Durham Field, The Rising in the North,* and *Edom O'Gordon.* This is perhaps the largest group.

(4) The ballad of love and adventure, e.g. *Sir Eglamour, Sir Thomas and Fair Annie, The Nut-brown Maiden.*

(5) The ballad of faery, including such examples as *The Lyke-Wake Dirge, The Twa Corbies, The Wife of Usher's Well.*

(6) The carol, the lullaby, the lament, and the hymns to the Virgin, of which two: *I synge of a Mayden* and *Adam lay i-bowndyn* are of such exquisite melody and feeling that they may be taken as representing, as Sir E. K. Chambers has said, "the highest level of lyrical beauty of which medieval poetry was capable."

The Two Streams of Poetry

The stream of pre-Renaissance poetry thus ran along two channels. One was the tradition of courtly poetry, continental in origin, in which the treatment conformed to the conventions established during the literary efflorescence of the tenth century. The authors were aware of themselves as belonging to this tradition and continually refer to their great exemplars. This self-conscious poetry tended towards prolixity and sententious moralizing, and was marked by the use of an "aureate" bookish or Latinized vocabulary, as in the following lines—

> The fyrst of them was called Veryte,
> And the second Good Operacion
> And the thirde cleped Fydelyte,
> All they at ones with good opinion
> Did geve to me great laudacion,
> And me beseched with her hert entere
> With them to rest, and to make good chere.
>
> STEPHEN HAWES: *Passetyme of Pleasure*

The other channel was the popular tradition of song and story, springing from unlettered sources, spontaneous and redolent of life, economical of words, dramatic in movement, and concrete in detail. The vocabulary was predominantly Anglo-Saxon. With the lines quoted above compare the opening lines of Sir Patrick Spens—

> The King sits in Dumferline town
> Drinking the blude-red wine;
> "O whaur will I get a skeely skipper
> To sail this ship o' mine?"

It was at the confluence of these two streams that the broad estuary of our English poetry opened out in the sixteenth century.

SUGGESTIONS FOR FURTHER READING

Sir E. K. Chambers: *English Literature at the Close of the Middle Ages* (Oxford Univ. Press).

G. C. Coulton: *Chaucer and His England* (Methuen).

R. M. Wilson: *Early Middle English Literature* (Methuen).

J. Livingstone Lowes: *Geoffrey Chaucer* (Oxford Univ. Press).

G. H. Gerould: *The Ballad of Tradition* (Oxford Univ. Press).

H. S. Bennett: *Chaucer and the Fifteenth Century* (Oxford Univ. Press).

M. J. C. Hodgart: *The Ballads* (Hutchinson).

CHAPTER VI

RENAISSANCE HUMANISM

D URING the second half of the fifteenth century and through the
sixteenth, the educated peoples of western Europe were
stirred into a vigorous intellectual and emotional activity.
To describe this the term Renaissance came into use about a hundred
years ago, meaning variously the historical period itself, or the forces
which were at work in that epoch, or again the changes which those
forces brought about. It is impossible to say whether the remarkable
achievements of the age in science, in exploration, in religion, in
philosophy, in statecraft, and in art and letters ought to be regarded as
causes or effects. They were summed up by a French writer as "man's
discovery of himself." The phrase implies that men gained a new
confidence in their own powers, and using those powers, opened up
vast new regions of speculation, of aesthetic enjoyment and of social
conduct. For a thousand years the Church had directed man's gaze
outwards towards the offices and consolations of religion as providing a
sufficient rule of life. Now he looked inwards into his own soul,
seeking the meaning of experience in terms of his own free individu-
ality. The new attitude of mind, implying a revolt against medieval
scholasticism, emphasized the dignity of the human personality.
Knowledge and speculation were now believed to derive their importance from their relation to human affairs, and man took his place
in the centre of the universe.

Man's concern with himself as an object of contemplation is called
Humanism, and the studies which arise are called the Humanities.
A student of the Humanities is known as a Humanist. In a narrower
sense, the Humanist is one who devotes himself to the study of classical
antiquity, since at the period of the Renaissance the only important
body of recorded knowledge and speculation contributing to the
study of the nature of man, rather than of the nature of the divinity,
was contained in the writings handed down from Greek and Roman
times.

It was in Italy that the first great triumphs in the field of Humanism
were won: Dante, Petrarch, and Boccaccio had prepared the way
in the fourteenth century. They "opened wide the gate for the

measureless devotion to antiquity in the fifteenth century."[1] From Italy the movement spread northwards and westwards over the Alpine routes to France, Spain, Western Germany, the Low Countries, and England.

It is possible to distinguish within the humanistic movement a number of subordinate trends all focusing interest on "the proper study of mankind."

The Discovery of Classical Antiquity

First in importance was the rediscovery of classical antiquity, and particularly that of ancient Greece. The Roman tradition had not been forgotten in Italy and in the lands of the Empire. Tales from Ovid formed an important element in medieval story-telling: Chaucer made considerable use of them. Material survivals of Roman magnificence were everywhere to be seen. Though its study was not based on the best classical models, but on the debased styles of later centuries, the Latin language was universally used by lettered men for purposes of religion, scholarship and business. The "new learning" restored the study of the writers of the Golden and Silver Ages of Latin literature, and Cicero in particular provided material for the new study of rhetoric.

The knowledge of Greek had disappeared altogether from the western world, and only in the fifteenth century was its study introduced into the curriculum of the Universities. The influence of Greek letters was felt immediately and profoundly. The free-ranging, liberal tone of the old Greek world reacted on the modern world now emerging from tradition-bound medievalism, and Humanism found in the spirit of Athenian democracy, and in its eager quest for beauty, its own justification and pattern.

The discipline of Greek studies was introduced into Oxford by William Grocyn but the first Englishman who can be said to have written under their influence was Sir Thomas More. His Utopia[2] written in Latin, was doubtless suggested by Plato's Republic. The important place which classical Greek and Latin assumed in English education in the sixteenth century may be gathered from Roger Ascham's Scholemaster, which is largely devoted to consideration of the best methods of teaching the classics. Many attempts were made to acclimatize classical metres in English poetry, while the great epics and

[1] Burckhardt: The Civilization of the Renaissance in Italy (Phaidon Press), p. 121.
[2] The word does not mean "an ideal place" as is usually supposed, but "no place at all."

tragic dramas provided an inexhaustible reservoir of themes on which the poets and the dramatists of the Renaissance could draw.

The experiments in the introduction of classical metres and literary modes were not persisted in after it had become clear that the genius of the English language was unsuited to them. But nevertheless there went on a gradual process of adaptation of native and classical elements. For example, Spenser, in the *Shepherd's Calendar*, borrowing from Virgil the idea of the pastoral eclogue, or dialogue in verse, used it in an entirely different spirit. While Virgil's peasants spoke the language of cultivated Rome, those of Spenser used rustic forms of speech. In fact, the poet was a more faithful disciple of Chaucer than of Virgil; the February fable of the oak and the briar was told in the Chaucerian manner, with a touch of humour which was entirely absent from the Virgilian model.

The unquestioning acceptance of the critical rules of the ancients by Sir Philip Sidney in his *Defence of Poesie* might seem to have indicated the deliberate choice of classical principles for poetry and drama. Yet when we consider that Sidney was writing about 1580, *before* the astonishing literary outburst in the closing decades of the century, his leanings are easily understood. The great triumphs of Shakespeare and his contemporaries which were to follow were an expression of native genius, and had Sidney written a generation later, he would have had these wonderful examples of the romantic spirit in literature to match against the classics.

In general the great Elizabethans, while respectful of the classical models, challenged their authority with something of the assured and independent spirit of Drake in face of the overwhelming power of the Spanish empire. They were confident of their own world and its values.

The Development of a Scientific Outlook

The second prominent aspect of Humanism was the discovery of the external universe, the study of its significance for humanity, and the representation of it through literary and visual media. The first scientific academy for stellar observation was established at Naples late in the fifteenth century, just about the time when Columbus was discovering America. Thus there were set on foot two great quests of the very first importance for the future of the human race. The Copernican system replaced astrology by astronomy, while the opening-up of access to the Seven Seas radically altered the balance of political power in Europe.

The scientific movement hardly touched England during the sixteenth century; her energies, being thrown into geographical discovery, were directed rather on colonization, and prepared her for her future role as a world power. For one allusion to the advances in natural science which can be found in the pages of Elizabethan and Jacobean literature, there are scores which reflect the exciting news of the wide world brought by the seamen. Sir Walter Raleigh stands as a great example of the explorer-poet. Hakluyt spent his life "making diligent inquiry of such things as might yield any light unto our western discovery in America" and his great work entitled *The Principal Navigations, Voyages, Traffiques and Discoveries of the English Nation* has been called a national "prose epic." It supplied material to Shakespeare for *The Tempest*, and to Beaumont and Fletcher for *Sea Island*, and it is quite natural that Bacon should have placed his imaginary commonwealth, the *New Atlantis*, in the distant West.

While the imagination of some thinkers and reformers was stirred by the contemplation of new life developing in the new lands, others were moved towards the scientific study of the past. So far there had been no systematic approach to history. Of chronicles there were many, and we know what excellent use our writers made of them. Sir Thomas North's translation of Plutarch's *Lives* (1579) was abundantly used by Shakespeare. An earlier translation by Lord Berners of the *Chronicles* of Froissart (1523) satisfied a demand for historical adventure, while Foxe's *Book of Martyrs* (1563) served for religious biography. But perhaps the first approach to serious historical analysis was made by Bacon in his *History of the Reign of Henry VII* (1622).

The Study of Human Personality

We have been considering the humanist looking outward at the universe and backward into history, and speculating on their significance for mankind. But he directed his gaze also inward, and became deeply interested in the problems of human personality. In the pages of earlier literature (allowing for the creations of Chaucer as rare exceptions) we find types rather than individuals. In medieval morality plays, the characters are mostly personifications: Fellowship, Kindred, Knowledge, and the like. The humanist, as a convinced believer in the dignity of man, was interested in the expression of personality; that is to say, of that group of qualities which distinguishes one human being from another and gives to each the uniqueness which may be called his individual soul. This explains why it was that humanism set such store by education. Sir John Colet, a pioneer of the New Learning in England, founded St. Paul's School. He was one of a long line of educationists who advocated the discipline of the humanities as the basis of an intellectual and moral training, and meanwhile did not neglect the cultivation of the body. Ascham's *Scholemaster* has, as a kind of companion volume, a treatise on archery, called *Toxophilus*. Between them they suggest the blend of studies and games which is characteristic of our system of education.

The sixteenth century was a testing time when the possibilities of the human personality were being explored in all sorts of ways: physical, intellectual, and moral. Just as there were trials of physical endurance made by the intrepid navigators who went out into the unknown with gay and confident hearts, so there were probations of the mind and spirit. It is not surprising that the literary essay should have emerged at such a time, since it is, as its name implies, also a species of trial or endeavour, in which individual experience, private meditation, wit and fancy are together matched in a kind of contest against a subject chosen at random. The essay became thus in essence a touchstone of the quality of the writer's mind, as well as being an assay or testing of the possibilities of the theme.

The essays of Bacon and of Montaigne were self-revealing. But there was another species of occasional writing which arose from the interest in personality, deriving its value from close observation of the external behaviour of men and women. The publication of the *Characters* of Sir Thomas Overbury, beginning in 1614, set a fashion in a new kind of literary composition, in which a portrait of a human "type" was attempted in a few brief strokes. "Characters" were often issued singly in pamphlet form, printed in large type for window display. Examples of Overbury's *Characters* are the *Good Wife*, the *Worthy Commander*, the *Affectate Traveller*, the *Milk Maid*, and the *Critic*. There were numerous imitators, of whom the most popular was John Earle, the author of *Microcosmographie* (1628). His characters, including such well-known portraits as those of the *She Hypocrite*, the *College Butler*, the *Church Papist*, give us a lively idea of the manners of the time. Altogether some two hundred of such collections were published during the seventeenth century.

Though the character-writers occasionally illuminated human nature with flashes of insight, they were usually content with generic descriptions. The characters were therefore akin to the "humours" on which Ben Jonson's comedies were based. Taking some idiosyncrasy, folly, affectation or overmastering passion as a starting point, he worked this up into a dramatic portrait, filling out the detail with every circumstance which might throw the "humour" into relief. This static conception of character-drawing allows no place for development or modification under the stress of events, which is so notable a feature of Shakespeare's dynamic method. It may be admitted that for Ben Jonson's dramatic purpose, which was derived from the practice of the ancients, the type was preferable to the individual. He was by disposition a satirist and accordingly found it convenient to isolate certain traits, rather than to present the whole man with his virtues as well as his vices.

These were by no means the only literary evidences of the absorption of the humanist in the study of human personality. Christopher Marlowe probes down into the deep places of passion. His heroes are monstrosities, creatures of illimitable lusts and ambitions, products of convulsive upheavals in human nature. Tamberlaine conquers, hates, and loves with ungovernable intensity. Barabas, the Jew of Malta, is possessed by an uncontrolled thirst for wealth, to be satisfied without mitigation of conscience or any other human attribute. Dr. Faustus too is portrayed in undiluted colours, consumed as he was by an insatiable appetite for knowledge, experience, power, and the gratification of the senses. He gathered up in himself the vital energy of a whole epoch.

Shakespeare revealed himself as a more consummate artist than either Marlowe or Jonson, because his perceptions were more subtle. They were more scholarly than he, but their learning was carried as a burden and weighed them down. Shakespeare's intellect and spirit were free and untramelled. His genius, illuminated by the purer flame of the Renaissance, enabled him to see life whole, and to present it to us in his plays "in the round." He too could delineate passion, but it was the passion that belongs to creatures of flesh and blood, neither the superhuman creatures of Marlowe's glowing imagination nor the abstractions of Jonson's cold logic.

It was this same awakening of personality, this same new passion for life, which gave us the exquisite lyrical poetry of the Elizabethan Age. The will to live and to savour all that life could offer was a prominent feature of the Renaissance mind; but this is not the full expression of it. For we discern also in the poets of the time an ever-present awareness of the imminence of death and decay, which gives a poignancy to all their zest and exuberance.

The Cultivation of the Sense of Beauty

The fourth aspect of the humanistic movement which we shall discuss is the enhanced sensitiveness to formal beauty, and the cultivation of the aesthetic sense. Formal art in the Middle Ages was the handmaid of religion. It was justified by something which lay outside itself. Renaissance art rested secure in its own laws, and the feeling for beauty spread over the whole of life. It showed itself in a new ideal of social conduct, that of the courtier. The exemplar was sketched by Castiglione, an Italian diplomat and man of letters, in his treatise entitled *Il Cortigiano* ("The Courtier"), written in 1514, and afterwards translated into English. Here we have the pattern of gentlemanly deportment and feeling upon which the conduct of such men as Sir Philip Sidney and Sir Walter Raleigh was modelled. The ideal embraced not only a dignified courtliness of bearing, but also standards of physical perfection, of moral compunction, and of personal honour. It came to literary expression in numerous forms. It is significant that George Puttenham, the author of *The Arte of English Poesie* (1589), with whom systematic theorizing on problems of style begins in English literature, passes quite naturally from the consideration of poetry and rhetoric to the analysis of manners. "Style," he wrote, "is the image of man," anticipating by many years the saying of Buffon: *Le style c'est l'homme.*

The desire to add beauty and colour to life brought about the development of carnivals or pageants, an important feature in the town life of Renaissance Europe. They drew upon all the arts: architecture, sculpture, painting, music, dancing, mime, drama, and costume, to produce effects of fantasy, allegory, or scenic magnificence. It is to this taste that we must ascribe the popularity of the Masque. These were court spectacles intended to satisfy the love of glitter and novelty. They had, at first, no dramatic element, and were used for the most part as elaborate compliments on occasions of high ceremony. The masquers entered, posed, offered their homage and withdrew, or joined with the company in a dance. Later the dramatic element was added, as in George Peele's *Arraignment of Paris*, wherein Paris amends his ancient fault in awarding the apple to Venus by giving it to "Eliza." An example of the earlier kind of masque may be studied in Shakespeare's *Henry VIII*, Act I, Scene 4. Of the later kind Ben Jonson was the most prolific writer. Between 1604 and 1630 he wrote thirty masques, many in collaboration with Inigo Jones. The vogue passed quickly but not before it had enriched our literature with the magnificent poetry of Milton's *Comus*, written in compliment to the Earl of Bridgewater for presentation at Ludlow Castle in 1634. After the Restoration, the demand for lavish spectacle, associated with music and dancing, was met by opera and pantomime.

We shall discuss later how the cult of elegance in prose-writing produced the exaggerations of Euphuism. But whatever views are held as to the merit of Lyly and his imitators, there can be no doubt that English prose gained in pithiness and harmony as a result of their efforts to introduce order and balance into it.

Moral and Religious Aspects

Our analysis of Humanism brings us now to a consideration of the moral and religious character of the age and of its expression in literature. In the new movement, the emphasis was not on the practical sanctions of morality and religion as embodied in the teachings of the Church and its sacraments, but on the ultimate sources of their authority, and on the problem of reconciling the principle of private judgment with an *a priori* system of morality, based on concepts of absolute good and absolute evil. The mood of the time was tinged with paganism, or at any rate with rationalism. Men came to be regarded as responsible for their own actions:

> The fault, dear Brutus, is not in our stars,
> But in ourselves, that we are underlings.

Authority was to be found within; guidance was from the light in the heart of Everyman. Lyly's romance of *Euphues* was written not as a mere exercise in a new kind of prose, but with the serious purpose of inculcating righteousness of living, based on self-control. Sidney's *Arcadia* also used fiction to expound an ideal of moral excellence. Spenser's plan for the *Faerie Queene* borrowed from all the great ethical systems. Temperance or Self-Control was typically a Greek virtue; Holiness was Christian; Courtesy belonged to medieval Chivalry. Spenser's many-sidedness accorded with the intrepid, inquiring, adventurous genius of the Elizabethan age.

We do not look for direct moral teaching in Shakespeare, because his dramatic instinct was too sound to allow him to become didactic. But nevertheless there is, underlying his work, the same profoundly moral attitude to the world. He showed the same eclecticism as Spenser. His characters derive their impulses not wholly or even principally from Christian teaching, but from varied sources, among which the example of the great men of pagan antiquity is important. Shakespeare's was not a conscious paganism, and there is much to suggest that he was a completely orthodox adherent of the newly established Church. But this does not prevent his interpreting life in terms other than those of the conventional morality of goodness rewarded by happiness, and sin visited by retribution. His tragedies are crowded with characters who notwithstanding their essential goodness are destroyed by a moral defect which is brought into fatal prominence by a special set of circumstances.

The first important attempt to interpret in humanistic terms the great controversial questions which the Reformation left as a legacy to future ages was made by Richard Hooker in his *Laws of Ecclesiastical Polity* (1594). The "judicious Hooker" was writing in defence of the Anglican Church, but his work is characterized by the broad tolerance of Humanism, and by his insistence that the individual conscience is the supreme guide of conduct. The second quarter of the seventeenth century produced a group of outstanding thinkers whose reflections on religion and morality are expressed in prose of sustained dignity and beauty. Jeremy Taylor in his *Liberty of Prophesying* (1647) and *Holy Living and Holy Dying* (1650) revealed the same breadth of outlook as Hooker. He asserted the humanist claim for intellectual freedom, untrammelled by the traditional concepts of medieval scholasticism. Sir Thomas Browne's *Religio Medici* has been called "a diary of the soul." It has a quality of humour which was also in strong evidence in Robert Burton's *Anatomy of Melancholy*. A third writer also possessing humour in great measure, though lacking the depth of Browne and Burton, is Thomas Fuller, the author of numerous prose works of which the most noteworthy is *The Worthies of England*.

SUGGESTIONS FOR FURTHER READING

Cambridge History of English Literature, Vol. III, Chapter I (Cambridge Univ. Press).

WALTER PATER: *The Renaissance* (Macmillan).

J. A. THOMSON: *The Classical Background of English Literature* (Allen & Unwin).

GILBERT MURRAY: *The Classical Tradition in Poetry* (Oxford Univ. Press).

BURCKHARDT: *The Civilization of the Renaissance in Italy* (Allen & Unwin).

CHAPTER VII

THE ELIZABETHAN TRADITION IN POETRY

OUR knowledge of the poetry of the reign of Henry VIII we owe in the main to the enterprise of Tottel, a London publisher, who collected a number of poems which had not previously been printed, and issued them first in 1557 as *Tottel's Miscellany of Songs and Sonnettes, written by the ryght honorable Lorde Henry Howard Late Earle of Surrey.* He gathered the poems from various private "commonplace books" of his friends, in which the owners had copied out and preserved verses circulated in manuscript. The original edition of the *Miscellany* contained 271 poems, of which forty were attributed to Howard, ninety-six to Sir Thomas Wyatt, forty to Nicholas Grimald, and ninety-five to other unspecified authors. Nearly all the poems were posthumous. In later editions the contents were varied, possibly as further commonplace books were drawn upon and as the authorship of anonymous poems became known. The poems are printed without any indication of chronological order.

The Courtly School of Poetry

It appears that there was, moving in and around the royal Court, a group of about a score of brilliant young amateurs of poetry. Puttenham refers to them as "a new company of courtly makers." They were scions of noble families, among whom writing was a graceful accomplishment rather than a serious form of art. They brought to their writing the kind of training and the same general attitude to life and society which Roger Ascham, appointed private tutor to Queen Elizabeth in 1558, describes in *The Scholemaster.* They were all influenced by the spirit of Humanism, and on their private and diplomatic travels, many of them had acquired a taste for Italian and French literary modes.

Sir Thomas Wyatt

The special reference to the Earl of Surrey on the title page of *Tottel's Miscellany* was probably intended as a compliment to one who ranked so high in society (his sister had been Queen Catherine Howard). But the first of this group of poets in point of date and of importance is Sir Thomas Wyatt (1503–42). His genius was essentially lyrical, and his great achievement is to have introduced into our literature the "singing note." Generally the inspiration was the tenderness or passion of love, but there is also an undercurrent of meditation upon the deeper meaning of life and death. He used numerous metrical forms, among which the sonnet is by far the most important. Except that he ended the sestet with a couplet, his sonnets were written mainly on the Petrarchan model. Several were translations or adaptations, but there was an independent note as well, for the sonnets were not all literary exercises on an abstract theme. The emotions described seem to express real and poignant experience, and the images employed are original. Other innovations which we owe to Wyatt are the employment of the Italian *terza rima* for satire and for renderings of the Penitential Psalms.

Henry Howard, Earl of Surrey

The Earl of Surrey (1518–47) is said to have gleaned where Wyatt reaped. But while much of his work was on similar lines, he made contributions of his own to our literature. First of these in importance was his employment of blank verse. Perhaps it should be called an invention, because we have no earlier example of it in English. But it may well be supposed that Surrey, in translating the second and fourth books of Virgil's *Aeneid*, should have attempted to come nearer to the spirit of the classics by refraining from the use of rhyme, a literary device unknown to the ancient poets, and now condemned by scholars of the New Learning as "rude, beggarly ryming, first brought into Italie by the Gothes and Hunnes when all good verses and all good learning too were destroyed by them." The same thing had occurred to some Italian poet-dramatists of the time, and it is really of little importance to speculate whether Surrey adopted a timid suggestion of unrhymed decasyllabic verse from the Italians, or was following an inspiration of his own. What is important is that our literature at this critical moment should have been endowed with a prosodic measure which proved to be so admirably suited to the genius of the language, and one in which our noblest poetry has found expression. Surrey's use of blank verse was wooden and it was the work of the century which followed his death to discover and exploit its rich potentialities. (See p. 49.) One further innovation of Surrey's is of interest. It was he who broke up the sonnet into three quatrains and a couplet, and set the example which Shakespeare followed.

Sir Thomas Sackville

The work of Wyatt and Surrey was followed up at the distance of a few years by that of Sir Thomas Sackville (1536–1608), later Earl of Dorset. In his *Induction* to the *Mirror for Magistrates*, which was written in Chaucerian stanzas, he showed a masterly power of poetic utterance. The plan of the poem is based on Dante's *Inferno*, and is an account of the poet's descent into the underworld guided by Sorrow, where he encounters the gruesome shapes of Misery, Revenge, Care, War and others. The easy flow of the verse wedded to the imaginative sweep of the conception produced a poem far in advance of anything the century had yet seen—

> Lastly stood War, in glittering arms yclad,
> With visage grim, stern looks, and blackly hued;
> In his right hand a naked sword he had,
> That to the hilts was all with blood imbrued;
> And in his left (that Kings and Kingdoms rul'd)
> > Famine and fire he held and therewithal
> > He razed towns, and threw down towers and all.

Unfortunately Sackville gave himself up to public affairs, and the loss to our literature it is impossible to compute.

The Miscellanies

The popularity of the "new poetry" may be inferred from the number of *Miscellanies* which followed Tottel's. Their compilers vied with each other in finding attractive titles: *The Paradise of Dainty Devices*, *The Gorgeous Gallery of Gallant Inventions*, are examples.

While under the early Tudors poetry was thus a fashionable accomplishment of the nobility and gentry, under Elizabeth it became, along with drama, the principal cultural expression of a wider social circle. England was likened to "a nest of singing birds." By the end of the third quarter of the sixteenth century the efforts of the poet-humanists to impose a discipline of form on the refractory language, and to mould a completely native idiom, were well-nigh accomplished. All that had been learned from the Romance literatures had been thoroughly assimilated, and the materials were available out of which marvels of literary art were shortly to be created.

Edmund Spenser

The first full expression of Renaissance poetry in England was attained by Edmund Spenser (1552–99). His first important poem, *The*

Shepherd's Calendar, was dedicated to Sir Philip Sidney in 1579. It was a work which pointed both backwards and forwards. Spenser was steeped in the classics and was a lover of Chaucer from whose language he borrowed in order to give to his own the romantic appeal of the archaic. But he was at the same time using poetry in a new way. The pastoral eclogue was new to our literature, as were the touches of rustic realism which are scattered throughout the poem. Spenser himself illustrated a new development in respect of his relation to his poetry, for he was possibly our first professional man of letters, a seeker of patronage, and (though he had political ambitions too) an aspirant for poetic fame.

The Faerie Queene (1590) is prefaced by a letter addressed to Sir Walter Raleigh in which the poet's purpose is stated and the plan of the work outlined. The purpose is moral instruction, through examples of virtuous conduct conveyed in the form of romantic allegory. Twelve "books" were planned, twelve being the traditional number of sections (often called fyttes or cantos) in works on an epic scale since Homer's *Iliad*. Each of the twelve was to deal with some one aspect of virtuous conduct as practised by the individual, such as Holiness, Justice, and Courtesy. Another twelve books were contemplated, to deal with these virtues from the political angle. Each virtue was to be embodied in a separate hero. The figure of the Faerie Queene is not introduced at all, but Prince Arthur appears in each of the six finished books.

The allegory is complex, and Spenser's own explanations of it do not help us much. But though he himself set such store by the ethical purport, the poem is treasured not for this but rather for its intrinsic beauty, its imaginative force, and its magical music. Charles Lamb's reference to Spenser as "the poet's poet" is supported by a long line of writers who, from Milton onwards, have returned to him as to a perennial spring of word melody, sensuous image, and imaginative suggestion.

Two other poems by Spenser must be mentioned, as worthy to stand beside anything in the language for their flawless perfection. They are the marriage songs: *Epithalamion* (1594) and *Prothalamion* (1596). Spenser uses for these an irregular rhymed metre of exquisite melody—

> There in a meadow, by the Rivers side,
> A Flocke of Nymphes I chaunced to espy,
> All lovely Daughters of the Flood thereby,

With goodly greenish locks all loose untyde,
As each had been a Bryde;
And each one had a little wicker basket,
Made of fine twigs entrayled curiously,
In which they gathered flowers to fill their flasket;
And with fine fingers, cropt full feateously
The tender stalks on hye.
Of every sort, which in that Meadow grew,
They gathered some, the Violet pallid blew,
The little Dazie, that at evening closes,
The virgin Lillie, and the Primrose trew,
With store of vermeil Roses,
To decke their Bridegromes posies,
Against the Brydale day, which was not long:
    Sweete *Themmes* runne softly, till I end my Song.

Prothalamion

The same love-episode celebrated in the *Epithalamion* was the basic theme of Spenser's sonnet sequence *Amoretti* (1595). This was one of many such sequences which appeared during the last decade of the sixteenth century.

Elizabethan Songs and Sonnets

This decade was one of the most distinguished in the history of English poetry. It was a time when the sonnet blossomed in richer profusion than in any other age.

But the sonneteers were not more remarkable than the song-writers, many of whom were anonymous. They had an extraordinary gift for writing light, tripping verses, eminently capable of being set to music, or on the other hand for fitting suitable words to airs.

Why the mood of the country should thus have expressed itself in the lyric, spoken or sung, it is not easy to explain. But there may be some significance in the sudden lifting of dread when the Spanish Armada was destroyed in 1588. It was just then too that there occurred the rise of a great school of English Chamber Music, associated with the names of Tallis, Byrd, Dowland, Morley, and Orlando Gibbons. "It was necessary," says Sir Edmund Gosse, "to find words for these airs, and the poems so employed were obliged to be lucid, liquid, brief and of a temper suited to the gaiety and sadness of the instrument. The demand created the supply, and from having been heavy and dissonant to a painful degree, English lyrics suddenly took a perfect art and sweetness."[1] A contemporary poet and musician, Thomas

[1] Sir Edmund Gosse: *Modern English Literature*, p. 89.

Campion, wrote: "I have chiefly aimed to couple my words and notes lovingly together, which will be much for him to do that hath not powers over both."

The almost unvarying theme of the sonneteers of the earlier years of this remarkable decade was love. In long sequences they analysed the passion in the abstract, or again described it in terms of their real feelings. Sidney set the fashion with *Astrophel and Stella*, which was published in 1591, though written for private circulation some time earlier, and his example was followed by Constable (*Diana* 1592), Daniel (*Delia* 1592), Lodge (*Phyllis* 1593), Drayton (*Idea* 1594), Spenser (*Amoretti* 1595). Altogether about a thousand sonnets have survived from this short period. The fashion soon went out, but the writing of miscellaneous lyric verse in the courtly tradition continued without interruption until the great outburst of Cavalier poetry in the time of the early Stuarts.

The most important collection of these lyrics were *The Passionate Pilgrim* (1599), *England's Helicon* (1600) and *Poetical Rhapsody* (1602). It must be remembered that there was at this time no law of copyright, and compilers of anthologies used material from any source, whether in print or in manuscript, without acknowledgment. It is therefore not surprising that the authorship should often be unknown or be wrongly stated. Nevertheless, our debt to the anthologists is incalculable, for without their enterprise, we might have lost many of our richest gems of poetry. Their authors were, as a rule, indifferent about publication, and each wrote only for a private circle. Puttenham refers to those who "have written excellently well, as it would appear if their doings could be found out and made public with the rest." The three collections referred to are important because of their comprehensiveness and the excellent judgment of their compilers. Among the poets represented are Spenser, Sidney, Raleigh, Drayton, Lodge, Greene, Peele, Watson, Shakespeare, and Barnfield.

While much of this "new poetry" is full of charm and melody, it is questionable whether it can be considered to have reached, except occasionally, the highest levels of lyrical emotion. The writers had certainly acquired a trick of throwing off poetical "devices" with a dexterous touch; but it seems after all to have been little more than a trick. Writing was an exercise in a prevailing mode, and the results have the stamp of the artificial rather than of the spontaneous. There was no lack of heartiness and vivacity, and fancy was quick and sparkling.

Shakespeare's Poems

The non-dramatic poetry of Shakespeare (1564–1616) was comparatively youthful work, contemporaneous with his earliest plays. In 1593 *Venus and Adonis* was published and in the following year *The Rape of Lucrece*. Both were twice-told tales, as old as Ovid, and known in translations and adaptations. They were narrative poems, encumbered with rhetorical ornament in the Renaissance tradition. Yet Shakespeare was not entirely imitative. Born and bred in Warwickshire, he knew, for example, the points of a horse—

> Round-hoof'd, short-jointed, fetlocks shag and long,
> Broad breast, full eye, small head, and nostril wide,
> High crest, short ears, straight legs and passing strong,
> Thin mane, thick tail, broad buttock, tender hide:
> Look, what a horse should have he should not lack,
> Save a proud rider on so proud a back.

and he does not hesitate to introduce such realistic detail into a story so utterly remote from life. The stanza of *Venus and Adonis* is made up of six decasyllabic lines, rhyming *a b a b c c*. That of the *Rape of Lucrece*, in rime royal, has more strength, and the euphuistic quality of the earlier poem here gives place to a more robust rhetoric. But neither poem is to be considered anything more than an exercise in a conventional manner, with no claim to originality.

Most of the *Sonnets*, though not printed until 1609, and then probably without leave, are known to have been in circulation in manuscript at least ten years earlier. Francis Meres in his *Palladis Tamia* (1598) refers to Shakespeare's "sugred sonnets among his private friends." It is because the plays throw comparatively little light on Shakespeare's personality that so much speculation has been rife regarding the autobiographical element of the *Sonnets*. Though their secret has never been revealed, it is at least probable that the first 126 were addressed to a man and the remaining 28 to a woman (the "dark lady").

There is certainly more of the poet's passionate experience here than in the typical sonnet-sequence of the time; yet it is possible to study and appreciate the *Sonnets* without having to adopt any of the theories which have been advanced to explain them. In any case, all attempts to interpret them as a chronological record of the development of the poet's feelings have to be discounted, since it may be assumed that the piratical publisher had no special knowledge to assist him in arranging the sonnets in the order in which they are printed.

If there is a basic theme in the *Sonnets* it is the lament that love and beauty should be perishable things. But the sadness of mortality is tempered by the hope which is married to immortal verse—

> Since brass, nor stone, nor earth, nor boundless sea,
> But sad mortality o'ersways their power,
> How with this rage shall beauty hold a plea,
> Whose action is no stronger than a flower?
>
> O, how shall summer's honey breath hold out
> Against the wrackful siege of battering days,
> When rocks impregnable are not so stout,
> Nor gates of steel so strong, but Time decays?
>
> O fearful meditation! where, alack,
> Shall Time's best jewel from Time's chest lie hid?
> Or what strong hand can hold his swift foot back?
> Or who his spoil of beauty can forbid?
>   O, none, unless this miracle have might,
>   That in black ink my love may still shine bright.
>
> *Sonnet* No. 65

This note is often struck in the sonnets of the age, and gives some support to the view that there may be more of literary convention in them than of authentic feeling. The last two of the sequence (Nos. 153 and 154) are obviously elaborations of "conceits" in the prevailing fashion, and are devoid of feeling. But these can be matched with others in which the utterance bears all the marks of passionate intensity. Among these may be mentioned "Shall I compare thee to a summer's day?" (18); "When in disgrace with Fortune and men's eyes" (29); "When to the sessions of sweet silent thought" (30); "Full many a glorious morning have I seen" (33); "Since brass, nor stone nor earth nor boundless sea" (65); "Let me not to the marriage of true minds" (116); "The expense of spirit in a waste of shame" (129); "Two loves I have of comfort and despair" (144). It is such sonnets as these that make the problem of Shakespeare's personality such an intriguing one.

Samuel Daniel and Michael Drayton

A pair of writers whose work (apart from that of Shakespeare) spans the years between Spenser and Milton are Samuel Daniel (1562–1619) and Michael Drayton (1563–1631). They attempted to carry on the epic tradition, with England and her story as the basic theme. Daniel's *Civil Wars*, a poem of 900 eight-lined stanzas, deals with the Wars of the Roses; Drayton's *Polyolbion*, "my strange

Herculean task" as he called it, is a "choreographical description" of the scenery and rarities of "this renowned isle," which only occasionally reaches the level of poetry. Each of these writers had nevertheless the stuff of poetry in him. Daniel's sonnet-sequence and Drayton's *Ballad of Agincourt* are esteemed among the highest in their respective kinds.

The School of Spenser

Those who regarded themselves as followers of Spenser wrote with a greater seriousness than the generality of Elizabethan songsters. The work of most of them continued into an age when the high spirits of the closing years of the sixteenth century had abated, and a probing, questioning mood had succeeded. The nation was heading towards a period of political and religious strife. Some of the poets got caught up in the bitter conflict of the Civil War, others deliberately chose a life of rustic seclusion, shutting their ears to the din of controversy. They were all profoundly religious in spirit, and occupy a position in our literary history mid-way between their master, Spenser, and Milton. In contrast to the earlier lyrists, who excelled in the writing of crisp, pretty airs and ditties, the poetic idiom of the Spenserians was inclined to be diffused and they easily slipped into prosiness. They made considerable use of the pastoral and allegorical conventions.

Among the most prominent of this group were the brothers Giles and Phineas Fletcher. The former (1585–1623), in his *Christ's Victory and Triumph*, has many passages which have the sensuous beauty of *The Faerie Queene*. In the *Purple Island* of the latter (1582–1650), the allegory of the human anatomy fails to inspire the imagination of the reader. William Browne (1591–1643) was a Devonian who copied from his master the spirit of the pastoral eclogue in *Britannia's Pastorals* (1613) and *Shepherd's Pipe* (1614). George Wither (1588–1667) did something similar in *Shepherd's Hunting* and *Fair Virtue*. Sir John Davies (1567–1626) had affinities with Spenser in his philosophic moods: in his *Nosce Teipsum* (1599) he set out the arguments for the immortality of the soul and countered the objections, thus anticipating eighteenth-century expository verse.

Among the formative poets whose influence was powerful through most of the seventeenth century we have so far considered only Spenser. But there were two others, towards whom later writers of verse turned with no less admiration for their example and respect for their authority. These were Ben Jonson (1573–1637) and John Donne (1573–1631). Each of them struck out in a new direction.

Ben Jonson

Jonson's lyrics are mostly contained in his plays and masques, and in two small collections: *The Forest* and *Underwoods*. In early Jacobean days he was the acknowledged mentor of literary taste, and his prestige was so great that it could survive the publication of verse marred by many lame rhymes. His attitude to poetry may be inferred from a passage in *Timber* where he enumerates the attributes of a poet, who should have (1) goodness of natural wit, (2) patience to exercise his art, "to bring all to the forge and file again," (3) imitation, "to be able to convert the substance or riches of another poet to his own use," and (4) "exactness of study and multiplicity of reading which maketh a full man." There is little here to suggest the spontaneity of poetry: all these attributes can be brought to perfection by art. Jonson's mind was rational, analytical and epigrammatic; he worked towards an ideal of clarity, a quality belonging pre-eminently to prose. It is therefore not surprising that Jonson should have been acclaimed by the writers of the Augustan age (see page 192.)

The following example of Jonson's verse may be studied as showing the lyrical mind of the poet at work, under the restraint of his feeling for the "majesty of art set high in spirit with the precious taste of sweet philosophy"—

> It is not growing like a tree
> In bulk, doth make men better be;
> Or standing long an oak, three hundred year,
> To fall a log at last, dry, bald and sere:
> A lily of a day
> Is fairer far in May,
> Although it fall and die that night;
> It was the plant and flower of light.
> In small proportions we just beauties see
> And in short measures life may perfect be.

Jonson was the poet of "*just* beauties," censorious of redundance of ornament, of disproportion of thought and expression, and of obscurity. He disciplined his verse to the severe economy and balance of the classics.

John Donne

John Donne (1572–1631) was a complete rebel against the courtly poetry and the light airy madrigals of the Elizabethans, with their conventional terms of love and grief, their hackneyed conceits and their florid prettiness. He differed from them in a number of ways. Firstly, with respect to prosodic form: he cared little for the smoothness and sweetness of the song-like lyrics which appeared in such quantities in his youth. His own versification was often harsh and knotted. Secondly, the emotions he described were his own. The Elizabethan love lyric is impersonal; Donne "looks into his heart and writes." Thirdly, the imagery was freshly imagined, being no longer an echo of the classical tropes which had done duty for so long. Fourthly, his urge to write was intellectual; no parallel that his wit could conceive was too fantastic and ingenious to use. He took an intellectual pleasure in extorting from a juxtaposition of ideas all that it could yield in support of some hyperbolic fancy. The following lines are part of a poem in which one at the point of death urges that there shall be no parting or farewell—

> Our two souls therefore, which are one,
>   Though I must go, endure not yet
> A breach, but an expansion,
>   Like gold to airy thinness beat.
>
> If they be two, they are two so
>   As stiff twin compasses are two,
> Thy soul the fixt foot, makes no show
>   To move, but doth, if th'other do.
>
> And though it in the centre sit,
>   Yet when the other far doth roam,
> It leans, and hearkens after it,
>   And grows erect as that comes home.
>
> Such wilt thou be to me, who must
>   Like th'other foot, obliquely run;
> Thy firmness makes my circles just,
>   And makes me end, where I begun.

We have in these lines two daring images, one of friendship beaten out like gold to gossamer thinness, to bridge the span between life and death, the other concerned with the movements of the two legs of a pair of compasses. It is such "conceits" that Dryden had in mind when he coined the description "metaphysical" when discussing Abraham Cowley and other imitators of Donne. In the example given, the parallels are concrete enough; but sometimes they are recondite and lost among abstractions.

Frequently Donne lights up his themes with a brilliant white light,

and then he attains heights of creative insight and imagination as
outstanding as any in the language—

> Go and catch a falling star,
>   Get with child a mandrake root,
> Tell me where all past years are,
>   Or who cleft the devil's foot,
> Teach me to hear mermaid's singing,
>   Or to keep off envy's stinging,
>   And find
>   What wind
> Serves to advance an honest mind.

Donne has served in the history of English poetry as a touchstone of
taste. Until the Restoration he was extravagantly admired. Ben
Jonson declared him to be "the first poet in the world in some things"
though he "for not keeping of accent deserved hanging." His influence
was strong on the religious poets of the Caroline period, one of whom,
Thomas Carew, wrote an elegy on him which ended with the lines—

> Here lies a king that ruled as he thought fit
> The universal monarchy of wit.

More particularly the spirit of Donne was shared by the group of
religious poets containing Herbert and Vaughan. John Cleveland
(1613–58) and Abraham Cowley (1618–67) carried the taste for
"conceits" to an absurd excess. Notwithstanding the considerable
vogue they enjoyed as poets during the period of Puritan domination,
they rank as intellectuals rather than as artists. Addison, while drawing
attention to his extravagant fancy, admits Cowley to have "as much
true wit as any author that ever writ," and Dr. Johnson considered
him to be the chief of the "metaphysicals."

With the cult of a new idiom of poetry in the changed atmosphere
of Restoration times, Donne's reputation suffered eclipse. Those who
adopted the ideal of correctness did so largely by way of reaction
against the exasperating subtleties and the broken and shapeless music
of Donne and his school. For his obscurity they substituted clarity;
for his ingenuities, directness; for his wayward passion, order; and for
his metrical ruggedness, smoothness. The neglect of Donne continued
through the eighteenth century into the nineteenth century, and it is
only in our generation that he has entered into his own again. Certainly
his age had much in common with ours. The joyous eagerness of the
Elizabethans had given place to a certain disillusionment. The fine
frenzy was over. The new age was one in which it seemed that there

were no more heroic deeds to be done, and derring-do gave place to endless discussion of such matters as the proper limits of the King's prerogative. Donne has been called the true poet of a decadent age, when pessimism and brooding doubt clouded the mind. He may well be termed "metaphysical" in another sense than that which Dryden and Dr. Johnson had in mind, because his tortured mind was pre-occupied with the meaning of the universe and man's place in it, and with the problems of life and death.

No circumstance in the history of literary taste in this country is more striking than the manner in which Donne has again in our own day become significant as a poet. He represents the "poetry of wit," that is to say the poetry which uses the intellect to build up complex unities of thought out of materials which are conventionally non-poetic. By the juxtaposition of ideas which seem at first sight unrelated and even violently discordant, and by their reconciliation in the white heat of the poet's imagination, a more coherent and organic body of truth is achieved than is attainable by the use of familiar comparisons. The obscurity of Donne is of the same nature as the obscurity of some of the moderns. It arises from the sudden leaps and jerks of the imagination. The effort to wrest a meaning out of intractable material at times involves the doing of violence to syntax, and the cheating of anticipations of rhythmical sequence.

SUGGESTIONS FOR FURTHER READING

C. S. Lewis: *The Allegory of Love* (Oxford Univ. Press).
Bruce Pattison: *Music and Poetry of the English Renaissance* (Methuen).
A. H. Bullen: *Elizabethans* (Chapman & Hall).
Seccombe and Allen: *The Age of Shakespeare: I—Poetry and Prose* (Bell).

CHAPTER VIII

CAVALIER AND PURITAN POETRY

THE dominating influences on the poets known as the Caroline Lyricists were, as we have seen, those of Ben Jonson and John Donne. Their revolt against the polite conventions of the Elizabethan lyric was altogether to the taste of the younger generation, who had not directly experienced the *élan* of the age of Spenser, Sidney, and Shakespeare. They had a considerable vogue in the Universities and among soldiers and clergymen, who stood towards the lyric very much in the position in which Wyatt and Surrey and their following stood nearly a century earlier. These did not write as professionals for publication, but as amateurs of poetry; nearly all of their work appeared posthumously.

The Metaphysicals

We can distinguish two groups. Firstly, the religious group also known as the "fantastics," consisting of George Herbert (1593–1633), Francis Quarles (1592–1644), Richard Crashaw (1612–49), Henry Vaughan (1622–95) and Thomas Traherne (1634–74). Secondly, the Cavalier group, gallant, aristocratic men of fortune, including Thomas Carew (1589–1639), Sir John Suckling (1609–42) and Richard Lovelace (1618–58). Robert Herrick (1594–1674) and Abraham Cowley shared the characteristics of both groups. All these poets were Anglicans, and supported the royal cause in the struggle between King and Parliament. What these poets have of smoothness, clarity, ease and dignity they have in common with Jonson; what they have of compactness, quick-darting imagery and subtle contortions of thought they share with Donne; what they have of song-like quality they derive from the Elizabethans.

Andrew Marvell and Edmund Waller

There was one of the religious group who was on the anti-royalist side: namely Andrew Marvell (1621–78), an official colleague of Milton in the Latin Secretaryship during the Commonwealth. His *Horatian Ode*, a panegyric on Cromwell, is unequalled in its kind in English. Marvell's verse, like that of Milton, falls easily into two divisions: his youthful poems such as *To His Coy Mistress* are in the spirit of the Caroline lyrists, light-hearted and "fantastic," while in those written after the Restoration he turned towards political satire. His use of the heroic couplet for this purpose pointed the way to the Augustans. So also did his qualities of urbanity, poise, and classical detachment.

A second influence which counted for much in giving a new direction to poetry was that of Edmund Waller (1606–87). Though his life lies quite outside the reign of Elizabeth, he can in one aspect of his work be reckoned as the last of the Elizabethans. His poem *Go Lovely Rose* has taken its place in our literature as his best lyric. But he is particularly interesting to the literary historian because of the high polish he gave to the heroic couplet. Dryden acknowledged his debt to Waller on the ground that he "first made writing an art," and this was the judgment of his time. Waller aimed above all things at "correctness." By this was meant chiefly two things. One was smoothness and epigrammatic and antithetical force, achieved through making the unit of meaning correspond with the metrical unit of the couplet. The divisions were clearly marked by the use of strongly-stressed rhymes—

> Stronger by weakness wiser men become
> As they draw near to their eternal home.
> Leaving the old, both worlds at once they view
> That stand upon the threshold of the new.

The other quality aimed at was lucidity. Waller can thus be regarded as at the same time a disciple of Jonson and a critic of Donne. His taste was for verse which showed the sharply-cut features of a classical profile, and he was the acknowledged founder of the Augustan school of English poets.

John Milton

Milton (1608–1704) had as his background the whole body of classical and medieval European literature and history, in which he was profoundly learned, and to this he added a knowledge of the Hebrew writings. He was moreover a child of the Renaissance, the last of the early English humanists. Notwithstanding the remark of Dryden: "Milton has acknowledged to me that Spenser was his original,"[1] it is impossible to discuss a poet of such towering genius as a member of any group or "school." He was independent of traditions

[1] Dryden: *Preface to Fables.*

and influences except those of the widest scope. Literature was to him the serious business of life, compact with moral purpose. In the glow of his poetic imagination he fused a dogmatic Puritan outlook with a pagan feeling for sensuous beauty.

The three divisions of Milton's writing correspond chronologically with three phases of our national history: pre-Commonwealth, Commonwealth, and post-Commonwealth. To the first period belong most of his lyric and elegiac poems: *The Hymn on the Nativity* (1629); *L'Allegro, Il Penseroso* (1632); *Lycidas* (1637); and *Comus* (1634).

In the second he turned from poetry to polemical prose in defence of civil and religious liberty, some of it undertaken as a duty incumbent on him as Latin Secretary to Cromwell, some of it arising independently. The third phase of his writing, which occupied the blind poet from 1660 till his death, consists of the two epics: *Paradise Lost* (1667) and *Paradise Regained* (1671), and the tragedy of *Samson Agonistes* (1671).

Milton's Lyrical Poetry

The *Hymn*, written at the age of twenty-one, shows that Milton's lyric genius was already highly developed. The sublime splendour of its conception can hardly be matched in the language, but it is possible to detect in the latter part of the poem something of the prevalent liking for "conceits," or far-fetched images—

> So when the sun in bed,
> Curtained with cloudy red,
> Pillows his chin upon an orient wave. . . .

The complementary poems *L'Allegro* and *Il Penseroso*, in octosyllabic couplets, contain delightful descriptions of rustic scenes and pastimes in Springtime and Autumn. The mood of *L'Allegro* is gay, positive, and active, as the name implies. It is a pastoral romance in the classical tradition, painting an idealized picture of rural life from dawn to dusk.

Il Penseroso is essentially a meditative poem, its theme being the passive joys of the contemplative life. It extols the recluse who spends his days in solitary reflection amid the calmer beauties of nature—

> Or, if the air will not permit,
> Some still removed place will fit,
> Where glowing embers through the room
> Teach light to counterfeit a gloom,
> Far from all resort of mirth,
> Save the cricket on the hearth,
> Or the bellman's drowsy charm
> To bless the doors from nightly harm.

We have in these two poems Milton's lyrical genius at its best. The learning that they contain, whether it is of classical legend, medieval romance or English folk-lore, is no pedantic excrescence; it is of the very stuff of the poem.

Lycidas is the greatest pastoral elegy in the English language. It was written at a time when the poet was about to be caught up in the political strife which tore the nation asunder, and it is not surprising that the poem should reflect something of his partisanship. The grief of the poet occasioned by the death of his friend, Edward King, alternates with savage denunciation of the "hireling" clergy and regret for the loss of true religion in the State Church. The poem is in irregular metre, with six-syllabled lines frequently interspersed with lines of ten syllables; the rhymes occur sometimes in couplets, sometimes apart—

> Thee, Shepherd, thee the woods and desert caves,
> With wild thyme and the gadding vine o'ergrown,
> And all their echoes, mourn.
> The willows, and the hazel copses green,
> Shall now no more be seen
> Fanning their joyous leaves to thy soft lays.
> As killing as the canker to the rose,
> Or taint-worm to the weaning herds that graze,
> Or frost to flowers, that their gay wardrobe wear
> When first the white-thorn blows;
> Such, Lycidas, thy loss to shepherd's ear.

Comus (1634) marks an important stage in the development of Milton's thought. It shows him in transition from the pastoral, idyllic manner of his early poems towards the greater purpose which informed his mature work. It is noticeable that he had by now abandoned rhymed for blank verse except in the songs which are interspersed in the masque. The poem shows that Milton had taken up a position strongly antagonistic to the ruling temper of Caroline society and it echoes the growing Puritan protest against its dissoluteness. Though marked by high seriousness, and didactic in aim, *Comus* is no tract, but one of the highest poetic achievements in our literature, in which Milton's lyricism is enriched by a—

> divine Philosophy
> Not harsh and crabbed as dull fools suppose,
> But musical as is Apollo's lute
> And a perpetual feast of nectared sweets
> Where no crude surfeit reigns.

The gap of years between the poetry of these lyrics and that of the great epics is to some extent bridged by a few great sonnets such as *When the Assault was intended to the City, To the Lord General Fairfax, On his Blindness,* and *On the Late Massacre in Piedmont,* the last two being surely among the half-dozen finest sonnets ever written, proceeding out of an emotion deeply and nobly felt. In all his sonnets Milton used the strict Petrarchan form.

The Epical Works

The end of Milton's work was present in the beginning, for even in his youth he dedicated himself to preparation for the great task which was to crown his days. Not until quite late in his life did he decide upon its subject and form, save that he intended it to be of large design. His note-books show that at one time he contemplated writing an epic on the Arthurian legends, and at another he was working on drafts for a tragedy in the Greek manner with the Fall of Man as the subject. The choice of the theme of *Paradise Lost* was made even while he was pre-occupied with the polemics of the Commonwealth. But on Cromwell's death in 1658 the work of composition began. Milton having become totally blind six years earlier, it was his habit to dictate a few lines daily to some member of his family or to a chance caller.

In *Paradise Lost,* Milton uses the classical conventions of form, but the spirit is that of the Hebrew Scriptures. The subject, Man, is seen against the Ptolemaic cosmogony. The "things unattempted yet in prose or rhyme" are the casting out from Heaven of the apostate angels, their planning of revenge in Hell, Satan's flight, Man's temptation and fall from grace and the promise of redemption. Against this vast background Milton projects his own philosophy of the purposes of human existence.

Paradise Regained is in four books. Without rising to the heights of the greater epic, the poem nevertheless registers rather a change of mood than a decline in poetic power. The subject gives less room for sublimity and is altogether in a quieter key. It is strongest in the narrative passages.

Reference is made elsewhere to the metre of the poems. Their principal ornament is the rich imagery, used to enhance the majesty of the basic conception. Much of this is contained in extended metaphors of the kind met with in classical epics, and derived from history, mythology, personal observation and literary and biblical suggestion.

The following examples may be compared—

> Angel Forms, who lay entranced
> Thick as autumnal leaves that strow the brooks
> In Vallombrosa, where the Etrurian shades
> High over-arched embower; or scattered sedge
> Afloat, when with fierce winds Orion armed
> Hath vexed the Red-Sea coast, whose waves o'erthrew
> Busiris and his Memphian chivalry,
> While with perfidious hatred they pursued
> The sojourners of Goshen who beheld
> From the safe shore their floating carcases
> And broken chariot wheels.
>
> *Paradise Lost I*

> As bees
> In spring-time, when the Sun with Taurus rides,
> Pour forth their populous youth above the hive
> In clusters; they among fresh dews and flowers
> Fly to and fro, or on the smoothed plank,
> The suburb of their straw-built citadel,
> New rubbed with balm, expatiate, and confer
> Their state-affairs; so thick the aery crowd
> Swarmed and were straitened.
>
> *Paradise Lost I*

SUGGESTIONS FOR FURTHER READING

BASIL WILLEY: *The Seventeenth Century Background* (Chatto & Windus).

E. M. W. TILLYARD: *Milton* (Chatto & Windus).

D. SAURAT: *Milton: Man and Thinker* (Dent).

DOUGLAS BUSH: *English Literature in the Earlier Seventeenth Century* (Oxford Univ. Press).

JOAN BENNETT: *Four Metaphysical Poets: Donne, Herbert, Vaughan, Crashaw* (Cambridge Univ. Press).

L. C. KNIGHTS: *Explorations: Essays in Criticism* (Chatto & Windus).

G. WILLIAMSON: *The Donne Tradition* (Oxford Univ. Press).

EDMUND GOSSE: *The Jacobean Poets* (Murray).

J. H. B. MASTERMAN: *The Age of Milton* (Bell).

CHAPTER IX

AUGUSTAN POETRY

THE Augustan age was so called by later literary historians because it seemed to embody some of the characteristic features of the culture of the age of the Roman Emperor Augustus (27 B.C.–A.D. 14), made illustrious by such writers as Virgil, Horace, Ovid, and Livy. The description Augustan is rather loosely used, since it sometimes connotes the whole period from the Restoration of 1660 to the middle of the eighteenth century, corresponding roughly with the age of Dryden and Pope, and sometimes is confined to a smaller part of this, namely the period of Queen Anne's reign when the vogue of the essayists was at its height.

The New Pattern

The wider use of the term is justified on the ground that most of the literature produced under the late Stuarts and the early Hanoverians conformed to a new pattern of taste. It was a pattern which set less store by the imagination and more by the critical faculty. There was a decline in the primary impulses which go to the making of poetry and a falling back on the secondary. Epic poetry was displaced by satirical, argumentative or expository, lyric by epigrammatical, tragic by heroic and rhetorical. The typical man of letters was a classical scholar, ever looking back—though usually through French spectacles —to models bequeathed by Rome.

During the Commonwealth, the living tradition of English poetry had been well-nigh forgotten. There was some neglected work by poets of an older manner, such as Robert Herrick. Milton was, in a poetic sense, almost mute. When the Restoration came, and the pulse of the nation beat normally again, a fresh start was necessary. The cultural atmosphere was changed with the return of the arbiters of taste and fashion from France, bringing with them a predilection for classical modes. The social atmosphere also was changed, as consequence of the resumption of court life, surrounded as it was by well-bred, dilettante coteries, cultivating manners as an art. A new kind of poetic inspiration was demanded, one which set a value on urbanity and good form, on order and proportion. As we have seen, there were models at hand which served to give a lead. Waller and Denham were already turning out work more or less in the disciplined and restrained manner of the French, and it needed only the emergence of a more robust talent to erect a method into a system.

John Dryden

This talent was forthcoming in John Dryden (1631–1700), a man of massive intellect and bold, critical judgment, who established himself as the greatest man of letters of his day. In poetry and criticism he was supreme; in drama he was at any rate among the leaders of taste. There is hardly a figure in our literary history who can be matched against him for many-sidedness.

Our concern in this section is only with his achievement in non-dramatic verse. Two early poems: *Heroic Stanzas* (1658), written on the death of Cromwell, and *Annus Mirabilis* (1666), dealing with the Dutch War and The Fire of London, were exercises outside his true bent. They were disfigured by absurd images and false sentiment, which show clearly that Dryden was not yet master of his method—

> While by the motion of the flames they guess
> What streets are burning now, and what are near,
> An infant, waking, to the paps would press
> And meets instead of milk a falling tear.

Almost the only other non-dramatic verse he produced during the first twenty years after the Restoration consisted of the prologues to the heroic tragedies, and in these he shows his liking for the conversational idiom, without any of the affectations or tricks of versifying. He was also gaining skill in using the rhymed couplet—

> Ladies! (I hope there's none behind to hear)
> I long to whisper something in your ear,
> A secret, which does much my mind perplex:
> There's treason in the play against our sex.
> A man that's false to love, that vows and cheats,
> And kisses every living thing he meets.
>
> *Prologue to The Princess of Cleves*

Political Satire

In 1681 Dryden turned to a new kind of poetry and at once struck a rich vein. This was political satire, and it engaged most of his energies during his middle period (1681–88). *Absalom and Achitophel* was his first effort in this kind and it was received with enthusiasm. The King's party welcomed it for its advocacy of the royal cause, but more generally the poem was acclaimed for its brilliant satiric portraiture of such contemporary figures as the Duke of Monmouth and the Earl of Shaftesbury. The poem was quickly followed by *The Medal*, *Mac-Flecknoe* and *Religio Laici*, written in the same spirit of vigorous argument mingled with biting invective against stupid and wrong-headed opponents.

In these poems the heroic couplet reached perfection. Smoothly and easily it penetrated like a steel rapier into the heart of the matter, whether this were a political doctrine or a fellow-poet's reputation—

> Shadwell alone of all my sons is he
> Who stands confirmed in full stupidity.
> The rest to some faint meaning make pretence,
> But Shadwell never deviates into sense.
> Some beams of wit on other souls may fall
> Strike through and make a lucid interval;
> But Shadwell's genuine night admits no ray;
> His rising fogs prevail upon the day.

The *Hind and Panther*, a defence of the Roman Church, followed in 1687. The political swing to Whiggery in 1688 affected Dryden's fortunes and he had to abandon his polemical writing. To the last few years of his life we owe the great translations, imitations, and modernizations of earlier poets. These included the *Æneid* of Virgil, the *Odes* of Horace, the *Satires* of Juvenal, and the *Translations* from Boccaccio and Chaucer.

For his satirical poetry, on which his claim to eminence as a poet mainly rests, Dryden's chief model was Juvenal. He and the Latin poet are alike in their vehemence, but differ in the objects of their attack. While Juvenal is a misogynist and is consumed with hatred of the social trends of his age, Dryden's shafts are directed mainly to his personal enemies and the opinions they hold. In his *Discourse concerning the Original and Progress of Satire* (1692), which he prefaced to a translation of Juvenal, he remarks that "the nicest and most delicate touches of satire consist in fine raillery . . . Neither is it true that this fineness of raillery is offensive. A witty man is tickled when he is hurt in this manner, and a fool feels it not."

Dryden distinguished his own method of satire from the "former sort . . . which is known in England by the name of lampoon." He used a rapier rather than a bludgeon, to the end that the malefactor should "die sweetly." It was to his credit that he recognized in the heroic couplet the weapon ideally suited for his purpose. It was clean and polished, and its use was consonant with the manners of a gentleman.

Alexander Pope

The literary career of Alexander Pope (1688–1744) began after Dryden's was ended. Roughly, they are separated in time by the consummation of the Whig revolution, which established in Britain a constitutional monarchy supported by the mercantile classes, the new nobility and the Puritans. Ranged in opposition to the Hanoverians were the country gentry and the rural clergy with their flocks. As urban life developed, the reading public expanded, a circumstance of some importance for literature. While Dryden had to rely on the stage to provide him with an income, Pope was able to amass a fortune from the sale of his poetry alone. Dryden's range was nevertheless wider, and his appeal was to a more varied circle. Pope was the poet of the Club, of the fashionable drawing-room, and of the literary circle; his audience was made up of intellectuals, who relished his epigrammatic wit and his easy optimism. Drawing in to himself the ideas which were floating about, Pope gave them back to his world in terse and polished language, easily remembered and quoted—

> Two principles in human nature reign:
> Self-love to urge, and Reason, to restrain;
> Nor this a good, nor that a bad we call,
> Each works its end, to move or govern all:
> And to their proper operation still,
> Ascribe all Good; to their improper Ill.
>
> *Essay on Man, Epistle II*

After some early work, *The Pastorals* and *Windsor Forest*, which, although but prentice efforts, already show him to be an accomplished versifier, his first characteristic poem was *The Essay on Criticism*, published when he was twenty-four years of age. In this he set out the entire body of "rules" which should govern the practice of the art of poetry. The ideas are not original, being derived from Horace's *Ars Poetica* and Boileau's *L'Art Poétique*, but the *Essay* stands as a testament of English classicism.

It will be useful to compare Pope's use of the heroic couplet with Dryden's. Dr. Johnson in his *Lives of the Poets* makes this comparison: "Dryden's page is a natural field, rising into inequalities and diversified by the varied exuberance of abundant vegetation; Pope's is a velvet lawn, shaven by the scythe and levelled by the roller." In another passage he says: "The method of Pope was to write his first thoughts in his first words, and gradually to amplify, decorate, rectify and refine them." The "inequalities" and "diversities" which Pope was so assiduous in removing were the use of *enjambement* (or the running on of the grammatical sentence beyond the limits of the couplet), of the occasional triplet and of the Alexandrine, as illustrated in the following—

> Waller was smooth; but Dryden taught to join
> The varying verse, the full resounding line,
> The long majestick march, and energy divine.

He disliked hiatus (or the elision of vowels), inversions, expletives and monosyllabic lines. Some of these faults he exemplifies in a well-known passage—

> But most by numbers judge a Poet's song;
> And smooth or rough, with them is right or wrong:
> In the bright Muse though thousand charms conspire,
> Her voice is all these tuneful fools admire;
> Who haunt Parnassus but to please their ear,
> Not mend their minds; as some to Church repair,
> Not for the doctrine, but the music there.
> These equal syllables alone require,
> Tho' oft the ear the open vowels tire;
> While expletives their feeble aid do join;
> And ten low words oft creep in one dull line:
> While they ring round the same unvary'd chimes,
> With sure returns of still expected rhymes;
> Where-e're you find "the cooling western breeze,"
> In the next line, it "whispers through the trees":
> If crystal streams "with pleasing murmurs creep,"
> The reader's threaten'd (not in vain) with "sleep":
> Then at the last and only couplet fraught
> With some unmeaning thing they call a thought,
> A needless Alexandrine ends the song
> That, like a wounded snake, drags its slow length along;
> Leave such to tune their own dull rhymes, and know
> What's roundly smooth or languishingly slow;
> And praise the easy vigour of a line,
> Where Denham's strength, and Waller's sweetness join.
> True ease in writing comes from art, not chance,
> As those move easiest who have learned to dance.
>
> *Essay on Criticism*

It was by the shedding of such "exuberances" that Pope sought to achieve "correctness." He added to the clipped effect of his verse by keeping the cæsura within narrow bounds, usually after the fourth, fifth or sixth syllable, and often using the two halves of his lines for antithesis—

> Poets themselves must fall, like those they sung;
> Deaf the praised ear, and mute the tuneful tongue.
>> *Elegy to the Memory of an Unfortunate Lady*

His rhymes are made to fall mostly on monosyllables, so that they may have the maximum of stress and accentuate the "clinch" of the couplet.

Another work of Pope's early period was *The Rape of the Lock* (1712), the best example in English of the mock-heroic— "filigree-work," as Hazlitt called it. It is an exquisite piece of raillery and wit, so perfect in form that the delight it affords the reader even to-day is unfailing. The following passage from Canto II (there are five Cantos) describes the supplication of the "advent'rous Baron," intent on winning the lock of Belinda's hair—

> For this, ere Phoebus rose, he had implor'd
> Propitious heav'n, and ev'ry pow'r ador'd,
> But chiefly Love—to Love an Altar built,
> Of twelve vast French Romances, neatly gilt.
> There lay three garters, half a pair of gloves;
> And all the trophies of his former loves;
> With tender Billet-doux he lights the pyre,
> And breathes three am'rous sighs to raise the fire.
> Then prostrate falls, and begs with ardent eyes
> Soon to obtain, and long possess the prize:
> The pow'rs gave ear, and granted half his pray'r;
> The rest the winds dispers'd in empty air.

The translations of Homer's *Iliad* and *Odyssey* established Pope's reputation and fortune. Dr. Johnson said of the *Iliad*: "It is certainly the noblest version of poetry which the world has ever seen; and its publication must therefore be considered as one of the greatest events in the annals of learning." Again a comparision with Dryden's translation of Virgil's *Æneid* is suggested. Modern criticism takes the view that, Dryden's genius being closer to Homer's and Pope's to Virgil's it would have been better had the two translators chosen differently. The resourcefulness of the poet is shown by the production, even while he was busy on *The Iliad*, of two such finished elegiac poems as *Eloisa to Abelard* and the *Elegy to the Memory of an Unfortunate Lady*.

Pope's attention was directed towards satire and polemics partly by the example of Swift, Arbuthnot, Gay, Congreve, and others whom he used to meet at the Scriblerus Club, and partly through a disposition to misanthropy fed by brooding on wrongs done to him by jealous literary competitors. Members of the Scriblerus Club had joined in a "scheme to ridicule all false tastes in learning." In 1728 appeared Pope's *Dunciad*, a satire on pretentious dullness, in which Theobald, who had published an important work of criticism, *Shakespeare Restored*, was enthroned as King of the Dunces. The satire includes an element of personal spleen, but also there was sound castigation of bad manners in literature. Pope carried on in a vein of satirical moralizing and philosophizing with his *Epistles, Satires, Moral Essays*, and *The Essay on Man*, which occupied the last ten years of his life.

Pope's reputation has passed through many vicissitudes. The tide of a new romanticism which had begun to flow even during his lifetime was against him, and there was hardly one except Byron in the full flood of the Romantic Movement to speak for him. But he has found in our own day many readers, sensitive to form and proportion in poetry, who place him high among English poets, if not in the first rank. The essential beauty of his poetry, which is the beauty dependent on restraint and on the "expected resolution" (as with the music of Mozart), is now appreciated. Although Pope represents in our literature the spirit of elegance and urbanity, this is by no means a complete measure of his range of thought and feeling. He could command the tragic as well as the satiric mood, and had a passionate hatred of sham and corruption. He was an apostle of intellectual and moral integrity. The following passage from Epistle III of the *Moral Essays* illustrates Pope's realism—

> In the worst inn's worst room, with mat half-hung,
> The floors of plaister, and the walls of dung,
> On once a flock-bed, but repair'd with straw,
> With tape-ty'd curtains, never meant to draw,
> The George and Garter dangling from that bed
> Where tawdry yellow strove with dirty red,
> Great Villiers lies—alas! how changed from him,
> That life of pleasure, and that soul of whim! . . .
> No Wit to flatter left of all his store!
> No Fool to laugh at, which he valu'd more.
> There Victor of his health, of fortune, friends,
> And fame, this lord of useless thousands ends.

SUGGESTIONS FOR FURTHER READING

A. BELJAME: *Men of Letters and the English Public in the Eighteenth Century* (Oxford Univ. Press).

H. V. D. DYSON AND JOHN BUTT: *Augustans and Romantics, 1689–1830* (Cresset Press).

EDMUND GOSSE: *Eighteenth-century Literature, 1660–1780* (Macmillan).

OLIVER ELTON: *The Augustan Ages* (Blackwood).

R. GARNETT: *The Age of Dryden* (Bell).

J. DENNIS: *The Age of Pope* (Bell).

EDITH SITWELL: *Alexander Pope* (Faber & Faber).

T. S. ELIOT: *Homage to John Dryden* (Hogarth Press).

THOMAS QUAYLE: *Poetic Diction* (Methuen).

LESLIE STEPHEN: *English Literature and Society in the Eighteenth Century* (Duckworth).

CHAPTER X

THE APPROACH TO ROMANTICISM
IN POETRY

W E have now to trace the course of the gradual, but progressive recovery of imaginative power in literature. Changes in literary modes do not occur abruptly, nor are these modes, when established, so dominant that there are no writers who remain unaffected by them. Long before the Augustan principles of Reason and Correctness came to be challenged on a broad front, a new spirit was beginning to be felt in poetry. It was not that poetry had any new tricks to learn; but values which Pope and his followers had discarded were coming into their own again. There were deeper cords in the heart to be stirred than the poetry of wit had been able to touch.

Aesthetic taste swings from delight in form to delight in feeling and back again like a pendulum. Greatness in art can be reached along either the classical or the romantic path. "In its central nature, great art is at once romantic and classical, yet characteristically neither. It has the virtues of both."[1] When either principle is urged too far, it begins to engender forces which favour its opposite, and a reaction is inevitable.

We can distinguish three prominent features of the movement towards the second great outburst of romanticism in our literature: the return to Nature, the return to Feeling, and the return to Romance. These were linked expressions of a single poetic mood in conflict with tired conventions.

The Return to Nature

Pope, as we have seen, used the term "Nature" in a special sense to imply the view of the world which we attain by the exercise of reason as contrasted with that which we reach by our intuition. He and other neo-classic poets opposed "Nature" to fantasy, extravagance, exaggeration, and all that was unbalanced and uncontrolled (or, in the parlance of the eighteenth century, "enthusiastic"). The Romantics used the word in quite other meanings. One was that expressed by Byron in the lines—

[1] Gotshalk: *Art and the Social Order* (Univ. of Chicago Press), p. 224.

There is a pleasure in the pathless woods,
    There is a rapture on the lonely shore,
There is society where none intrudes,
    By the deep Sea, and music in its roar;
I love not Man the less, but Nature more,
    From these our interviews, in which I steal
From all I may be, or have been before,
    To mingle with the Universe, and feel
What I can ne'er express, yet cannot all conceal.

Childe Harold, Canto IV

Here it is the world without Man and his works. Another meaning underlies much of Wordsworth's poetry. Nature to him is that part of existence which refuses to yield up its secrets to conscious reasoning, but which may sometimes be illuminated in flashes of insight—

That blessed mood
In which the burden of the mystery,
In which the heavy and the weary weight
Of all this unintelligible world,
Is lightened.

WORDSWORTH: *Tintern Abbey*

According to this view, "the inward eye" reveals truths beyond the reach of the intellect. Romantic poetry finds its themes and its inspiration therefore in the countryside rather than in the town, in the simple faith of childhood rather than in sophisticated manners, in primitive elemental things rather than in a refined civilization. A supreme poet like the Milton of *L'Allegro* and *Il Penseroso* could include all these things in a single imaginative apprehension of life.

The earliest eighteenth-century poet to use in his work a first-hand observation of nature was James Thomson (1700–48). In *The Seasons* he shows himself deeply sensitive to the moods of the sky, the fields, the woods and the brooks, and enters fully into the delights of out-of-door sports and avocations. Wild creatures are described not as a mere background to human life, but as having their own life—

But let not on thy hook the tortured worm
Convulsive twist in agonizing folds.

Thomson, by using blank verse, goes back to the Miltonic tradition, but he is at the same time subject to the influences of his own time insofar as he succumbs to the vogue of artificial periphrases, and avoids the straightforward and concrete word: thus fish are "the finny drove," birds "the feathered tribe," and frost "the rigid influence."

Every object named has to have its conventional epithet: "the dimpled water," "the shelving shore," "the shadowy clouds," "the pendant trees," "the barbed hook." There is something of the Miltonic manner in this too, but while Milton was using sonorous latinized epithets in the grand style appropriate to the sublimity of his theme—

> There lands the Fiend, a spot like which perhaps
> Astronomer in the Sun's lucent orb
> Through his glazed optic tube yet never saw. . . .

Thomson, whose themes were less elevated, had no such justification.

In *The Castle of Indolence*, Thomson employs the dream-allegory so popular in medieval literature and he was wise enough to choose the Spenserian stanza as his medium. The poem represents a still bolder break with the current mood. Such a passage as the following gives us vague outlines and dim suggestions which would have meant little to a writer of the Augustan school—

> Full in the passage of the vale, above,
> A sable, silent, solemn forest stood;
> Where nought but shadowy forms were seen to move,
> As Idless fancied in her dreaming mood:
> And up the hills, on either side, a wood
> Of blackening pines, aye waving to and fro,
> Sent forth a sleepy horror through the blood;
> And where this valley winded out below,
> The murmuring main was heard, and scarcely heard, to flow.
>
> THOMSON: The Castle of Indolence

The Return to Feeling: Gray and Collins

The second prominent feature of the reaction was the return to feeling or sentiment. This took a number of forms, not less various than the gamut of human emotions. The note of the Augustan writers was one of emotional restraint; a tight rein was kept on any manifestation of deep feeling. The publication of John Dyer's poem, *Grongar Hill* (1726), in the metre and spirit of *Il Penseroso*—

> Grongar, in whose mossy cells
> Sweetly musing Quiet dwells:
> Grongar in whose silent Shade
> For the modest Muses made,
> So oft I have, the Even still,
> At the fountain of a Rill
> Sat upon a flowery Bed,
> With my Hand beneath my Head.

and more particularly of Edward Young's *Night Thoughts* (1742), showed that there were more vibrant chords ready to be touched. The latter poem, in blank verse, dealing with death and immortality, is gloomy in the extreme. Yet its extraordinary popularity, both in England and on the Continent, suggests that it matched the spirit of melancholy brooding which for some time past had been abroad. It accounts for the frequency with which twilight and evening are apostrophized in the poetry of the time. This mood is found again in Thomas Gray's *Elegy Written in a Country Churchyard*, and in William Collins's *Ode to Evening*—

> Now air is hush'd save where the weak-eyed bat
> With short shrill shriek flits by on leathern wing,
>   Or where the beetle winds
>   His small but sullen horn . . .

Solitude and quietude are valued by these poets because they afford opportunity for the contemplative life.

In Europe a whole literature sprang up associated with the cult of seclusion and melancholy, taking many forms, sedate, mystical or ecstatic. The supreme expression of this mood was the German romance: *Werthers Leiden* (The Sorrows of Werther), written by Goethe in 1774, but the impulse came from England. The novels of Richardson had given a strong lead to the literature of sentiment or *Schwärmerei* (meaning the over-indulgence of emotion), and Sterne's *Sentimental Journey*, which dealt less with the writer's observations than with his feelings, followed by Mackenzie's *Man of Feeling*, had confirmed the vogue.

The poetry of nature and of feeling constantly holds up to admiration a golden age of antiquity, when the virtues of simplicity and human equality were thought to govern conduct. Collins ends *The Passions* with the lines—

> O bid our vain endeavours cease,
> Revive the just designs of Greece,
> Return in all thy simple state,
> Confirm the tales her sons relate!

This heralds the revolutionary strain of Rousseauism, which was to be heard through the whole of later romantic poetry from Burns to Byron and Shelley. Rousseau maintained that man in the "state of nature" was good, because as such his behaviour was regulated only by instinctive feeling. He postulated an earlier simple society, free from the perversions to which modern civilization gave rise, and held up the "noble savage" as the happiest and wisest of mankind. This idealization of primitive simplicity had a profound effect, not only on political thinking, but on literature also.

The Return to Romance

The third aspect of the reaction against the spirit of Augustan poetry we have called the turn to Romance. This too found expression in many different ways. It was a reaction against canons of taste based on the example of the classical writers. But fundamentally, it was a turning away from sophistication—

> 'Tis fancy's land to which thou sett'st thy feet;
> Where still, 'tis said, the fairy people meet.

Collins in these lines from his *Ode on the Popular Superstitions of the Highlands of Scotland* was urging the claims of "themes of simple, sure effect" on the poet's attention. While he looked to Scotland, Gray looked to Wales and Iceland as lands of "fancy." *The Bard* is inspired by Welsh medieval legend and *The Descent of Odin* by Norse tradition. The *Rowley Poems* by the Bristol boy, Thomas Chatterton (1752–70), written in pseudo-Chaucerian English, and fictitiously claimed to be the work of a fifteenth-century monk, are, notwithstanding the forgery, evidence of the strong appeal of medievalism or, as it was generally called, "the Gothick"—

> His cloak was all of Lincoln cloth so fine,
>   With a gold button fastened near his chin,
> His autremete was edged with golden twine,
>   And his shoe's peak a loverde's might have been;
>   Full well it shewn he thoughten cost no sin.
> The trammels of his palfrey pleased his sight,
> For the horse-milliner his head with roses dight.
>
> *An Excellente Balade of Charitee*

The publication of Bishop Percy's *Reliques of Ancient Poetry* in 1765 contributed greatly to the romantic mood by reviving interest in our ballad literature. The ancient ballads were instinct with those qualities of nature, feeling, and romance, which were now rising so strongly to recognition in poetry, and although Percy was apologetic about his work, as being "among the levities (I had almost said follies) of my youth," he helped to release the pent-up spirit of lyric poetry.

The "Gothick"

These expressions of the Gothic spirit belong principally to the decade 1760–1770, and it was then also that the strange outpourings called the *Works of Ossian* astonished the literary world. James Macpherson (1738–96) was a Scottish schoolmaster who published selections of what purported to be translations of Gaelic folk-literature which centred around a third century Celtic hero. The originals on which these renderings were said to be based were never in fact produced, and it is probable that Macpherson had woven into a romance of his own various scattered elements of Celtic folk-lore. The style was a kind of rhapsodical prose, impregnated with moonlight melancholy and ghostly romantic suggestion—

> Nathos is on the deep, and Althos, that beam of youth. Ardan is near his brothers. They move in the gloom of their course. The sons of Usnoth move in darkness, from the wrath of Cairbar of Erin. Who is that, dim by their side? The night has covered her beauty! Her robe streams in dusky wreaths. She is like the fair spirit of heaven in the midst of his shadowy mist.

Whether these prose-poems were in fact translations, or adaptations, or downright forgeries (as Dr. Johnson was convinced), it is not of the greatest moment to decide. What it is important for the student of literature to appreciate is their widespread influence. By European *savants*, Ossian was acclaimed the Celtic Homer, and for a time he out-topped even Shakespeare in reputation. Schools of Ossianic poetry and prose romance arose in a dozen languages. Wordsworth, looking back on this period half a century later, wrote: "Whatever men may now think of them, there cannot be a doubt that these mountain monotones took the heart of Europe with a new emotion, and prepared it for that passion for mountains which has since possessed it."[1]

The "return to romance" is sometimes described as the "renascence of wonder." Along with the revival of romance there arose a cult of the supernatural. We have seen how in Collins and Gray superstitious legend was exploited for poetic purposes, but these were only early examples. Ossian is full of the mystery of waste lands. The "Gothic" novel (see page 225), beginning with Horace Walpole's *Castle of Otranto* (1764), is largely concerned with the world which is beyond experience. It was, however, in the work of William Blake (1757–1827), a visionary mystic, that metaphysical poetry found its most potent expression. "The revolt of the eighteenth century," wrote G. K. Chesterton, "did not merely release naturalism, but a certain

---

[1] *Poetic Interpretation of Nature.*

kind of supernaturalism also. And of this particular kind of super-naturalism, Blake is particularly the heir."[1]

William Blake

In some of his work, including *Songs of Innocence* and *Songs of Experience* which contain the poems *Little Lamb, who made thee?* and *Tiger, Tiger burning bright*, it is the surprising lyrical quality which compels our admiration. But in another part of his work, known as the "prophetic" writings, *The Book of Thel, Marriage of Heaven and Hell* and others, he expresses his meaning in terms of elaborate trans-cendental cosmogonies, which have affinities with the Swedenborgian conceptions of the nature of the universe.

With Blake, English poetry finally shook itself free of Augustan influences. Not a trace of their spirit remained. In the *Prophetic Poems* there is no rhyme, and the measure is a kind of blank verse so loosely constructed as to resemble prose—

> Thou fair-hair'd angel of the evening . . .
> Smile on our loves and while thou drawest the
> Blue curtains of the sky, scatter thy silver dew
> On every flower that shuts its sweet eyes
> In timely sleep.

and again

> Fearing that Albion should turn his back against the Divine vision,
> Los took his globe of fire to search the interior of Albion's
> Bosom, in all the terrors of friendship, entering the caves
> Of despair and death, to search the tempters out, walking among
> Albion's rocks and precipices, caves of solitude and dark despair.

In language such as this Blake indulges his gift of inspired, or as T. S. Eliot calls it, hallucinated vision.

Robert Burns

Robert Burns (1759–96) was not so completely emancipated. He wrote in two idioms, one Scots, one English. He can, strangely enough, change from the one to the other within the same poem and even in successive stanzas—

> Wee, sleekit, cow'rin, tim'rous beastie,
> O what a panic's in thy breastie!
> Thou need na start awa sae hasty,
>   Wi' bickering brattle!
> I wad be laith to rin an' chase thee
>   Wi' murd-ring pattle.

[1] G. K. Chesterton: *William Blake*.

> I'm truly sorry man's dominion
> Has broken Nature's social union,
> An' justifies that ill opinion
>   Which makes thee startle
> At me, thy poor earth-born companion
>   An' fellow-mortal.

In the one stanza we have genuine feeling expressed in the vernacular, in the other artificial sentiment cast in the mould of rhetoric. Yet notwithstanding the hold which the eighteenth century had on him, Burns is to be reckoned as belonging to the new movement. He lived close to nature and believed in human dignity and equality—

> A man's a man for a' that.

Romanticism had, as we have seen, a political side, and even before the French Revolution had given it a creed and a programme, Burns was possessed by its spirit. He was romantic, too, in his rejection of prudential motives and his submission to instinctive feeling. His poems match his impassioned moods; his large-heartedness made him acutely sensitive to cruelty, falsity, and want. With this humanity he had a lyric gift, an ear for melody in verse, which made his *Songs* among the greatest we have.

William Cowper

Two other writers who were active late in the century can be counted among those who represent the middle phase in the movement towards romanticism. One was William Cowper (1731–1800), a pious recluse of unstable mind, often tortured by religious obsessions, but in periods of normal mental health a genial, kindly soul. He is known to literature chiefly by his private letters, which are characterized by great charm of expression. His poetry also has its place in the movement of reaction against classicism. In much of it he used a conventional diction but he had command of another style as well, as in *To Mary*—

> Thy needles, once a shining store,
> For my sake restless heretofore,
> Now rust disused, and shine no more,
>   My Mary!
>
> For though thou gladly wouldst fulfil
> The same kind office for me still,
> Thy sight now seconds not thy will,
>   My Mary!

Cowper in *The Task* used blank verse to describe homely scenes and the pleasures and pains of simple humanity. He is a master of the serio-comic manner, as shown in *John Gilpin*. His poetry was written from the heart, and much of it had an autobiographical interest.

George Crabbe

The other was George Crabbe (1754–1832). He too stood midway between the Augustans and the Romantics. In diction he inclined to the former; in the temper of his mind and in his realism he may be reckoned with the latter. He used the heroic couplet much on the approved pattern, though with less precision—

> Darkness begins to reign; the louder wind
> Appals the weak and awes the firmer mind.
> But frights not him, whom evening and the spray
> In part conceal—yon Prowler on his way.

A large number of lines show enjambment. But it is in his attitude to nature and to feeling that Crabbe is to be classed with Cowper. Each of them described nature at first hand rather than bookishly, and each employed the pathetic fallacy. Crabbe had no use for pastoral idealizations of the countryside—

> Yes, thus the Muses sing of happy swains,
> Because the Muses never knew their pains:
> They boast their peasants' pipes; but peasants now
> Resign their pipes and plod behind the plough;
> And few, amid the rural-tribe have time
> To number syllables and play with rhyme.
>
> CRABBE: *The Village*

Nature was thus no longer a literary accessory. It was at least on the way to becoming what it was in the poetry of Wordsworth: a "presence," "a motion and a spirit," and "the soul of all my moral being," in a mystical union with man.

Samuel Johnson

Notwithstanding the effort made by Thomson in *The Seasons* to break away from it, the reign of the heroic couplet stretched out for some years longer because of the support given to it by Samuel Johnson (1709–84). An uncompromising classicist, he found in satire his most congenial theme. He was didactic and sententious, but as the objects of his scorn were manners rather than people, he came nearer to Juvenal than to Dryden or Pope. In his two satires *London* and *The Vanity of Human Wishes*, Juvenal was translated into terms of modern life. The verse exhibits the characteristic diction of rhetorical poetry in full play—

> personification:
>> Here Beauty falls betray'd, despis'd, distress'd
>> And hissing Infamy proclaims the rest.

> antithesis:
>> See nations slowly wise and meanly just
>> To buried merit raise the tardy bust;

> slurred syllables:
>> To Int'rest, Prudence: and to Flatt'ry, Pride;

> tautological expression:
>> Let observation, with extensive view
>> Survey mankind, from China to Peru;

> epigram:
>> To point a moral or adorn a tale;

> classical allusion and invocation:
>> Once more, Democritus, arise on earth;

> paradox:
>> With cheerful wisdom and instructive mirth;

> rhetorical question:
>> But did not Chance at length her error mend?
>> Did no subverted empire mark his end?

> conventional adjectives:
>> passing world, triumphal show, regal palace.

In general, the idiom is latinized. The abstract is preferred to the concrete, giving us such impossible mental pictures as "confiscation's vultures," "contagion of the gown" and "congratulating Conscience." Music is described as "the tuneful levities of pain." In short we have not poetry but rhetoric.

These examples can be multiplied from the poets of the eighteenth century, who were imitating the sonorous diction of Milton, but using it for unsuitable purposes. There are passages in Johnson in which his style is vigorous and pungent, and free from such faults, as in the following from *London*, where he is describing the dangers of the streets—

> Prepare for death, if here at night you roam,
> And sign your will before you sup from home.
> Some fiery fop, with new commission vain,
> Who sleeps on brambles till he kills his man;
> Some frolick drunkard, reeling from a feast,
> Provokes a broil, and stabs you for a jest.

Oliver Goldsmith

Oliver Goldsmith (1730–74) used the heroic couplet with more grace. He wore his classicism with a difference, for its ideals of correctness and restraint were modified by the subjective quality of a man who looked out on the world with tolerant humour and sensibility. In *The Traveller* and *The Deserted Village*, which together represent the greater part of his poetical output, the verse is handled still with true eighteenth-century lucidity, but it is warm with human sympathy and gentle irony. The monotony of the abstract diction is varied by touches of realism—

> The white-washed wall, the nicely sanded floor,
> The vanish'd clock that click'd behind the door;
> The chest contriv'd a double debt to pay,
> A bed by night, a chest of drawers by day;
> The pictures plac'd for ornament and use,
> The twelve good rules, the royal game of goose.

Goldsmith's independence is further shown by his use of a cantering anapaestic measure for his short poem *The Retaliation*, in which he gives us imperishable portraits of his friends and associates, such as this of Edmund Burke—

> Here lies our good Edmund, whose genius was such,
> We scarcely can praise it, or blame it too much;
> Who, born for the Universe, narrow'd his mind
> And to party gave up what was meant for mankind.

SUGGESTIONS FOR FURTHER READING

BASIL WILLEY: *The Eighteenth-century Background* (Chatto & Windus).
K. CLARK: *The Gothic Revival* (Constable).
DOUGHTY: *The English Lyric in the Age of Reason* (Daniel O'Connor).
W. L. PHELPS: *The Beginnings of the English Romantic Movement* (Green).
THEODORE WATTS-DUNTON: *The Renascence of Wonder in Poetry* (Chambers Cyclopaedia of English Literature, III).
LORD DAVID CECIL: *Two Quiet Lives: Dorothy Osborne, Thomas Gray* (Constable); *The Stricken Deer: Life of Cowper* (Constable).

CHAPTER XI

THE AGE OF ROMANTICISM

THE full flowering of Romanticism took place in the quarter-century which lies between the publication of the *Lyrical Ballads* of Wordsworth and Coleridge in 1798, and the death of Keats in 1821, of Shelley in 1822, and of Byron in 1824. Wordsworth, although he lived on until 1850, had completed all his important poetical work by 1814. Similarly all the great poems of Coleridge, who died in 1834, were written within the short space of time when he was closely associated with Wordsworth, that is, between 1797 and 1803. Southey, too, had completed his main work in poetry by 1822, and thereafter concerned himself mainly with prose.

We can classify the poets of the high romantic age as (1) the lake school, consisting of Wordsworth, Coleridge and Southey, (2) the Scott group, including Campbell and Moore, and (3) the group comprising Byron, Shelley, and Keats. The first two groups were distinctly earlier than the third, so that we have two eight-year flood periods of supremely great poetry, namely 1798–1806 and 1816–1824, separated by a middle period when by comparison creative energy had ebbed.

The Lake Poets

The Lake Poets formed a "school" in the sense that they worked in close collaboration. Wordsworth had already published his *Poems written in Youth* and completed *The Borderers* (in which he rejected the philosophy of the French Revolution), before his long association with Coleridge began in Somerset. After a joint visit to Germany in 1798, Wordsworth made a new home in Grasmere, and within two or three years Coleridge and Southey became his near neighbours at Keswick. Southey was not himself distinguished by creative imagination, and supported rather than added to what the more original genius of the other two had achieved. The literary revolution which we associate with their names had in fact been accomplished by 1800, when the second edition of the *Lyrical Ballads* appeared, with an expanded statement of the critical doctrines of the authors in the preface.

The genesis of the poems is best described by Coleridge in his *Biographia Literaria* (1817)—

> During the first year that Mr. Wordsworth and I were neighbours, our conversations turned frequently on the two cardinal points of poetry: the power of exciting the sympathy of the reader by a faithful adherence to the truth of nature, and the power of giving the interest of novelty by the modifying colours of imagination. . . . The thought suggested itself that a series of poems might be composed of two sorts. In the one, the incidents and agents were to be, in part at least, supernatural; and the excellence aimed at was to consist in the interesting of the affections by the dramatic truth of such emotions as would naturally accompany such situations, supposing them real. . . . For the second class, subjects were to be chosen from ordinary life; the characters and incidents were to be such as will be found in every village and its vicinity, where there is a meditative and feeling mind to seek after them, or to notice them, when they present themselves. In this idea originated the plan of *Lyrical Ballads*; in which it was agreed that my endeavours should be directed to persons and characters supernatural. . . . Mr. Wordsworth on the other hand, was . . . to give charm of novelty to things of every day.

That explains the framework; as for the style, we may refer to the famous *Preface*, wherein Wordsworth says that the poems were published—

> as an experiment which, I hoped, might be of some use to ascertain how far, by fitting to metrical arrangement a selection of the real language of men in a state of vivid sensation, that sort of pleasure and that quantity of pleasure may be imparted, which a poet may rationally endeavour to impart.

In particular Wordsworth had in mind the language actually spoken by peasants and such as lived closest to nature, claiming that their direct and artless expressions of feeling were nearer to poetry than the speech of educated people.

> Low and rustic life was generally chosen, because in that condition the essential passions of the heart find a better soil in which they can attain their maturity, are less under restraint, and speak a plainer and more emphatic language.

Wordsworth was thus making a protest against the use of an artificial "poetic diction." He declared "there neither is, nor can be, any essential difference between the language of prose and metrical composition." He entered upon his poetic career in the spirit of a crusader, convinced that this duty called him to lift poetry up from the condition of "depravity" to which it had sunk. A new spirit was needed to restore the true values of poetry.

He amplified his point of view by quoting a sonnet of Thomas

Gray, a poet whom he considered more than any other "curiously elaborate in the structure of his own poetic diction"—

> In vain to me the smiling mornings shine,
> And reddening Phoebus lifts his golden fire:
> The herds in vain their amorous descant join,
> Or cheerful fields resume their green attire.
> These ears, alas! for other notes repine;
> *A different object do these eyes require;*
> *My lonely anguish melts no heart but mine;*
> *And in my breast the imperfect joys expire;*
> Yet morning smiles the busy race to cheer,
> And new-born pleasure brings to happier men;
> The fields to all their wonted tribute bear;
> To warm their little loves the birds complain.
> *I fruitless mourn to him that cannot hear,*
> *And weep the more because I weep in vain*

and adds this comment—

> It will easily be perceived that the only part of this Sonnet which is of any value is the lines quoted in Italics: it is equally obvious that, except in the rhyme, and in the use of the single word 'fruitless' for fruitlessly, which is so far a defect, the language of these lines does in no respect differ from that of prose.

Wordsworth thus makes it clear that what he has in mind when he writes of "the language of prose and metrical composition" is the diction which is "the very language of men," free from the mechanical devices consciously used to elevate the style, "a family language to which writers in metre seem to lay claim to by prescription."

Wordsworth's Poetry

While Wordsworth on the whole succeeded in his mission, it cannot be said that his practice corresponded at all times with his theory. He achieved here and there a nobility of utterance, in language that was simple and free from artifice, but often in the quest for plainness, his inspiration failed him, and the result was banal. Examples of such banality have already been given (see p. 26). They suggest that no sound theory of poetic language can ever be erected upon a merely negative consideration—the avoidance of this or that in diction.

Wordsworth admits that ideas should be "expressed in language fitted to their respective importance," and remarks: "If the Poet's subject be judiciously chosen, it will naturally, and upon fit occasion, lead him to passions the language of which, if selected truly and

judiciously, must necessarily be dignified and variegated, and alive
with metaphors and figures." This is the justification for the kind of
elevation of style which is seen in such a poem as the *Ode on Intimations
of Immortality from Recollections of Early Childhood.* In such lines as—

> The cataracts blow their trumpets from the steep;
> No more shall grief of mine the seasons wrong;
> I hear the Echoes through the mountains throng,
> The Winds come to me from the fields of sleep
> And all the earth is gay.

There are no words other than those one might readily use in prose
and no poetic dialect.

Yet the characteristic note of his poetry is to be found, in fact, not
so much in the poems written to his prescription of high thinking and
plain writing, but in those in which he gives philosophic expression
to the two deep convictions which possessed his soul. The one, a
belief in the essential dignity of man, will be found in such a poem as
Michael; the other is a sense of serenity and power, both moral and
intellectual, flowing into his being from Nature—

> I had been taught to reverence a Power
> That is the visible quality and shape
> And image of right reason. . . .
>
> *The Prelude*

This means for Wordsworth much more than the simple naturalism
of Rousseau. His "right reason" is a pantheistic philosophy, based on a
belief in the one-ness of nature (including man)—

> And I have felt
> A presence that disturbs me with the joy
> Of elevated thoughts; a sense sublime
> Of something far more deeply interfused,
> Whose dwelling is the light of setting suns,
> And the round ocean and the living air,
> And the blue sky, and in the mind of man,
> A motion and a spirit, that impels
> All thinking things, all objects of all thought,
> And rolls through all things.
>
> *Tintern Abbey*

Primarily, Wordsworth was a nature mystic, and his great power
was his ability to communicate his mystical experiences in poetry.

The Prelude is a retrospective account of the stages by which Wordsworth's mind matured, passing from the revolutionary ardour of

youth, through disillusionment, to withdrawal into a life of contemplation. He planned a vast edifice of poetry to be called *The Recluse*, likening it to "the body of a gothic church," with which his minor pieces were to stand in comparison like "cells, oratories, and sepulchral recesses." Of this "long and laborious work" only the middle part, "the anti-chapel," called *The Excursion*, was actually accomplished. The theme was "the sensations and opinions of a poet living in retirement." Unfortunately, by the time this project was formed, Wordsworth's creative urge had weakened. *The Excursion* contains long passages of pedestrian verse of a laboured "moralistic" kind, relieved only occasionally by genuine spontaneous poetry. The philosophy in it counted for more than the imagination, the judgment more than the feeling.

Wordsworth's standing as one of the half-dozen major English poets must not be supposed to rest upon the validity of a theory of poetic diction, or upon the truth of a philosophic system. Ultimately it can rest only upon the absolute power of his poems to produce the kind of aesthetic pleasure which we look for from poetry. We may nevertheless distinguish certain of those "powerful feelings" which spontaneously overflowed into poetry: firstly, his vision of the beneficent forces of Nature which, wedded with the creative imagination, yields spiritual health and consolation, peace and cheerfulness to the mind exposed to their ministration "with a wise passiveness;" secondly, his discovery of the emotional quality in the lives and speech of rustic folk; thirdly, his sense of the wonder and romance of—

> Old, unhappy, far-off things
> And battles long ago;

and fourthly, his passion for human freedom, as expressed in some of his Sonnets, e.g.—

> Two Voices are there; one is of the sea,
> One of the mountains; each a mighty Voice:
> In both from age to age thou didst rejoice,
> They were thy chosen music, Liberty!

Coleridge

The genius of Samuel Taylor Coleridge (1772–1834) was complementary to that of Wordsworth. While the prevailing mood of the latter was loftily reflective, his art controlled and disciplined, his purposes defined and steadily pursued, the poetic mind of Coleridge was less restrained. His imagination carried him unresisting into strange worlds, vaguely outlined by "the light that never was on sea or land." Of these he gave us but transitory glimpses, for his visions quickly faded. Coleridge's principal contribution to *The Lyrical Ballads* was *The Ancient Mariner*, a poem unique in literature, where pure fantasy unites with verbal melody and dramatic intensity in a poetic amalgam so subtly concocted as to defy all analysis. The other great poems which establish his place as a lyrical poet are *Christabel* and *Kubla Khan*, each of them a witchery of word-music, and each of them quite essentially romantic, the nearest things we have to "pure poetry." There is not in either poem a sound or image to disturb the atmosphere of faerie. Here the rational yields place to the irrational, the consequent to the inconsequent. The logic is not that of the syllogism; it is of a different order. Their coherence and lucidity belong entirely to the world of dreams. If we but accommodate ourselves within the "frame of reference" and yield ourselves willingly to the magic of words, we can do no other than give absolute credence to all that happens.

Though these three poems, and a few shorter ones (e.g. *Love*) are all of Coleridge's poetical work that really matters, it is he rather than Wordsworth who influenced the younger group of romantic poets. It was not that his contemporaries were immediately held by the witchery of the *Ancient Mariner* when it appeared. Most of them were at first unresponsive, and even hostile. Coleridge's influence was exerted through his critical prose, consisting of essays, lectures and miscellanies, in which he expounds (without accepting) the Wordsworthian thesis, and develops his own philosophical conception of the nature of poetry.

Southey

Of Southey little need be said; his talent was purely derivative, and although he borrowed the trapping of the romantics, he lacked the higher qualities of poetry. Early in life he formed grandiose plans for encompassing the outstanding mythologies of the world in a series of epic poems. But he was without the intellectual grasp, to say nothing of the poetic sympathy, to succeed, and he achieved only dullness occasionally relieved by some fine rhetoric. *Thalaba, Madoc, Roderick* were portions of the task he set himself, and *The Vision of Judgment* is notable because it drew a mischievous parody from Byron under the same title.

The Scott Group

Sir Walter Scott (1771–1832) was caught up in the romantic movement through an antiquarian love of old English ballads and through
an interest in German poetry of the *Sturm und Drang* tradition, which
corresponded to the "Gothic revival" in our literature and art. Starting
as a translator and a collector, he applied a talent for writing stirring
rhymes to historical subjects which caught his imagination. *The Lay
of the Last Minstrel* was his first full narrative of Border chivalry, and
this was followed by *Marmion, The Lady of the Lake, Rokeby, The
Lord of the Isles,* and others in similar vein.

These poems represented something new in romanticism—story-
telling in verse, with vivid descriptions of feudal customs, supernatural
solicitings, love and adventure, flavoured with a touch of archaism.
His verse-form owes something to *Christabel,* which Coleridge
described as follows: "The metre is not properly speaking irregular
though it may seem so from its being founded on a new principle:
namely, that of counting in each line the accents, not the syllables.
Though the latter may vary from seven to twelve, yet in each line the
accents will be found to be only four."

> And Christabel saw the lady's eye,
> And nothing else saw she thereby,
> Save the boss of the shield of Sir Leoline tall,
> Which hung in a murky old niche in the wall.
> "O softly tread," said Christabel,
> "My father seldom sleepeth well."

The following passage of *The Lady* will show how Scott used this
accentual metre—

> The Ladye steps in doubt and dread,
> Lest her watchful mother heard her tread;
> The Ladye caresses the rough blood-hound,
> Lest his voice should waken the castle round;
> The watchman's bugle is not blown,
> For he was her foster-father's son;
> And she glides through the greenwood at dawn of light,
> To meet Baron Henry, her own true Knight.

Scott, in an estimate of his own poems, said that what merit they
had was in "a hurried frankness of composition which pleases soldiers,
sailors, and young people of bold and active disposition." He popularized romanticism, and created a reading public of his own, more
numerous and nation-wide than any of our poets had reached. After
1815 Scott wrote little poetry and turned to the prose-romance.

The vogue of Scott stimulated a host of lesser poets to attempt versified romance; among them the most successful in their day were Thomas Campbell and Thomas Moore. Campbell wrote *Gertrude of Wyoming* in Spenserian stanzas, but it is his patriotic war-songs which have survived: e.g. *Ye Mariners of England, Hohenlinden* and *The Battle of the Baltic*, and ballads such as *Lord Ullin's Daughter*. Moore established himself as a poet by starting the publication of a long series of *Irish Melodies*, words written to music, vivacious or sentimental. He then turned to the luscious imagery of Oriental tales, collected under the title *Lalla Rookh*. The rest of his work consisted of literary squibs and satires. His popularity in his day was enormous, but it survives principally in Ireland.

The Second Blossoming of Romanticism

The three poets Scott, Campbell, and Moore bridged the years which preceded the second outburst of high creative activity in this age of romantic literature. Lord Byron (1788–1824), though he had already, in his satiric *English Bards and Scotch Reviewers* (1809), gained a reputation for invective in the style of *The Dunciad*, leapt into sudden fame three years later with the appearance of the first two cantos of *Childe Harold*. This poem was a running commentary on travels in Europe, written in the Spenserian stanza, interesting not only because it touched on places and people of contemporary interest but also because it revealed a new type of romantic personality. Byron followed up his early success with melodramatic tales of Eastern crime, intrigue and battle, *The Gaiour, The Corsair, Lara*, and *The Siege of Corinth*, dashed off in periods reckoned in days rather than weeks. His enduring work belongs to the eight years which remained to him after his quitting England in 1816 with scorn and bitterness in his heart. Thereupon he threw himself tempestuously into the wider world, intent on savouring love and life and art and war without reck or heed of conventional morality or prudence. His combination of misanthropy with passion and egoism produced in his readers a kind of mental intoxication, extraordinarily acceptable to the taste of the age, and Byron has remained ever since in the imagination of Europe the dynamic Englishman and, as a poet, second only to Shakespeare.

In 1816–17 *Childe Harold* was completed. *Beppo*, a Venetian story in serio-comic vein, followed. For this he used an adaptation of the Italian *ottava rima*, or stanza of eight eleven-syllabled lines (see page 54). Byron reduced the line to ten syllables, with the rhyming scheme *a b a b a b c c.* Finding it so suitable for his facetious wit, he used it again in *Don Juan*, a meandering narrative interspersed with caustic and cynical comment on the ways of men and women, tender sentiment and ribaldry. In this poem Byron most clearly reveals himself, flippant and sarcastic, brilliant and profligate.

Byron was too subjective an artist to succeed as a dramatist. His historical play *Sardanapalus* (1821) and the two tragedies, *Manfred* (1817) and *Cain* (1821) are to be considered rather as dramatic poems than as stage-pieces.

His heroes Manfred and Cain are but projections of himself, the proud, self-centred, tortured outcast in revolt against the tyranny of social order and authority, his mind aglow with the Promethean spark, and hurling defiance against the cruel destiny which compels mankind to face life and death with half-knowledge—

> I feel the weight
> Of daily toil and constant thought; I look
> Around a world where I seem nothing, with
> Thoughts which arise within me, as if they
> Could master all things.

This is the figure of the Byronic hero, "dwelling in his despair," which impressed itself so powerfully on the mind of Europe, and gave rise to many national schools of neo-romantic writers, united not by reaction against classicism in a literary sense but by a will to challenge accepted principles in government, conduct, and religion.

Byron's masterpiece in satire is *The Vision of Judgment* in which he pilloried Southey, the Poet Laureate, and Farmer George, as the late King George III was known. His lyrical pieces, e.g. *When We Two Parted, She Walks in Beauty*, and *Maid of Athens* have a kind of prettiness, but it is clear that Byron's genius did not lie in the direction of the lyric.

Shelley

While in Switzerland and in Italy Byron spent some time as a member of the Shelley circle. Shelley (1792–1822), too, chose self-exile after a legal action which deprived him of the custody of his children, and he lived for the last four years of his life in Italy. His first important poem, *Alastor*, in blank verse, appeared in 1816 and ranked with the best that the romantic movement had yet produced. In it we can already discern the poet's passion for humanity and his belief that only through the imagination can man be healed of his "gloom and misanthropy." "A man to be greatly good," he said, "must imagine intensely and comprehensively . . . The great instrument of moral good is the imagination; and poetry administers to the effect by acting upon the cause" (*Defence of Poetry*). Shelley believed in the perfectibility of man. He was thus truly in the tradition of Rousseau and the French Revolution. Yet he sought the salvation of the human soul, not through programmes and creeds, but through intellectual beauty, which he identifies with abstract love. His religion developed into a kind of pantheism based on the hypothesis of a pervading Spirit. Shelley's philosophy, fully elaborated in *Prometheus Unbound*, envelops all he wrote with a kind of iridescent haze.

The only poem belonging to Shelley's youth in England which need be mentioned here, other than *Alastor*, is *The Revolt of Islam*, a romance in Spenserian stanzas, which is also a manifesto for revolutionaries. His greatest works were written abroad: the dramas, *Prometheus Unbound* and *The Cenci*; the lyrics, *The Cloud*, *Ode on the West Wind* and *The Skylark*; the elegy on Keats, *Adonais*; the political poem, *The Masque of Anarchy*, and the Platonist love-song *Epipsychidion*, which contains the essence of Shelley's mature philosophy.

Prometheus Unbound is possibly the greatest product of Shelley's lyrical and philosophical genius. The myth which was the basis of the play by Aeschylus is here transformed into an allegory of man's destiny, and in it we have the finest expression of the poet's cosmic conception of nature. *The Cenci* written in the same year (1819), is modelled rather on Shakespeare than on the Greek playwrights, and contains scenes reminiscent of parts of *Macbeth* and *Othello*. The story is Italian and the treatment is more realistic than in any other work by Shelley. The characters are of flesh and blood, and in Beatrice we have a figure of great dramatic force. *The Cenci*, even if it be difficult to act, is held by many to come nearer to being a tragedy of the first order than anything written in England for a century and a half previously.

Adonais (1821) is an elegy modelled on Bion and Moschus who had also served Milton for his *Lycidas*. Bion, of the third century B.C., was a pastoral poet of Sicily who wrote a lament for Adonis, and Moschus was his disciple. But Shelley is less classical in spirit. In place of the fauns and satyrs he uses spiritual presences and mourners—

> And others came. . . . Desires and Adorations,
> Winged Persuasions and veiled Destinies,
> Splendours, and Glooms, and glimmering incarnations
> Of Hopes and Fears, and twilight Phantasies;
> And Sorrow, with her family of Sighs,

And Pleasure, blind with tears, led by the gleam
Of her own dying smile instead of eyes,
Came in slow pomp;—the moving pomp might seem
Like pageantry of mist on an autumnal stream.

The phrase "pageantry of mist" will serve to describe the atmosphere of Shelley's poetry; and a stanza near the end of the poem will equally serve to sum up his philosophic outlook—

The One remains, the many change and pass;
Heaven's light for ever shines, earth's shadows fly;
Life, like a dome of many-coloured glass,
Stains the white radiance of eternity,
Until Death tramples it to fragments.—Die,
If thou would'st be with that which thou dost seek!
Follow where all is fled!—Rome's azure sky,
Flowers, ruins, statues, music, words, are weak
The glory they transfuse with fitting truth to speak.

Keats

John Keats (1795–1821) was the third poet of this group, and he too represents a particular aspect of romanticism. He had a high sensitiveness to the sights and sounds of the world, and a quick intuition of beauty of form, colour and melody. "Keats," said Matthew Arnold, "is abundantly and enchantingly sensuous." He found in Spenser and in the Greek poets his principal models and sources: the former he admired for the external beauty of faerie, the latter for the beauty of myth and legend.

Endymion (1818), one of his early poems and written in heroic couplets, is a story of a soul seeking to realize dreams of an ideal loveliness. The allegory is confused, since Keats, not content to keep his attention fixed on the nature-myth of Endymion and the Moon, introduces a bewildering gallery of mythological figures which have little connexion with the main narrative. The poet, it seems, could not resist the attraction of so much beauty. The poem, classical in theme, is Elizabethan in its richness of imagery.

In *Hyperion*, published two years later, Keats makes a second attempt to "touch the beautiful mythology of Greece." The story is based on the Greek sun-myth, and this time Keats abandons rhymed for blank verse, which he uses in close imitation of the Miltonic manner. The poem is epic in conception, but Keats abandoned it midway through the third book. "I have given up *Hyperion*," he wrote, "there were too many Miltonic inversions in it—Miltonic verse cannot be written but in an artful, or rather, artist's humour. I wish to give myself up to

10

other sensations. English ought to be kept up." Notwithstanding this, Byron matched the poem for sublimity with the poetry of Aeschylus, and Shelley said, "If the *Hyperion* be not grand poetry, none has been produced by our contemporaries."

The third of Keats' great poems is *The Eve of St. Agnes*. In this his feeling for sensuous beauty and for the music of words has full play. He "loads every rift with ore." We are compelled to think of Spenser, not only because of the use of the stanza of the *Faerie Queene*, but also because of the vivid apprehension of sights and sounds which fed his imagination's yearning for the beautiful—

> A casement high and triple-arch'd there was,
> All garlanded with carven imag'ries
> Of fruits, and flowers, and bunches of knot-grass,
> And diamonded with panes of quaint device,
> Innumerable of stains and splendid dyes,
> As are the tiger-moth's deep-damask'd wings;
> And in the midst, 'mong thousand heraldries,
> And twilight saints, and dim emblazonings,
> A shielded scutcheon blush'd with blood of queens and kings.

It is possible to consider the Keats of the *Ode to a Nightingale* and particularly of *La Belle Dame sans Merci* as the poet who came nearest, along with the Coleridge of *Kubla Khan*, to finding the perfect expression of romanticism—the song—

> that oft-times hath
> Charm'd magic casements, opening on the foam
> Of perilous seas, in faery lands forlorn.

In the *Ode*, Keats, yielding to his "drowsy numbness," is approaching subliminal experience; in *La Belle Dame* he is completely over the boundary which separates the waking from the dreaming state. Nevertheless, we accept the Knight-at-arms, the lady in the meads, the elfin grot and the pale kings as realities, and the incidents as being as circumstantial as any we have known in our actual experience. The poem, that is to say, answers the great test, in that it presents a world of the imagination to us in credible symbols which carry not only meaning but emotion.

Hellenism

A different facet of romanticism is presented by the *Ode to a Grecian Urn*. This was Hellenism, from which Gray and Collins, among the precursors of the romantics, had drawn inspiration in the mid-eighteenth century. Early in the new century, the Greek spirit began to be a powerful cultural force. The Elgin Marbles had been brought to London. Ancient Greece was idealized as the cradle of political freedom—

> The mountains look on Marathon—
> And Marathon looks on the sea;
> And musing there an hour alone,
>   I dream'd that Greece might still be free;
> For standing on the Persians' grave,
> I could not deem myself a slave.
>   BYRON: *Don Juan, Canto III*

But while it was the example of Athenian democracy which fed the revolutionary ardour of Byron[1] and Shelley, it was Hellenism as the cradle of art and legend that attracted Keats. The *Grecian Urn* has the austere and stately beauty of Greek sculpture. Compared with the *Ode to the Nightingale* it is remarkable for the absence of warmth and colour. Instead, the suggestion is of calm serenity—

> O Attic shape! Fair attitude! with brede
> Of marble men and maidens overwrought
> With forest branches and the trodden weed;
> Thou, silent form, dost tease us out of thought
> As doth eternity: Cold Pastoral!

The impact of the Hellenic spirit on the romantic mind was thus to suggest the greater permanence of beauty based on truth, compared with that which arose from "breathing human passion." A further typically Romantic notion was that the incomplete is better than the complete, and aspiration better than attainment—

> For ever panting, and for ever young.

It comes to expression again frequently in Browning's work.

SUGGESTIONS FOR FURTHER READING

MARIO PRAZ: *The Romantic Agony* (Oxford Univ. Press).
MALCOLM ELWIN: *The First Romantics* (Macdonald).
G. WILSON KNIGHT: *The Starlit Dome* (Oxford Univ. Press).
OLIVER ELTON: *A Survey of English Literature* (1780–1830) (Edward Arnold).
C. H. HERFORD: *The Age of Wordsworth* (Bell).
EDMUND BLUNDEN: *Shelley* (Collins).
J. BRONOWSKI: *A Man Without a Mask* (Secker & Warburg).
DENIS SAURAT: *Blake and Modern Thought* (Constable).
J. LIVINGSTONE LOWES: *The Road to Zanadu* (Constable).

[1] Byron died of fever while he was in Greece, helping the insurgents in their struggle for independence.

CHAPTER XII

POETRY IN THE VICTORIAN AGE

THE passing of Keats, Shelley, and Byron in the early eighteen-twenties was followed by a period of some fifteen or twenty years when the fine frenzy of the high romantics subsided, and a quieter mood ensued. The revolutionary fervour had abated. Wordsworth's inspiration had deserted him and he had come down from the summits on to the flats. There he found himself in company with a host of writers of moderate talent, such as the peasant poet, John Clare, the writer of *Poems descriptive of Rural Life and Scenery*, and the factory poet, Ebenezer Elliott, famous for his *Corn-Law Rhymes*. The neo-hellenists, Thomas Love Peacock (1785–1866) and Walter Savage Landor (1775–1864), were at work countering the exuberant fancies and loose texture of romantic poetry with the austerity and discipline of classical art. Others of note were John Keble (1792–1866), the author of *The Christian Year* and the hymnologist of the Oxford Movement; James Hogg (1770–1835), the "Ettrick Shepherd," who drew inspiration from Scott; Thomas Hood (1799–1845), known to-day by his *Song of the Shirt* and *Bridge of Sighs*, poems expressive of the "sorrow barricadoed ever more Within the walls of cities."

The Changing Social Background

Reference has been made elsewhere to the rapid growth of the reading public. It affected mainly the middle range of society, corresponding to that part which was enfranchised by the Reform Act of 1832. Being thus made free of the political heritage of Britain, the middle classes aspired also to a share of the literary heritage. Poetry could no longer survive as an aristocratic prerogative. It had to learn to speak to a larger audience, and touch on the wider concerns of society. The conditions were favourable for a great outburst of literary activity. The idea of progress was in the air. Science and exploration were rapidly extending the horizons of knowledge; an era of international peace was dawning; the standards of living were rising, and it needed only the abolition of the Corn Laws in 1846 to set the nation fairly on the road of social amelioration. Although popular education was still backward, the "public schools" of the middle classes were rapidly gaining in importance, under the leadership of Dr. Arnold of Rugby.

There was an increasing demand for periodical literature. The "quarterlies" gradually developed into "monthlies" and the "monthlies" into "weeklies." The dissemination of literature was enormously helped by the inauguration of the "penny post" in 1840. All this meant that authors had no longer to depend on patronage for their livelihood. Financial rewards were not great, except for some exceptional writers such as Dickens and George Eliot, but on the whole they were dependable, and as the century wore on, the profession of "man of letters" attracted a growing number.

As education spread, the demand for knowledge became an insatiable urge. Content in writing became more immediately important than form. The new public had little time to bestow on art for art's sake (a phrase in any case not yet invented), and clamoured for books which either set out the findings of the latest researches into history, biology, political science, geography, anthropology and the like, or applied them to the problems of the time. The demand, in short, was for instruction and "improvement." The attempt to comprise the utmost possible within the scope of the work led to a certain diffuseness in Victorian literature. In fiction, the characteristic product was the "three-decker" novel but the same profusion is to be observed in all forms of Victorian art, from the ornament applied to household furniture to the Albert Memorial. John Ruskin may stand as an example of the encyclopaedic Victorian mind at work in literature. Didactic, discursive and opulent, he wrote on aesthetics, history, social ethics, literature, economics, religion, and education, all with a sincere passion for the spiritual regeneration of the nation. Herbert Spencer's was another synthetic mind, ranging boldly over every department of knowledge as he reached out for comprehensive explanations. As the railways pushed their way into every corner of the land, the fixed patterns of social life tended to break down. Greater mobility brought more varied human contacts, and the diversification of experience could not but express itself in a vast expansion of the domain of literature.

Victorian Romanticism

Tennyson and Browning, both representative poets of the Victorian Age though standing in many respects as contrasts, matured during the thirties. The publication of a volume of *Poems* in 1842 brought to an end the nine years' silence of Tennyson after the death of his friend, Arthur Henry Hallam, who was the subject of his elegiac poem *In Memoriam*. This was published in 1850, the year in which Tennyson succeeded Wordsworth as Poet Laureate. Browning's recognition by the public came about the same time, with the appearance of *Dramatic Lyrics* (1842), although *Paracelsus* and *Sordello* had already been published. Elizabeth Barrett, at the time of her marriage to Browning (1846), was already accepted as the foremost woman poet of the age, but her best work, including *Sonnets from the Portuguese* and *Aurora Leigh*, was yet to come.

The eighteen-forties was therefore a period when a new impulse was given to romantic poetry. It was, however, romanticism with a difference. Tennyson recognized an affinity with Byron and Keats, Browning with Shelley, but romanticism no longer implied an attitude of revolt against conventional modes. It had itself become a convention. The revolutionary fervour which had inspired so much of the poetry of the first quarter of the century had given place to an evolutionary conception of progress, propagated by the writings of the Darwinians and the Benthamites. The tendency to seek material for the imagination in remote, shadowy fields persisted, but the pressure of the contemporary age was also strong, and the marvels of science offered no less promising a starting point for excursions into the regions of fancy. On the whole the period looked forwards rather than backwards. "The best is yet to be" was the dominant note of Browning, and Tennyson found spiritual consolation in contemplating the—

> one far-off divine event .
> To which the whole creation moves,
>
> *In Memoriam*

The earlier years of the Victorian age were thus marked by faith in the reality of progress. The questionings, although they may be found in Tennyson, were voiced more urgently by Matthew Arnold, the supreme poet of doubt, and these became the characteristic mode of expression during the later or so-called "decadent" period, the *fin de siècle* phase of disillusionment.

Alfred Tennyson

A study of Tennyson's work, produced during sixty long years of poetic activity, shows that his art was maintained on remarkably level standards throughout. Except for the deep and ineffaceable emotional experience which came to him when Hallam died, there was no violent turmoil of heart or mind to turn aside the even current of his life. He lived in and for his age, and remains for us its supreme representative, because he was content to use his art as a means of interpreting in terms of poetry what seemed to him to be significant movements going on all around him and his readers. Tennyson was, like Milton and Wordsworth, a consecrated or Messianic poet. He laid upon himself a mission to exalt the people through the example of a life dedicated to truth, love and beauty, and of an art seeking no other thing. To achieve his purpose, he had to cultivate clarity of thought and of expression. He found his intellectual and moral satisfaction in observing more closely what was already familiar. Not content, as most poets might have been, to refer to the russet tints of the fall of the year as evidence of the fact of natural decay, Tennyson traces the detailed progress of decay—

> As a leaf in mid-November is
> To what it was in mid-October.

He observes nature with so great a degree of accuracy that we are startled into recognition. Yet his observation is not with the eye and intelligence of the scientist, but with those of the artist and the seer. When he uses a discovery to emphasize a situation, its significance comes upon us with the force of a revelation—

> beneath a whispering rain
> Night slid down one long stream of sighing wind.

This clarity of Tennyson derives also from his diction. While he avoids the commonplace, he never becomes "precious." He prefers the monosyllabic English word to the longer word of Romance origin. It would, for example, be difficult to find in any other poet so sustained a monosyllabic style as in the poem *Break, break, break.* Another example is *Ring Out Wild Bells.* It is no small part of Tennyson's artistic skill that he should, with such simple linguistic material, so often have achieved a stately dignity of utterance.

Tennyson, said Sir Edmund Gosse, held "English poetry stationary for sixty years, a feat absolutely unparalleled elsewhere; and the result of various revolutionary movements in prosody and style made during the Victorian age was merely in every case temporary. There was an explosion, the smoke rolled away and Tennyson's statue stood exactly where it did before."[1] Until 1847, all his poems were short; they include narrative poems with romantic and classical subjects (*The Lady of Shalott, Oenone, Ulysses*); lyrics (*The Lotus Eaters*); and such poems as *The Two Voices* and *The Palace of Art*, which strike a deeper chord.[2]

The Princess, which appeared in 1847, was Tennyson's first elaborate poem, and this was soon followed by *In Memoriam*, a profound analysis of the poet's speculations on life and death, written in a hundred and thirty sections, each of which could stand as a separate poem, yet falling into a unity by reason of their sustained topic and mood. The stanza used in the poem consists of four octosyllabic lines rhyming *a b b a* and although it can be found in the work of Ben Jonson may be considered to have been re-invented by Tennyson—

> This truth came borne with bier and pall,
> I felt it when I sorrowed most;
> 'Tis better to have loved and lost
> Than never to have loved at all.

The work which made the name of Tennyson a household word was *The Idylls of the King*. It appeared in instalments between 1859 and 1872. The theme, the body of Arthurian legend, had epic possibilities, but these were not realized. The failure arose partly from a defect in structure, for there is a want of coherence. Each idyll is an episode, standing alone, even though related to others by the comradeship of the heroes at the Round Table and by their connexion with a penumbral allegory. The chivalric code with which medieval romancers had already overshadowed the semi-barbarism of the historic Arthurian epoch (fifth or sixth century) was now in its turn overshadowed by the moral complacency and self-righteousness of the mid-nineteenth century. The result does not carry conviction and we are left with a loose collection of romantic tales. Their merit is in the melody and smoothness of the verse and the consummate skill which transforms literary artifice into artistry. The *Idylls* are, with the exception of Wordsworth's *Prelude*, the greatest achievement in sustained blank verse which our literature has to show since *Paradise Lost*.

The dramatic work of Tennyson is touched on in another section. It formed a clear-cut part of his literary activity during the "seventies,"

[1] Gosse: *Modern English Literature*, pp. 360–1.
[2] The student who is interested in the study of the working of the poet's mind would find in a comparison between Tennyson's *Poems, Chiefly Lyrical*, published in 1830 and 1833, and his *Poems* of 1842, a fruitful field of interest. Some half a dozen earlier poems reappear in a revised form, being substantially added to, subtracted from, rearranged and re-expressed. To attempt to evaluate these changes in terms of poetic art would be a useful exercise.

but afterwards he resumed his lyrical, narrative and philosophical poetry with little loss of skill. In *Locksley Hall Sixty Years After* he tried once more to assess the movements of his age.

Robert Browning

While Tennyson reflected Victorian moods and manners in their public aspects, Robert Browning (who was born three years later and died three years earlier) was a robust individualist. He stood in many respects in sharp contrast to his contemporary. The outlook of Tennyson was insular, that of Browning cosmopolitan. Tennyson's strength was in objective description, conveyed in verse of liquid smoothness; Browning's poetry was introspective and speculative, and couched in a style wherein the language chases the flying, twisting thought with little hope of ever quite catching up with it.

> But whom at least do you admire?
> Present your own perfections, your ideal,
> Your pattern man for a minute—oh, make haste?
> Is it Napoleon you would have us grow?
> Concede the means; allow his head and hand,
> (A large concession, clever as you are)
> Good! In our common primal element
> Of unbelief (we can't believe, you know—
> We're still at that admission, recollect)
> Where do you find—apart from, towering o'er
> The secondary temporary aims
> Which satisfy the gross tastes you despise—
> Where do you find his star? his crazy trust
> God knows through what or in what? it's alive
> And shines and leads him and that's all we want.
> Have we ought in our sober night shall point
> Such ends as his were, and direct the means
> Of working out our purpose straight as his,
> Nor bring a moment's trouble on success
> With after-care to justify the same?
>   BROWNING: *Bishop Blougram's Apology*

Most of the reputed obscurity of Browning arises from his use of colloquial diction. Real conversation is helped along by facial expression, gesture, and nuance. These to a great extent bridge over the gaps in thought, and account for the fact that rapid changes of viewpoint can take place when two persons familiar with every detail of an incident and of its background are discussing it. Much may meanwhile remain incomprehensible to the listening stranger.

We are here near an explanation of Browning's most characteristic poetic conception, that of the dramatic lyric. In an introductory note to *Dramatic Romances and Lyrics* (1845) Browning wrote: "Such poems as the following come properly enough, I suppose, under the head of 'Dramatic Pieces'; being, though for the most part lyric expression, always dramatic in principle, and so many utterances of so many imaginary persons, not mine." It is strange that, though he considered all poetry to be "dramatic in principle," he was not successful with drama in the sense of the stage-play. His interest lay, not in action, but in speculation on the motives of action, and on the emotions which accompanied action. He found that the dramatic monologue was exactly suited to his genius. Taking a subject from history (preferably of the Italian Renaissance) or inventing a story, he selected a critical moment in his hero's experience, and then set him talking in character. In *Men and Women* (1855), *Dramatis Personae* (1864), *The Ring and the Book* (1868-9), *Dramatic Idylls* (1879), Browning used this method.

The Ring and the Book is a poem in ten books, together with a prologue and epilogue. They consist of a series of dramatic mono- logues, all dealing with a single set of incidents, the record being traversed ten times over, each time from the standpoint of a different narrator, who by his attitude to the affair reveals his or her inward mind. The poem, which runs to 21,000 lines of blank verse, stands as Browning's greatest achievement, absolutely original in conception, and one through which he managed to convey his own deepest thoughts about life, while never deviating from dramatic truth and consistency.

In the poetry of Browning's last twenty years there was no change of method, but he was all the time educating his own public. His output was enormous, and to the end his vigour showed no abatement. Possibly his own philosophy lay rather more heavily on his later poetry and in this his eccentricity of expression was carried still further. His employment of grotesque rhyming is shown in the following lines from *The Glove*—

> For De Lorge, he made women with men vie,
> Those in wonder and praise, these in envy;
> And in short stood so plain a head taller
> That he wooed and won. . . . How do you call her?
> The beauty, that rose in the sequel
> To the King's love, who loved her a week well; . . .

Browning's optimistic outlook on the world has often been

commented on. But probably more characteristic was his proneness to idealize imperfection striving towards the perfect—

> But what's whole, can increase no more,
> Is dwarfed and dies, since here's its sphere.

The fragmentary experience, the unfulfilled aspiration has in it still the promise of something more excellent. This thought recurs in the many poems on the subject of unrequited love, and also in the poems inspired by Italian art such as *Old Pictures in Florence* where the finished work of art is contrasted with human imperfection—

> To-day's brief passion limits their range;
> It seethes with the morrow for us and more.
> They are perfect—how else? they shall never change:
> We are faulty—Why not? we have time in store.
> The Artificer's hand is not arrested
> With us; we are rough-hewn, no-wise polished:
> They stand for our copy, and once invested
> With all they can teach, we shall see them abolished.

Matthew Arnold

The principal years of Arnold's poetic activity lay between 1842 and 1867, years which were also important in the work of Tennyson and Browning. *The Strayed Reveller and other Poems* appeared in 1849, *Empedocles on Etna* in 1852 and *New Poems* in 1867. Even when put together, the bulk is small. But the place of Arnold's work in the canon of English poetry is nevertheless secure. His taste was austere and led him to put a low estimate on the lavish ornament and fluid style of Tennyson and on the periphrastic, iconoclastic idiom of Browning. Arnold stands in our literature, along with Landor, as a representative of the classical spirit. Fastidious in style and stoical in outlook, he conceived of poetry as a ministration: "The greatness of a poet lies in his powerful and beautiful application of ideas to life." He was an apostle of culture, and saw in intellectual integrity, and in clear restrained thinking, the only hope of salvation of Victorian society, distracted as it was by political, religious and economic problems. To the practical solution of these he brought no suggestion. As a poet, it was not his function to do so, but he knew that it was essential for the men of the age "to possess their souls again." In his prose his criticism becomes more constructive, though its value is limited by the inadequate technical equipment of one who was pre-eminently a man of letters for confronting the complex problems of modern society.

Arnold essayed poetic drama in the Greek style in *Merope*, but without success. The play lacks action and movement. There are two romantic narratives, *Sohrab and Rustrum* and *Balder Dead*, again not wholly successful, perhaps because Arnold seems to be adopting a pose. We feel there is too deliberate an attempt to weave into the telling of the stories certain epic conventions such as the extended metaphor. The best work of Arnold is in the poetry of reflection, and more particularly in that which sounds the elegiac note. His *Thyrsis*, commemorating his friend Arthur Hugh Clough, places Arnold alongside Milton, Shelley and Tennyson as a master of this literary form. But we have in addition *Rugby Chapel*, where the subject is his father, and *A Southern Night*, dedicated to his brother. *The Scholar Gipsy*, *Resignation*, the *Obermann* poems and *Dover Beach* are others which are touched with the same sense of loss and which repeat—

> the undertone which flows
> So calmly sad

through all the substance of the poet's thought.

The Pre-Raphaelite Movement in Poetry

The term Pre-Raphaelite came into use in the year 1848 when a group of artists, who shared a certain outlook, banded together in a Brotherhood. They were intent on bringing back into art the qualities of the primitive Italian painters before Raphael, in particular their close fidelity to nature, their simplicity, sincerity and spiritual intensity. The leading spirit in the Brotherhood was Dante Gabriel Rossetti (1828–1882), whose forbears were mostly Italian. He, like several other members, combined the arts of painting and writing, and thus there came about a fresh penetration of poetry by romantic medievalism, a movement implying the repudiation of Renaissance classicism. What was characteristic of the Pre-Raphaelite group was a common method of approach; the content of their thought was of great diversity. As in painting, so in poetry, the effect was attained by the careful elaboration of detail—

> The blessed damozel leaned out
>   From the gold bar of Heaven;
> Her eyes were deeper than the depth
>   Of water stilled at even;
> She had three lilies in her hand,
>   And the stars in her hair were seven.
> Her robe ungirt from clasp to hem,
>   No wrought flowers did adorn,

But a white rose of Mary's gift,
  For service meetly worn;
The hair that lay along her back
Was yellow like ripe corn.
            The Blessed Damozel

Rossetti represents that part of the romantic movement which has been called the Renascence of Wonder, and in him the revival reached its culmination. It is this which gives to his *Sister Helen, Eden Bower, Troy Town*, the poem quoted above and others, their close kinship in spirit with *Christabel, Kubla Khan* and *La Belle Dame sans Merci*. They belong to the category of dream poems in which the magical element is on the point of passing into the mystical—

Vaporous, unaccountable,
  Dreamworld lies forlorn of light,
Hollow like a breathing shell.
  Ah! that from all dreams I might
Choose one dream and guide its flight!
  I know well
What her sleep should tell tonight.
            D. G. ROSSETTI: *Love's Nocturne*

William Morris

Closely associated with D. G. Rossetti in the Pre-Raphaelite movement was William Morris (1834–1896), a man of wide range, being not only artist-craftsman, scholar, poet, and novelist, but social prophet as well. He breathed the chivalric air of Chaucer and Froissart, and besides derived imaginative sustenance from the Arthurian and Icelandic sagas. In *The Defence of Guinevere, The Earthly Paradise*, and *Sigurd the Volsung*, he brought together stores of medieval romance, with plenty of word-painting to match the rich designs of the tapestries which he used to weave on his hand loom. *Sigurd the Volsung* was projected on an epic scale, but though it has something in it of primitive heroic vigour, it is defective in structure, and the poet lingers too much over the decorative parts while the action languishes. There is interest in the metrical form, which is an anapaestic measure, with lines of irregular length—

Then Sigurd leapt from Greyfell, and men were marvelling there
At the sound of his sweet-mouthed wisdom, and his body shapen fair.
But Heimer laughed and answered: "Now soon shall the deeds befall,
And tonight shalt thou ride to Lymdale, and tonight shalt thou bide in my hall,
For I am the ancient Heimer, and my cunning is of the harp,
Though erst have I dealt in the sword-play, while the edge of war was sharp.

Algernon Charles Swinburne

Algernon Charles Swinburne (1837–1909) was a third Victorian poet who is reckoned among the Pre-Raphaelites, though his association with them was personal rather than literary, and belonged to the later stages of the movement. Along with poetry, he practised the sister art of music instead of painting. His breath-taking advent as a poet with the publication of *Atalanta in Calydon* (1865), and of *Poems and Ballads* a year later, has often been compared with that of Byron when he published the first two cantos of *Childe Harold*. Like Byron, Swinburne was a rebel. He revolted against Victorian prudery in England and against political tyranny in Europe. In the matter of technique, he set his face against the hegemony of iambic measures in our poetry, and used his skill as a metrist to rehabilitate in English verse a wide variety of rhythmical forms. Though he had a faultless ear, there was little that was original in his measures: his merit was that by demonstrating the abundance of metrical patterns available to the English poet, he profoundly influenced our later poetry. He was one of the first in England to appreciate the qualities of the belated French romantic school, the historical side of which was led by Victor Hugo, and the morbidly introspective side by Baudelaire. Notwithstanding the fact that Swinburne's mind was cast in a revolutionary mould, he was always intensely patriotic, and in the early years of the present century, his voice rang out in championship of imperial and monarchic England. His passionate love of the sea was also a significant aspect of his "Englishness."

The principal works of Swinburne's middle period are *Songs before Sunrise* (1871) and *A Century of Roundels* (1883). Each of these gives evidence of his virtuosity as a metrist. Each also reveals his weakness as a poet, namely his liability to lose grip on meaning when deliriously gliding along on currents of sensuous verse.

Swinburne's *Tristram of Lyonesse* (1882) is of interest for several reasons. The story is told without the moral inhibitions of Tennyson; it shows a new way of using the heroic couplet, here turned to lyrical and romantic effect; and it illustrates again the strong hold of sea-scapes on his imagination.

Swinburne appears to have nursed ambitions as a dramatist, hoping to achieve something not unworthy of the great tradition of the Greek and the Elizabethan tragic playwrights for whom he had a genuine and understanding love. His plays make up a considerable part of the bulk of his published work, but they are deficient in the prime essentials of stage art, and what value they have is lyrical rather than dramatic. *Atalanta in Colydon* and *Erechtheus* are efforts in the Hellenic manner, while his trilogy of plays on the theme of Mary, Queen of Scots, namely *Chastelard, Bothwell,* and *Mary Stuart,* and his *Marino Faliero* (based on the same Venetian story as Byron some sixty years earlier had used for a historical tragedy with the same title) are in the Elizabethan manner.

The work of Swinburne's last period was prolific, but added little to his reputation.

Two more major writers bring up the history of English poetry to the end of the nineteenth century and carry it into the twentieth. These are George Meredith (1828–1909) and Thomas Hardy (1840–1928).

George Meredith

Meredith's early poetry (*Poems* 1851), including *Love in a Valley,* was compared by Charles Kingsley to that of Herrick, and his *Modern Love* (1862) contains fifty sixteen-lined "sonnets" which can stand among the most poignant tragic poetry of the century. Yet his chief occupation in these early years was with fiction, and it was not until the eighties, when his finest period as a novelist was over, that he turned his main attention to verse. In 1883 he published *Poems and Lyrics of the Joy of Earth,* in which his philosophy of life finds expression, though the language is cryptical and the meaning clogged by the onrush of thought. Meredith made no concessions to the reader, of whom he demanded an intellectual effort to match his own. In his belief in the communion of man with nature he was Wordsworthian, but his penetration went deeper. Earth and the natural life are there to assist man to realize the highest potentialities of his own being. There was a Celtic strain in Meredith, and his strong intuitions rendered him impatient of the slow processes of reason. He ranks close to Swinburne as a metrist who was always seeking to find new rhythmical effects, but in his indifference to verbal music he is akin to Browning.

Thomas Hardy

Like Meredith, Hardy was a poet-novelist whose literary work falls into two well-defined periods. His work on the novel ended in 1895 with the publication of *Jude the Obscure.* Three years later appeared

Wessex Poems, some of which had been written thirty years earlier. In these we see already the determinism and fatalism which coloured all his writing—

> Our incorporeal sense,
> Our overseeings, our supernal state,
> Our readings Why and Whence,
> Are but the flower of man's intelligence;
> And this but an unreckoned incident
> Of an all-urging Will, raptly magnipotent.
>
> *The Dynasts, Part I, Act VI, Scene 8*

The Dynasts, published in parts between 1903 and 1908, is called by Hardy an "epic-drama," a "chronicle piece" and "a panoramic show." It is considered here rather than under Drama because, with its nineteen acts, one hundred and thirty scenes and many characters, it has no relation to a stage-play. As the preface says: "By dispensing with the theatre altogether, a freedom of treatment was attainable in this form that was denied where the material possibilities of stagery had to be rigorously remembered." The drama was "intended for mental performance," and in point of literary form, "the scheme . . . was shaped with a single view to the modern expression of a modern outlook, and in frank divergence from classical and other dramatic precedent which ruled the ancient voicings of ancient themes."

The theme is the story of Napoleon's struggle to master Europe between 1805 and his fall in 1815: "The Great Historical Calamity, or Clash of Peoples." The scenes are laid in the Overworld, in Parliament, in ships, in inns and clubs, on battlefields, in boudoirs and ball-rooms, and along the roads of Europe from Russia to Spain. The characters are the great historical figures, soldiers, and citizens, abstractions such as Woman, Boy, Gentleman, Lord and Spirits: Spirit Ironic, Spirit of Rumour, Spirit of the Years, and the like, which supply the chorus-element. Many of the scenes consist in part or wholly of dumb-show, in which there are strange premonitions of the future technique of documentary films.

The whole constitutes one of the most elaborate poetical works in our literature. The normal measure is a flowing blank verse, interspersed with prose spoken by the unheroic characters (very much in the Shakespearian manner), and with a variety of metres for the choric passages. The following is a passage spoken by Napoleon to Josephine—

I must dictate some letters. This new move
Of England on Madrid may mean some trouble.
Come, dwell not gloomily on this cold need
Of waiving private joy for policy.
We are but thistle globes on Heaven's high gales,
And whither blown, or when, or how, or why,
Can choose us not at all! . . .
I'll come to you anon, dear.

The Dynasts, Part II, Act II, Scene 6

Several volumes of occasional poems appeared in the twenty years
which were still left to Hardy, and on these rests his principal claim to
be reckoned among our great lyrical poets. These volumes include
Satires of Circumstance (1914), *Moments of Vision* (1917), and *Late
Lyrics* (1922). *Winter Words* was published posthumously. In all these
the prevailing mood is of brooding interrogation, or wistful musing
on missed happiness.

Fin de Siècle

During the eighteen-nineties our literature passed through a phase
variously described as "decadent," *fin de siècle* and aesthetic. Artists
and writers of the time who were influenced by this movement, such
as Whistler, Aubrey Beardsley, and Oscar Wilde, pursued an ideal of
"Art for art's sake," a rather too self-conscious cult of daring cleverness
and languid preciosity, which was burlesqued in Gilbert and Sullivan's
comic opera *Patience*. Wilde, who wrote *The Ballad of Reading Gaol*,
several witty comedies, and the fine prose of *De Profundis*, was most
typically representative of the period. Others of the group were
Ernest Dowson and John Davidson. These and Arthur Symons were
deeply affected by three French poets of the nineteenth century,
Baudelaire, Verlaine, and Mallarmé, who are known as Symbolists.
Much of the work of the English decadents was published in *The
Yellow Book*.

Contemporary with these, but quite different in spirit were the
mystical poets, such as Francis Thompson and Alice Meynell and
Coventry Patmore, who has been called the last of the Pre-Raphaelites.
Rudyard Kipling (1865–1936) was a portent of "the century of the
common man." Rejecting the outlook and the diction of the poetry
of "loves and doves," he brought in the rhythms and slang of the
military parade, of the engine-room, and of the far ways of Empire
and trade.

11

SUGGESTIONS FOR FURTHER READING

EDITH BATHO AND B. DOBRÉE: *The Victorians and After* (Cresset Press).
F. L. LUCAS: *Decline and Fall of the Romantic Ideal* (Cambridge Univ. Press).
Ed.: G. M. YOUNG: *Early Victorian England* (Oxford Univ. Press).
H. WALKER: *The Literature of the Victorian Era* (Cambridge Univ. Press).
O. BURDETT: *The Beardsley Period* (John Lane).
HOLBROOK JACKSON: *The Eighteen-Nineties* (Cape).
HAROLD NICHOLSON: *Tennyson* (Constable).
W. H. GARDNER: *Gerard Manley Hopkins* (Secker & Warburg).
BASIL WILLEY: *Nineteenth Century Studies* (Poetry) (Chatto & Windus).

CHAPTER XIII

TWENTIETH-CENTURY POETRY

THE poets who helped to bridge the transition from the Victorian to the Georgian era were Robert Bridges, A. E. Housman, and W. B. Yeats.

Transitional Poets

Robert Bridges (1844–1930) was a poet and scholar, and represents a return to classicism. He was led to poetry, he said, by "the inexhaustible satisfaction of form." He had a deep interest in the problems of literary criticism, particularly of prosody, and he used, as well as advocated, a more rational spelling of English words. In 1913 he succeeded Alfred Austin as Poet Laureate, having become known by the collection of his published poems in a single edition in 1912. As he himself tells us, he "felt no call to poetry" for some years, and he became known as "the dumb laureate." His outstanding contribution to our poetry was the *Testament of Beauty*, published in 1929, six months before his death.

The poem is a philosophical dissertation on the stages of human progress, and the function of the artistic spirit in leading mankind towards self-knowledge and self-control. The immediate popularity of the poem, which was reprinted fourteen times in the first year, indicates that Bridges had a message for the times, but doubtless many read it without concerning themselves with the prosodic experiments which the poet was making. Ever since, half a century earlier, he ventured into print with his sonnet-sequence, *The Growth of Love*, Bridges had had a classical scholar's interest in the problems of metre. His metrical innovations were directed to the breaking down of the domination of the syllabic system of versification, overruling it by a stress-prosody wherein natural speech-rhythms should find their proper values. Though there existed, as he pointed out, no recognized prosody of verse based on accent, he was nevertheless convinced that only through the resuscitation of the principle of quantitative stress could any advances in English versification be expected.

In the "loose Alexandrines," as he called them, of the *Testament of Beauty*, Bridges aimed at this perfected prosody. The degree of success which he achieved may be left to individual judgment; but it is already certain that his abiding place in the tradition of English poetry will owe far less to this poem with its neo-metrics and its comprehensive philosophy of human endeavour than to his early lyrics. In these he sang of familiar things simply, with a fine reticence in the employment of words, and a subtle music.

A. E. Housman (1859–1936) produced *A Shropshire Lad* in 1896, and *Last Poems* in 1922. He too was a classical scholar and, rejecting the ecstasies of romantic poetry, used a style of austere purity. His exacting standards prevented him from writing much, but his influence has been out of all proportion to the small bulk of his poetry. He gave back to his age its mood of philosophic "despair," which he expressed with the utmost simplicity and restraint, paring away everything that was merely ornamental.

W. B. Yeats (1865–1939) was the founder of the Celtic movement in poetry and drama, a phase of romanticism which had not been much exploited hitherto. The rise of the new Irish school was signalled by the publication of his *Poems* in 1895 and *The Wind among the Reeds* four years later, but Yeats' main activities were directed towards the establishment of an Irish literary theatre, for which he wrote poetic dramas. In this effort he was helped by Lady Gregory and J. M. Synge. Yeats sought his themes in Irish mythology, a region as far removed from the world of science, technology and progress as might well be imagined. There, he said, lived "the last folk tradition of Western Europe." He was drawn into the Irish nationalist movement, and many of his poems touch on the politics of the rebellion; yet it seems that in the end Yeats gladly put all this aside. In one later phase, represented by the poem *Sailing to Byzantium*, he indulged in Oriental dreams. But generally he fell in with the intellectual mood of his age, and his latest work was surrealist.

The Spirit of Revolt

Even before the end of the nineteenth century a spirit of revolt against Victorianism was spreading. In it there was something of impatience with the didacticism of the great Victorian poets who had set up to be the prophets of their time. Tennyson, Browning, and Arnold, even Swinburne and Meredith, each felt that it was incumbent on him as a poet to take up an attitude on the questions which divided men, and in doing so they were, in the view of the rebellious youth of the ebbing century, false to their lights as poets. In this view the poet's business was to be uniquely himself, and to project his own personality through the medium of his art. Poetry was not a medium for philosophy and other extraneous matters; nor was it "idle singing." It was a method first of discovering one's self, and then a means of projecting this discovery.

The problem was, how to arrive at a completely individual expression of oneself in poetry? It could plainly not be solved by using the language of universals. To abstract from objects or scenes those qualities which logical analysis showed to be common to all, and as true for one observer as for another—that was a function which belonged to science. Equally it could not be solved by the use of a poetic diction, which registered a kind of vision which had become stereotyped among poets. Certain forms of utterance had become inseparably associated with certain conceptions of the function of poetry. Consequently, changes in those conceptions implied that an attempt was required to discover new techniques of communicating meaning. Hence there arose a new attitude towards emotion. It was felt that the emotions of the Victorians, too easily degenerating into a kind of sugary sentimentalism, and dissipating themselves in an all-too-conscious effort to "tune in with the Infinite," corresponded with nothing that was felt in the inner core of being.

Imagism and Symbolism

Out of this rather vague defiance of accepted standards arose the movements known as Symbolism and Imagism. Symbolism was of French origin, and was associated in its beginnings with Mallarmé (1842–98). The Symbolist is concerned wholly with registering his individual sensations and perceptions in language which seems best adapted to convey their essential quality, regardless of conventional cadences and syntactical structure. His purpose is not to communicate logical meaning, but to induce states of mind in the reader. The Imagists, a school founded by an American writer, Ezra Pound, at the time of the outbreak of the First World War, aimed at clarity of expression through the use of hard, accurate, and definite images. The soul of poetry was expressed, it was claimed, not in the elaborated similes of a Milton, or in poems which are little more than extended metaphors, but in the recording of the rapid impingement of images on the consciousness, setting up in the mind fleeting complexes of thought and feeling. In poetry which would capture such instantaneous states of mind, there is no leisure for "emotion recollected in tranquillity."

Suggestion is paramount; of patient, objective description there is little or none. Ornament is pruned back to the stem of meaning.

T. S. Eliot

It was the appearance of T. S. Eliot's *The Waste Land* in 1922 which signalled the emergence of symbolist poetry in England into the full light of day. But that deep forces had been at work for a considerable time before is evident from the fact that Gerard Manley Hopkins (1844–89), a Jesuit priest, whose poems were not published until thirty years after his death, was possessed of the Symbolist spirit well within the Victorian age. Hopkins and Eliot had together a profound influence on English poetry between the two wars.

The technique of symbolist writing is impressionistic and non-representational. In their anxiety not to allow any direct statement of experience to get in the way of emotive suggestion, the symbolists prefer to wrap up meaning in obscurity. The obscurity may be partial, but relieved, as in editions of *The Waste Land,* by notes explaining the erudite allusions; or it may be a total eclipse, as in some of the poetry of E. E. Cummings or Gertrude Stein. There is also in symbolist poetry a strong element of incantation, due partly to an attempt to imitate music, which of all the arts is least representational. Repetition is an ancient device, normally used either for emphasis, or for the pleasure derived from the sound pattern, as in the famous death-bed scene in Marlowe's *Tamburlaine the Great,* with its line—

> To entertain divine Zenocrate,

recurring like a refrain;
or again as in Tennyson's *The Marriage of Geraint—*

> Forgetful of his promise to the King
> Forgetful of the falcon and the hunt,
> Forgetful of the tilt and tournament,
> Forgetful of his glory and his name
> Forgetful of his princedom and its cares.

But the repetitive rhythms of the symbolists have in them a hypnotic quality as well, and they recall the texture of dreams and of sub-conscious states of mind and may be accompanied by patterns of onomatopoeic sound—

> Inside my brain a dull tom-tom begins
> Absurdly hammering a prelude of its own
> Capricious monotone. . . .
>
> ELIOT: *Portrait of a Lady*

On the one hand the repetitive design is subject to abrupt breaks to suggest the lack of continuity of the images of the dream-consciousness. On the other hand, the frequent absence of punctuation gives to language the fluid texture of a consciousness which knows no intermission, the "stream-of-consciousness"—

> Will the veiled sister between the slender
> Yew tree pray for those who offend her
> And are terrified and cannot surrender
> And affirm before the world and deny between the rocks
> In the last desert between the last blue rocks
> The desert in the garden the garden in the desert
> Of drouth, spitting from the mouth the withered apple-seed.
>   T. S. ELIOT: *Ash Wednesday*

The symbolists have admitted into poetry concepts which traditionally have been outside its purview. They have done so in the cause of fidelity to private or abstract experience. The object or the situation is a matter of indifference to them; what is important is the subjective vision of it. In art, beauty or ugliness inheres not in the object or situation depicted, but in the form in which communication is effected. To express successfully in art what is sinister, nauseating or selfish in conduct is to create beauty just as surely as to express successfully their opposites. The tragedy of *King Lear* will not be denied beauty because of the heartrending cruelty and anguish which Shakespeare depicts. That has always been true of art, but the symbolists, in their reaction against romanticism, have found an intense satisfaction in ridding their minds of the obsession of the conventionally beautiful, and in groping for a principle of beauty in every detail of our work-a-day surroundings. Here is a field for "challenge and response" which evoke the greatest art. The intractability of the material calls for a deeper penetration, a more sensitive approach.

In symbolic method, what applies to the object of thought and emotion applies also to the language in which they find expression. Here, too, fresh ground has to be broken. Every word in the language, being a coin of utterance, is held to have its value for poetry as well as for prose. And since the hitherto rejected among words and idioms would be ill at ease in the conventional surroundings of romantic poetry, a new prosody must be contrived to accommodate vocables and speech rhythms which were till now considered to be beyond the pale. There are in poetry no longer privileged topics, diction, and rhythms.

SUGGESTIONS FOR FURTHER READING

E. R. Leavis: *Revaluation: Tradition and Development in English Poetry; New Bearings on English Poetry* (Chatto & Windus).

Ruth Bailey: *A Dialogue on Modern Poetry* (Oxford Univ. Press).

C. M. Bowra: *The Heritage of Symbolism* (Macmillan).

J. Livingstone Lowes: *Convention and Revolt in Poetry* (Constable).

Herbert Read: *Form in Modern Poetry* (Sheed & Ward).

G. Bullough: *The Trend of Modern Poetry* (Oliver & Boyd).

Cleanth Brooks: *Modern Poetry and the Tradition* (Oxford Univ. Press).

Charles Williams: *Poetry at Present* (Oxford Univ. Press).

Louis MacNiece: *The Poetry of W. B. Yeats* (Oxford Univ. Press).

Edwin Muir: *The Present Age from 1914* (Cresset Press).

CHAPTER XIV

DESIGN IN DRAMA

A CERTAIN difficulty arises in any discussion of Drama as a branch of literature, because its true essence lies not in words but in action. The consummation of Drama is achieved on a stage, before an audience. As an art-form it is a composite product, requiring contributions from the visual arts such as architecture and painting, as well as sometimes from music and dancing. Drama may even attain many significant values without the use of speech at all. The advocates of symbolism in the theatre invite us to envisage a non-literary dramatic art. "We will surround the people," says Gordon Craig in *The Mask*, "with symbols in silence: in silence we will reveal the Movement of things . . . this is the nature of our art."

Our present concern is nevertheless with the literature of Drama, that is to say with writings which, though intended to be, or capable of being, spoken by actors as dialogue in the presence of a public audience, are fully intelligible to the private reader.

Essentials of Dramatic Structure

The essentials of dramatic structure comprise first a theme, sometimes called the "fable," but usually known as the "plot." This is a continuous stream of action, a single chain of cause and effect, leading gradually to the "climax," after which comes the more rapid "fall" or close, called in a tragedy the "catastrophe," or more generally the *dénouement*. The material being human life with its infinite variety, some measure of unity has to be imposed by selection and concentration. The principal limitation is the dramatic idea, in virtue of which occurrences which from one point of view are trivial may from another be invested with the utmost significance. Since the scope of drama is limited in practice by the possibility of enactment on a stage in a single session of not more than three or four hours (although there are exceptions), it follows that a rigid economy must be exercised by the playwright in determining what characters, what events, and what speech may be admitted to produce the maximum effect. It was in the interests of this economy that the theory of the "dramatic unities" (viz. the unities of place, of time, and of action) was evolved.

The action of a play is presented, not directly through description by an omnipresent observer, as in most novels, but indirectly through the speech, movements and gestures of the characters themselves, either alone or in the presence of each other. It is thus in soliloquy or dialogue that we learn what is happening, and obviously if dramatic probability is to be achieved, the characters have to speak in a way which is consistent with their personalities. We have here therefore the second essential element in dramatic structure: the characters who are to carry the action along. They have to be sufficiently distinctive in their persons, their outlook, their conduct and their modes of utterance to be instantly recognizable, and their behaviour (including their speech) must either determine, or at any rate, harmonize with, the general movement of the action. The requirement of consistency. however, is not to be taken to mean that a character is necessarily static. In plays in which the interest is mainly in action, character will tend to be fixed; but in the psychological drama, character will be dynamic, and will evolve as the action unfolds itself.

The third essential of dramatic composition is the dialogue, through which the movement of action and character is amplified and made manifest. Here again the playwright has to achieve economy by compression without destroying the illusion that the language is taken from real life. No soldier, to be sure, has ever spoken in hexameters on a battlefield, as Achilles does in the *Iliad*; no advocate has ever addressed the plaintiff in blank verse as Portia does in the *Merchant of Venice*. But the illusion is there notwithstanding. The skill of the dramatist is exercised to the end of inducing us to "suspend our disbelief." He does so by means of suggestion. Translating his idea into symbols (on the printed page or on the stage), the dramatist persuades us to put aside reason, and to accept the symbols as real existences. That done, verisimilitude lies in the consistent use of the symbols. The truth of the action or of the language used is in the assumption we are induced to make, namely, that *given* such a situation and such people, they would have acted and spoken in this way and no other.

The last essential element in our analysis of dramatic structure is the setting, or the *mise-en-scène*. Unless, as in plays constructed on the classical model, the action takes place on one spot, there has to be a division into acts and scenes, to allow of changes of stage scenery and costume, and to suggest the passage of time. This involves suspension of the action, possibly repeated several times. In the conditions of the open-air amphitheatre of the Greeks, continuous action was necessary.

Division into acts was a device adopted when theatres became enclosed, and movable scenery and properties began to be used. The invariable five-act division of the Shakespearian plays is a convention borrowed from the Roman playwright, Plautus.

Dramatic Conventions

Such are the basic elements which have to be organically combined by the dramatist in the fashioning of a play. There are four principal conventions within which he can work: the classical, the realistic, the romantic, and the symbolist or expressionist.

The classical convention is to be seen in its most fully developed form in the tragic drama of ancient Greece. It is concerned with the presentation of epic themes, with figures larger than life, and has an aspect of ritual, being associated with popular religious myths. Speech is declamatory, and by the employment of a chorus to report related happenings off-stage, the necessity of complicating the stage action is avoided. Structure consequently remains simple and unitary.

The realistic convention is based on the view that the function of the artist is to observe closely the life he sees around him and, as faithfully as his art allows him, to reproduce the form and features of his age. According to this conception, art is representation, and its quality is to be judged by its truth to the detail, even the trivial detail, of actual life. The dramatist therefore who aims at realism has first to observe minutely and set down what he sees, without allowing his subjective attitudes to give colour to his presentation, and without allowing his imagination to exaggerate or distort.

In the romantic convention there is called into existence a new world of people and circumstances. The dramatist,

> giving to airy nothing
> A local habitation and a name,

puts on the stage an "insubstantial pageant" which, when the dramatic purpose is achieved, fades and "leaves not a wrack behind." Yet even this world, however remote it be from that which we know, must have in it a principle of truth. It must obey the principle of consistency. The agents and incidents in the romantic play have to convince the audience, "by the dramatic truth of such emotions, as would naturally accompany such situations, supposing them real." These words were used by Coleridge with reference to the introduction of supernatural elements in poetry, but they apply equally well to all those idealized worlds beyond the range of normal experience, to which the art of the dramatist (or other artist) gives momentary existence.

The fourth of the principal conventions which the dramatist may choose is one in which the truth to be aimed at is not that of objective appearances, but something deeper and more fundamental. External actions are notoriously unsure pointers to the real motives of human behaviour. The symbolist or expressionist playwright therefore attempts to isolate in his art what is significant, ruthlessly rejecting those superficial aspects of life which, so far from being realistic, tend only to obscure realities.

It is the province of the study of Æsthetics to inquire into the value of these conventions for the purposes of art. But it may briefly be remarked here that every play which has dramatic merit uses something at any rate of the last three of them. Even the realist play can never be a photographic transcript from life: there must have been selection, exclusion, compression, and reconstruction of the elements of experience. On the stage nothing can be so unconvincing as actuality. Nor can the idealized world of romance be divorced completely from our own. There may be differences of proportion, with kings who are humble and beggars who are proud, but humility and pride are still human attributes. In a romantic setting the familiar ingredients of our workaday lives are recombined into novel patterns, and thus they minister to our delight in strangeness as long as they do not pass beyond certain limits. Again, both the realist and the romantic in drama may be aiming at something beyond illusion, at something more than the telling of a tale in a convincing manner. If they believe in a world behind appearances, not observable by the senses, and, using their art to draw aside the veil, afford us a glimpse of the ultimate, and thereby enlarge our spiritual experience, then they are expressionist. Shakespeare is realist, romanticist and expressionist in one. His plays have in them the truth of the world of the senses, of the imagination and of the spirit.

Tragedy and Comedy

Tragedy according to Aristotle meant, in brief, drama which is concerned with life in its ultimate aspects, as contrasted with comedy, which depicts the accidentals of life, "the mistakes of an afternoon." In general, tragedy uses material drawn from human experience at the heroic level, whereas comedy prefers the lower scale of experience, where chance and the clash of idiosyncrasy can create grotesque or romantic situations. The distinction is not to be found in the power of tragedy to draw tears, or of comedy to evoke laughter. It is something more fundamental. Tragedy has a serious purpose in view, called by Aristotle the "catharsis" or purging of the emotions. There has been much discussion of his meaning, but it is generally assumed to refer to the release of our own repressions by the moderate indulgence which is involved in witnessing the uninhibited expression of emotion on the stage. Such release provides us with a moral-aesthetic satisfaction which is the "pleasure" we derive from tragic drama.

The more modern view of the essential purpose of Tragedy does not distinguish it greatly from that of Comedy. They are both a means whereby we enlarge experience. This may also be said of literature in general. By the reading of fiction or poetry or drama, we range beyond the boundaries of our normal existences, and are admitted to a share in the writer's deeper penetration into the mysteries. Each form of literature thus in its way enables us to have life more abundantly.

The ancient Greeks made such a sharp distinction between Tragedy and Comedy that their great playwrights wrote exclusively in the one form or the other. As long as the classical tradition continued to influence drama in Renaissance times, there was a tendency to maintain this distinction, but the general movement of drama under the lead of Marlowe and Shakespeare was towards a mixed type, known as "romantic," in which tragic and comic elements were mingled. In France, where the authority of the Academy upheld classical principles of dramatic construction long after they had been discarded elsewhere, the demarcation between the types was closely observed, until the final triumph of romanticism marked by the production of Victor Hugo's *Hernani* in 1830.

The Chronicle Play

The growth of national consciousness in England in the sixteenth century showed itself in the development of a historical sense, which in drama produced a kind of play unknown to the ancients, namely the Chronicle History. Being episodical in structure, and having no "plot" in the sense of a knot to be tied and then untied, the chronicle play in its crude form was not true drama. Historical annals represent life in a continuous perspective; there is no resting point for the imagination. It is the function of the historical chronicle to record events, not to organize them into patterns, and it stands, therefore, closer to epic than to drama. The earlier chronicle plays introduce little else than an element of dialogue into the record. Not being divided into acts and scenes, they lack even a rudimentary structure, though of necessity some effort of selection has been made from the mass of material offered.

The imposition of true dramatic form on such brittle material is a task calling for great boldness and skill, and we find that in the most successful examples of the chronicle play, the dramatist has refused to be trammelled by the requirements of historical accuracy. Not only are dates and events altered in perspective, but also character is modified. Non-historical figures are introduced and incidents are invented for which there is no authority in recorded annals. All this is done in the interests of dramatic unity. The historical playwright makes no claim to be writing authentic history, but filters history through his imagination, and what he offers is not historical truth but a work of art.

Melodrama

The word melodrama implies a combination of two arts: music and drama. The form appeared in England in the eighteenth century and consisted of speech and action accompanied by instrumental music, or interspersed with it, as in Gay's *Beggar's Opera*. The two were not yet closely integrated, as in modern opera and musical comedy.

In nineteenth-century and modern melodrama, the presence or absence of music is irrelevant, and the term is employed to describe a form of drama in which tense situations are built up by stock-figures and sensational effects are achieved by the employment of stage devices. The action follows a conventional pattern, with strongly contrasting hero and villain, a heroine in distress and a scheming adventuress, the unmasking of crime, comic relief and the like, all presented in a vein of crude exaggeration and carried to a happy ending with honour vindicated, persecution revenged, misunderstandings resolved, and virtue rewarded. The appeal of melodrama is to primitive emotions such as love, pity, fear and revenge; its pathos is spurious, and its sentiment false.

SUGGESTIONS FOR FURTHER READING

U. ELLIS-FERMOR: *The Frontiers of Drama* (Methuen).
F. L. LUCAS: *Tragedy* (Hogarth Press).
ALLARDYCE NICOLL: *British Drama* (Harrap).
C. E. VAUGHAN: *Types of Tragic Drama* (Macmillan).
A. H. THORNDIKE: *Tragedy* (Constable); *English Comedy* (Macmillan).
SIR H. GRANVILLE BARKER: *On Dramatic Method; The Use of Drama; On Poetry in Drama* (Sidgwick & Jackson).

CHAPTER XV

EARLY DRAMA

To understand the development of drama in the western world we have to begin with ancient Greece, where each of its great branches, Tragedy, and Comedy, was in its beginnings an aspect of religious ritual. To accommodate the vast throngs which gathered to celebrate the great religious festivals, the amphitheatres were built, sometimes seating as many as 24,000 people. In the earliest times the ritual consisted of scenic choral dances; then sacred singing (the dithyramb) was introduced, and this eventually became the function of a standing chorus of satyrs (in form part human, part god-like) attendant on Dionysus, or Bacchus. Their incantations were called by the Greek word for tragedies, signifying goat-songs. They were lyrical rather than dramatic; the evolution of dramatic dialogue belongs to a later period and is associated with the wandering minstrels of Ionia, who added interest to the ritual by the alternate recitation of passages borrowed from the epic poets.

Greek Tragedy

The invention of tragedy is attributed to Thespis (sixth century B.C.) who introduced on the stage the first actor. It was the exchanges of this actor with the leader of the satyric chorus which constituted the first dramatic dialogue, and his impersonation of the great legendary heroes may be said to be the first example of character-acting. But the lyrical element continued to be the principal component of drama until Æschylus (early fifth century B.C.) brought in a second actor and tilted the balance towards dramatic dialogue. When Sophocles, his successor (later fifth century B.C.), added a third actor, the predominance of dialogue and action was assured. The chorus, now much contracted in size, withdrew from its prominent position in the arena, and was used to comment on the action or to describe happenings off-stage. The third of the great Greek dramatic writers, Euripides, was a contemporary of Sophocles. His genius was more varied, his social sympathies wider, and he did much to reveal the possibilities of drama as a medium for dealing with the problems of normal human existence. Music and the dithyrambic ecstasy gradually gave place to talk, and literary drama entered into possession of the theatre.

With these writers the limits of development in Greek tragic drama may be said to have been reached. Most of the plays which brought them victory in the festival competitions at Athens have been lost, but we still have seven by Æschylus, seven by Sophocles, and nineteen by Euripides.[1]

Greek Comedy

Greek comedy had its origin in the popular and extempore revels which accompanied the organized celebrations of the Dionysian rites. A usual feature was the singing procession, or *comos*, chanting ribald verses and flinging about scurrilous abuse. Their song or *ode*, along with a kind of mummery or play-acting imported from the villages, developed into the "old" comedy of Athens, which found in Aristophanes its first great exponent. Much of the character of its origins was retained in his comedies,[2] especially the unlicensed personal invective and parody which he directed particularly against Euripides. The transition to Middle Comedy was marked by a greater reticence and a preference for themes which raised important social issues. The satire became impersonal, and being directed to types rather than to individuals, pointed the way towards the Comedy of Manners.

The third phase was known as the New Comedy, dating from the rise of Macedonia. The best known writer was Menander whose plays we have principally in Latin translations by Plautus and Terence. The love intrigue, which had no place in Greek tragedy, nor hitherto in Comedy, now became the dominant theme. After the death of Menander (early third century B.C.) Greek comedy declined rapidly.

The Dramatic Unities

The organization of the Greek theatre and the methods of presentation are related to theatrical rather than to literary art, but since they have relevance to the Aristotelian canon of the Dramatic Unities, it is necessary to consider them briefly. The *Poetics* of Aristotle, written about 330 B.C., has come down to us either as an unfinished work by the philosopher-critic, or possibly as a disciple's notes of his lectures.

[1] The best-known are: Æschylus—*The Persians, The Seven against Thebes, Prometheus Bound, The Suppliants, Agamemnon, Eumenides*; Sophocles—*Oedipus Rex, Antigone, Electra, Ajax*; Euripides—*Alcestis, Medea, Hippolytus, Iphigenia in Tauris, The Trojan Women, Orestes, The Bacchae.*

[2] Among the comedies of Aristophanes, the following may be mentioned: *The Frogs, The Clouds, The Wasps, The Birds, Lysistrata, Peace.*

The work consists of a discussion of the methods used by the great masters of epic-poetry and drama, particularly the tragedians, and it is noted that in the construction of their plays certain guiding principles are observable. They all tend to emphasize the unity which is an essential attribute of drama. The action is confined to a single place, the events happen within the space of a single day, and the continuity of the action is preserved by the exclusion of themes or plots which do not contribute directly to its progress. These are the Unities of Place, Time, and Action which French critics of the seventeenth century, forgetting that they were no more than practical expedients relating to the special conditions of the Greek amphitheatre, raised to the dignity of sacrosanct rules for tragic drama.

If it be agreed, on aesthetic grounds, that the impression made by any work of art should be complete and harmonious, it can be allowed forthwith that the principle of unity of action is one of universal validity. In Aristotle's phrase, the work of art should be capable of being apprehended as a single whole; the aesthetic satisfaction arises from the total effect, rather than from a sum of partial effects. There is less to be said for the Unities of Place and Time. Shakespeare has demonstrated once for all that totality of effect is not sacrificed by the dispersal of the action over many times and places. If drama is to draw its material from life, it must recognize that no arbitrary limits of place and time can be set to the unfolding of character and to the sequence of cause and effect in human affairs.

The Drama in Rome

After the decline of Greek drama the development of dramatic literature was carried on by the Romans. Though Italy has had a remarkable native skill in dramatic improvization from the earliest times, the literary drama in Rome was an importation from Greece via Tarentum, a Greek colony in Sicily, where the festival of Dionysus had always been celebrated. Accordingly, it is not surprising that the themes and their manner of treatment conformed to Greek models, and particularly, as we have seen, to those of the New Comedy of Menander. The characters were mostly stock figures, such as the comic slave, the braggart soldier, the conceited cook, the young lover and the heavy father, the hunch-back, the cuckold, the gallant, the courtesan, and the like, all familiar to us in the later history of Comedy.

The outstanding names in the history of Roman comic drama were Plautus (c. 200 B.C.) and Terence (c. 150 B.C.). Twenty plays of Plautus

12

are extant, including the *Menaechmi*, from which Shakespeare took the plot for *The Two Gentlemen of Verona*. Only six plays of Terence have come down to us and these are all close imitations of words by Menander. Terence was the principal link between the classical and the modern drama. Roswitha, the Saxon Nun, who wrote Latin plays in the tenth century, complained that the "inventions of Terence," a pagan, though his diction was sweet, were being read too often by Christians, wherefore she, imitating the manner, would amend the matter, and instead of wanton would offer chaste and godly examples of living.

The most important writer of Roman tragedy was Seneca, who flourished during the time of the Emperor Nero. He was a statesman and a philosopher of the Stoic school. His plays were not written for the stage, but were rather exercises in a kind of sententious moralizing thrown into dramatic form. In Italy, Seneca had a great vogue through the Middle Ages, and his ten plays, which were translated into English by the humanists during the early years of Elizabeth's reign, leapt into instant popularity, first in scholastic circles and in the court, and then in the popular theatre.

Native Religious Drama

There is very little to bridge the gap which yawns between the drama of Rome, cast out by the Church as a morally decadent pagan survival, and the medieval liturgical drama, sponsored by the same Church nearly a thousand years later as a method of teaching to an unlettered people the central events of the Bible story. If there can be said to have been any survival of the dramatic tradition of classical times, it must be sought either in the ritual of propitiation and thanksgiving which was associated with the seasons of ploughing, sowing of seed, and harvesting in towns and villages all over Europe; or among the strolling players, dancers and singers known as minstrels or *jongleurs* who clung to their art in the most forbidding circumstances.

About the tenth century there emerged in Europe a more clearly defined liturgical drama, which reached its highest point in the fifteenth century. In all the lands of Christendom its development showed substantially the same features; namely the shift of language from Latin to the vernacular, and the gradual secularization of the plays until drama became dissociated altogether from the Church and the theatre once again drew upon itself the disapprobation and the hostility of the clergy.

The earliest form of religious drama was ancillary to the principal Church festivals. To add force to a ritual observance the priest and worshippers would sometimes engage in a simple series of questions and answers which were intoned or chanted. A further development would be simple dialogue on the altar steps, supplemented by dumb-show. Eventually the participants moved to the church porch, for greater freedom of action. Meanwhile the *Mystery* proper, a dramatization of the central facts of the Christian tradition, such as the Nativity, the Crucifixion and the Resurrection, was developing into the *Miracle*, which went outside the revealed Scriptures for some of the themes and characters and found them in the lives of the Saints. By the fifteenth century the typical religious play was the *Morality*. Already the process of secularization had gone far, and a literary-allegorical element had crept in. The purpose of the *Morality* was no longer simply to give dramatic form to a known scriptural story; it was rather to inculcate virtue by showing the forces of Good and Evil in action. The characters were mostly personifications of abstract qualities and human characteristics. *Everyman*, the best known of the Moralities, contains such characters as Death, Fellowship, Good Deeds, Knowledge, Fine Wits, Beauty, and Confession. Often a Bible story, for example, the story of Noah, formed the basis of the play, but great freedom was allowed in the addition of other matter, including comic interludes. One must not suppose that the Moralities displaced the earlier forms of religious drama. All forms undoubtedly existed side by side until the end of the sixteenth century.

The Play Cycles

The presentation of Morality plays at public festivals, which coincided in medieval times with the religious "feasts," was principally in the hands of the craft-guilds. Many crafts had a kind of proprietary interest in certain themes or stories, and acquired suitable properties and wheeled platforms (called pageants) for mounting the plays. The most important collections or cycles of the guildsmen's plays are those of York (numbering 48), Towneley or Wakefield (32), Chester (25), and Coventry (42), and in addition we have many isolated examples. The plays were performed in the squares and at the cross-roads of the towns during all the daylight hours from early dawn to dusk, particularly on the festivals of Shrove Tuesday, Easter, Whitsun, and Corpus Christi. All the plays of the cycle were played in succession at each station, so that a large number was being simultaneously performed.

Mumming-plays, Motions, and Interludes

There were in addition to these liturgical and morality plays other kinds of folk-drama which had a secular origin: these included the Mumming-plays, the Puppet-plays, and the Interludes. The "mummers," particularly at Christmas, paraded through the streets in a spirit of carnival and visited the great houses wearing masks, or masquerading as animals, taking with them their crude charades or knock-about scenes, in which such popular figures as St. George and the Turkish Knight constantly appeared. On May Day, the exploits of Robin Hood provided the favourite theme. The mumming-plays were little more than the dramatization of popular ballads, which they closely resembled in style.

Competing for favour with the mummers were the puppet shows (or "motions"). These were related to pantomime, and may be traced to an origin similar to that of the more sophisticated *Commedia dell'Arte*, of Italy. The latter consisted of an extempore comedy or harlequinade of masked characters, linked together by the figure of Harlequin. Nothing but a brief scenario was written, and success depended on the ready invention of "business." Autolycus in *The Winter's Tale* refers to himself as having "compassed a motion of the Prodigal Son."

The origin of the term "Interlude" is in dispute, but it is generally used of a species of professional performance which was in request on occasions of ceremony or banqueting, when there were intervals to be occupied in the course of the more important business. The Interlude marks a definite advance towards a comedy which is organized and articulate. Earlier dramatic productions were limited by the necessity of keeping close to the traditional Biblical or legendary stories, since the expectations of the popular audiences could not be disappointed in such a matter. But the passage of drama from its liturgical and allegorical phase to the freer phase of realism, in which familiar types from contemporary life were introduced in place of Biblical characters, saints and personifications, gave scope for new contrivance in both plot and language. The interlude introduced also a changed conception of the purposes of drama, which gradually lost its didactic character and became a vehicle of secular entertainment.

The development of the Interlude is associated with the name of John Heywood (1497–1580). The most famous example of his work is *The Foure Ps.*, printed in 1569. Three characters: the palmer, the pardoner, and the potycary, vie with each other in telling the biggest lie while the fourth, the pedlar, adjudicates. The verdict goes to the palmer for his assertion that of the five hundred thousand women he has known, he had never seen one "out of patience." There is much in the humorous narrative and character delineation which is reminiscent of Chaucer. The verse consists mainly of decasyllabic rhymed couplets.

The Great Age of Drama

The great age of English drama, from the early years of the reign of Elizabeth to the closing of the theatres in 1642, fell into four phases, each lasting about twenty years.

The first phase (1560–80) was that of the scholastic or academic drama. This started under classical influences, but gradually assimilated native elements. The second (1580–1600) was the age of Marlowe, Kyd, Greene, Peele, and the earlier Shakespeare, and was the time when the romantic drama arose, and achieved the integration of humanism with the native tradition. The third phase (1600–20) was dominated in the first half by the mature work of Shakespeare. The spirit of adventure and the exuberant vitality of the late Elizabethans had by now been succeeded by a darker mood. In the work of Chapman, Webster, Tourneur, and others of this period there is a morbid preoccupation with decay and abnormality, and a tendency to excess which often characterizes decadent romanticism. The growth of doubt and disillusion took another form in the work of Ben Jonson, who exemplifies the revival of rationalism and of the critical spirit. His plays are in the classical tradition and their savage comment on contemporary society is an indication of the mood of the period. Finally, the fourth phase (1620–40), that of Philip Massinger, John Ford, and James Shirley, brings us to within two years of the closure of the theatres by an act of the Long Parliament. This period had all the marks of the final phase of a process of evolution. Poetry had become rhetoric, romance had become melodrama, invention had passed over into mere dexterity or sensationalism, with comedy often overstepping the limits of decorum and tragedy becoming horrific and revolting. The beauty is no longer something suffusing whole plays, but is found in isolated lines or passages as though a flame should flicker up now and again among dying embers. There is perhaps something to be said for the view that the closure of the theatres was in the interests of good drama. A vein of rich ore had been fully worked out and it was time to sink a new mine.

While this chronological progression may usefully be kept in mind, it will be better for our present purposes to adopt a rather different arrangement.

Transitional Tudor Drama

The influence of Humanism on the drama in England began to be strongly felt towards the middle of the sixteenth century, when it became usual to present Latin plays at Grammar Schools, Universities, and Inns of Court. The performances were often given by child actors, e.g. the "Paul's boys," organized as semi-professional companies and trained by the choir-master. From this it was an easy step to plays written in the classical manner. The first regular comedy in English was *Ralph Roister Doister*; it was by Nicholas Udall, Headmaster of Eton and later of Westminster, where it was produced at Christmas, 1553. Based on the *Miles Gloriosus* of Plautus, it uses the five-act structure which afterwards became for a long time an established convention in English drama. The types of the vainglorious soldier (Ralph) and of the parasitical adventurer (Merygreeke) were familiar on the Roman stage, but along with them in the play are figures straight out of English social life, such as the widow Custance and her nurse Madge Mumblecrust. The verse consists of irregular rhyming couplets. A second comedy, *Gammer Gurton's Needle* (first performed in 1566), whose authorship is in doubt, is also in the humanist tradition, although its incidents and characters are drawn from the English countryside.

The first English example of the Senecan drama is *Gorboduc* or *Ferrex and Pollux* by Thomas Norton and Thomas Sackville, which was based on a legend of early Britain, reminiscent of that of King Lear. It was first performed in the presence of Queen Elizabeth at the Inner Temple in 1562, and is almost completely in the classical manner, with its chorus, its dumb show, its declamatory monologues, its ghostly apparitions, the device of the play within a play, the absence of action on the stage and the motive of revenge and retribution. The monstrously violent crimes and incidents which fill the story of the unnatural feud of the two brothers are enacted off-stage and are narrated by messengers. In conscious imitation of unrhymed classical verse, the new blank verse recently introduced by Surrey was employed. In one respect, the play varies from the classical model: there is no observance of the unities of time and place.

The Senecan manner dominated English tragic drama for some

twenty years after the production of *Gorboduc*. At first it was favoured only by the learned coteries of the Court but after the appearance of *The Spanish Tragedy* the taste spread to the popular theatre. By virtue of this play, the author, Thomas Kyd (1558–94), occupies a unique place in literary history. The play was for half a century a prime favourite in the English theatre, and for much longer in the theatres of European countries. Kyd, who was also the putative author of the earlier *Hamlet*, of which traces remain in Shakespeare's play, used the Senecan recipe with such melodramatic extravagance, that it drew upon itself innumerable parodies. The "tragedy of revenge" became a distinct sub-species with a progeny reaching down to Victorian days.

Meanwhile the native tradition of drama had not died out; Miracle and Morality plays were performed throughout Tudor times, mostly in inn-yards on temporary stages, but occasionally in the permanent theatres which were now being erected.

In these the liking of popular audiences for visible melodramatic horrors could be indulged. For economic reasons the acting companies found themselves obliged to consult the tastes of their audiences. The pedantry which kept learned tragedy within a convention was here quite out of place. The London apprentices saw nothing incongruous in "mingling kings and clowns" or "matching hornpipes and funerals," which Sir Philip Sidney, in his *Defense of Poesie*, inveighed against as being injurious to "honest civility" and contrary to the august precepts of Aristotle. History relieved by clowning, tragedy intermixed with farce were favourite receipts for the popular stage. Whetstone's *Promos and Cassandra* (1578) illustrates this tendency towards the evolution of a romantic comedy of mixed moods and styles.

SUGGESTIONS FOR FURTHER READING

F. S. Boas: *Introduction to Tudor Drama* (Oxford Univ. Press).
Sir E. K. Chambers: *The English Folk Play; The Medieval Stage* (2 vols) (Oxford Univ. Press).
A. W. Reed: *Early Tudor Drama* (Methuen).
J. M. Manly: *Specimens of Pre-Shakespearean Drama* (Gunn).
Ed. Thorndike: *The Minor Elizabethan Drama* (Everyman, Dent).
Ed. F. J. Tickner: *Earlier English Drama* (Nelson).

CHAPTER XVI

THE SHAKESPEARIAN AGE

GEORGE PEELE (1558–97) inaugurated the second phase in the period of great drama with his *Arraignment of Paris*, produced in 1581. The play was not itself of outstanding merit, being a slight but graceful piece in the pastoral manner, written as a compliment to Queen Elizabeth, to whom Diana awards the golden apple over her rivals Juno, Pallas, and Venus. But it had poetry and wit and the dramatic interest is well sustained. Peele's scriptural play, *David and Bethsabe*, in blank verse, with its often quoted lines—

> To joy her love I'll build a kingly bower
> Seated in hearing of a hundred streams,

uses a typical Morality theme in the humanistic manner, and so serves to link up the old and the new in drama. *The Old Wives' Tale* is a caricature of dramatic fustian.

Robert Greene (1560–92), a leading "University wit," after some unsuccessful attempts to out-do Marlowe, struck in his *Friar Bacon and Friar Bungay* and *George a-Greene* a vein of romantic comedy which was peculiarly English. There are features in these works which point unmistakably towards Shakespeare; for example, Greene's skill in the delineation of his heroines, the pastoral charm of his settings, and his art in giving significance to both comic and serious situations by bringing them into relation with one another.

The genius of John Lyly (1554–1606) was not pre-eminently dramatic. He was a writer of pleasant and euphuistic prose trifles, performed by companies of child-actors for the amusement and flattery of the Court, the subjects being drawn from classical myths. He brought to his plays the same qualities of artifice which characterized his prose. In *Alexander and Campaspe*, *Endymion*, *Midas*, and other plays, he uses the witty, but rather too fine-drawn repartee of which there is more than an echo in Shakespeare's *Love's Labour's Lost*.

Christopher Marlowe (1564–93) was born in the same year as Shakespeare, but had wellnigh completed a brilliant career as a dramatist while his greater contemporary was barely out of his apprenticeship to the theatre. Soon after leaving Cambridge, Marlowe wrote the two parts of *Tamburlaine the Great* (1587), and these were followed by the

Jew of Malta (1589) and *Dr. Faustus* (1592). In these plays he enlarged the conception of tragedy by rejecting the limited medieval theories of the wheel of fate and the "fall of princes" as the chief themes for tragic drama. Instead he based his tragedies on the conflict between the insufficiency of the individual and his limitless desires, and on the disaster inevitable when a good principle runs to excess.

Tamburlaine is the ambitious man brought down by his over-weening thirst for power; Faustus is the embodiment of human intelligence seeking after the unattainable in knowledge and damned for his audacity; Barabas, the Jew of Malta, is consumed by avarice. But not one of these is a villain incarnate; in each there is an element of goodness. Tamburlaine is redeemed by his tender love for Zenocrate; Faustus was human in his yearning to know; Barabas is far from being the stock figure of the miser and can justify himself on scriptural grounds. Thus Marlowe, even if he allows these plays to be too powerfully dominated by a central character, yet gives to this character more than one dimension. We see it in its weakness and its strength, and are thereby brought closer to the dynamic characterization which is so important an element in Shakespeare's dramatic art. Marlowe's *Edward II* representing further development of the same kind leads us to the consideration of the evolution of the historical play.

From Chronicle Plays to Historical Drama

The origin of the chronicle play may be found in the pseudo-history of the mumming plays. A further stage in its development is marked by the use of authentic instead of legendary material. Bishop Bale, a convinced Protestant, was a prolific writer of historical plays with a propagandist purpose. In one of these, namely *King John* (1538), historical personages, among whom are Stephen Langton and Cardinal Pandulphus, mingle with allegorical figures such as "England," "Civil Order," and "Private Wealth." In this respect it resembles a morality play. The whole is a diatribe against Romanism, savage and bitter in tone. Another play on the same theme is *The Troublesome Reigne of King John*. This play, of unknown authorship, and written from the same anti-Papal standpoint, represents a considerable advance. Omitting all the fantastic abstractions of Bale, it introduces only characters known to history. *The Troublesome Reigne* was used by Shakespeare for his own *King John*; although Shakespeare organized his material with much greater consistency of aim and with more economy and dramatic sense, nevertheless he did not completely overcome its intractability.

These three versions of the same theme serve to illustrate sufficiently well three stages in the development of the chronicle play. Further illustration could be found in a comparison of the early play on the exploits of King Henry V, namely *The Famous Victories of Henry the Fifth*, with Shakespeare's *King Henry the Fifth*. The former is a particularly crude and shapeless dramatization of the story, but nevertheless it was used by Shakespeare, along with Holinshed's *Chronicles*. Again the result was a play which, since it has no plot, has more of epic narrative interest in it than of authentic drama. As the prologues suggest, it offers a sequence of historical tableaux.

The story of King Lear also was dramatized by some apprentice hand before Shakespeare began to work on it. *The True Chronicle History of King Lear* borrowed material from old ballads and from the *Historia Regum Britanniae* (History of the Kings of Britain) by Geoffrey of Monmouth (twelfth century). As it was produced in 1593, it was probably known to Shakespeare, but again he added material drawn from Holinshed. This time, however, the mature genius of Shakespeare completely transformed the material. The fact that the story was well known did not deter him from making important changes in it. For example, Lear in the chronicles is finally restored to his kingdom. Had Shakespeare been faithful to them, he could not have written that agonizing last scene, in which the daemonic tragedy of Lear's life ends with the pathos of weakness: "Pray you, undo this button." So the story has been transformed into a parable of human life in general, but of life raised by poetic imagination to the sublimity of a tempest, which wears itself out and ends with a sigh. In short the chronicle play had matured and become tragedy.

There are other writers who represent intermediate stages in the evolution of the historical play. George Peele's *The Chronicle of Edward I* (1590), and Christopher Marlowe's *Edward II*, produced very soon afterwards, stand somewhere between the embryonic types mentioned above and the work of Shakespeare. Peele's play shows a definite advance in dramatic conception over *The Troublesome Reigne of King John*, and it was written without too much consideration for historical accuracy. He managed the heroic line with careless ease, but fell far short of Marlowe in dramatic power. Marlowe's play comes within measurable distance of the greatness of Shakespeare's historical plays, and in particular challenges comparison with the latter's *Richard II*. The pathos of the scene in which King Edward is murdered is indeed far more affecting than the parallel scene in which

King Richard is the victim. In characterization, dramatic interest and imaginative intensity generally, there is little to choose between the two plays. In this instance the superior merit of Shakespeare is in the structural unity of his play.

In a century when so much store was set by classical learning it was unlikely that the rich quarry of ancient history, Greek and Roman, would be neglected by writers in search of subjects for historical plays. The principal classical influences came, as we have seen, from Seneca in respect of tragedy and from Plautus and Terence in respect of comedy. Their plots were sometimes borrowed direct (e.g. *Comedy of Errors*) and sometimes by way of some Italian adaptation (e.g. *Taming of the Shrew*). Moreover, the recent history of France, Spain, and the Netherlands offered in abundance themes capable of being presented in terms of romantic drama. Marlowe's last play *The Massacre at Paris* (1593) dealt with the aftermath of the events of the Eve of St. Bartholomew, when the Huguenots were destroyed. It was a throw-back to the style of the earlier chronicle plays, written with a pen dipped in anti-papal venom. But the personages of the play were actual and the play had a strong topical interest.

This kind of historical portraiture on the stage was the peculiar contribution of George Chapman (1559–1634) to drama. He was a humanist, hardly less steeped in classical learning than Ben Jonson, but he used his materials as freely as had Shakespeare in adapting Plutarch for the theatre. In *Bussy d'Ambois* and its sequel *The Revenge of Bussy d'Ambois* Chapman took a theme from contemporary French political life, which supplied at the same time many of the elements of a Senecan tragedy: ambition, murder and retribution. The style is forced and rhetorical, in accordance with Chapman's view of what was seemly in tragic drama, namely: "material instruction, elegant and sententious excitation to virtue and deflection from her contrary being the soul, limbs and limits of an authentic tragedy."

Shakespeare's Early Plays

Having attached himself to one or more of the acting companies about 1587, Shakespeare was soon busy refurbishing or amplifying old plays which were already in the repertory. Himself an actor, he brought to the task a sense of "theatre" which belonged only in a lesser degree to the "University wits" such as Robert Greene. It was Greene who complained that the prestige of the work of his friends, hitherto unquestioned, was being challenged by an interloper, whom he described as an "upstart crow, beautified with our feathers."

To distinguish the hands of various playwrights in a composite work is a matter of considerable difficulty, but critics are generally agreed in certain cases, For example, *Titus Andronicus*, an imitation of Seneca, though included in the Shakespeare canon, is known to be in fact only a revision of some amateur effort, designed to cater for the popular taste for horrors; and *Henry VI*, Part I, was also a touched-up version of an earlier play. The part which is most certainly Shakespeare's is the Temple Garden scene. By 1594, when *Henry VI*, Parts 2 and 3, were written, the poet had already discovered his own powers in the dramatic presentation of history. These plays followed *Richard II* and *Richard III*, and in the latter the influence of Marlowe is clearly visible.

The other apprentice work of Shakespeare in the early fifteen-nineties comprises *The Comedy of Errors*, *Love's Labour's Lost*, *The Two Gentlemen of Verona*, and *The Taming of the Shrew* (part only). In all these plays the lyrical impulse is more strongly marked than the dramatic. The song-dialogue of Spring and Winter which brings *Love's Labour's Lost* to a close with "When daisies pied and violets blue," and "When icicles hang by the wall," and the exquisite "Who is Sylvia?" in *The Two Gentlemen* bear witness to this. The lyrical touch is prominent also in *Romeo and Juliet* and in *A Midsummer Night's Dream*, both plays of this period, but showing nevertheless an obvious advance in dramatic skill.

Shakespeare's Maturing Genius

The second main division (approximately 1594–1600) comprises a more highly developed kind of history and comedy. The histories are *King John*, *Henry IV*, Parts 1 and 2, *Henry V*, and *Julius Caesar*. The comedies are *The Merry Wives of Windsor*, *Much Ado about Nothing*, *As You Like It*, *Twelfth Night*, and *The Merchant of Venice*, all gay with a rollicking humour, nimble with witty dialogue, and except for the darker passages in *Much Ado*, vital and confident in outlook. They offer us no deep problems to solve, but in richness of fancy, in close observation of character and in the brilliant texture of their poetry they are without rival in the dramatic literature of the world.

Shakespeare's Tragic Period

Some kind of a change came over the poet about the year 1600. His spirit became troubled, his outlook clouded. The malaise may have been due to personal troubles, or it may have been a result of the general climate of feeling at the turn of the century. Whatever the cause, the attention of the dramatist became fixed for some years (1600–09) on the profounder issues of human life. These were the years of the strong tragedies—*Hamlet, Othello, Macbeth,* and *King Lear,* and of the dark comedies—*Measure for Measure* and *All's Well that Ends Well.*

To this period also belongs *Troilus and Cressida,* which has been called "a comedy of disillusion," wherein the glittering pageant of chivalric romance is exposed as a sham. The play depicts the vulnerability of the chivalric ideal in the face of reality. The tragedy lies in the inability of the romantic to endure those imperfections which he cannot alter. The disparity between illusion and actuality shatters his mind—"there is no rule in unity itself."

The tragic mood of Shakespeare found still further expression in *Antony and Cleopatra, Coriolanus,* and *Timon of Athens,* for which the themes were borrowed from North's *Plutarch. Julius Caesar,* the earlier Roman play, was also based on Plutarch but it was less complex in its problems and characterization, although the tragedy of Brutus was also a tragedy of character. The three later Roman plays are concerned with the dire consequences which attend a moral defect or taint. In Corolianus it is overweening pride; in Antony it is—

The love of Love and her soft hours,

a gratification of the senses completely at variance with the ancient Roman idea of *virtus,* or moral excellence. Each of the four supreme tragic masterpieces has in it something pointing to the same principle, although it would be wrong to suggest that they can be reduced to so simple a formula of construction. Thus Othello's frank nature suffers excess, and deteriorates into culpable credulity; Macbeth is highly suggestible to the temptations of ambition; Lear commits a wilful folly by insisting unduly on his demand that Cordelia should declare her affection for him in extravagant terms; Hamlet's weakness is that of indecision.

Shakespeare: The Last Phase

The last phase of Shakespeare's work gave us the four romances: *Pericles* (which is of doubtful authenticity), *Cymbeline, The Winter's Tale,* and *The Tempest.* He wrote these plays between 1608 and 1612, when the mental discords which had affected him had been resolved. He had achieved the peace which comes from wholeness. The tenseness had gone, and his mood was now serene and grave. Accordingly he turned from tragedy to plays wherein he could express comedy, realism, phantasy, playful irony, "airy nothings," lyric passion, and mellow wisdom, mingled in a universe where factual reality counted for nothing. *The Winter's Tale* spanned twenty years, *The Tempest* was the depiction of the events of a single afternoon.

Professor Edward Dowden, writing of these last plays[1] remarks—

> When a man has attained some high and luminous table-land of joy or of renouncement, when he has really transcended self, or when some one of the everlasting, virtuous powers of the world—duty or sacrifice, or the strength of anything higher than himself—has assumed authority over him, forthwith a strange, pathetic, ideal light is shed over all beautiful things in the lower world which has been abandoned.

Over the enchanted island of *The Tempest* all objects are suffused in this luminosity. The action is completed within the three hours of brightest daylight, and Prospero's agent is Ariel, the air-spirit, and the embodiment of the poetic imagination. In the serene atmosphere of the play (and the same can be said of the other late plays) hatred and evil cannot exist. The prevailing note is of reconciliation and forgiveness. It is as if Shakespeare himself had achieved a harmonious adjustment of the warring impulses of his own being and now walked on the "high table-land" of a life purged of all bitterness.

Shakespeare's Themes and Plots

It is above all things in his power of creating character that Shakespeare's dramatic genius stands out so distinctly. To originality in the invention of plot and incident he was indifferent. He not only borrowed themes and situations from earlier books and plays, but used them repeatedly. For example, the familiar motive of lost children being restored to their parents is used in all three of the late Romances; while reconciliations after estrangements or misunderstandings are to be found in many of the plays: e.g. the reuniting of the lovers in *Midsummer Night's Dream*, also of Oberon and Titania; Brutus and Cassius; of Henry IV and Prince Hal; of Beatrice and Benedict; of Orlando and Oliver; of Bertram and Helena; of Claudio and Isabella; of Lear and Cordelia; and of Prospero and Antonio. The devices of mistaken identity, substitution and disguise are used over and over again, as in *The Comedy of Errors*, where twin masters are served by twin servants; *Twelfth Night*, where Viola masquerades as a page and resembles Sebastian, her twin brother; Rosalind in *As You Like*

---

[1] *Shakespeare: His Mind and Art*, p. 414.

It, putting on "a swashing and a martial outside"; Edgar's disguise as a peasant in *King Lear*; Portia's hoax in the Trial Scene of *The Merchant of Venice*, and so forth. Most of these impersonations involve the wildest improbabilities, and it is because of these inherent weaknesses of plot, that when the time comes for a play to be brought to a close, we so often find a *dénouement* which is psychologically absurd. This lack of psychological truth is shown also in other ways, e.g. the holding up of the action for indulgence in word-quibbles, rhetorical speeches or overwrought metaphor.

It is all the more remarkable that the plays should triumph over every such failure of plausibility and consistency. They were redeemed by Shakespeare's practical view of his function as a dramatic artist. Being essentially a man of the theatre, an actor-manager whose plays must needs "pay," he would obviously not have used incidents and situations more than once unless they continued to give delight to his audience. It has also to be remembered that dramatic truth is not the same thing as the truth which guides our actions in ordinary life. What takes place upon the stage is not to be judged except by a logic of its own. The improbabilities and incongruities are accepted as part of the world of make-believe. Shakespeare possessed a stage-intuition which carried him to success over all such obstacles. A more conscious artist might have hesitated to take the risks, and might have found himself bogged down in pedantry and dullness. Shakespeare's art was inspired and confident: he strode out without hesitation over the most difficult places.

Shakespeare's Romanticism

The only play of Shakespeare in which there is any observance of the unities of time, place and action is *The Tempest*, which in other respects is as far removed from the classical convention as may be imagined. He was essentially a romantic, concerned with the depiction of human nature in its infinite variety, including not only its central manifestations but its marginal aspects also. Here we find tragedy and comedy, as in real life, in close contact, each gaining in significance because of the nearness of the other. The classical insistence on the inviolability of the "kinds" had no meaning for Shakespeare. Romanticism implies variety and even a measure of excess.

Elizabethan audiences were avid for *incident* on the stage, a circumstance which may help to explain why it is that in one play there are often two or even more actions carried on side by side. In *The Merchant of Venice*, for example, besides the main Shylock-Antonio theme we have the Casket story (itself the plot of many an earlier play), the Lorenzo-Jessica romance and the subordinate Gratiano-Nerissa by-play. A play constructed in this way, with the interest constantly veering or being left in suspense, is an altogether different thing from the Greek play which moves on relentlessly to its resolution. Any claim which Shakespeare makes to excellence of construction arises from his skill in thus merging separate actions into a play which yet stands as a united work of art.

His romanticism is to be seen also in his mingling of elements drawn from different conventions, the realistic with the supernatural, the aristocratic and heroic with the plebeian, the idealistic with the commonplace, the imaginative with the pedantic. It is this breadth of treatment which gives to the plays their extraordinary fidelity to nature, so that we accept them as the supreme expressions of the spirit of humanity in literary art—

> What a piece of work is man! how noble in reason! how infinite in faculty! in form and moving how express and admirable!

Development of Form

Shakespeare is remarkable among our poets for the developing mastery of metrical art which distinguishes his verse in successive periods. This advance in technique runs parallel to the maturing of his skill in characterization, and to the enlargement of his conception of the potentialities of drama for the discussion of human problems. Our present purpose, however, is to touch on some aspects of his versification.

The analysis of Shakespeare's metrical forms has an interest for theorists of prosody, but it can also throw light upon the chronology of the plays. The evidence of prosodic changes bears out in a remarkable way the conclusions reached on other kinds of evidence, so that there has resulted a fair consensus of critical opinion regarding the dates of the plays and poems.

An examination of the following lines from an early play (*Two Gentlemen of Verona*) will reveal certain immaturities in metre—

> He wonder'd that your lordship
> Would suffer him to spend his youth at home,
> While other men, of slender reputation,
> Put forth their sons to seek preferment out:
> Some to the wars, to try their fortune there;
> Some to discover islands far away;
> Some to the studious universities.

> For any or for all these exercises,
> He said that Proteus your son was meet;
> And did request me to importune you
> To let him spend his time no more at home,
> Which would be great impeachment to his age
> In having known no travel in his youth.

It will be seen that the lines are mostly "end-stopped," that is, there is a tendency for the meaning to end with the line, which is both a sense-unit and a prosodic unit. The pauses within the line are few and not strongly marked and the lines usually end with strongly-stressed syllables. The rhythm lacks variety, the metrical pattern being hammered out with scarcely any inversions of stress except the repeated "some to." These and the three hypermetric syllables of the first, third and eighth lines are the only aberrant features to relieve the monotony of the iambic pentameters. The stresses are too even for any melodic quality to emerge. There is no rhyme in this passage, but rhyming couplets are frequent in the plays of the earlier period.

The following extract from a late play, *The Tempest*, will serve to mark the great changes which the blank verse of Shakespeare underwent during his lifetime—

> Bravely the figure of this harpy hast thou
> Perform'd, my Ariel; a grace it had, devouring.
> Of my instruction hast thou nothing bated
> In what thou hadst to say: so, with good life
> And observation strange, my meaner ministers
> Their several kinds have done. My high charms work,
> And these, mine enemies, are all knit up
> In their distractions: they now are in my power,
> And in these fits I leave them, while I visit
> Young Ferdinand, whom they suppose is drowned,
> And his and mine lov'd darling.

Here the sense runs on freely from line to line. The breaks come more frequently within the line than at the end. Several lines end with lightly-stressed syllables, the caesura falls variously, and a large proportion of the lines are hypermetric. The iambic pattern is constantly changed to produce a far higher quality of modulation and harmony than is to be observed in the earlier passage quoted. In the late plays, rhyme is rare, except of course in the songs.

The evolution of the verse-form thus shows a growth of freedom, and a greater integration of the thing said with the way in which it is said. The deeper spiritual perceptions of the poet are matched with language adequate for their expression. In the first passage, the thought is spun out thinly over a number of lines with wearisome reiteration. In the second the meaning is closely packed.

SUGGESTIONS FOR FURTHER READING

G. WILSON KNIGHT: *The Wheel of Fire* (Methuen).

DOVER WILSON: *The Essential Shakespeare* (Cambridge Univ. Press).

EDWARD DOWDEN: *Shakespeare: His Mind and Art* (Routledge & Kegan Paul).

A. C. BRADLEY: *Shakespearean Tragedy* (Macmillan).

E. M. W. TILLYARD: *The Elizabethan World Picture* (Chatto & Windus).

LOGAN PEARSALL SMITH: *On Reading Shakespeare* (Constable).

SIR H. GRANVILLE-BARKER: *Prefaces to Shakespeare* (Sidgwick & Jackson).

F. S. BOAS: *Christopher Marlowe: a Biographical and Critical Study* (Oxford University Press).

G. B. HARRISON: *Introducing Shakespeare* (Penguin).

SECCOMBE AND ALLEN: *The Age of Shakespeare: II—Drama* (Bell).

SIR E. K. CHAMBERS: *The Elizabethan Stage* (4 vols) (Oxford Univ. Press).

CHAPTER XVII

POST-SHAKESPEARIAN DRAMA

AFTER the turn of the century and the passing of Elizabeth, the theatre continued to command popularity, although the Puritan opposition was stiffening. But taste was changing; the audiences were asking for stronger fare. In their attempts to give it to them the playwrights of the time certainly achieved many striking dramatic situations, and occasionally attained to the heights of poetry, but such touches of genius were fleeting, and the drama of the time, other than the later work of Shakespeare, was lacking in the organic unity which any product of supreme art must possess. The occasional excellences (e.g. of Jonson's *Volpone* and *The Alchemist* and of Webster's *White Devil*) are balanced by crudenesses; passages of lyrical beauty are succeeded by rank declamation; the tenderness of love by the extravagances of passion; innocent comedy by the grotesque and the repulsive. It is as if there were a lack of control to restrain and to discipline thought and feeling in the interest of a totality of artistic effect.

Marks of the decline in standards can be discerned in three directions: in construction, in characterization, and in verse-form. Too often plot construction shows carelessness in detail, and a want of coherence. There are effective episodes but not structural growth. Characterization is deficient in light and shade and is conceived of as "datum," something "given," which it is the function of the play to sustain and to reinforce. Blank verse becomes so loose that it often degenerates almost into prose.

Ben Jonson

Shakespeare, notwithstanding his pre-eminence, founded no school, whereas Ben Jonson, who had a coherent critical theory of drama, did so. Not only until the closing of the theatres in 1642, but after their re-opening in 1660, his influence was powerful.

A profound classical scholar, whose mind was cast in a critical and dogmatic mould, he took up an attitude of protest against the formlessness of most of the Elizabethan dramas. Though he honoured the memory of Shakespeare "on this side idolatry," he was not blind to his defects—

> I remember the players have often mentioned it as an honour to Shakespeare that in his writing (whatsoever he penned) he never blotted out a line. My answer hath been, 'Would he had blotted out a thousand.' . . . His wit was in his own power; would the rule of it had been so, too! Many times he fell into those things, could not escape laughter. . . . But he redeemed his vices with his virtues.

Jonson poured scorn on the romantic as well as on the chronicle plays, with their lack of proportion and restraint, their ridiculous absurdities and their creaking mechanisms.

His own theory of comedy was set out in the well-known prologue to *Every Man in his Humour*—

> To make a child, now swaddled, to proceed
> Man, and then shoot up, in one beard, and weed,
> Past three score years: or, with three rusty swords,
> And help of some few foot-and-half-foot words,
> Fight over York, and Lancaster's long jars,
> And in the tyring-house bring wounds, to scars.
> He rather prays, you will be pleased to see
> One such to-day, as other plays should be;
> Where neither Chorus wafts you o'er the seas;
> Nor creaking throne comes down, the boys to please;
> Nor nimble squib is seen, to make afeard
> The gentlewomen; nor rolled bullet heard
> To say, it thunders; nor tempestuous drum
> Rumbles, to tell you when the storm doth come;
> But deeds, and language, such as men do use;
> And persons, such as Comedy would choose,
> When she would show an image of the times,
> And sport with human follies, not with crimes.

Jonson was clearly resolved to abjure cheap romantic effects and to keep his art within the limits set by reason and common sense. By so doing he aimed at achieving unity of effect, if not the "unities." He looked around him for his themes and characters, and created a comedy out of actualities. His genius was satiric rather than sympathetic, and his attitude to life that of an intellectual.

Jonson was not the inventor of the stock figure of drama which is called "the humour." It was known, as we have seen, in the *Commedia dell'Arte* and there are numerous examples in Shakespeare of clear-cut, static types alongside the dynamic characters, in the creation of which he was supreme. The word "humour" was originally a medical term signifying a propensity or affection. Character or disposition was thought to be determined by the predominance of one of four physiological elements of the body, viz. blood, choler, phlegm, and melancholy: producing respectively the sanguine, the choleric, the phlegmatic and the melancholic temperaments. When these elements or humours were mixed in due proportion, a perfect disposition resulted.[1]

The chief contribution which Ben Jonson made to dramatic theory and practice was to construct plays based on the "humours." He was an acute observer of social manners, and the main interest of his plays for us is in character rather than in plot. Every master-passion which he personifies is displayed in the light of a wide variety of realistic dramatic situations, the whole conveying a pungent criticism of society. In this way Jonson created a new type of comedy, distinctive in method, scope, and purpose. Although he drew upon Aristophanes, Plautus and the Italian theatre of the Renaissance for many of his stock figures, he placed them in a contemporary setting and added numerous types which came straight off the London streets. Realism in Shakespeare's plays was episodic rather than structural. His genius was essentially romantic. Jonson represents the breaking away from the romantic tradition.

Ben Jonson's five great comedies, written between 1598 and 1614, were *Every Man in His Humour*, *Volpone*, *The Silent Woman*, *The Alchemist*, and *Bartholomew Fair*. The scene of *Volpone* is Venice, but for the rest the setting is English. In making use of the figures and scenes of contemporary, and especially London, life, Jonson was staking out a new territory for comic drama. In exploiting this material he was followed by Thomas Dekker, Thomas Middleton, and Thomas Heywood.

The Contemporary Scene in Drama

Thomas Dekker (1570–1632) was a prolific writer, who in addition to his many plays wrote a considerable number of pamphlets in a vein of good-humoured satire. He knew and loved the London scene which was the background for his best known comedy, *The Shoemaker's Holiday*. In this and other plays he presents such a faithful account of the life around him, and especially the low life of the city,

---

[1] Antony's words over the fallen Brutus will be recalled.
> "His life was gentle; and the elements
> So mixed in him, that Nature might stand up
> And say to all the world, 'This was a man'."
> Shakespeare: *Julius Caesar*, V. 5

that he has been compared with Charles Dickens, whom he resembled in the breadth of his social sympathies. Dekker was a great collaborator, and at times joined with Webster, Middleton, Massinger, and Ford in writing for the stage. With Ben Jonson, on the other hand, he was involved in a long quarrel, and his play *Satiro-Mastix, or The Untrussing of the Humorous Poet*, was written as a burlesque of the Jonsonian style.

Thomas Middleton (1570–1627) was also a Londoner and a city official. His diverting comedies were extremely popular. He was resourceful in comic invention and his gallery of comic types can be compared with Chaucer's: many of them came from the underworld, the cheats, bullies, and gamblers, the bawds and highway-robbers mingling with over-fed magnates and shabby-genteel folk. Among the best of his comedies are *A Mad World My Masters*, *A Trick to Catch the Old One*, and *A Chaste Maid in Cheapside*.

Thomas Heywood (1575–1650) is the third of this group of writers of domestic and topical drama. His strength was in the portrayal of people of the middle station in society, and he wrote in a mood of quiet sentiment rather than with the gusto of Middleton. *A Woman Killed with Kindness* is a simple story of a happy home life destroyed by the betrayal of the husband by the wife, her removal, the onset of remorse, and forgiveness at the point of death. Though there is much in the character-portrayal which is psychologically unconvincing, a gentle spirit plays over the scene, and there is no hint of the Senecan formula of revengeful violence. When calling Heywood (who wrote in blank verse) a "prose Shakespeare," Charles Lamb implied that though his range was wide, his inspiration was weak. The first of his enormous output of plays—he claimed to have written 220 of them— was the extravaganza called *The Four 'Prentices of London*, which is of interest because it occasioned the writing of *The Knight of the Burning Pestle* by Beaumont and Fletcher, in which the preposterous alarums and excursions of the dramatic fare served out to the London apprentices is parodied.

Jacobean and Caroline Tragedies and Tragi-comedies

Any account of post-Shakespearian tragic drama must begin with Ben Jonson's two Roman plays: *Sejanus* (1603) and *Catiline* (1611), so classified even though they appeared while Shakespeare was still writing. Shakespeare carried over the Elizabethan tradition into the Jacobean era, but among his late contemporaries there was a new spirit evident, less buoyant, less self-possessed, and more introspective. Ben Jonson's learning lay too heavy on his spirit to enable him to rise to the heights of the greatest poetry. There was far more scholarship in *Sejanus* and *Catiline* than in *Julius Caesar* or *Coriolanus*, but far less art. The poetry was clogged by erudition, and though there was as much of Roman *gravitas*, there was but little *humanitas*. Notwithstanding his dominance over the literary coteries of London, Jonson represented no new method of tragedy, as he did of comedy, and his partiality for the classical rules found small echo in other writers of tragedy during the early Stuart period.

The further history of the tragedy of revenge may be traced in the work of John Marston, Cyril Tourneur, and John Webster. With the tragic motive there was usually associated an element of comic satire. Hence arose the tragi-comedy, which may be regarded as the typical product of the Jacobean age of drama. Thus Marston's *Antonio and Mellida*, written in two parts, has in the first a vein of romantic intrigue while the second is compact of tragic horror. *The Malcontent* combines a coarse and cynical humour with the motive of a blood feud. Tourneur's *The Revenger's Tragedy* and *The Atheist's Tragedy* suggest by their titles the pervading gloom, thickened with every circumstance of crime and perversion: murder, torture, and suicide, lust, and insanity, and such *Grand Guignol* effects as scaffolds, skulls, corpses, graveyards, midnight funerals, and female ghosts, to sustain the central theme of vengeance. Even so, there was a comic sub-plot.

With John Webster's *The White Devil* and *The Duchess of Malfi*, we reach the apotheosis of the tragedy of revenge. Notwithstanding defects of construction and weaknesses in characterization, such as were common among the Jacobean dramatists, these two plays show an imaginative grasp and an intensity of poetic feeling which lift them up very close to the Shakespearian level. The melodramatic horrors are still there, but they are transformed by the creative genius of the poet into artistic truth, and both works achieve a spiritual unity.

Beaumont and Fletcher

The famous collaboration of Francis Beaumont (1584–1616) and John Fletcher (1579–1625) lasted from 1607 to 1616. Each wrote also separately from the other, and Fletcher in particular had many other collaborators. They have in association an important place in literary history because of the popularity they achieved, not only among their contemporaries, but throughout the following century. Nearly all their plots were of their own invention, and having an acute sense of theatre they managed with great skill to provide effective dramatic situations and telling climaxes. The devices of surprise and suspense are worked to the full; and in the search for novelty, the ingredients of tragi-comedy are for ever being mixed in different proportions. The romantic or realistic elements are introduced, not as in Shakespearian plays to give roundness and depth to tragic situations, but rather to enable complicated situations to be built up and afterwards surprisingly and satisfactorily resolved.

Such complexities as we usually find in the plays of Beaumont and Fletcher arise from situations artificially contrived, and have nothing in common with those which lie in human character. The figures in the action are stock types: the soldier of fortune, the sentimental lover, the forlorn maid, the scheming woman, the pimp, the tyrant, the foppish courtier, the low-life comic, and so on. They are more like puppets than like real people. Yet the verse which is put into their mouths flows on with effortless grace; it is based on the cadences of normal speech, and answers to the Augustan test of "correctness." "I am apt to believe," said Dryden, in his *Essay of Dramatic Poesy* (1668), "that the English language in them arrived to its highest perfection . . . Their plays are now the most pleasant and frequent entertainments of the stage: two of theirs being acted through the year for one of Shakespeare's or Jonson's: the reason is, because there is a certain gaiety in their comedies, and pathos in their serious plays, which suits generally with all men's humours. Shakespeare's language is likewise a little obsolete, and Ben Jonson's wit comes short of theirs."

The general influence of Beaumont and Fletcher on English drama was, in respect of comedy, to enlarge the "comedy of humours" into a "comedy of manners." In respect of tragedy, it was to turn it into romantic and heroic courses.

Typical plays written in collaboration are *A King and No King*, *The Maid's Tragedy*, *Philaster*, and *The Knight of the Burning Pestle*, the first three being romantic dramas and the fourth, as we have seen, a burlesque on the excesses of romantic drama. *The Woman Hater*, which is pure comedy, is Beaumont's own work. Fletcher's individual output of plays was far greater and includes *The Faithful Shepherdess* (a rhyming pastoral play), *Wit Without Money* (a witty comedy of London life), and *The Captain* (a comedy of manners in an Italian setting).

SUGGESTIONS FOR FURTHER READING

U. M. Ellis-Fermor: *The Jacobean Drama* (Methuen).
L. C. Knights: *Drama and Society in the Age of Jonson* (Chatto & Windus).
F. S. Boas: *An Introduction to Stuart Drama* (Oxford Univ. Press).
Enid Welsford: *The Court Masque* (Cambridge Univ. Press).
T. S. Eliot: *Elizabethan Essays* (Faber & Faber).
E. H. C. Oliphant: *Shakespeare and his Fellow Dramatists* (Pitman).

CHAPTER XVIII

RESTORATION AND
EIGHTEENTH-CENTURY DRAMA

THE ordinance for the closing of the theatres, issued by the authority of the Long Parliament in 1642, had not resulted in the total suppression of stage plays in England, and further and stricter prohibitions were from time to time issued. Although magistrates were given power to beset suspected playhouses and to apprehend and sentence to public whippings any actors who were found— members of the audience were fined five shillings—surreptitious performances still continued to be given at fairs and remote taverns, and even sometimes, by connivance, in the great houses of the nobility. Before the end of the Commonwealth period Sir William D'Avenant found a way to circumvent the law by skilfully interpolating spectacle and musical entertainment into dramatic programmes, and thus, under the guise of Opera, was able to minister to the popular craving for theatrical entertainment. In 1656, at Rutland House, he produced *The Siege of Rhodes*, a "Representation by the Art of Perspective in Scenes and the Story sung in Recitative Music."

In so doing, D'Avenant achieved three important things. He carried on our ancient dramatic tradition; he introduced scenery into the theatre, and he pointed the way to the heroic drama of the Restoration. His introduction of scenery had the further effect of modifying stage architecture, the acting space being now withdrawn from the pit except for an "apron," so that spectators could no longer sit on all three sides of it. The proscenium curtain was still placed well back, but it was seldom used except for spectacular effects, and the action took place for the most part on the "apron." The new theatres were roofed in and lit with candles.

One of the first acts of the Restoration Parliament was to renew the licences of the pre-Commonwealth theatres and to grant patents to newly formed companies, such as D'Avenant's "Duke of York's Company," which took over a recently erected playhouse in Lincoln's Inn Fields. In the repertory of these theatres, the most popular favourites were, as we have seen, the plays of Beaumont and Fletcher. Shakespeare, too, was included, though often subject to violent adaptation. *Romeo and Juliet* became a comedy; *Macbeth* received "alterations, additions, and new songs;" in *The Tempest* (revised by Dryden) a sister is provided for Caliban, and Miranda loses her innocence.

The Theatre and Society

That such things should have been possible is a clear indication that there was after 1660 a new outlook on life, which could not but be reflected in the drama of the time. Of all the arts, drama is that which is most conditioned by the social *milieu*. The age was deficient in poetic feeling; it expressed itself naturally in prose, and even when verse forms were used, the themes were chosen and their treatment determined in an intellectual-critical rather than in a poetical-emotional spirit. The taste of society was aristocratic and the prevailing fashions and etiquette foreign and extravagant; the moral tone of the theatre-going public was frivolous and cynical. It is not to be supposed that the outlook of the whole nation was thus affected; there was always a hard core of Puritanic sentiment which abhorred what it considered to be the excesses of the arbiters of fashion and opinion. But, as is generally the case, drama easily took the imprint of the prevailing social manners. The theatre attracted chiefly a sophisticated and raffish section of the public. It ceased for a time to exercise a universal appeal, as it had done in Elizabethan times. For over two centuries, the attitude of the middle and lower classes of society to play-acting remained on the whole hostile, a fact which, by turning the stage into sterile courses, profoundly retarded the development of theatrical art in Britain.

At a time when fancy was not free because the feeling for poetry was inhibited, and imagination was regarded as vulgar "enthusiasm" by the dictators of the social code, the writers turned inevitably to the portrayal of actualities. But these were the actualities of the lives of the fashionable coterie only, and do not therefore give us a picture of the whole nation. The characteristic dramatic form was the Comedy of Manners, reflecting the gaiety, foppery, insolence and intrigue of an aristocratic group, which political changes had suddenly brought into prominence and authority. When we remember that outside London there was very little serious dramatic art, and that in London for many years it was confined to one or at the most two theatres we can the better understand how narrow the basis was.

The general tone of this drama was admirably summed up by Shelley—

> Comedy loses its ideal universality; wit succeeds to humour; we laugh from self-complacency and triumph, instead of pleasure; malignity, sarcasm and contempt, succeed to sympathetic merriment; we hardly laugh, but we smile. Obscenity, which is ever blasphemy against the divine beauty of life, becomes, from the very veil which it assumes, more active if less disgusting: it is a monster for which the corruption of society for ever brings forth new food, which it devours in secret.

The new trends in comedy are to be noted first in Dryden's *Wild Gallant* (1663) which, although it proved to be a relative failure, Pepys saying it was "as poor a thing as ever I saw in my life," showed a skilful contrivance of light intrigue in the manner of the Spanish drama. Etheredge's *The Comical Revenge or Love in a Tub* (1664), adopted the rhymed heroic verse which Dryden too had used in his second play, *The Rival Ladies* (1664). Etheredge's method may well be described in his own words, taken from the prologue to a later play: *The Man of Mode or Sir Fopling Flutter* (1676).

> 'Tis by your follies that we players thrive,
> As the physicians by diseases live:
> And as each year some new distemper reigns
> Whose friendly poison helps t'increase their gains,
> So among you there starts up every day
> Some new unheard-of fool for us to play.

The Comical Revenge had a mixed reception, since on the whole its airy, graceful wit showed rather too delicate a taste for the times. It stands in our literary history as the first of a type of classical comedy modelled on Molière. Etheredge was closely followed by Wycherley, whose career as a playwright was as brilliant as it was brief. Between 1672 and 1677 his four comedies were produced, of which two, namely, *The Country Wife* and *The Plain Dealer*, are the most typical products of the comedy properly called Restoration. Wycherley's merit was in his vitality and constructive skill, and it was by virtue of these qualities that his comedies continued to hold the stage for a century and a half, and have now come back into popularity.

Vanbrugh, Farquhar, and Congreve, usually classed with the playwrights mentioned above as Restoration dramatists, belong in fact to a later generation; they wrote during the closing years of the seventeenth and in the early eighteenth century, when the Glorious Revolution was consummated, and when the mood of the reign of Charles II was already passing. Whiggism had been born, and as the mercantile classes grew in wealth and influence, the social atmosphere underwent a gradual change.

The most gifted among all the post-Commonwealth dramatists was William Congreve (1670–1729). It is a remarkable fact that all his plays were written before he was thirty years of age. The change in the public outlook as the century came to an end may be measured by the different reception accorded to his plays: *Love for Love* (1695) and *The Way of the World* (1700). The former was a triumphant success; the latter, though now considered to be his best play, was a failure. Two years before it was performed, Jeremy Collier's *Short View of the Immorality and Profaneness of the Stage* had appeared, a savage attack on the licentiousness of the theatre, to which, probably mistaking cause for effect, the author attributed the low moral tone of society. The strictures of Collier were answered by Dryden, who accepted them on the whole as justified, and by Congreve who, though he defended himself vigorously, forthwith renounced the stage in dudgeon.

Among the qualities which put Congreve at the head of this remarkable age of drama, and give him a claim to be considered the greatest master of pure comedy in English, his style is outstanding. Sir Edmund Gosse says of it: "No one, perhaps, in any country, has written prose for the stage with so assiduous a solicitude for style. Congreve balances, polishes, sharpens his sentences till they seem like a set of instruments prepared for an electrical experiment; the current is his unequalled wit." Unfortunately Congreve reflected in his work the lax standards of a particular generation of the theatre-going public and while, therefore, his plays are valuable social documents, they lack the universal appeal of dramatists who are inspired by a love of their fellow-kind. Congreve, by excluding from his plays, as Charles Lamb put it, "not only anything like a faultless character, but any pretensions to goodness or good feelings whatever," fails to qualify for a place among the greatest; yet there is no one to come between him and Molière.

Too much need not be read into judgments such as this of Lamb or that of Shelley quoted above. They were thoroughgoing Romantics, and were pronouncing on work which belonged to the classical tradition. But the existence of these judgments is itself an evidence of the vicissitudes of literary taste, and so they have their value for the student of literature. Restoration comedy is to-day in considerable demand again, and many successful revivals have been staged in recent years.

The Heroic Convention in Tragedy

The romantic genius of Shakespeare and many of his contemporaries had seen no incongruity in mingling tragic and comic elements on the stage. They chose to derive their principles of dramatic composition from observation of life as it was lived around them, rather than from classical rules. But it was otherwise with the critical minds of the Restoration playwrights, many of whom had, during their French exile in the Commonwealth days, been conditioned by the theatre in Paris to prefer logic and correctness to what they considered to be the bizarre products of eccentric genius. Reason, no less than good breeding, put an emphasis on "form," whether expressed in conduct or in art. For that reason the century which began in 1660 is remarkable in our social history as an age of exquisite manners, superficial maybe, but having the merit of establishing a standard of urbanity and social discipline.

In the drama of the Restoration we notice first of all the firm line drawn between tragedy and comedy, precisely as it was drawn in France between Corneille and Racine on the one hand and Molière on the other. Next we notice that the tragedy is on the "heroic" level, "an imitation in little," as Dryden said, of an heroic poem. The themes chosen were of epic magnitude, the heroes and heroines figures of superhuman stature. The purpose was didactic: "to advance the characters of virtue in the shapes of valour and conjugal love." It was in accordance with the heroic convention derived from France that "heroic metre" should be used, that is the rhymed five-foot iambic couplet, the nearest possible English equivalent to the French rhymed alexandrines. Dryden defended his use of rhyme in breach of the English tradition by declaring: "Blank verse is acknowledged to be too low for a poem, nay more, for a paper of verses; but if too low for an ordinary sonnet, how much more for tragedy?"

Reference has already been made to the hold which the operatic convention had upon the English stage in 1660. This was partly due to the popularity of the earlier masques and partly due to the hybrid stage performances which D'Avenant had devised. Operatic technique calls for declamation rather than dialogue, and for rhapsody rather than natural expression. Heroic tragedy adopted to a great extent the bombast and exaggeration of opera, and used sensational effects whenever possible. There was no realistic characterization and, in contrast to the tragedy which springs from the observation of life, the endings were invariably happy and virtue was always rewarded.

Dryden

The principal practitioner of, and apologist for, heroic tragedy was Dryden. Under his leadership, it occupied the stage almost exclusively from 1660 to 1678. Then Dryden shifted his ground, dropping rhyme and questioning the validities of the "unities" in the conditions of the English stage. His play *Tyrannic Love* was his first important experiment in the heroic vein, and in *The Conquest of Granada* (1669) this type of play reached its culminating point. Dr. Johnson's judgment on this play will serve as a final summing up of the general character of the heroic convention—

> The two parts of *The Conquest of Granada* are written with a seeming determination to glut the public with dramatic wonders to exhibit in its highest elevation a theatrical meteor of incredible love and impossible valour, and to leave no room for a wilder flight to the extravagance of posterity. All the rays of romantic heat, whether amorous or warlike, glow in Almanzor by a kind of concentration. He is above all laws; he is exempt from all restraints; he ranges the world at will, and governs wherever he appears. He fights without inquiring the cause, and loves in spite of the obligations of justice and of prohibition from the dead. Yet the scenes are, for the most part delightful; they exhibit a kind of illustrious depravity, and majestic madness, such as, if it is often despised, is often reverenced, and in which the ridiculous is mingled with the astonishing.

The condemnation of heroic tragedy was not in fact delayed until this common-sense verdict of Dr. Johnson, given a century later, for a similar judgment was pronounced by Dryden's own contemporaries. George Villiers, Duke of Buckingham, wrote a play *The Rehearsal*, produced in 1671, which was a burlesque of the contemporary grand manner in tragedy, but aimed particularly at Dryden. The parody stung him to a spirited retort, but heroic tragedy was never quite the same afterwards. *Aureng-Zebe*, Dryden's last play in this manner, shows the greater restraint and decorum of the French classical tragedies and there is, moreover, the evidence of the Prologue to indicate a change of outlook, in the belated recognition of the possibility that Shakespeare's method had its merits. He confesses that he—

> Grows weary of his long-loved mistress Rhyme,
> Passions too fierce to be in fetters bound,
> And Nature flies him like enchanted ground;
> What verse can do, he has performed in this,
> Which he presumes the most correct of his;
> But spite of all his pride, a secret shame
> Invades his breast at Shakespeare's sacred name.

Dryden's *All for Love* (1678) which is based on the story of *Anton*
and Cleopatra gave further proof of his altered attitude. In the preface
he writes: "In my style I have professed to imitate the divine Shakespeare; which that I might perform more freely, I have disencumbered
myself from rhyme." Regarding the "fabric of the play," he declare
that the unities of time, place, and action are "more exactly observed
than perhaps the English theatre requires." On the question of the
authority of the French theatre, Dryden again shows that his view
are changing: "I desire to be tried by the laws of my own country
for it seems unjust to me, that the French should prescribe here, til
they have conquered." Among other important indications of a
turning away from the heroic convention of tragedy is the fact that
Dryden here abjures the happy ending.

Eighteenth-century Tragedy

The history of tragic drama after the death of Dryden may be
summed up as a struggle, continuing for the space of two or three
generations, in which the English and the French traditions contended
for dominion in the theatre. The native tradition was the Elizabethan
represented mainly by revivals of Shakespeare and Beaumont and
Fletcher. It was a drama of strong situations, crowded with incident
involving a large number of players and many and rapid shifts of
scenes. The plots were intricate, often doubled; comedy often became
farce; tragedy admitted horror and violence on the open stage. The
dialogue was broken and the diction suffused with poetry and passion.
In general this was the romantic pattern. The French tradition,
represented most typically by Racine, was restrained in taste, circum-
scribed in theme, and avoided violent action on the stage. Since the
scene was rarely changed within the acts, the actors, who were few in
number, held the stage for long periods, and declaimed their speeches
with few interruptions. No comic business or sub-plot was allowed
to disturb the quiet unfolding of the single action. This was the
classical pattern. The characteristic quality of the English type of
drama was energy, that of the French type decorum.

Three plays which held the stage throughout the eighteenth century
and gave occasion for some of the greatest acting by Mrs. Siddons
and Garrick, may also be regarded as rallying points of the respective
critical theories. The heroic drama, of which Dryden had been the
protagonist, found its most perfect expression in Congreve's *The*
Mourning Bride (1697), but thereafter the convention ceased to attract

playwrights and it took on gradually the aspect of an out-moded form appealing only to a specialized public. The traditional English pattern of drama was exemplified in Otway's *Venice Preserved*, which was if anything more Elizabethan than the Elizabethans. The classical rules, as interpreted on the French stage, were upheld in Addison's *Cato* (1713), a frigidly correct play, choked with sententious moralizing, yet brilliantly successful in the theatre.

Neither of the two modes which survived the decline of heroic drama remained uninfluenced by the other. While Shakespeare came back steadily into repute, it happened too often that he was subjected to a process of pruning and "correction" to bring him closer into line with the dramatic proprieties. This continued until the time of Garrick, under whose influence the texts were restored. On the other hand French plays, e.g. those of Voltaire, were adapted for the English stage by the contrary process of breaking up the long orations and interpolating stage business.

The most important successors of Addison in the classical tradition were James Thomson, the author of *Sophonisba* (1729) (containing that notorious line: "O Sophonisba, Sophonisba O"), and Dr. Johnson, who wrote *Irene* (1749). These plays and many others in the same *genre* are altogether without dramatic interest. It was abundantly clear that in the department of tragic drama the creative impulse had spent itself. In no period were there more tragedies written, but a gulf opened out between literary and stage drama. The stage was occupied after the middle of the eighteenth century increasingly by revivals of plays in the older tradition; most of the numerous plays of the new tradition were thrown off as *jeux d'esprit*, not by specialists in the art of the theatre, but by men of letters whose main concern was with other kinds of writing.

The Drama of Sentiment

The process of disintegration continued throughout the eighteenth century, and far into the nineteenth. The theatre gradually ceased to be the plaything of the Court, and the middle-class prejudices against it tended to grow rather than to diminish as the evangelistic movement and the various societies for the reformation of manners gained influence. The audience was changing, and the theatres, which in Restoration days under royal patronage had fostered serious drama though for a narrow social class, became places of trivial amusement. They were often invaded by young bloods, the "routs of Vandals," intimidating the actors and wrecking plays which incurred their displeasure, while the revived practice of allowing spectators to be seated on the stage itself contributed nothing to the serious practice of the art of acting.

It is not surprising that in such conditions taste should deteriorate. Classicism and heroics were spent forces and comedy tended towards farce and pantomime, except for the growth of a specialized kind based on sentimentality or "sensibility," a cast of mind equally distant from the fashionable affectation of cynicism and from the coarseness of low-life.

We may seek an explanation of the growth of sentimentality in literature in the weakening of the authority of reason, and the return to nature, feeling and romance. This movement of revolt against reason is more easily considered in relation to the development of poetry and has already been discussed. The effect of this trend on drama may be seen in the work of playwrights from Steele to Sheridan. A passage from one of Goldsmith's essays sets out the matter from the standpoint of a critic—

> A new species of dramatic composition has been introduced under the name of sentimental comedy, in which the virtues of private life are exhibited, rather than the vices exposed; and the distresses rather than the faults of mankind make our interest in the piece. These comedies have had of late great success, perhaps from their novelty, and also from their flattering every man in his favourite foible. In these plays almost all the characters are good, and exceedingly generous: they are lavish enough of their *tin* money on the stage; and though they want humour, have abundance of sentiment and feeling. If they happen to have faults or foibles, the spectator is taught, not only to pardon, but to applaud them, in consideration of the goodness of their hearts; so that folly, instead of being ridiculed, is commended, and the comedy aims at touching our passions without the power of being truly pathetic.[1]

There was a strong flavour of sentimentality in the tragedy of Otway, *The Orphan* (1681), and in the three comedies of Steele, written in the opening years of the eighteenth century, *The Funeral*, *The Lying Lover* and *The Tender Husband*. In writing these, Steele avowed a moral purpose, and tried to prove that morality was not synonymous with dullness. His best play, produced in 1722, was *The Conscious Lovers*. The mixed reception given to Steele's plays indicated the divided mind of the age. His good feeling and tenderness suited the taste of one section, while another found in his sentimental passages a disposition to sermonize.

[1] Goldsmith: *Miscellaneous Essays, XXII.*

The comedy of sentiment was continued by Colley Cibber (Poet Laureate and the hero of Pope's *Dunciad*), Mrs. Centlivre and many others and, even in plays which cannot be said to fall into this class, moral sentiments are frequently interjected. The four virtues which Steele had praised in his dedication to *The Lying Lover*: Simplicity of mind, Good-nature, Friendship, and Honour, were always held up as guiding principles for conduct, while tears of pity and emotion flowed profusely. Sheridan, in *The Rivals*, parodied the sentimentalists in the character of Lydia Languish, and in *The Critic* he held up to ridicule the affectations of the stage in general, including the excesses of sentimentality. His *School for Scandal* was a reversion to the manner of Congreve but without his coarseness. Though there is no moralizing in the play, at any rate Sheridan made a concession to changing taste by arranging that the intrigue should be unsuccessful.

Goldsmith was also in revolt against the invasion of the stage by sentimentality, even though in his novel *The Vicar of Wakefield* and in his poem *The Deserted Village* there are clear marks of a sentimental attitude to life. But in his play *The Good-Natured Man*, by portraying the character of Honeywood as unadulterated "good-nature," he covers it with ridicule. The rollicking comedy *She Stoops to Conquer* is quite free of the current mannerism. Henry Fielding was another who parodied the dramatic fashion of the time. He caricatured heroic tragedy in *The Life and Death of Tom Thumb the Great*, while George Colman satirized the sentimental comedy in *Polly Honeycombe*.

During the last quarter of the century drama was moving towards its lowest ebb. Plays written to please the taste of particular cultural groups are always apt to mistake a part of human nature for the whole, and by too close an observance of a formula, to exaggerate to the point of imbecility. Thus heroic tragedy and the comedy of sentiment were in turn laughed out of court. The Elizabethan and Jacobean plays were revived from time to time, but the theatre could not thrive on the past. The theatres themselves, kept few in number by the operation of the licensing laws, tended to become larger and consequently to favour spectacular production and plays which demanded no subtlety of acting. In such conditions, farce, pantomime and opera flourished at the expense of legitimate drama.

SUGGESTIONS FOR FURTHER READING

BONAMY DOBRÉE: *Restoration Comedy 1660–1720; Restoration Tragedy 1660–1720* (Oxford Univ. Press).

A. NICOLL: *A History of Restoration Drama; A History of Early Eighteenth-century Drama, 1700–1750; A History of Late Eighteenth-century Drama, 1750–1800* (Cambridge Univ. Press).

JOHN PALMER: *The Comedy of Manners* (Bell).

J. H. WILSON: *Influence of Beaumont and Fletcher on Restoration Drama* (Columbus).

LORD MACAULAY: *Essay on the Comic Dramatists of the Restoration* (Longmans, Green).

CHARLES LAMB: *Essays of Elia* ("*On the Artificial Comedy of the last Century*").

A. M. SUMMERS: *The Restoration Theatre* (Paul).

ALWYN THALER: *Shakespeare to Sheridan* (Oxford Univ. Press).

CHAPTER XIX

REVIVAL OF DRAMA

THE conflict between the licensed and the piratical theatre continued into the nineteenth century. Gresham's Law ("Bad currency drives out good") has an application also to drama. The low standards of the illegitimate theatre, which had found a way of defeating the regulations by the introduction of songs to the number of five into plays, depressed also the standards of the patent theatres. How low the dramatic art had fallen in public estimation may be gathered from a notice in *The Times*, dated 5th March, 1839, concerning a production at the Adelphi Theatre—

> A set of very diverting, if not very legitimate, performers made their first appearance last night on the stage of this theatre . . . to wit, the celebrated Parisian monkeys. Since quadrupeds of all sorts have, for some time, more than divided the plaudits of the town with biped players, it may perhaps be no intrusion for animals which sometimes walk on four legs and sometimes on two to put in their claim for the support and approbation of the lovers of the drama: and since many "walking gentlemen" and "low" comedians ape the characteristics of the monkey tribe in a manner occasionally so perfectly natural that the copies can hardly be distinguished from the originals and receive for their grimaces the encomiums of the spectators, neither they nor their admirers can complain that the monkeys should return the obligation. . . . The successors of Garrick, Kemble and Kean may be considered installed in their present situations.

It has been said that the greater part of the drama of the first half of the nineteenth century consists either of "plays which are not literature, or literary exercises which are not in the fullest sense plays." In the hands of M. G. Lewis, stage plays tended towards melodrama; Joanna Baillie and Sheridan Knowles attempted to lead drama back to Elizabethan courses; Shelley (*The Cenci*) and Byron (*Manfred, Cain, Sardanapalus*) wrote plays which could be read but scarcely acted. The most characteristic stage performances were in fact not properly dramatic at all, but rather spectacular and panoramic, exhibiting all sorts of ingenious effects produced by mechanical means, such as "vanishing scenes" and realistic snow-storms and waterfalls.

In the early Victorian age Bulwer Lytton wrote melodramas which reached a good average level of literary quality, for instance, *The Lady of Lyons* (1838) and *Money* (1840).

Tennyson and Browning both wrote verse plays, but neither had the proper feeling for the theatre, and their dramas have been seldom produced. Tennyson's best play is *Becket* (1884), based on the stress in the Archbishop's mind between his conflicting loyalties to Church and State. Browning in *Strafford* (1837) had attempted something of the same kind. It was abundantly clear that the old tradition of English drama was dead and that a new start would have to be made if vital drama was to become once again a part of our cultural life.

The Rebirth of Drama

The appearance in 1865 of *Society*, a play by Tom Robertson (1829–71), was a portent. Methods of production were transformed, realism came into the theatre and the actor-manager took charge. Instead of conventional types, the characters were recognizable individuals, and instead of a stilted stage-language they used the forms of current speech. Notwithstanding that there were some detractors of the "cup and saucer" comedy, the success of the play was instantaneous, and Robertson followed it up quickly with *Ours, Caste, Play, School*, and *M.P.* in ensuing years. In all of them the stage was used for the presentation and discussion of some social problem; thus there came about the combination of the play of ideas with realistic production and a new attitude to the theatre.

While Robertson was thus bringing a new spirit into English drama Henrik Ibsen in Norway was writing his lyrical drama, *Peer Gynt*. Within a few years he too entered the field of social drama with *The Pillars of Society* (1877), *The Doll's House* (1879) and *Ghosts* (1881). The excitement caused by these bold adventures in drama spread to England, and Arthur Wing Pinero and Henry Arthur Jones carried on to a further stage the work begun by Robertson. Pinero's *The Second Mrs. Tanqueray* (1893) was the first of our mature problem plays. These made demands on the intelligence of theatre audiences; while they amused, amusement was not the main purpose.

It was otherwise with the comedies of Oscar Wilde, *Lady Windermere's Fan* (1892), *A Woman of No Importance* (1893), *An Ideal Husband* (1895), and *The Importance of Being Earnest* (1895), all plays of scintillating wit. Wilde was a master of epigram and paradox, and in his gay persiflage he is reminiscent of Wycherley. Fundamentally he was a satirist, but his satire was mocking rather than serious. The popularity of his plays on the continent, and especially in France, is due to the fact that he shared the Latin attitude to moral problems, and enjoyed the game of pricking the bubble of Victorian pretensions to respectability. The plots of the plays are dexterous but do not count for much: the genius of Wilde was in his unfailing wit.

George Bernard Shaw

It required however the witty advocacy and example of George Bernard Shaw to establish the theatre as a place in which serious ideas could be discussed. He popularized dramatic criticism with his *Quintessence of Ibsenism*, and by articles in the periodical reviews. At the same time he invaded the theatres with plays such as *Widowers' Houses* and *Mrs. Warren's Profession*, which dealt with social evils. In his later plays the range of interest broadened out, while plot and action tended to become subservient to the dialogue. *Caesar and Cleopatra* (1898), and *St. Joan* (1924) offered historical characterization in the light of the modern comic spirit. In *Androcles and the Lion* (1912) and *Back to Methuselah* (1921), Shaw dealt with religious and philosophical aspects of life. Social satire was prominent in *Major Barbara*, *The Doctor's Dilemma* (1906), *Misalliance* (1910), and *Pygmalion* (1912). The political scene was presented in a number of late plays: *The Apple Cart* (1929), *Geneva* (1938), and *In Good King Charles's Golden Days* (1939). All these plays are written with admirable gusto and show a profound sense of theatrical values.

Other dramatists who exploited the drama of ideas were Sir H. Granville-Barker, who was also a distinguished critic, and John Galsworthy. The former's *The Voysey Inheritance*, *Waste*, and *The Madras House* all present problems of conduct in a contemporary setting, without offering solutions. Galsworthy's sympathies with those who are ground under the wheels of industry, or become victims of the soulless mechanism of the modern State, are evident, yet he was not a propagandist. In *The Silver Box*, *Strife*, *Justice*, *The Skin Game*, and *Loyalties*, the drama of social reform is directed towards specific problems, such as solitary confinement in prisons and industrial strife. While Shaw's manner was exuberant and facetious, Galsworthy's was intensely earnest, making no concession to the demand for humour or prettiness. Plays of this kind were particularly suited to the repertory companies which began to spring up early in the century under the leadership of the Abbey Theatre in Dublin. They depended for success not on glamour and elaborate *décor*, but on good all-round acting. The repertory companies found further useful material in the historical reconstructions of John Drinkwater, such as *Abraham Lincoln, Mary Stuart*, and *Cromwell*, plays which answered the mood of the years immediately following the First World War, and which called for a rededication of the nation to sound political principles.

Poetic Drama

The Abbey Theatre movement brought in its train a revival of poetic drama which was, however, short-lived. W. B. Yeats took the view that drama should turn away from rationalism and realism and achieve its results, as in the greatest days of the theatre, through the emotions, that is to say, most directly and surely through poetry. A group of Irish poets, including Yeats, J. M. Synge, and Lady Gregory, turned the Celtic revival to good effect by writing plays based on old legends, either in verse or in a kind of prose which, echoing the idiom and cadences of peasant speech, suggests that there was a good deal of truth in Wordsworth's contention regarding the proper language of poetry. The first of these, produced at the opening of the Irish Literary Theatre, was Yeats's *Countess Cathleen* (1892). During the opening decade of the present century Yeats wrote *Deirdre*, and Synge *The Shadow of the Glen, Riders to the Sea, The Playboy of the Western World*, and *Deirdre of the Sorrows*. There was a strong vein of imaginative feeling also in Seán O'Casey's *Juno and the Paycock* (1925) and *The Plough and the Stars* (1926), written in a prose which was instinct with poetry and symbolism.

In England poetic drama in the present century is represented by the work of Stephen Phillips (1866–1915), the author of several blank verse plays, among them *Nero, Herod*, and *Paolo and Francesca*; and of John Masefield, who wrote *Philip the King* and *A King's Daughter*. Masefield's *Tragedy of Nan* uses a poetic prose. It would seem from the slight success won by these plays on the public stage that the taste of the age had definitely moved away from a long tradition, but there have been several recent experiments in verse drama which at least call such a judgment into question. These include T. S. Eliot's *The Rock* (1934), *Murder in the Cathedral* (1934), *The Family Reunion* (1939), *The Cocktail Party* (1950); Auden and Isherwood's *The Ascent of F.6.*, in verse and prose; Christopher Fry's *The Lady's not for Burning* and *Venus Observed*, and many others, which must await judgment. It does, however, appear that poetic drama is returning to the popular stage.

SUGGESTIONS FOR FURTHER READING

A. Nicoll: *A History of Early Nineteenth-century Drama*, 1800–1850 (2 vols); *A History of Late Nineteenth-century Drama*, 1850–1900 (2 vols) (Cambridge Univ. Press).

Ernest Reynolds: *Early Victorian Drama*, 1830–1870 (Heffer, Cambridge); *Modern English Drama* (Harrap).

James Agate: *A Short View of the English Stage* (Herbert Jenkins).

Ernest Short: *Introducing the Theatre* (Eyre & Spottiswoode).

Frank Vernon: *The Twentieth Century Theatre* (Harrap).

A. E. Morgan: *Tendencies of Modern English Drama* (Constable).

CHAPTER XX

THE EVOLUTION OF PROSE STYLE

I N all known literatures of the world the development of prose occurs later than that of poetry, which in the ritual and religious ceremonies of primitive societies was associated with music. The repetitive rhythms were accompanied by dance movements and were essential to the incantatory purpose of the ritual. Songs and incantations were associated also with occupational activities, and in some cases became completely secular, but this was a later development.

The Nature of Prose

It would be altogether too great a simplification to think of prose as a kind of writing which is not verse, as if the only difference were in the length of line or in the rhythmical pattern. It is true that verse has some structural features which are absent in prose, but for the due appreciation of prose we require to study the qualities it possesses rather than those which it lacks. Wordsworth indeed will not have it that there is any contradistinction between Poetry and Prose. In his view the distinction that ought to be made is a philosophical (i.e. logical) one, between Poetry and Matter-of-fact or Science. He allows that an antithesis exists between Prose and Metre; though this is not in fact strictly valid "because lines and passages of metre so naturally occur in writing prose that it would be scarcely possible to avoid them, even if it were desirable."[1]

Most modern critics would refuse to admit that metrical passages in prose writing could ever be desirable as such. That is far from saying that there are no rhythms in prose. Our speech is full of rhythm, and without a rhythmical utterance much of what we say would be robbed of meaning. It is impossible to exchange the time of day without using a rising or a falling inflection. English broadcasters are inclined to say "Good night" with trochaic force; American broadcasters prefer the iambic stress. But this speech rhythm is to be distinguished from a recurring metrical pattern. When the reader of prose has his attention distracted from meaning to manner and is forced by repetition of a formal design of syllabic stresses to switch

---

[1] *Preface to Lyrical Ballads.*

over mentally to a different kind of attitude to what he is reading, then unquestionably the prose is defective. The problem of *metrical* prose is to be distinguished from that of *poetic* prose. Provided that the conceptions are such as match an elevated style, there is no reason why the prose in which they are communicated should not give us aesthetic pleasure of the same order as poetry does.

Early English Prose

In England, it was not until the end of the ninth century that a vernacular prose began to be used for sustained literary work. King Alfred set on foot the great enterprise of the compilation of the Anglo-Saxon Chronicle, which was not altogether abandoned until the middle of the twelfth century. On this account he has been called the Father of English Prose. The title has less justification than such titles usually have because of the great structural changes which the language was destined to undergo before a prose medium for literary uses could be created.

The Chronicle, being the work of many hands over many succeeding generations, and its authors having no consistent principle to guide them, lacks the unity of style and conception which a true piece of literature must possess; nevertheless it stands as an important link between pre-Norman and post-Norman writing.

Before a continuous tradition of English writing could be said to have been created, the language itself had, so to speak, to find itself. It did so in three ways: firstly, as we have already seen, by changing from an inflected grammar to one in which the functions of words in a sentence were for the most part determined by position; secondly, by the absorption of a great number of new words of Latin or Romance origin, to match growing needs as civilization developed; thirdly, by the adoption of a new regulating principle of speech based on rhythmically organized syllabic stresses.

Middle English Prose

By about the year 1200 the process had gone far enough to provide a medium of expression in English which could begin to compete with the Latin which had served almost exclusively hitherto for the work of prose. The *Ancrene Riwle*, a book of devotional exercises and guide to everyday conduct, written early in the thirteenth century for the private instruction of three anchoresses in a Dorset hermitage, shows a notable advance in the power of using English, as well as an enlarged conception of its possible uses.

Not however until the age of Chaucer had the process of language-consolidation gone so far that it could be said that English was well on the way to displace Latin and French for general purposes. Chaucer himself demonstrated its value for scientific writing in his *Treatise of the Astrolabe*, and for philosophical writing in his translation of the *Consolations of Boethius*. Wycliffe's use of English in his popular Lollard tracts and sermons was proof of its power for invective and persuasiveness in furtherance of a cause. In the translation of the Holy Scriptures which he instituted, there was still more evidence of the possibilities of the language. The Bible is itself a library in miniature, containing history and prophecy, poetic drama, narrative, philosophy, mysticism, proverbial wisdom, biography, epistles, and much else.

The same period is notable for the compilers of romantic stories in prose. The most remarkable among these collections is the *Travels of Sir John Mandeville*. The tales and marvels he recounted are a curious mixture of the genuine and the fabulous, and mystery surrounds the author, but there is no doubt about the enormous popularity of the book. It has been called the first book of *belles lettres*[1] in the English language, and it gave us once for all the idiom of story-telling, marked by simple construction of co-ordinate sentences—

> On the other side of Calde toward the south side is Ethyope a great lande. In this lande on the south are the folke right blacke. In that side is a well that on the day the water is so colde that no man may drinke thereof and on the night it is so hote that no man may suffer to put his hand in it. In this lande the rivers, and all the waters are troublous and some dele salt for the great hete, and men of that land are lightly dronken and have little appetite to meate, and they have commonly the flixe of body and they live not long. In Ethyope are such men that have but one foote and they go so fast that it is a great marvaill and that is a large foote that the shadow thereof covereth the body from the son or rayne when they lye upon their backs, and when their children be first borne they loke like russet, and when they waxe old than they be all blacke.

Pre-Renaissance Prose

The same tradition of the simple, unadorned narrative style is found in Wycliffe's translation of the Gospels later in the same century, and in Malory's *Morte d'Arthur*, which Caxton printed in 1485. This was

---

[1] *Belles lettres* is defined as the more imaginative and artistic kinds of literature, including poetry and romance. as distinguished from the more utilitarian or informative.

undoubtedly the greatest literary work of the fifteenth century, and represents the high-water mark of pre-Renaissance prose. The style is remarkable for its concreteness, the gusto of its vernacular mono-syllabic idiom, and its rigid economy of language which never holds up the speed of the narration by a single word too many—

> So Sir Tristram rode along after this strong knight. And at last he saw where lay a lady overthwart a dead knight. Fair lady, said Sir Tristram, who hath slain your lord? Sir, said she, there came a knight riding as my lord and I rested us here, and asked him whence he was, and my lord said of Arthur's court. Therefore, said the strong knight, I will just with thee, for I hate all these that be of Arthur's court. And my lord that lieth here dead mounted upon his horse and the strong knight and my lord encountered together and there he smote my lord through out with his spear. And thus he hath brought me in great woe and damage.

Humanist Influences

From the beginning of the sixteenth century, we find a new influence at work, profoundly affecting English prose. The classical Renaissance had the effect of rendering our writers acutely conscious of style. The study of the classical literatures of Greece, and particularly Rome, taught them to value manner as much as matter. The earlier prose had been colloquial and unstudied; now prose began to put on airs and to seek rhetorical effects. The most powerful influence on the new academic prose was the oratorical style of Cicero which, being graceful, balanced and persuasive, provided the humanists with their ideal of clarity and elegance.

We find, therefore, in sixteenth-century English prose a conflict, which was now and again resolved into a vigorous unity, between the natural movement of native idiom and the studied cadence of learned prose. We have already seen how the vocabulary of English was enlarged and enriched by direct borrowings from Latin. Occasion-ally the use of bookish words became an obsession. But when discreetly used, the new words gave an added strength and a more varied rhythm to English prose, and carried it one step further towards the perfection of style which it eventually attained.

As an example of a humanist who attempted to preserve a just balance between the native and the borrowed elements, Roger Ascham may well be chosen. He uses a vocabulary reinforced, though not encumbered, by Latinisms, but on the other hand he is too prone to express himself in a diction which is derived from classical sources.

The following passage from *The Scholemaster* illustrates Roger Ascham's periodic sentence structure—

> And to saie all in shorte, though I lacke Authoritie to giue counsell, yet I lacke not good will to wisshe, that the yougthe in England, speciallie Ientlemen, and namelie nobilitie, shold be by good bringing up, so grounded in judgement of learninge, so founded in loue of honestie, as, whan they shold be called forthe to the execution of great affaires, in seruice of their Prince and contrie, they might be hable, to vse and to order, all experience, were they good were they bad, and that, according to the square, rule, and line, of wisdom learning and vertue.

It will be noticed that Ascham makes considerable use of antithesis e.g. "I lacke Authoritie . . . I lacke not good will; so grounded in judgement of learning . . . so founded in loue of honestie; were they good were they bad." The passage contains also the rhetorical device of the three-pronged phrase, e.g. square, rule, and line; wisdom, learning, and virtue. The whole is a highly wrought, balanced and cadenced piece of writing, devised to give pleasure as much by its form as by its content.

Euphuism

It was the exaggeration of antithesis and parallelism, with the artifice of alliteration superimposed, which produced among the writers who stood around the court of Queen Elizabeth, the curious literary vogue of the years 1580–90. The fashion was set in its extreme form by the publication of John Lyly's pseudo-romance *Euphues*. To our ears the unending pendulum swing of phrase quickly becomes wearisome, and so does the continual reference to classical exemplars, and the use of conceits or similes drawn from the medieval-bestiaries, with which the most commonplace of statements are supported.

The following passage will serve as an example of the Euphuistic manner—

> Too much study doth intoxicate their brains. For, say they, although iron the more is used the brighter it is, yet silver with much wearing doth waste to nothing: though the cammock (= *crook*) the more it is bowed the better it serveth, yet the bow the more it is bent and occupied (= *used*) the weaker it waxeth; though the camomile the more it is trodden and pressed down the more it spreadeth, yet the violet the oftener it is handled and touched the sooner it withereth and decayeth. . . . The scythe cutteth far better than the saw, the wax yieldeth better and sooner to the seal than the steel to the stamp or hammer, the smooth and plain beech is easier to be carved and occupied than the knotty box.

Euphuistic prose passed through all the phases which belong to the history of extravagant fashions, until finally it became meet for parody. The trick of singularity was affected by most of Lyly's contemporaries, and not only by such lesser figures as the pamphleteers Greene, Lodge, and Nash, but also by so critical a writer as Sir Philip Sidney. In his *Arcadia* we find Euphuism with a difference. There is still an excess of ornament, such as alliterative balance, and words are tossed about as jugglers throw their balls, and catch them to throw again. But now there is added the artifice of the pastoral and chivalric conventions. Arcadianism, with its idealized rusticity, and its courtly amours presented in the guise of the loves of shepherds and shepherdesses, became a vogue no less universal than that of Euphuism. Each of these modes of expression is to be found in Shakespeare's plays, notably in *Love's Labour's Lost*, *Two Gentlemen of Verona*, and *Romeo and Juliet*. The figure of Jaques in *As You Like It* is conceived entirely in the convention, but Shakespeare's use of Euphuism and Arcadianism has always a sufficient dramatic motive. In *Henry IV*, Part I, we find Falstaff using the idiom in a mock-heroic parody—

> Harry, I not only marvel where thou spendest thy time, but also how thou art accompanied: for though the camomile, the more it is trodden on, the faster it grows, yet youth, the more it is wasted, the sooner it wears. . . . I do not speak to thee in drink, but in tears; not in pleasure but in passion; not in words only, but in woes also.

It has to be remembered, notwithstanding the extravagances of euphuism, that the fashion bequeathed something of value to English prose style. It substituted design for formlessness, and demonstrated the importance of precision, proportion, and rhythmical balance. These were essential elements in the aesthetics of prose.

Search for the Plain Style

The search for a prose-style which would be adequate to the growing demands made upon it was partly the cause, partly the result, of a sharpening of the critical sense. The revival of letters, while it made "polite" learning synonymous with the study of the classics, had an influence also on the study of English. Caxton in his *Prefaces* had quite early begun to consider the problem of how to achieve a "pure" English style. But the greatest critical work of the English renaissance was Sidney's *Defense of Poesie*, which stands as an early example of prose conforming to the new pattern of elevation and stateliness.

> Now therein of all sciences . . . is our poet the monarch. For he doth

not only shew the way, but giveth so sweet a prospect into the way, as will entice any man to enter into it: Nay, he doth, as if your journey should lie through a fair vineyard, at the very first, give you a cluster of grapes; that, full of that taste, you may long to pass farther. He beginneth not with obscure definitions; which must blur the margent with interpretations, and load the memory with doubtfulness; but he cometh to you with words set in delightful proportion, either accompanied with, or prepared for, the well enchanting skill of music; and with a tale forsooth, he cometh to you, with a tale which holdeth children from play, and old men from the chimney corner; and pretending no more, doth intend the winning of the mind from wickedness to virtue; even as the child is often brought to take most wholesome things by hiding them in such other as have a pleasant taste.

The plain style continued to be practised, and was carried to a point of perfection in Richard (the "judicious") Hooker's *Laws of Ecclesiastical Polity* (1594). He was a humanist, and echoed the formal abstract Latin idiom rather than the concrete and racy native speech rhythm. But at the same time, he was always master of his medium, and used it with consummate art to give us a clear and controlled prose, with thought and expression truly matched. He can rise to levels of sublime eloquence, or can write easily and forthrightly, as the subject requires.

The king is not subject unto laws; that is to say, the punishment which breach of laws doth bring upon inferiors taketh not hold on the King's person; although the general laws which all mankind is bound to do tie no less the King than others, but rather more. For the greviousness of sin is aggravated by the greatness of him that committeth it: for which cause it also maketh him by so much the more obnoxious unto Divine revenge, by how much the less he feareth human.

Sir Francis Bacon

The next outstanding name in the development of prose is that of Francis Bacon. He wrote far more in Latin than in English, and rarely attempted verse. "I have," he wrote, "taken all knowledge to be by my province," and by dint of the most painstaking care he brought his style to such a fullness of meaning, as prompted Ben Jonson to declare in one of his aphorisms—

No man ever spake more neatly, more presly, more weightily, or suffered less emptiness, less idleness in what he uttered. No member of his speech but consisted of his own graces. His hearers could not cough, or look aside from him, without loss. He commanded where he spoke. . . . The fear of every man that heard him was lest he should make an end.

Timber

We do not read Bacon for any quality of melody in his style, but rather for "high sentence" or practical wisdom expressed with the utmost economy of language and with all the wisdom of the proverb. He has two styles: the one is the casual detached style of the *Essays*, the other the more consciously developed expository style of such philosophical writings as *The Advancement of Learning*. As examples the following two passages may be compared—

There is a wisdom in this beyond the rules of physic: a man's own observation, what he finds good of, and what he finds hurt of, is the best physic to preserve health. But it is a safer conclusion to say, "This agreeth with me not well, therefore I will not continue to use it," than this, "I find no offence of this, therefore I may use it." For strength of nature in youth passeth over many excesses, which are owing a man till his age. Discern of the coming on of years, and think not to do the same things still; for age will not be defied. Beware of sudden change in any great point of diet, and if necessity enforce it, fit the rest to it. For it is a secret, both in nature and state, that it is safer to change many things than one. Examine thy customs of diet, sleep, exercise, apparel, and the like; and try, in any thing thou shalt judge hurtful, to discontinue it by little and little; but so as, if thou dost find any inconvenience by the change, thou come back to it again: for it is hard to distinguish that which is generally held good and wholesome, from that which is good particularly, and fit for thine own body. To be free-minded and cheerfully disposed at hours of meat and of sleep and of exercise, is one of the best precepts of long lasting.

Essays: Of Regiment of Health

It appeareth likewise that I have assigned to summary philosophy the common principles and axioms which are promiscuous and indifferent to several sciences: I have assigned to it likewise the inquiry touching the operation of the relative and adventive characters of essences, as quantity, similitude, diversity, possibility, and the rest: with this distinction and provision; that they be handled as they have efficacy in nature, and not logically.

The Advancement of Learning

Bacon has been called the inventor of the literary essay; but it is impossible to overlook the importance of Ben Jonson in its history. His method was probably not unlike that of Bacon; each formed the habit of making jottings of his random thoughts, and occasionally of "essaying" to develop them into more systematic theses. Collected under the title *Timber or Discoveries* are Ben Jonson's notes in every stage of their evolution, from single sentences and brief paragraphs into short essays. The style is in the plain rather than in the "aureate" tradition, as will be seen from the example quoted above.

The English Bible

The greatest single and omnipresent influence on modern prose style has been that of the Authorized Verson of the Scriptures, which was published in 1611. It was not the first translation into English. Early writers such as Caedmon had produced paraphrases of scattered passages, rendered in verse, and Bede had translated part of the Gospel of St. John. The first complete version in English was the work of Wyclife and his followers, dating from the late fourteenth century. All these were based on the Latin text, known as the Vulgate, which was issued by St. Jerome early in the fifth century.

The first English version of the New Testament translated from the Greek text was that of William Tyndale (d. 1536), who also made a translation of the Pentateuch (the first five books of the Old Testament) and of the Book of Jonah from the Hebrew. In 1535 a complete Bible in English was printed, attributed to Coverdale; it was not based on the original texts, but some use was made of Tyndale's translation as well as of Luther's version in German. Cranmer's *Great Bible* was issued in 1539.

At the end of the century there appeared to be a need for a new translation which would be equally acceptable to both High Church and Low Church parties. At a Conference held at Hampton Court in 1604, the venture was launched. Fifty-four eminent scholars and divines took part, forming small groups which undertook the revision or retranslation of particular sections. It is a very remarkable circumstance that, notwithstanding this communal method, the work as a whole should show such unity of style and feeling. This is due in large measure to the fact that the cadences of Tyndale's prose were carried over into the new version, and also to the chance that the native idiom of English was at that particular period of history at its freshest: vigorous, concrete, clear, and rhythmical. Its ornament was kept within bounds by a classical restraint and by a humble reverence which abhorred affectation, and the imagery had not yet been staled by use.

The language of the Authorized Version, as it came to be called, along with that of the Collects which are distinguished by the same kind of verbal harmony, became familiar to generations of English-speaking peoples, by reason of its being read and re-read daily in their churches and their homes. For many men and women who attained eminence as writers, orators, and leaders, it remained the one book which nourished their spirits: for Cromwell, Bunyan, Wesley,

Browning, Ruskin, and John Bright in England, and for Emerson, Walt Whitman and Abraham Lincoln in America, the Bible was the chief formative influence in shaping their outlook, their manner of speech and writing. Moreover the phraseology and the metaphor of the Scriptures has become so closely knit with the texture of current speech that there are countless Biblical expressions in common use, whose origin is unsuspected by many of the present generation to whom the Bible has become a closed book.

The "Periodic" Style

The prose of John Milton, written during his middle years, has the fault of excessive Latinity, in both vocabulary and syntax. While there are passages in *Areopagitica* and the *Tractate on Education* which are as eloquent and sublime as anything in the language, it cannot be said that Milton contributed to the evolution of English prose style anything of permanent value. We treasure Milton's prose for the revelation it affords of a mind passionate in its advocacy of great causes, and superbly independent in judgment, rather than for grace and harmony. The following brief passage, which concludes Milton's preface to *Samson Agonistes*, will serve as an example of his more informal prose manner—

> Of the style and uniformity, and that commonly called the plot, whether intricate or explicit—which is nothing indeed but such economy or disposition of the fable, as may stand best with verisimilitude and decorum—they only will best judge who are not unacquainted with Aeschylus, Sophocles and Euripides, the three tragic poets unequalled yet by any, and the best rule to all who endeavour to write Tragedy. The circumscription of time, wherein the whole drama begins and ends, is, according to ancient rule and best example, within the space of twenty-four hours.

The seventeenth century produced several other great prose writers whose normal unit of expression was the elaborate period. Robert Burton's *Anatomy of Melancholy*, Sir Thomas Browne's *Religio Medici* and *Hydriotaphia or Urn Burial*, Jeremy Taylor's *Holy Living* and *Holy Dying*, and Thomas Hobbes's *Leviathan* are all monumental works, distinguished for their high seriousness and . stately rhetoric. These writings were products of the late Renaissance in England and stood midway between the Elizabethan phase of eager trial and error, where every experiment inaugurated a new, if brief, fashion, and the more assured, urbane, conversational diction of the Restoration period.

Dryden, Father of Modern English Prose

If anyone can be said to be the Father of Modern English Prose, it is John Dryden. We owe to him the creation of a workmanlike medium of expression, which was flowing, transparent, and completely free from affectation. It was a prose style for every occasion, a flexible instrument, apt for use by the periodical essayist, the novelist, the scientist, the historian, the philosopher, the critic, the letter-writer and a hundred and one others who wrote with the idea of clarifying their ideas or communicating them to others. It is an extraordinary thing that Dryden should have found the perfect medium without groping for it. He had no need to serve an apprenticeship to the craft of prose-writing, because from the first his skill was consummate.

The following passages of Hobbes and Dryden respectively are quoted in order to illustrate the advance which was made during the latter half of the seventeenth century—

> Whatsoever therefore is consequent to a time of war, where every man is enemy to every man; the same is consequent to the time, wherein men live without other security, than what their own strength and their own invention shall furnish them withal. In such condition, there is no place for industry; because the fruit thereof is uncertain: and consequently no culture of the earth; no navigation, nor use of the commodities that may be imported by sea; no commodious building; no instruments of moving, and removing such things as require much force; no knowledge of the face of the earth; no account of time; no arts; no letters; no society; and which is worst of all, continual fear, and danger of violent death: And the life of man solitary, poor, nasty, brutish and short.
>
> HOBBES: *The Leviathan* (1651)

> I have almost done with Chaucer, when I have answered some objections relating to my present work. I find some people are offended that I have turned these tales into modern English; because they think them unworthy of my pains, and look on Chaucer as a dry, old-fashioned wit, not worth reviving. I have often heard the late Earl of Leicester say, that Mr. Cowley himself was of that opinion; who, having read him over at my Lord's request, declared he had no taste of him. I dare not advance my opinion against the judgment of so great an author; but I think it fair, however, to leave the decision to the public. Mr. Cowley was too modest to set up for a dictator; and being shocked perhaps with his old style, never examined into the depth of his good sense. Chaucer, I confess, is a rough diamond, and must first be polished ere he shines.
>
> DRYDEN: *Preface to the Fables* (1700)

It is obvious that with Dryden we have reached modern prose. Its negative merits are the apparent absence of effort and the freedom from any idiosyncrasy which by interposing itself between the mind of the writer and that of the reader might tend to obscure the meaning. Its positive features are the intimate, confidential manner, the use of a natural speech rhythm, the simple diction and the pleasant variety in the length of sentences. This has been called the Middle Style of prose. It is based on the racy flow of good talk among equals and has nothing in common with the one-way utterances of moralists, scholars and rhetoricians demonstrating, scolding or persuading *ex cathedra*. The Middle Style is unselfconscious; its pace and emphasis correspond to the rhythm of conversation. It prefers homely metaphor, and a wisdom rather proverbial than recondite and sententious.

The subsequent history of the development of prose style will be incidentally considered in the sections on the Novel, the Essay, and Literary Criticism which follow.

SUGGESTIONS FOR FURTHER READING

HERBERT READ: *English Prose Style* (Bell).
A. C. WARD: *Foundations of English Prose* (Bell).
EDWIN MUIR: *Structure of the Novel* (Hogarth Press).
GRAVES AND HODGE: *The Reader over your Shoulder* (Jonathan Cape).
R. G. MOULTON: *The Literary Study of the Bible* (Harrap).

CHAPTER XXI

THE EVOLUTION OF THE NOVEL

The beginnings of prose fiction are to be found in primitive story-telling and story-writing, but the novel, which is a product of conscious literary art, is a much later development. It emerged in England only after a considerable degree of maturity and differentiation had been achieved in other branches of literature. The evolution of the novel depended on writers having a certain mastery of character analysis and organized narrative, and an adequate prose style. Once these conditions existed, rudimentary novels began to appear, and in time a new literary mode was established. It was a form which developed slowly and its extraordinary potentialities as a means of expression were not explored at all fully until well on in the nineteenth century. The early history of the novel gives little indication of the variety and complexity the form was to attain in modern times.

Early Story-telling

The story is the most prominent element in Malory's *Morte d'Arthur*, the style in Lyly's *Euphues* and Sidney's *Arcadia*, and human personality in the seventeenth-century collections of "characters." Although Malory, Lyly, and Sidney are often referred to as the progenitors of the novel, their claims are in fact no stronger than those of Greene, Lodge, and Nash, who all wrote meandering tales in a euphuistic style. Greene's *Pandosto* and Lodge's *Rosalynde* have achieved immortality through being sources for *A Winter's Tale* and *As You Like It* respectively, and Nash's *The Unfortunate Traveller* is interesting as being an early example of the picaresque.

All of these lack shape and proportion. Action is held up by long, moralizing discourses. There is little or no skill shown in the management and distribution of crises in the story. Characterization is crude, and of the interplay of character and situation there is no indication. Even more important is the absence of any critical interpretation of manners and behaviour by the writer. There is, in fact, nothing to reveal his attitude to the events he narrates. The novel proper, on the other hand, is touched by the author's outlook and personality, and the aesthetic pleasure which it gives comes not only from its content but also from the illumination it affords of the writer's mind.

John Bunyan

For any advance in the art of fiction-writing we have to move forward the best part of a century, to Bunyan's *Pilgrim's Progress* which appeared in 1678, followed two years later by *The Life and Death of Mr. Badman*. Bunyan himself did not regard his work as fiction, but rather as a record of his own spiritual experiences. Although he wrote in the form of allegory, every detail of character and incident is realized with vivid intensity, and the dialogue is natural. With him "personifications," as Macaulay said, "became men. A dialogue between two qualities, in his dream, has more dramatic effect than a dialogue between two human beings in most plays." Further, the books tell us as much about Bunyan himself as about any one of his creations. Though he thus made a considerable advance towards the fully-developed novel, it would be wrong to class Bunyan as a novelist. His purpose in writing and his attitude to the story and to the reader were didactic and arose from his religious outlook; any advances he made in the art of fiction were inadvertent.

Daniel Defoe

The publication of Defoe's *Robinson Crusoe* (1719), *Colonel Jack*, and *Moll Flanders* (1722), and numerous other romances of the type which purports to describe actual events, marks another stage in the development of the novel. If we accept for a moment the limited definition of a novel as a story of considerable length which, though not historically true, might very well be so, since it arises out of normal experience and is based on actual manners and credible people, then Defoe may properly be said to have created it as a literary form. He had the trick of verisimilitude to perfection. His *Journal of the Plague Year*, a narrative of events which happened when he was a child of four years, carries all the conviction of a record of authentic experience, and is an admirable illustration of the saying: Truth hath no greater enemy than verisimilitude.

Yet to adopt this quality of truth-seeming as a criterion of literary fiction would be to isolate one aspect, if a very prominent one, of the novel, and so to exaggerate its importance. Defoe's romances lacked a more important quality: they were not integrated. Events set in an unbroken line succeed one another in time, and there is no attempt to indicate a relation between cause and effect, or to analyse the thoughts and feelings of the characters. Later novelists freed themselves from chronology in order to supply their own comment and interpretation, and thereby to suggest the "frame of reference" within which the novel is constructed.

Beginning of the Novel

Samuel Richardson (1689–1761) wrote the first English novel in which human relationships play an important part, and in which there is a degree of emotional unity. This development came about almost accidentally. Richardson had written a book called *The Moral Letter Writer*, which was intended to be instructional. He then transformed the material into a series of letters passing to and fro among imaginary characters, in which a sentimental love-story is developed.

The result was *Pamela or Virtue Rewarded* (1740), the first love-novel in English and perhaps in European literature. Of incident there is little, but analysis of character and of motive is carried to extravagant lengths and executed with meticulous refinement. Every circumstance of the relationship between Pamela, the demure serving maid, and the master of the house is set down and rehearsed over and over again, in interminable letters written by herself, her parents and her friends, until finally she is triumphantly justified in her resistance to importunity by winning her pursuer in wedlock, and finding herself mistress of a fine establishment.

Richardson soon realized that he was engaged in a "new species of writing." It was new in that it combined in a single work of literary art a record of the unfolding of external events, with a description of the inner states of thought and feeling which accompanied these events, and gave them their significance. The instantaneous appeal of *Pamela* led to the writing of *Clarissa Harlowe* (1748), Richardson's masterpiece in realistic fiction, and to *Sir Charles Grandison* (1753) in which the level is not sustained. But the novel of sentiment or sensibility was now fairly launched on its way and within a very short time there were numerous imitators.

The example of Richardson was enough to establish the vogue of the epistolary novel for a time, but its inherent limitations and absurdities before long produced a reaction in favour of a less artificial method.

Henry Fielding

Henry Fielding, a stipendiary magistrate of Westminster, entered the field of novel writing with *Joseph Andrews* (1742), which began as a parody of *Pamela*, but then developed on original lines. The narrow domesticities of Richardson's world are replaced by a scene thronged with characters who enjoy their open-air life without inhibitions. The humour is sometimes by our standards coarse, but it springs from the vigour of animal spirits. Parson Adams is one of the great comic figures of literature and the first of such to be presented in a novel.

In *Tom Jones* (1749) Fielding reveals his skill as a novelist even more fully, and this is considered by some to be the greatest literary work of the century. The canvas on which he depicts the pulsating life of the English countryside is of epic dimensions: Thackeray called *Tom Jones* "the greatest comic epic," and Byron called Fielding "our prose Homer." As a picture of manners, the novel is unsurpassed, and takes its place beside Hogarth's drawings as an eighteenth-century social document. But the importance of *Tom Jones* is not in its content alone; it is remarkable also for its structure and for the skill with which the principal plot and the lesser plots are managed. Fielding uses the device of the omniscient narrator, but he succeeds in making the pattern of events objective, so that they move from stage to stage by virtue of an inner necessity. Character is revealed indirectly through action, and both take on thereby a deeper meaning. *Tom Jones* is thus an essentially realistic novel, and its consistency is marred only by the introduction of moral invocations, which were a characteristic of the literature of the period.

Tobias Smollett

The possibilities of the novel were still further extended in the work of Tobias Smollett (1721–71), who was first a ship's, then a London surgeon. He made a worthy third in this trinity of early novelists. *Roderick Random* appeared in 1748, and *Peregrine Pickle* in 1751, and near the end of his life he wrote *Humphrey Clinker*. The autobiographical element gives to his novels a basis of realism, but Smollett was attracted by eccentricity rather than by normal humanity. Often this taste for the grotesque led him into coarse vulgarity. His humour was of the practical joke variety and showed little regard for the susceptibilities of the squeamish. The merit of Smollett was in bringing to the novel of adventure the special knowledge he had gained from his own experiences. It is no accident that many of his most successful creations, such as Trunnion and Tom Bowling, are sailors.

Laurence Sterne

Laurence Sterne (1713–68) is usually classed as a novelist, though in fact his *Tristram Shandy* is so formless that it does not lend itself to easy classification. There is no coherent narrative, for the story, such as it is, is continually being interrupted while the author indulges his fondness for digressions. In these Sterne uses material borrowed from out of the way literary sources, whose only relevance is that they feed his appetite for the whimsical and sentimental. The Shandean attitude to life involves an excess of sentiment, tearful or boisterous as the case may be. Some situations are met with inconsequent foolery, some with recondite allusions; others with ribald innuendo and even with complete absence of mind. There is, in short, a total surrender to the moods of a capricious sensibility.

Tristram Shandy appeared in instalments over a period of years (1759–67), and readers in England and France devoured them eagerly on publication. The mannerisms of the writing, which were a complete denial of the values of the Augustan school, seemed to suit the taste of the age. The "man of sensibility" had displaced the "man of reason" as the most approved type. But, for later readers, the value of Sterne lies in his consummate literary art. When we have discounted the crude buffooneries, the blank spaces, the asterisks, the chapter titles without chapters, the nonsense jingles and the like, there remains a style of considerable distinction, and a power of using the language to provide exquisite pleasure.

The following passage concerns the preparations made by Uncle Toby for taking the field (his kitchen garden) by way of recapitulation of the glorious campaigns he had fought with Marlborough—

The eve which preceded, as my Uncle Toby went to bed, he ordered his Ramillie wig, which had lain inside-out for many years in the corner of an old campaigning trunk which stood by his bedside, to be taken out and laid upon the lid of it, ready for the morning; and the very first thing he did in his shirt, when he had stepped out of bed, my Uncle Toby, after he had turned the rough side outwards, put it on. This done, he proceeded next to his breeches, and having buttoned the waistband, he forthwith buckled on his swordbelt, and had got his sword half way in, when he considered he should want shaving, and that it would be very inconvenient doing it with his sword on, so took it off. In essaying to put on his regimental coat and waistcoat, my Uncle Toby found the same objection as in his wig, so that went off too; so that, what with one thing and what with another, as always falls out when a man is in most haste, 'twas ten o'clock, which was half an hour later than his usual time, before my Uncle Toby sallied out.

Bridging the period between the four great founders of the modern novel, Richardson, Fielding, Smollett, and Sterne, and the great Victorian novelists, there are several writers who each in a special way exploited this new literary form and turned it to account. Three principal lines of development may be distinguished.

Firstly, there is the novel of Terror and Mystery, sometimes described as the Gothic Romance. We have already seen how writers who shared the new romantic spirit, which came to expression midway through the eighteenth century, found in medieval manners, legends and scenes a prolific source of interest and inspiration. The new attitude was a reaction against the rationalism and materialism of Hanoverian England.

The "Gothic" Novel

The first important product of this cult of medievalism was Horace Walpole's *The Castle of Otranto* (1764). Walpole was an important figure in the literary and artistic life of the mid-Georgian period, and he was largely responsible for the craze for antiquarianism which arose at this time. The content of *The Castle of Otranto*, the scene of which is laid in the Italy of the twelfth century, is at the opposite extreme from the drawing-room and kitchen intimacies of *Pamela*. It was an attempt to exploit the possibilities of Gothic mystery and romance as a basis for fiction. Walpole's use of the supernatural was often clumsy and obvious, but he set a fashion which was widely copied both in England and on the Continent.

Clara Reeve's *The Old English Baron* was a direct imitation of Walpole, but better known are the books of Mrs. Radcliffe and "Monk" Lewis, who were typical exponents of the novel of Mystery and Horror. *The Monk* by Lewis is an extreme example, with black magic, murder and lust as its main themes. Mrs. Radcliffe's *The Mysteries of Udolpho* (1795) resembles *Otranto* in its use of conventionally crude means of suggesting terror: dark passages, fearsome dungeons, shadowy effects, mysterious footsteps and so forth, but because of her careful building up a romantically emotive background, she stands high among writers of "thrillers." A very remarkable work in this *genre* was Mary Shelley's *Frankenstein or The Modern Prometheus* written, at the suggestion of Byron and her husband, to beguile the time during a wet season in Switzerland. Frankenstein, a student of science, fashioned a monster by animating dead bones, but was then terrorized and murdered by the unnatural creature to which he had given life.

The Novel with a Message

The second line of development was the didactic novel, or novel with a message. It was not to be expected that an instrument so handy, and so admirably suited to the purpose of proselytizing, should have been neglected by those who had political or other doctrines to inculcate. The novel found its way into large numbers of domestic circles, and the practice of reading aloud in family groups ensured that whatever influence it had should be widespread. Rousseau had set out his views on education in two novels: *La Nouvelle Héloise*, and *Emile*, and William Godwin, Shelley's father-in-law, who was strongly influenced by French revolutionary views, wrote *Caleb Williams or Things as They Are* to give currency to the opinions expressed in his philosophical treatise, *Political Justice*. Other writers who followed Godwin with novels of ideas were Robert Bage, the Quaker freethinker (*Man as He Is* and *Hermsprong or Man as He Is Not*), Mrs. Inchbald (*A Simple Story*), Hannah More (*Cælebs in Search of a Wife*), and Thomas Holcroft (*Anna St. Ives*). The propagandist novel tends by its very nature to be ephemeral. The problems it discusses cease after a time to agitate people either because they are solved or because more compelling ones arise. The books mentioned in this paragraph are now seldom read, but nevertheless they have historical importance because of the persistence of the novel with a message through the nineteenth century. We shall see later how Charles Dickens preached social reform in his novels, and how Disraeli used fiction to propagate his political views. There were also such novelist-reformers and moralists as Charles Kingsley, F. D. Maurice, and George Eliot.

The Novel of Manners

We have now to consider the third line of development, the novel of manners, lightly touched with a vein of satiric humour. The prototype is Oliver Goldsmith's *Vicar of Wakefield* (1766), which depicts the country life of England as seen from the point of view of the rectory. Fanny Burney, whose diary is one of our precious literary legacies, wrote several novels, including *Evelina*, in which the town is regarded from the standpoint of the country. The heroine, a country girl, tells in a series of letters her impressions of London and how she adapts herself to its life. It is a comparatively small jump from Fanny Burney to Jane Austen, in whose hands the domestic novel reaches perfection.

The possibilities of the novel were far from being exhausted during these comparatively early days of its evolution. Maria Edgeworth was the originator of two new types: the first was the novel which derives its inspiration from a particular place and uses local colour, speech and manners to give additional interest to the story. *Castle Rackrent* has its setting in Ireland, and reconstructs for us the life of the Irish squires and peasants. This is done with humour, and insight into the unhappy social conditions resulting from absentee landlordism. The influence of the book in opening up a new vein of fiction cannot be better illustrated than by Sir Walter Scott's statement in a preface to *Waverley*: "I felt that something might be attempted for my own country, of the same kind with that which Miss Edgeworth so fortunately achieved for Ireland." Since then, the *genius loci* has inspired thousands of novels ranging from those which, like Scott's *Heart of Midlothian*, are based on national sentiment and behaviour, to those on a smaller canvas, such as Mrs. Gaskell's *Mary Barton*, which deals with factory life in Manchester. The Wessex novels of Hardy are outstanding examples in this kind.

The second notable contribution made by Miss Edgeworth is the novel of childhood, in particular, tales about children for children. One of these, *Rosamund of the Purple Jar* (1801), may be regarded as starting a long line of children's books, which in due time gave us such imperishable works as Lewis Carroll's *Alice in Wonderland* and Kipling's *Jungle Books*. Much of Miss Edgeworth's work is in the form of the short story (e.g. *Popular Tales*) and here again she showed the way to an important new literary development.

SUGGESTIONS FOR FURTHER READING

E. M. Forster: *Aspects of the Novel* (Edward Arnold).

A. S. Turberville: *English Men and Manners in the Eighteenth Century* (Oxford Univ. Press).

Lord Ernle: *Light Reading of our Ancestors* (Hutchinson).

W. M. Thackeray: *English Humorists of the Eighteenth Century* (Murray).

Henry James: *Art of the Novel* (Scribner's).

V. S. Pritchett: *The Living Novel* (Chatto & Windus).

CHAPTER XXII

THE NOVEL: NINETEENTH CENTURY

MANY causes contributed to the popularity of the novel and the enlargement of its scope during the nineteenth century. Firstly, there was the expansion, due to the spread of literacy, of the reading public. Secondly, by serializing books in cheap monthly parts, or printing them in magazines, they were made accessible to large numbers of people who could not afford the heavy expense of single volumes, let alone the "three-deckers." Novel-writing as an art doubtless suffered from publication in instalments, because of the bad effect on structure, and of the temptation to "write down" to the reader, but nevertheless many of the greatest Victorian novels appeared first in the pages of periodicals.

The Expansion of the Novel

The subject-matter of the novel was quickly extended to cover almost every aspect of social life. Dickens descended into the subterranean life of poor-law London for themes; Trollope depicted the typical society of cathedral towns; Thackeray wrote about the upper classes; Charlotte Brontë seldom ventured beyond her own personal experience; Mrs. Gaskell, as we have seen, found material for some of her novels in the conflicts of labour and capital in a manufacturing town. There emerged also the novels of warfare, of crime and detection, of treasure-hunting adventure, of exploration and countless other types, for all of which readers were found. The general tendency was towards realism, though with this there was often mixed a romantic treatment of empire-building, and of scientific discovery and speculation.

We may conveniently consider the nineteenth-century novel in three periods: the pre-Victorian (1800–37), the early Victorian (1837–70), and the later Victorian (1870–1900). In the pre-Victorian period, the great names are those of Jane Austen (1775–1817) and Sir Walter Scott (1771–1832).

The Pre-Victorian Novel: Jane Austen

Jane Austen was wise enough to know her limitations. She was interested in people of her own time and station, and these she depicted "with so fine a brush," as she said, "on a little bit (two inches wide) of ivory." She was completely unmoved by current events although she lived against the background of the Napoleonic wars and the Industrial Revolution. She was extraordinarily immune also to the influence of the fashionable novels of her day, the Gothic romances, the moralizing or reforming novels and the historical tales, and in the disciplined economy of her writing she was near in spirit to the Augustans. Through precision of style, balance of structure, and unity of effect, Jane Austen gives her readers a rare aesthetic experience, the sense of form inseparable from content. In her greatest novel, *Pride and Prejudice*, the pride of the hero and the prejudice of the heroine suggest "upreared and abutting fronts" of rock fretted and eventually undermined by the rhythmical wash of waters at the base. The progression of events is that of a well-constructed play. With her lively sense of dialogue, Jane Austen might have won an equal success in the field of comic drama. All six of her novels were published anonymously between 1811 and 1818: *Sense and Sensibility, Pride and Prejudice, Mansfield Park, Emma, Persuasion*, and *Northanger Abbey*.

Sir Walter Scott

Sir Walter Scott's qualities as a novelist were vastly different from those of Jane Austen. Where she was precise, he was diffuse; while she painted domestic miniatures, he depicted the pageantry of history on broad canvases. With her we share the quiet intimacies of English rural life; he stimulates us with a sense of multitude and the excitement of action. Scott was a romantic nurtured on the ballad poetry of the Lowland and Border country, and his best novels are those which reflect the life of the Borderers, among whom he spent much of his youth, studying their manners and recording their folk-lore. Among the novels with a local interest and based on personal observation are *Guy Mannering, The Antiquary, Old Mortality*, and *The Heart of Midlothian*.

During his first five or six years of novel-writing Scott confined himself to familiar scenes and characters. His first attempt at a historical novel was *Ivanhoe* (1819), followed by *Kenilworth* (1821), *Quentin Durward* (1823), and *The Talisman* (1825). He returned to Scottish antiquity from time to time as in *The Monastery* (1820) and *St. Ronan's Well* (1823).

In these and other novels Scott revealed himself as a consummate tale-teller. Without being in the strict sense a historian, he had a sense of period, and this he conveyed to the reader with boundless vitality, a wealth of colourful description, and with much humour and sympathy. His gallery of imperishable portraits challenges comparison with that of Shakespeare and includes Queen Elizabeth, Mary Queen of Scots, Bonnie Prince Charlie, Graham of Claverhouse, and such creatures of the imagination (though often based on actuality) as Meg Merrilees, Dominie Sampson, and Dandie Dinmont. Scott wrote out of the super-abundance of his material, and his fecundity may well explain a certain looseness in the texture of his writing. Except in his dialogue, which is invariably true to character, his prose resembles the formal diction of the mid-eighteenth century as used by Dr. Johnson in *Rasselas*. His leisurely unfolding of the story allows of digressions, particularly in the description of natural scenery or of interiors. In this respect again, his method stands in sharp contrast to that of Jane Austen, who rarely bestows as much as a glance at the surroundings in which her creatures disport themselves.

Jane Austen stands alone and apart; she founded no school. Scott on the other hand had a great following. Most of the outstanding Victorian novelists, though they are not classed as historical novelists, did each in fact produce at least one major work in this category, for example Dickens's *Barnaby Rudge* and *A Tale of Two Cities*, Thackeray's *Henry Esmond*, George Eliot's *Romola*, Charles Reade's *The Cloister and the Hearth*, and Charles Kingsley's *Westward Ho!* and *Hereward the Wake*. While Scott looked on history as a pageant of romantic stories, the Victorian attitude was increasingly influenced by the theories of the evolutionary scientists, which gave rise to a general interest in the study of origins.

The variety of the novel in the first half of Queen Victoria's reign, and the fact that many novelists worked in more than one convention, renders classification difficult. There are, however, four outstanding writers: Charles Dickens, William Makepeace Thackeray, and Charlotte and Emily Brontë, whose original genius carried the literary novel to a point beyond anything so far reached. Around these four most of the rest can be grouped.

The Early Victorian Novel: Charles Dickens

Charles Dickens (1812–70) produced *The Pickwick Papers* in the year of the Queen's accession, and thereby his fame was once and for all established. Except for contributions to magazines, collected as *Sketches by Boz*, he had passed through no period of apprentice authorship. His first book was the masterpiece with which his name is universally associated. Strangely enough, *The Pickwick Papers* were intended merely as the letterpress for a series of comic sporting pictures which were published at intervals, but the genius of Dickens made them into the greatest book of humorous fiction in the language. He brought back the "humours" of Ben Jonson and the oddities of Smollett, but used them in a different way. They no longer served to ridicule and castigate society, but were presented with a tolerant and imaginative sympathy. The idea of the Pickwick Club possibly owed something to the Spectator Club of Steele and Addison.

The Pickwick Papers was followed by *Oliver Twist*, in which Dickens introduced his first protest against social evils. In this instance, it was the Poor Law workhouse which was held up to obloquy. In later novels the satire was directed against the tyranny of the charity school, the "Circumlocution Office," and the prison system. But the real interest of Dickens's novels is not in their social teaching, but rather in character and incident. Dickens has peopled our imagination with hundreds of his creations, many of which have become proverbial: Bill Sykes and Uriah Heep, Mrs. Gamp and Little Nell, Sam Weller and Pecksniff embody conceptions of character and conduct which are more clear and positive than any we could have formed from observation of real life.

Most lovers of Dickens would rank *David Copperfield* as his best novel. It has a considerable autobiographical element, and a gallery of imperishable comic creations. Travels in America suggested *Martin Chuzzlewit*, and it was perhaps his visits to the Continent and the publication of Carlyle's *French Revolution* which led to the writing of *A Tale of Two Cities*.

The weaknesses of Dickens are due partly to the circumstances of his own upbringing in a poor and feckless household, and to the limitations which that childhood imposed on his outlook; and partly to the journalistic background of his writing. He had no deep psychological or philosophical insight, and his approach to life is often marred by mawkish sentimentality and excessive pathos.

Practically all the novels of Dickens are badly constructed. Although some of them have highly complicated plots, their characteristic form is picaresque or peripatetic. In a typical example the hero is involved in a succession of loosely connected episodes which are interrupted by numerous digressions, and there is no attempt to present a unified action in which cause and effect have an organic and not merely a mechanical relationship.

16

Thackeray

The structure and style of Thackeray's novels show that he was a more sensitive artist than Dickens, but his interest in and feeling for humanity is more restricted. Thackeray's upbringing was among gentlefolk, and his novels deal exclusively with the life of the upper classes. Like Dickens, his work had a journalistic background,[1] but although all his great novels (except *Henry Esmond*) were serialized before publication, his feeling for form, while not highly developed, was strong enough to give his books a certain architectural and sculptural quality.

Thackeray's reputation rests on five great novels: *Vanity Fair* (1848), *Pendennis* (1849), *Henry Esmond* (1852), *The Newcomes* (1854), and *The Virginians* (1859). In these he shows a remarkable feeling for period, particularly for the eighteenth century. An enemy of sentimentality, he ignored or ridiculed the Romantics, and was much closer in spirit to the Augustans. He lacked the warm human sympathy which Dickens revealed even when dealing with deformity and obliquity; he had no illusions, and the spectacle of human weakness and hypocrisy saddened or soured his spirit. He aimed at realism in the manner of Fielding: "I would have history familiar rather than heroic: and think that Mr. Hogarth and Mr. Fielding will give our children a much better idea of the manners of the present age in England than the *Court Gazette*."

Thackeray's method of narration was that of the omniscient and ubiquitous spectator who does not hesitate to interpose himself between the reader and the story. There are frequent conversational asides which draw the reader's attention to some turn of events, ask his advice, or justify the author's manner of telling the story.

> We must now take leave of Arcadia . . . to enquire what has become of Miss Amelia. "We don't care a fig for her," writes some unknown correspondent with a pretty little handwriting and a pink seal to her note. "She is *fade* and insipid," and adds some more kind remarks in this strain.

Trollope

Anthony Trollope is another Victorian writer who favoured realism. He was a conscientious literary craftsman, and the account in his *Autobiography* of his systematic method of work is well known. He regularly turned out 750 words in three hours' writing in the very early morning, before going to his work as a Civil Service inspector.

---

[1] Thackeray was one of the earliest contributors to *Punch*.

It may be that the decline of his reputation soon after his death was partly due to the effect on his readers of this frank confession.

His attitude to his writing was completely matter-of-fact: he would entertain no notions of "divine afflatus," and took the reader into his confidence even more than Thackeray did. Commenting on his method he said—

> The novelist desires to make his readers so intimately acquainted with his characters that the creatures of his brain should be to them speaking, moving, living, human creatures. This he can never do unless he know these fictitious persons himself. . . . They must be with him as he lies down to sleep, and as he wakes from his dreams. He must learn to hate them and to love them. He must argue with them, quarrel with them, forgive them, and even submit to them.

The creatures with whom Trollope thus lived in his imagination were chiefly the inhabitants of Cathedral closes and country houses, whose love affairs, bickerings, gossip, and local intrigues he described in a leisurely way which was in keeping with the tempo of their lives. The six "Barsetshire" novels beginning with *The Warden* (1855) contain his best work. The others were *Barchester Towers, Framley Parsonage, Doctor Thorne, The Small House at Allington*, and *The Last Chronicle of Barset* (1867). These novels are given a loose unity by the introduction of several of the principal characters in several or all of them.

Trollope stands in the second rank of our novelists. His range was limited. He had the good sense not to attempt what was beyond his powers and his books have an even quality which is often lacking in the work of greater writers. His values were positive and consistent and his technique masterly; with these qualities he was able to create an imaginative world which, though restricted, had its own artistic validity.

Charlotte Brontë

In the novels of Charlotte Brontë, realistic and romantic elements are in close conjunction. But the realism has little in common with that of the three writers who have just been considered. It was not concerned with truth to externals, based on the observation of human idiosyncrasy, but with the workings of the emotions. Charlotte Brontë brought passion (even if it was prim and timid) back into the novel. She was essentially a subjective writer, and her intensity and outspokenness on matters about which the Victorian conventions enjoined silence shocked her generation.

Her revolt was thus both literary and social. At the same time she asserted the reality of the primal instincts of woman, and drove the romantic heroine out of serious fiction. Charlotte Brontë's reputation rests on three novels, *Jane Eyre*, *Shirley*, and *Villette* published between 1847 and 1852. In all these the autobiographical element is strong.

Emily Brontë

Emily Brontë (1818–1848) had little in common with her sisters. She collaborated with both Charlotte and Anne in issuing a volume of verse in which her contribution was alone worthy of notice, and a year later she and Anne published *Wuthering Heights* and *Agnes Gray* respectively in a three-volume edition. Emily's novel has an assured place in the tradition of English fiction, because of its unique qualities. "No coward soul is mine," she wrote in her poem *Last Lines*, and her fierce independence of spirit lights up the passionate tragedy of the Yorkshire moors with stabbing flashes of insight. Nothing in the range of the romantic novel approaches *Wuthering Heights* in its evocation of an atmosphere of gloom and tempest, within the hearts of the characters as well as without.

George Eliot

It will be convenient here to touch on another woman novelist, most of whose work falls into the early Victorian period: George Eliot (1819–80).

George Eliot still holds a high place among the women novelists of England, although the extravagant adulation of her contemporaries rapidly abated in the next generation. She was an intellectual, a radical and a freethinker, and, in contrast to Trollope, regarded her work as a novelist in the light of a mission. There was, however, another aspect of her personality, revealed in her writing by quick intuition and a sympathetic humour in describing the life she knew at first-hand.

> I find a source of delicious sympathy in these faithful pictures of a monotonous homely existence, which has been the fate of so many more among my fellow mortals than a life of pomp or absolute indigence, of tragic suffering or world-stirring actions. I turn, without shrinking, from cloud-borne angels, from prophets, sibyls and heroic warriors, to an old woman bending over her flower-pot, or eating her solitary dinner. . . .
>
> *Adam Bede:* Chapter entitled, "The Story Pauses a Little"

Undoubtedly her best work was done in this spirit. She depicted the homely rural life of England with deep understanding, and a gentle pity for the sorrows and tragedies which followed from error or weakness. The novels which show these qualities best are *Adam Bede, The Mill on the Floss, Silas Marner,* and *Middlemarch.* These, the product of her natural talent, are more successful than the novels which resulted from the exercise of her acquired accomplishments.

The other side of George Eliot's genius is that of the scholar, philosopher, and teacher. The more concerned she is with instruction, the less she succeeds as an artist. *Romola* falls short of being a great novel, notwithstanding the pains which were taken to make it a faithful reproduction of the spirit of Florence at the time of the Renaissance, or perhaps because of this fact. In *Daniel Deronda* the theme of the Jewish racial problem is pursued with laboured gait, and ingenuity does not atone for the absence of spontaneity. This novel is, however, redeemed by the portrait of Gwendolen, who is one of the many superbly imagined women characters in George Eliot's novels.

George Meredith

A wholly serious attitude to the novel as an art-form was shown also by George Meredith. Beginning with *The Ordeal of Richard Feverel* in 1859, the year in which *Adam Bede* appeared, he devoted himself unhurryingly to the craft of letters until his last book, *The Amazing Marriage,* was published in 1895. Like George Eliot he was an intellectual, and like her he used the novel, not merely for the delight of story-telling, but as a means of studying the workings of the human spirit. In 1877 he wrote an essay entitled *The Idea of Comedy,* in which he set out what he considered to be the uses of the Comic Spirit. He found in it the prophylactic against humbug, sentimentality, pretentiousness, and pessimism. He propounded a gospel of common sense, the assertion of the claims of sane and normal humanity as material for art, and the rejection of excess and eccentricity out of which nothing but disaster could arise. This essay lays down the general principles which inspired Meredith's novels, and which gave them solidity and significance.

Meredith disdained popularity and because of the obscurity of his writing his audience has always been a special one. The originality of his style results partly from compression but more from his very individual use of the extended metaphor, which often gave to his language an essentially poetic quality. His novels are almost the only

lyrical novels in English. We are accustomed to find poetry packed
with meaning, with overtones echoing through the plain sense of the
words and sentences. With Meredith we have something similar in
prose. His elliptical, allusive and aphoristic style cannot be read quickly,
and people who are accustomed only to simple prose may not make the
effort of concentration necessary to enjoy his subtleties.

Meredith's aim was to present a reasoned criticism of life based on a
system of moral philosophy, and therein he differs from many of
the novelists discussed above. He was deeply interested also in the
emergence of women as independent human beings; some of his
best portraits are of female characters, and in intellect and judgment
they are often better endowed than their male counterparts. The
work which best illustrates Meredith's original use of language is
One of Our Conquerors, one of his last books. His theory of comedy influenced all his novels, but the fullest embodiment of it is in *The
Egoist*. It is impossible to say that any one of Meredith's books is the
best; all his mature work shows remarkable intellectual and imaginative force, and his extension of the language of prose has had an
incalculable effect on English literature.

Thomas Hardy

Thomas Hardy's novels also are unified by a coherent philosophy
of life. In his case the unifying factor is really metaphysical rather than
philosophical, for he is concerned with the relation of man to the
Universe rather than with social or individual ethics. A superficial
unity results from his choice of Wessex as the setting for his stories,
and from his preoccupation with the primal and universal aspects of
the life of his characters, who inhabited the farms, villages and small
towns of this part of England. There is one silent participator in all his
stories about the Wessex folk, at one time savage and sinister, at another
kindly and caressing, or again brooding with ancient inscrutable
thoughts on their follies, and that is the spirit of the heathland, of the
quiet woods and fields and of the deep roads and foot-paths. This
does not constitute a mere decorative background; it enters into every
human situation as an active agent, and makes its inexorable claims.

A further principle of unity arises from Hardy's philosophical
attitude to the life he depicts. The novel for him is concerned with an
interpretation of life, and his interpretation is tinged with pessimistic
irony. He stresses man's puny insignificance in the struggle with
natural forces, whose tyranny of blind chance he calls Fate. In general,

though touched with humour, his novels are concerned with the tragedy of life.

Hardy's reputation was soon won. His first novel was *Desperate Remedies*, published in 1871, and the chief of the Wessex novels are *Far from the Madding Crowd*, *The Return of the Native*, *The Mayor of Casterbridge*, *The Woodlanders*, *Tess of the D'Urbervilles*, and *Jude the Obscure* (1895). The relative frankness of *Jude* shocked the Victorian world, whose inhabitants had no wish for free discussion of the social problems which it raised. Hardy was rendered angry and contemptuous by its reception and wrote no more novels. Thereafter he published only poetry and poetic drama, but many of the poems had been written much earlier, and this must be remembered in studying the development of his novels.

Other Victorian Novelists

Around these great figures in the history of the literary novel clustered many who in occasional works reached a high level, but whose talent was generally of the second rank. Among these Charles Kingsley, Robert Louis Stevenson, and R. D. Blackmore were in the romantic tradition. Wilkie Collins developed the type of novel in which the plot is all-important, and he created suspense and mystery in a way which foreshadowed the technique of the modern detective story. Charles Reade was nearer to the manner of Dickens, in so far as his novels were social documents—he called them "matter-of-fact romance." The beginnings of photographic realism, and of the objectivity which is typical of twentieth-century fiction, are to be found in the work of George Gissing. Rudyard Kipling was another born story-teller. Many of his novels were set in the Empire, and particularly in India, and were about the people who administered the imperial lands. William Morris and Samuel Butler used the novel to depict Utopias and their intentions were mainly didactic. Another group who achieved considerable popularity in their day were the Scottish novelists, Barrie, Crockett, and Maclaren.

SUGGESTIONS FOR FURTHER READING

LORD DAVID CECIL: *The Early Victorian Novelists* (Constable).

ANTHONY TROLLOPE: *Autobiography* (Oxford Univ. Press).

GEORGE MEREDITH: *An Essay on Comedy and the Uses of the Comic Spirit* (Constable).

BASIL WILLEY: *Nineteenth-century Studies: The Novel* (Chatto & Windus).

CHAPTER XXIII

THE NOVEL: TWENTIETH CENTURY

THE popularity of the novel did not decrease after the turn of the century, and notwithstanding the variety of forms it had already assumed during Victorian times, there was no halt to its development in the hands of the new generation of writers of prose fiction. There was a tendency at this period for the novelist to branch out into other literary forms. Meredith and Hardy wrote memorable poetry; H. G. Wells was a sociologist, historian, and scientist as well as a novelist; John Galsworthy achieved as much distinction in drama as in fiction; and G. K. Chesterton and Hilaire Belloc were essayists, historians, and versifiers.

The Novel of Ideas

The characteristic Edwardian novel was concerned with the discussion of ideas: scientific, social, political, industrial, psychological, and so forth, and was designed for the large middle-class public which had grown up during the nineteenth century, and was now well established. The smug complacency of the Victorian age was being disturbed here and there by anxious questionings as to the validity of the institutions and conventions which had upheld the old order. The emancipation of women was proceeding apace; the hold of the Church on the allegiance of the people was waning; the motor-car and the aeroplane brought increased social mobility, and this was intensified by a war fought by citizen armies. There was a vast accession of state-educated readers to the ranks of the fiction lovers,. and the spread of public libraries and the publication of cheap editions gave them easier access to books. These readers, enjoying the thrill of living in an expanding age, needed the support of general notions for their intellectual life, but were not sufficiently trained to seek their sustenance in specialist books. It was the novel of ideas which provided them with the tonic they needed, in the right doses and in the right strength.

H. G. Wells was outstanding in this work of popular enlightenment. He was a missionary among novelists, teaching and healing, and propagating a gospel of life and conduct for the New Age. He began with a scientific extravaganza: *The Time Machine* (1895) and followed this up with other romances founded on an imaginative treatment of science, such as *The War of the Worlds* and *The Food of the Gods*, mostly written before 1908. Thereafter Wells mingled novels of humorous social satire, such as *Tono-Bungay* (1909) and *The History of Mr. Polly* (1910), with novels of ideas. The latter included *Anne Veronica* (1909), a study of the modern feminist movement, *The Passionate Friends* (1913), which discussed the problem of marriage, *Mr. Britling Sees it Through* (1916), dealing with the roots of patriotism, and *Joan and Peter* (1918), in which education is the theme. Some of Wells's novels have a large autobiographical element, e.g. *Love and Mr. Lewisham* (1900), *Kipps* (1905), and *The New Machiavelli* (1910).

Arnold Bennett and John Galsworthy, both born in 1867, a year after Wells, shared his popularity. Bennett's reputation has sunk low since his death in 1931, while that of Galsworthy, a much greater artist, has not been fully maintained. Bennett declared that he worked under the spell of those French and Russian novelists who aimed at an objective naturalism, independent of moral issues. He recorded what he saw in life and was not moved to take sides, to make protest or to indulge his emotions. By selecting his narrow native world of the Five Towns (which to-day constitute Stoke-on-Trent) as the scene of three of his novels, he was the better able to reflect with faithful accuracy both the external details of the place and the twists and turns of thought and speech of the people. Of these three novels *The Old Wives' Tale* stands out as the greatest. In his later novels Bennett turned away from this familiar ground and lost his sureness of touch. In *Riceyman Steps*, however, where the scene is a London slum area, he was again successful in his portrayal of sordidness.

John Galsworthy had a wider range and a firmer grasp. In the novels which constitute the *Forsyte Saga* (1922), he pictured upper middle-class English life during the generations which lived on either side of the "Great Divide," in other words the close of the Victorian era. On the far side, there were the certitudes and the fancied security of the third quarter of the nineteenth century, changing, as the century wore on, to the weary doubts of the transition years and finally to the violent collapse of conventions and accepted moral sanctions during the period of the First World War and after. Galsworthy was a man of aristocratic temper and with a social conscience. He did not allow his obvious sympathies with the submerged to carry him either into agitation for reform or into sentimentality, but, trained lawyer as he was, he preserved a judicial temper, content with establishing the facts after setting forth the evidence. Galsworthy resembles Trollope in making the novel an inventory of the modes of life of a recognizable social group, and like him he created a novel-cycle by taking his principal characters through one book after another. But Galsworthy differed from Trollope in presenting his characters against the background of a changing environment, and he was thus able to give a fuller assessment of their attitudes and conduct.

The Experimental Novel

No revolutionary changes in the conception of the novel as a literary form were introduced by Conrad, Somerset Maugham, Sir Hugh Walpole, E. M. Forster, and Ford Madox Hueffer, but each wrote books of considerable distinction, original in technique and in content. An outstanding example is Forster's *Passage to India*. There remain to be considered a few authors who looked upon the novel in a completely new way. The novel, like the stage-play, entered on an experimental phase when writers began to seek for a profounder interpretation of the workings of the human mind by using the discoveries of the psychoanalysts.

D. H. Lawrence (1885-1930) was in revolt against the domination of life by the intellect, by prudential morality, and by conventional sentiment. He traced the springs of conduct to Freudian depths, and his heroes and heroines were prompted by dark urges springing up from their subconscious selves. His novels were not concerned with telling stories, but with the study of inner conflicts and their resolution. He was acutely conscious of the unhappiness which comes from the divided mind, and he sought to restore wholeness. Lawrence was the most prominent of the novelists who were influenced by the psychoanalysts. His first great novel was *Sons and Lovers* (1913), and this was followed by *Aaron's Rod, Kangaroo, Lady Chatterley's Lover*, and others. In his style he often does violence to the normalities of prose, and seeks to produce startling effects by the use of incongruous phrases.

His outspokenness on sexual relations went beyond anything so far known in English fiction, and he was interested in the perverse and the neurotic. Lawrence's work was in line with other anti-rationalist tendencies, which he influenced and from which in turn he derived strength. His importance in the second and third decades of the twentieth century extended beyond the confines of the novel and for younger artists and thinkers of every kind he was the symbol of a new movement.

James Joyce (1882–1941) completely rejected the traditional conception of the novel. In the first place he uses the expressionist technique by which characters are projected not by reporting their actions and sayings, as observed from without by an omniscient recorder, but by making the characters themselves reveal their inmost thoughts, moods and feelings, however inconsequent, fragmentary, and fleeting these may be. The expressionist sees a man's life not as a sequence of separate acts and emotions, each capable of analysis in isolation, but rather as a "stream of consciousness" eddying and flowing in a perpetual flux, which is only partly manifested in what he says and does. Consequently Joyce had to evolve a new kind of language in which normal syntax was abandoned and the sentence was no longer the basic unit of expression. He discarded the traditional methods of composition and employed a language in which words were torn from their customary associations, mutilated, coined afresh, and sent chasing helter-skelter after the elusive shreds of meaning. It was, in fact, not the dictionary meaning of a word which mattered to Joyce, as much as the associations with which it is encrusted in the mind of the individual.

Joyce's main works are *Dubliners*, a book of short sketches (1914), *A Portrait of the Author as a Young Man* (1916), *Ulysses* (1922), and *Finnegan's Wake* (1939).

Ulysses is a record of a single day in the lives of a group of people in Dublin in 1904. In language and structure it is one of the outstanding achievements of modern literature. It is divided into eighteen episodes, and each carries three layers of allegorical meaning, apart from the superficial story, and is related organically to the whole. This extremely elaborate plan is executed with unfaltering brilliance, and the final effect of the book is one of extraordinary richness and depth. As with most great works of art, its full significance is not perceived at the first acquaintance. Over *Finnegan's Wake* obscurity lies heavy; the book attempts to express the workings of the unconscious mind in sleep, and uses words as though they were notes in music—that is to say, they are chosen for the emotive power of their sound rather than for their logical meaning.

Virginia Woolf (1882–1941) never ceased to experiment with the novel. She rejected realism and that meant for her the rejection, too, of conventional plot, of objective characterization, sequential narrative, and description. Having thus effectually disembowelled the novel, she set to work to re-create it on new structural principles. In this new form, actions do not simply happen to people; rather are actions inferred through the mental states which they produce in the protagonists. The conception of progression in time, which in the traditional novel is fundamental, is thus reduced to small importance. The focus oscillates between present and past as the consciousness ebbs and flows. In life a casual remark or chance appearance will often bring back to a person's memory the "feel" of some past episode, the details of which have been quite forgotten; but though forgotten the experience has been formative, and remains an element in the mental constitution. Mrs. Woolf attempted to present the creatures of her imagination in their true inwardness, and gave to external events only a secondary importance. The four novels on which her reputation will rest are: *Jacob's Room* (1922), *Mrs. Dalloway* (1925), *Orlando* (1929), and *The Waves* (1931).

SUGGESTIONS FOR FURTHER READING

EDWIN MUIR: *Transition* (Hogarth Press).
D. DAICHES: *The Novel and the Modern World* (Cambridge Univ. Press).
D. M. HOARE: *Some Studies in the Modern Novel* (Chatto & Windus).
H. E. BATES: *The Modern Short Story* (Nelson).

CHAPTER XXIV

ESSAYS AND OTHER PROSE WRITINGS

WE have seen in an earlier chapter that the essay as a literary form in English originated with Sir Francis Bacon. It is quite probable that he was acquainted with some of Montaigne's *Essais*, which were published in France between 1580 and 1595 and translated into English in 1603. Montaigne had not the intellectual grasp of Bacon, but he was a more consummate literary artist. His characterization of himself (in the words of John Florio's translation): "I have a mind free and altogether her owne; accustomed to follow her owne humour," is an admirable summing up of the attitude of the true essayist. But though Bacon treated of some topics which we find also in Montaigne, there is reason to think that he worked out the shape of the essay as an art-form for himself. Beginning with ten examples in 1597, he revised, rewrote, and added until the final edition of fifty-eight essays appeared in 1625. In his dedication to the Duke of Buckingham, he remarks on the popularity the earlier essays had won: "for that, as it seems, they come home to men's business and bosoms."

The style of Bacon was so spare, so austere, so pregnant, that no further development in the direction he had taken was conceivable, and in fact there have been no imitators. But while the *Essays* remain unique in our literature, Bacon had demonstrated once for all that there was a use of prose for instruction and delight which had hitherto not been imagined. By means of the essay, the writer's personal experience and reflection, the play of his thoughts and feelings even about trivial matters which have captured his attention, can be made to promote the enrichment of the reader's mind. It remained only to find the perfect style to match the relaxed and companionable atmosphere in which the occasional essay could be enjoyed.

Steele and Addison

Dryden, in discovering a style which answered his own purposes also provided Steele and Addison with what they required. Their public consisted mainly of the habitués of the London coffee-houses, of which many hundreds are known to have existed in the time of

Queen Anne. Though not exclusive, they served as clubs for people of like tastes and opinions. There the daily newspaper, a recent innovation, could be read and gossip exchanged. These conditions were perfect for the vogue of the essay, and Richard Steele (1672–1729) seized the opportunity with both hands. In 1709 *The Tatler* was launched, a journalistic venture intended to supplement the news-sheets, on three days a week with "advices and reflections," not forgetting "entertainment to the fair sex." Joseph Addison (1672–1719) was a contributor, and wrote "with such force of genius, humour, wit and learning that," said Steele,"I fared like a distressed prince who calls in a powerful neighbour to his aid; I was undone by my auxiliary."

In the beginning of 1711 *The Tatler* ceased publication, and a few weeks later *The Spectator* began to appear daily. The *Tatler* had addressed his readers now from one coffee-house, now from another, according to the theme under discussion. The *Spectator* wrote from an imaginary club, whose members are described in the second paper. The new venture ran for eighteen months under the joint auspices of Addison and Steele, and for another six months under Addison's sole direction. Altogether 635 papers were issued. Of these Steele's share was 240, Addison's rather more, while a hundred or more papers came from other contributors. The initiative usually came from Steele, whose genius was the more original; but Addison's intellectual and moral backing was necessary to sustain the effort.

The aims of *The Spectator* were, in Addison's words—

> . . . to march boldly in the cause of virtue and good sense . . . if I meet with anything in cities, court or country, that shocks modesty or good manners I shall use my utmost endeavours to make an example of it . . . I promise . . . never . . . to publish a single paper that is not written in a spirit of benevolence, and with a love to mankind.
>
> *The Spectator*, No. 34

The topics were therefore concerned largely with fashions and foibles, with morals and religion, and with literature and other matters of taste. Occasionally a paper was devoted to some tale or allegory (e.g. *The Vision of Mirzah*, No. 159). Party politics were barred. "I would recommend this paper," said Addison, " to the daily perusal of . . . everyone that considers the world as a theatre, and desires to form a right judgment of those who are the actors on it." The sequence of papers dealing with the figure of Sir Roger de Coverley, published at intervals, constitute in themselves an embryo novel of exquisite charm, and the collected papers on *Paradise Lost* offer us an important body of literary criticism.

Jonathan Swift

While Steele and Addison were thus winning over their readers to an urbane outlook on the world by the use of genial humour and tolerant raillery, Dean Swift (1667–1745) was using the Essay and other occasional forms of writing for a different purpose. An embittered and disappointed misanthrope, he lashed about him in a spirit of hatred and scorn, holding up to contempt and obloquy the whole human race. He achieved this, not through direct censure of the failings and vices of mankind, but by the subtler method of ridicule disguised as gravity. The story of *Gulliver's Travels* (1726) is told in an artless, matter-of-fact style, and can be read by children for sheer amusement; but the book is in fact an exposure of human littleness and treachery, with particular reference to the vices of his contemporaries.

Swift was perhaps the greatest pamphleteer in English. He took a share in all the controversies of his day. In the *Battle of the Books* he defended the Moderns against the Ancients and in the *Tale of a Tub* he attacked corruptions in religion and learning. He joined in the political struggle on the side of the Tories, and wrote a powerful indictment of Whig policy—*The Conduct of the Allies*. With the six *Drapier's Letters*, published during 1724, which fulminated against the issue of "Wood's halfpence," he roused all Ireland to a state of passionate protest, and became a popular hero. Swift's sharpest weapon was irony, used sometimes with tragic and sometimes with comic effect. A completely different side to his nature is revealed in his *Journal to Stella*, a series of letters in which the gossip of Dublin town is conveyed with a charming simplicity, which is in the strongest contrast to the savage indignation of his satirical writing. But whatever disagreement there may be as to the value of his criticism of life, no one can dispute the supreme excellence of Swift's style. More than any other writer he fostered the purity and dignity of the English language; his prose is lucid, vigorous and rhythmical; the sentences are perfectly balanced and there is an inevitability about his choice of words which is truly classical.

Dr. Johnson and Oliver Goldsmith

The Spectator found many imitators. Dr. Johnson began his occasional writing by reporting (and often fabricating) the speeches in Parliament ("the Senate of Lilliput") in the *Gentleman's Magazine*. In 1750 he launched *The Rambler*, which appeared twice weekly until 1752, when he became much occupied with work on his *Dictionary* (published in 1775). His next journalistic venture was a series of weekly essays contributed to the *Universal Chronicle*, over the signature "The Idler".

At the same time Oliver Goldsmith's essay-periodical, *The Bee*, was appearing, and in 1760 he contributed to the *Public Ledger* the series of "Chinese Letters," which was afterwards republished under the title *The Citizen of the World*. Goldsmith's general aim was similar to that of Steele and Addison, and in structure and mood he introduced little that was new. The soul of the essay, however, is the revelation it affords of the writer's personality. Johnson was a literary dictator, unequivocal and didactic in manner, lacking in grace, yet withal of great intellectual strength. Goldsmith was entirely different; he had an easy, tolerant humour; too tolerant in fact, since it led him into improvident courses. His sweetness, gentleness, and engaging simplicity are reflected in all he wrote, in the *Deserted Village* and *The Vicar of Wakefield* no less than in his essays.

The following passages, in the ponderous style of Johnson and the mellower style of Goldsmith, may be usefully compared—

As in every scheme of life, so every form of writing, has its advantages and inconveniences, though not mingled in the same proportions. The writer of essays escapes many embarrassments to which a large work would have exposed him; he seldom harasses his reason with long trains of consequences, dims his eyes with the perusal of antiquated volumes, or burdens his memory with great accumulations of preparatory knowledge. A careless glance upon a favourite author, or transient survey of the varieties of life is sufficient to supply the first hint or seminal idea, which, enlarged by the gradual accretion of matter stored in the mind, is, by the warmth of fancy, easily expanded into flowers, and sometimes ripened into fruit. *The Rambler*, No. 184

As he had fancied himself quite unperceived, he continued, as we proceeded, to rail against beggars with as much animosity as before: he threw in some episodes on his own amazing prudence and economy, with his profound skill in discovering imposters; he explained the manner in which he would deal with beggars were he a magistrate, hinted at enlarging some of the prisons for their receptions, and told two stories of ladies that were robbed by beggar-men. He was beginning a third to the same purpose, when a sailor with a wooden leg once more crossed our walks, desiring our pity, and blessing our limbs. I was for going on without taking any notice, but my friend, looking wistfully upon the poor petitioner bid me stop, and he would show me with how much ease he could at any time detect an imposter.

The Man in Black (from *The Citizen of the World*)

The Formal and the Informal Essay

These two passages will serve to indicate the broad division which was opening out between the essays which were informative, expository or persuasive, and those which were written to divert the reader and beguile an idle hour. They may be called respectively the formal and the familiar essay. The formal essay, with its kinship to scientific writing, may or may not belong to literature. To be so considered, it would have to do more than serve a useful, practical end; it would require to have some quality of style and presentation which would satisfy the aesthetic sense. Such a quality is to be found in many different kinds of formal essay, including the critical writings of Hazlitt, the *Rural Rides* of Cobbett, Macaulay's essays on history, Ruskin's on aesthetics and sociology, and Carlyle's shorter writings on philosophy. Each of these writers looked on the world from an individual standpoint and our interest in their reports of it is less in the truth of what they say than in the attitudes which reveal their personal outlooks.

Charles Lamb

The development of the informal essay was continued with distinction by Charles Lamb (1775-1834). He found relief from long hours of office drudgery at East India House in a correspondence carried on with Coleridge, who had been at Christ's Hospital with him, and also in critical studies of the early dramatic literature, of which he edited *Specimens* (1808). His "Essays of Elia", which appeared in the *London Magazine* between 1820 and 1823, were afterwards issued as a volume, and ten years later a second series appeared. In these the genius of Lamb found its most perfect expression.

The basic quality of Lamb's mind was an imaginative and poetic humour which touched on simple and familiar topics in an easy discursive spirit, making no claims to profundity, and satisfied to enable the reader to share his quiet reveries, his frolicsome jests, and his hovering, wistful fancies. The topics he touched on might be in themselves unimportant, but a magic web was spun over them by Lamb's own personality. With seeming artlessness, but with consummate artistry, he drew upon his memories and played on his emotions, without ever losing touch with the actualities which started him off on his voyages of discovery. In his critical essays, he reveals himself as a thorough-going Romantic, having closest affinities with the eccentrics of the seventeenth century.

17

Victorian Essayists

There were several other practitioners of the familiar essay during the early Victorian period who, without approaching Lamb in delicacy of touch, nevertheless achieved considerable success. The one who resembled Lamb most closely was Leigh Hunt, an adept in the writing of easy and graceful pieces, but master of many moods. Yet on the whole the Victorian essayists were more attracted by the formal essay. The age took readily to being lectured and instructed, and generally preferred to have its entertainment stiffened with a little solid mental fare. Among the writers of this miscellaneous prose whose essays are still read are John Ruskin, Matthew Arnold, and Walter Bagehot.

The number of periodical journals increased and these were largely literary and scientific; it was an age of tracts. Books of travel and biography, consisting often of collections of essays, were numerous: R. L. Stevenson's *Travels with a Donkey in the Cevennes* (1878) and *Virginibus Puerisque* (1881) are typical instances. While this kind of essay has never since lost ground, it was not until the twentieth century that the informal essay became popular once again, through the work of Max Beerbohm, G. K. Chesterton, E. V. Lucas, Robert Lynd, and many others.

Other Prose Writings

The dividing line between literature and other writing is finely drawn, and is not the same in all epochs nor even for all readers within an epoch. It is generally the fate of second-rate verse to be forgotten entirely, but often a prose work may live, if not for its literary quality, then for some significance which posterity will value in its content. Such writings as Malthus's *Essay on Population*, Godwin's *Political Justice*, John Stuart Mill's *On Liberty*, and Darwin's *Origin of Species* belong to the history of ideas. They are seminal writings, and they have exerted and still exert a profound influence on human thought. Consequently they are assured of immortality, even though few have found pleasure in reading them for qualities which can strictly be called literary. Whether they are admitted into the canon of our literature or not is largely a matter of definition. De Quincey thus distinguished between the literature of knowledge and the literature of power—"The function of the first," he said, "is *to teach*; the function of the second is *to move*; the first is a rudder, the second an oar or sail. The first speaks to *mere* discursive understanding; the second speaks, ultimately it may happen, to the higher understanding or reason, but always *through* affections of pleasure or sympathy." (*Essays on the Poets: Alexander, Pope*). Yet in another passage in his *Letters to a Young Man*, he remarks: "All that is literature seeks to communicate power: all that is not literature seeks to communicate knowledge."

We need not attempt to pronounce on a question in regard to which De Quincey, along with numerous other critics, takes such an uncertain stand; yet we may usefully review briefly some of the prose writings in English which, although they stand outside the principal categories of literature, and are ostensibly concerned with knowledge rather than power, nevertheless have claims to a place in the living tradition of English letters.

Seventeenth-century Prose Writings

The seventeenth century gave us Bacon's *Advancement of Learning*, which advocated empirical methods in scientific inquiry. Sir Walter Raleigh's *History of the World* rises in some passages to a noble eloquence. *The Compleat Angler, or the Contemplative Man's Recreation* by Izaak Walton has long been recognized as a minor classic; it was intended as a practical handbook of the art of fishing, but, in the words of the author, it was also concerned with "the thoughts and joys that have possest my soul." Hobbes's *Leviathan* is an essay in political philosophy, and the Earl of Clarendon's *History of the Grand Rebellion* is a valuable aid to the study of that period, Bunyan's *Pilgrim's Progress*, for a long time the most popular book in the English language after the Bible, had the very practical purpose of winning souls to goodness by allegorizing and dramatizing the author's own religious experiences. It survives because of the emotive force of its incomparable style. John Locke's *Essay Concerning Human Understanding* and his letters and treatises on toleration, government, and education set the tone of most of the philosophical thought of the century which followed.

Eighteenth-century Prose Writings

The advance of the scientific spirit was a marked feature of the eighteenth century, and it influenced the writing of history. Hume's *History of England* is the first piece of historical writing in English which has pronounced literary merit.

The political writings of Burke, among them the *Thoughts on Present Discontents*, and *Reflections on the French Revolution*, advocated reverence for tradition and for established institutions; they are magnificent pieces of rhetoric, in a style which is both overwhelmingly persuasive and of a lofty dignity. *The History of the Decline and Fall of the Roman Empire* by Edward Gibbon is a monumental achievement, in which the style matches the vast scope of the events narrated. Gibbon's prose is in the grand manner. His unit of composition was the paragraph rather than the sentence, and he built up his rolling cadences with such artistry that the effect is often reminiscent of a chorus from a Greek play. The science of political economy dates from Adam Smith's *Wealth of Nations*, in which there is contained the doctrine of economic *laisser-faire* which governed policy during the nineteenth century. Jeremy Bentham held similar views, and in his *Fragment on Government* he elaborated the ethical system of Utilitarianism and founded an important school of political thought known as that of the Philosophical Radicals. Near the end of the century appeared Malthus's *Essay on the Principles of Population*, with its pessimistic conclusion that through the operation of natural laws mankind in the mass was destined to live for ever at the lowest level of subsistence.

The eighteenth century gave us one outstanding biography: Boswell's *Life of Johnson*, perhaps the greatest in any language. The merit of Boswell is that he succeeded in getting into his book his own intense interest in the Doctor, and thereby has kindled in readers a similar zest and enjoyment—a striking example of the creative artist's power to evoke in other minds a feeling akin to his own.

Nineteenth-century Prose Writings

The range of prose writing broadened out very considerably in the nineteenth century, with the development of education and the growth of the reading public. The Rev. Sidney Smith founded the famous *Edinburgh Review* in 1802, a Whig journal which did much to promote the humanitarian movement. It had its importance for literature also, since it decried the poetry of the romantics, and drew upon itself a vehement reply from Byron (*English Bards and Scottish Reviewers*). The Radical point of view in politics was urged by William Cobbett, whose *Rural Rides* first appeared in the *Weekly Political Register*.

The Victorian age was remarkable for a mass of historical, scientific, and philosophical writing, of much importance in the evolution of ideas, and occasionally rising to the level of great literature, but for the most part it was destined to be forgotten. Few people to-day read those typical "great Victorians"—Carlyle, Macaulay, and Ruskin—for doctrine, though for the connoisseur of style their writings are of considerable interest. Carlyle's main works are *The French Revolution, Heroes and Hero-Worship, Past and Present, Sartor Resartus* and the *History of Frederick the Great.* He was a kind of modern prophet, preaching a doctrine of work and aspiration. He used an idiom full of German constructions, invented many new words, and tormented the body of our familiar syntax until it yielded to his imperious demand for more emphasis. Macaulay (*History of England, Essays*), the most readable of all historians, had a style of the utmost clarity, balanced and antithetical, for ever mounting to climaxes in the manner of rhetoric by an orderly progression of positive statements offered with conviction. Ruskin (*Modern Painters, Unto This Last, Sesame and Lilies*) took up an Olympian standpoint in many departments of knowledge, and though his judgments on economics and on art are to-day outmoded, he expressed them in a colourful prose that revealed a poetic vision and sensitivity to beauty. Like Carlyle, he was a prophet, calling upon his age with glowing earnestness to repel the influences which he believed were destroying human happiness.

At a time when the urbanization of England was proceeding apace, there were still many who tried to express the consolations and joys of natural things in literary form. The tradition of the literature of the open air, to which *The Compleat Angler* belonged, was carried on by Gilbert White in his *Natural History of Selborne* (1789), an unaffected description of the wild life of the birds and animals of the district he knew so well, and by Richard Jefferies (1848–87) in *Wood Magic, Bevis: the Story of a Boy*, and *The Story of My Heart*. The second and third of these books constituted a spiritual autobiography of one who had "three giants" dragging him down—disease, despair, and poverty —but who perpetually restored himself through a mystical communion with the life of the fields.

The preoccupation of the Victorians with the foundations of religion produced a spate of writings, in which the claims of Authority were weighed against the claims of Reason. Among these was John Henry Newman's *Apologia pro Vita Sua*, a sincere record of the spiritual experiences which led him into the Roman Church. In this, and in his *Grammar of Assent*, he used a pure, lucid prose, the product of a cultured taste. Liberal Christianity (the "Broad Church") was represented by the writings of F. D. Maurice, Mark Pattison, and Thomas Hughes of Rugby, the author of *Tom Brown's Schooldays*. The evolutionary theory, which was propounded scientifically by

Charles Darwin, and T. H. Huxley, was developed in the direction of sociology, education and psychology by Herbert Spencer, who aimed at a synthesis of knowledge based on the evolutionary hypothesis. Spencer's *Autobiography* (1904), which he called "the natural history of himself," revealed him as a cold and unemotional thinker, without humour, but relentless in his pursuit of truth.

There was a side of the Victorian mind which was very different from that of the strenuous seekers and teachers who have been mentioned above. It is represented by the laughter-makers, the creators of nonsense-worlds based on inverted values and pure inconsequence. The greatest of these in prose was "Lewis Carroll" (1832–98), who wrote *Alice's Adventures in Wonderland* and *Through the Looking Glass*, which are outstanding classics of children's literature.

SUGGESTIONS FOR FURTHER READING

B. DOBRÉE: *English Essayists* (Collins).

LESLIE STEPHEN: *History of English Thought in the Eighteenth Century* (Murray); *The English Utilitarians* (Duckworth). Ed. Aitken; *English Letters of the Eighteenth Century* (Penguin); *English Letters of the Nineteenth Century* (Penguin).

Ed. A. C. WARD: *A Miscellany of Tracts and Pamphlets from John Knox to H. G. Wells* (Oxford Univ. Press).

Ed. MAKOWER and BLACKWELL: *A Book of English Essays* (1600–1900) (Oxford Univ. Press).

CHAPTER XXV

LITERARY CRITICISM: RENAISSANCE

THE function of the literary critic is the evaluation of what has been written, in terms of aesthetic principles appropriate to literature. Every separate art has its own standards, and the term literature is a broad one which embraces many distinct arts, such as those of poetry, of the drama, of fiction, of the essay, of biography, and so on. Although all these use the same basic material, namely words arranged in significant ways, each is judged by its own canons of criticism, because each aims at a different kind of excellence. Literature is the most complex of all the arts, and its values are least capable of being reduced to rule and measure.

The Difficulties of Criticism

The difficulties in the path of the critic are many. One arises from the fact that literature is a transcript of life, and accordingly it offers so many angles from which judgment might start, that no critic can possibly encompass them all. That is why evaluations so often conflict. A feature which one critic considers worthy of admiration, another may regard with indifference or even dislike. There are therefore no final judgments; all are relative and conditional, and often subjective. They depend on the critic's own knowledge and experience, on his natural bias, and on his power to yield himself up to the influence of a literary work as a whole.

Further, there is the fact that any literary work which extends to more than a few lines is difficult to hold steadily and completely in the mind's eye. Let us suppose that Shakespeare's *Julius Caesar* is under consideration. The critical mind can isolate in turn and examine the structure and plot, the characterization, the language (including vocabulary, prosody, and imagery), the central meaning of the play, its place in the development of Shakespeare's dramatic skill, his treatment of his sources, the question of fidelity to historical facts, the political bias of the play if any, and many other matters. All these aspects cannot be comprehended in a single view, nor can they be made the subject of a single judgment.

But there is another obstacle, and this applies to art criticism in general. There is a constant shift of taste as one generation succeeds another. It is a commonplace of literary history that the critics have failed, times without number, to acclaim as great literature works which have since become a priceless part of our heritage. Often they and the public have extravagantly praised works which, within a decade, have become unreadable. That is not to say that criticism is useless. It only points the lesson that criticism is related to a particular time and place, as well as being influenced by the subjective equipment and outlook of the critic. Thus, in delivering to a reader his own interpretation of a book and his own judgment upon it, the critic is not supposed to be giving a final opinion, nor attempting to establish a set of values which shall be universally binding. But he will, by restating from time to time the aesthetic principles which he considers appropriate to the work, and examining it in relation to these principles, be assisting others to a fuller appreciation.

The qualities required in a critic are primarily sensitivity, imagination, knowledge, and judgment. His equipment should include a just perception of the "value-possibilities" of the art and a capacity for judging how near the intrinsic qualities of the work which is under examination come to realizing these potentialities. A good critic must possess also a strong historical sense, else he may fall into the common error of attributing to a writer of the past opinions and feelings which belong to his own time.

In the later part of the seventeenth century, and during the eighteenth, critics were bred in the classical tradition, and considered that it was their function to encourage the artist to conform to fixed canons and accepted traditions, and to assess his work according to the degree of conformity to these standards.

In the modern era the tendency of criticism has been to deny the universal validity of such standards, and to question their authority. The philosopher Kant claimed that beauty was a matter of taste, and that taste was subjective. The critic who saw beauty in an object of art, and the critic who saw none might both be right. This kind of criticism resolved itself into "a record of personal adventures among masterpieces" and could easily degenerate into an outpouring of uncritical enthusiasms and aversions. To-day the best criticism has a firm historical basis: its aim is to deepen understanding of the meaning of works of art by relating them to the spirit and circumstances of their periods. The study of background is often accompanied by a consideration of the artist's personality, using all the resources of modern psychology, and this can be helpful, provided it is not carried to excess, and is employed only in suitable cases. The chief merit of historical criticism is that it cuts through accretions formed by prejudice, and provides a detached evaluation of whatever work is being studied.

Criticism as Literature

Much literary criticism, as much writing of any kind, is ephemeral. Yet there exists a great body of critical comment in English which is not only about literature, but *is* literature in its own right. It may be found in systematic expositions of theory, such as Sir Philip Sidney's *Apologie for Poetrie*; in private note-books, such as Ben Jonson's *Discoveries*, in prefaces such as Dryden's *Preface to the Fables*, in essays such as Addison's *Spectator* paper *On Popular Poetry*, in poems such as Pope's *Essay on Criticism*, in biographies such as Dr. Johnson's *Lives of the Poets*, in journals such as *The Edinburgh Review* and in scattered places in letters and diaries and memoirs. Sometimes valuable literary criticism is embedded as *obiter dicta* in writings which are concerned with other matters, e.g. Hamlet's advice to the players, or Anthony Trollope's asides on the working out of his story in *Barchester Towers*. Writers are deeply concerned with the principles which govern their art, and have always been ready to enter the lists in defence of their own practice. Whenever they have done so, they have thrown a light upon themselves, and the understanding of literary art has been promoted by having abstract principles so closely associated with concrete examples.

In the following pages, a brief outline is given of some of the *loci classici* of literary criticism in English, beginning with Sir Philip Sidney and ending with T. S. Eliot. Here are no academic pronouncements, delivered with unassailable authority. England has never had an institution resembling the French Academy, which, during its long history dating from 1630 has acquired the character of a "high court of letters," to use the phrase of Matthew Arnold. Its influence on the whole has been used in a manner favourable to tradition. To it, in large measure, must be attributed the interest which the French people have in the preservation of the purity of their language, and their jealously guarded standards of literary taste. In England the question of literary aesthetics has never been treated in this manner; it has been left to the play of opinion, and no literary mode has ever commanded more than a partial obedience, or been able to claim the sanction of authority, unless it were the authority derived from the classical literatures.

Literary Criticism in the Age of Humanism

The approach of the English humanists of the sixteenth century to the principles governing the art of letters was strongly influenced by the prestige in which the Latin orators, in particular Cicero, were held. Cicero became the accepted exponent of the Latin style at its highest pitch of excellence. Latin had been studied in the monastic schools all through the Middle Ages, but the examples used there were those derived from a period when the language had become debased. The humanists were concerned to use and teach only a Latin style which was copied from the most perfect models. Cicero was an orator, and the analysis of the Ciceronian diction and syntax became in Renaissance times, under the general description of "rhetoric," the core of a "polite" education. The best educated man was one who could on any and every occasion adduce from Cicero or one of his school a quotation to clinch an argument.

The greatest English teacher of humanistic learning in the early sixteenth century was John Colet, founder of St. Paul's School, who was helped by Erasmus, the man of no country and of all. Together they promoted the study of classical Greek in England; and thus examples of Ciceronian oratory were reinforced by those drawn from Demosthenes. Similarly, as the study of poetry began to overtake that of oratory, the study of the Virgilian epic was helped by that of the Homeric poems.

These early critics of literary style wrote in Latin, the universal language of scholarship. But it is important to mention their writings here for two reasons: one is that they taught a *method* of criticism which could be applied to works written in the vernacular, as well as to the classics. The other is that they opened up a vast quarry of literary material, out of which modern writers might dig for themes and exemplars.

If English was to develop its full potentialities as a literary medium, it was necessary that it should "go to school" and be disciplined. There was, to begin with, the problem of the vocabulary. A compromise had to be reached between reliance on native Anglo-Saxon, with its limited scope, and on the "aureate" style, which was affected by the Latinists. Borrowings there had to be, but not all Latinisms could be assimilated. Just as the Ciceronians were quick to eject barbarous expressions from their system, so English stylists too had to acquire a fastidiousness of taste and habit, so that nothing harmful to the genius of the language might enter and remain. English writers, moreover, had to be taught to appreciate the value of the old rhetorical devices which tended to aptness and clarity and required the judicious selection of material and the well-ordered disposition of its parts, as well as the temperate use of ornament. Though Erasmus insisted that the models to be copied should be the best, he was by no means inclined to be a mere imitator. He knew that the excellence of a literary work was relative to the age in which it was produced, and that it had in it also something of the personality of the writer.

It is to the rhetorical tradition that we must ascribe the prestige attached to oratory, as compared with poetry, among the four kinds of writing which early criticism distinguished; when poetry was mentioned by the humanists, it was usually in a tone of disparagement. The other two—history and philosophy—were reckoned as of still less account. Poetry was regarded as in many respects an inferior art, even when it was not condemned outright, as by the Puritans. The gravamen of the charge against poetry was that it set forth vanities and lying examples, and was therefore subversive of morality. The ornament of verse was regarded as no more than a meretricious embellishment, detracting from rather than adding to the dignity which true eloquence should possess.

Poetry as a Courtly Accomplishment

In the second half of the sixteenth century, we notice the beginning of a change of attitude. The scholarly ideal of the gentleman began to give place to the courtly ideal, and poetry became one of the accomplishments of the fashionable courtier. Interest had been stimulated by the discovery of the text of some fragmentary notes of Aristotle, known as the *Poetics*. He had stood for centuries as a philosopher of such unquestioned repute that his speculations on the nature of the art of poetry supplied the impetus which was required. Numerous writings appeared in "defence" of poetry, answering the detractors, and making positive assertions which indicated a new assessment of poetry as the supreme literary art. Such were Thomas Lodge's *Defence of Poetry* (1579) and Sir Philip Sidney's *Apologie for Poetrie*, written soon afterwards for private circulation, though not published until 1595. Two works of a more systematic character were William Webbe's *Discourse of English Poetrie* (1586) and George Puttenham's *Art of*

English Poesie (1589). Puttenham's work was the more comprehensive, being arranged in three parts: the first, "of poets and poesies," was a history of poetry and a division of it into the "kinds;" the second, "of proportion," dealt with metre, rhyme, and accent and included a discussion of quantitative verse, the use of which had been urged on Edmund Spenser by Gabriel Harvey; the third part, "of ornament," was concerned with style, including figures of speech.

Sidney's "Apologie for Poetrie"

Sidney's *Apologie* merits a somewhat fuller discussion, because it is literature, and not merely of historical interest. He wrote it as a dignified retort, when a pamphlet entitled *The School of Abuse*, "a pleasant invective against Poets, Pipers, Players, Jesters, and such Caterpillars of a Commonwealth," was dedicated to him without permission by the author, Stephen Gosson. Sidney was still a youth in his twenties when he wrote his reply, a fact which makes the display of learning in the *Apologie* all the more astonishing. He first shows how poets were honoured by the ancients as having the attributes of prophets. Then he turns to the true nature of poetry and asserts that "rhyming and versing" are not essential to it. These devices may, he allows, have a practical use as helps to the memory, and may give a kind of pleasure, but the real essence of poetry is in its power to instruct and delight at the same time. Sidney passes next to a question which occupied much of the attention of early literary critics, namely, the distinction which ought to be made between the "kinds" of writing, and particularly the "kinds" of poetry. His own classification is confusing, since it involves a cross-division. It is based partly on metrical structure and partly on subject matter.

Sidney turns next to a vindication of poetry against the disparagements of those who have called it "the mother of lies," but at the same time he acknowledges the defects of English poetry from Chaucer to Spenser. Referring to *The Shepherd's Calendar*, he says: "That same framing of his stile to an old rustick language, I dare not alowe, sith neyther Theocritus in Greeke, Virgil in Latin, nor Sanazar in Italian, did affect it," and later he refers with contempt to the "tingling sound of rhyme." The deference paid in the above passage to the authority of classical and Italian models is characteristic. It occurs also in Sidney's treatment of English drama. He is strongly in favour of the Unities, holding up to ridicule the extravagances of romantic plays, in which the complex plots range over time and place, disregarding the limits set by reason. Sidney's strictures on the literary failings of his time include an attack on preciosity of style. Lyly's *Euphues* had just been published, and this was certainly in Sidney's mind when he derided tinsel and decoration as a tiresome substitute for eloquence.

The great value of the *Apologie* lies in the fact that it treats of literature in the spirit of an artist, rather than in that of a scholar. It restores poetry to a worthy place among human activities, and makes claims for English as a medium which, "equally with any other tongue in the wc rld," is capable of sustaining the highest flights of fancy and verbal melody," "uttering sweetly and properly the conceits of the mind." At the same time Sidney's limitations of outlook must be remembered. To him all poetry found its justification in its quality of "vertue-breeding delightfulness . . . voyde of no gyfte, that ought to be in the noble name of learning." In thinking thus, he revealed a prejudice of long standing, nourished by the Church in the Middle Ages, which regarded all forms of art as the handmaidens of morality.

In addition to discovering general principles, Sidney began to apply the critical method to particular works. In a well-known passage, he praised Chaucer, who "undoubtedly, did excellently in hys *Troylus and Crisseid*; of whom, truly I know not, whether to merveile more, either that he in that mistie time, could see so clearly, or that wee in this clear age, walke so stumblingly after him." Sidney proceeds to mention with approval the *Mirror of Magistrates* and "the Earle for Surrie's *Liricks*," and then follows the reference to Spenser's *Shepherd's Calendar* quoted above.

The University Wits

This fashion of commenting on the literature of the day found many followers; it brought criticism out of the scholar's study into the market-place or the tavern, where opinions on the latest author, book, poem or play became the current coin of conversation among the critics. The performance of Marlowe's *Tamburlaine the Great* (Part I) on the stage in 1587 set them talking vigorously. To be sure, Marlowe had thrown down a challenge—

> From jigging veins of rhyming mother-wits,
> And such conceits as clownage keeps in pay,
> We'll lead you to the stately tent of war,
> Where you shall hear the Scythian Tamburlaine,
> Threatening the world with high astounding terms.

These "high astounding terms" Thomas Nash, one of the "University wits," preferred to call "swelling bombast," and the use of blank verse, which was so startling an innovation after the "jigging veins" of rhymed verse, he stigmatized as "bragging" and "the spacious volubility of a drumming decasyllabon." In these opinions, and others contained in his pamphlets, he was supported at first by Robert Greene, another of the inn-parlour critics, who later, in a pamphlet entitled *A Groatsworth of Wit bought with a Million of Repentance*, written just before he died in 1592, made amends to Marlowe, and claimed him as one of those who, along with Nash and Peele, had reason to protest against the growing popularity of a new school of playwrights, "antics garnished in our colours." One of these in particular incurred his jealousy: "an upstart crow, beautified with our feathers, that with his tiger's heart wrapped in a player's hide, supposes he is as well able to bombast out a blank verse as the best of you: and being an absolute *Johannes Factotum*, is in his own conceit the only *Shakescene* in the country."

Greene's pamphlet is addressed to George Peele, who is abjured to share the author's repentance for a life misled. Peele's interlude, *The Old Wives' Tale*, is of interest because it uses parody as an instrument of criticism.[1] In it rustic dialogue is used side by side with the affected diction of the overdrawn characters of romance, with the obvious intention of poking fun at a certain style of writing. The noisy controversy which the University Wits as a group were waging with the pedantic Gabriel Harvey, "father of the hexameter in English," is recalled by the preposterous use of mock-classical metres by the clown Huanebango—

> Dub dub a dub, bounce, quoth the guns, with a sulphurous huff-snuff:
> Waked with a wench, pretty peat, pretty love, and my sweet pretty pigsnie.

Rhyme and No-rhyme Controversy

Notwithstanding the appearance of so many excellent rhymed lyrics and other verse in the last twenty years of the sixteenth century, which might have been expected to settle the controversy of rhyme and no-rhyme, the debate broke out afresh at the start of the new century. It is surprising that there should have been on the side of the no-rhymesters so sweet a singer of rhymed lyrics as Thomas Campion, the author of—

---

[1] *The Old Wives' Tale* gave Milton the idea for *Comus*.

There is a garden in her face,
Where roses and white lilies grow;
A heavenly paradise is that place,
Wherein all pleasant fruits do flow,
    There cherries grow that none may buy,
    Till Cherry-ripe themselves do cry.

That he could also write charming unrhymed verse is shown by his often-quoted *Rose-cheek'd Laura*, with its opening stanza—

Rose-cheek'd Laura, come;
Sing thou smoothly with thy beauty's
Silent music, either other
Sweetly gracing.

The position taken up by Campion in his *Observations on the Art of English Poesie* (1602) was in fact a middle one. Rhyme, he considered, was no more than one of many figures of rhetoric, to be moderately used lest it should result in "tedious affectation." He was at pains to show that it was no more than "a vulgar and unartificial custom," since it was possible for English verse to capture the beauty of unrhymed classical metres, except the dactylic hexameter which, he conceded, was "altogether against the nature of our language." Campion's disparagement of rhyme was little more than the last flicker of a Renaissance prejudice. It required only the reply which Daniel issued immediately afterwards to snuff it out, and in general to dispel the notion that literary excellence was most surely to be achieved through the imitation of ancient models. In his tractate entitled *Defence of Rhyme* Daniel used not only the historical argument—that the use of rhyme was universal and of great antiquity, and consequently might be supposed to indicate some favourable disposition towards it in the human mind—but also the aesthetic argument. Rhyme, he contended, "giveth wings to mount." Let the world "enjoy that which it knows and what it likes, seeing that whatsoever force of words doth move delight and sway the affections of men . . . is true number, measure, eloquence and perfection of speech." The importance of Daniel was that he brought critical theory into line with practice. English poetry, like English drama, had grown up without the support of "rules," or rather in spite of them, to heights which no other literature in the world had reached. Criticism was no longer merely negative and defensive, but was now beginning to be directed to the end of promoting appreciation.

Jonson's Classicism

Ben Jonson, every inch a critic, left us no systematic work on criticism, though it is possible that such a work was lost in the burning of his library. His views are contained in his *Conversations with Drummond*, and in his notebook: *Timber: or Discoveries*, which was not intended for publication. Jonson was accepted in the literary circles of the time ("the tribe of Ben") as a veteran arbiter of taste, a position which no modesty of his own prevented him from filling. Having strong likes and dislikes, he asserted his opinions somewhat aggressively. *Timber* consists of aphoristic jottings on men and manners, only some of which touch on literary matters. There is no logical arrangement, and it is possible therefore to give only a few unconnected examples of the opinions expressed. Criticizing romantic dramatists he says: "Though his (i.e. the playwright's) language differs from the vulgar somewhat, it shall not fly from all humanity, with the Tamerlanes and Tamerchams of the late age, which had nothing in them but the scenical strutting and furious vociferation to warrant them to the ignorant gapers." Regarding the authority of ancient writers: "It is true they opened the gates and made the way, that went before us; but as guides, not commanders . . . Truth lies open to all." On polemical writers: "Their arguments are as fluxive as liquor spilt upon a table, which with your finger you may drain as you will." On the acquisition of style: "For a man to write well, there are required three necessaries, to read the best authors, observe the best speeches, and much exercise of his own style." Though his scholarship was deep, Jonson was no Dr. Dryasdust. His wit and shrewdness saved him from pedantry. "Writings," he said, "need sunshine." "Ease and relaxation are profitable to all studies." He was a classicist by conviction, ranking the qualities of clarity, reason and discretion in writing above those of variety, spontaneity, and exuberance. "The sum of all is," he concluded, "ready writing makes not good writing, but good writing brings on ready writing."

With *Timber* the era of Elizabethan criticism comes to an end. Ben Jonson had a grasp of critical method which might have carried literary studies to a very advanced point. He also had before him for observation a plethora of literary products to which he might have applied his critical probe. But whether material or psychological circumstances were the cause, the method was never fully worked out, and we are left with only fragmentary glimpses of his views on literature.

Dramatic Criticism

The development of dramatic criticism ran roughly parallel with that of poetic criticism. We have seen that before there could be any adequate consideration of the nature and art of poetry, the question of why it should exist at all had to be answered. It was to this question that Sidney had addressed himself in his reply to Gosson's frontal attack. The earliest controversies regarding drama were concerned with whether or not stage-plays should be regarded as "instruments of Satan," used for the perversion of the nation. The assault was launched by the Puritans, whose hostility to the theatre was strong enough to secure the passing of repressive laws. In 1572, players, other than those attached to companies under dignified patronage, were classed as "rogues, vagabonds, and sturdy beggars," and although in 1576 a licence was given for the building of the first permanent theatre, it was erected outside the boundaries of the City of London, in Shoreditch.

The defence of play-acting followed the usual lines: namely, that public performances had the sanction of ancient custom, and had in general tended towards the inculcation of virtue. When plays had dealt with themes of wantonness, they were to be interpreted allegorically, as warning examples. While the debate continued, and the attackers were using the same arguments as they applied to dicing, gaming, and such idleness, neither the livery actors in the new theatres, nor the "common players" clandestinely strutting the boards in remoter places, were unduly disturbed, and the development of drama continued without interruption.

The beginnings of real dramatic criticism are to be found not in formal treatises, but in the day to day exchanges in which the eager practising playwrights of the fifteen-nineties hurled invective at each other. The discussion centred for the most part on what concessions ought to be made to the liking of the theatre groundlings for melodramatic rant, bloodshed, and clowning. There were none to defend in principle this craving on the part of the London citizen, but nevertheless most playwrights made concessions to it. The attitude of Shakespeare is summed up in Hamlet's address to the Players—

Hamlet. Speak the speech, I pray you, as I pronounced it to you, trippingly on the tongue: but if you mouth it, as many of your players do, I had as lief the town-crier spoke my lines. Nor do not saw the air too much with your hand, thus; but use all gently: for in the very torrent, tempest, and as I may say, the whirlwind of passion, you must acquire and beget a temperance that may give it smoothness. O it offends me to the soul to hear a robustious periwig-pated fellow tear a passion to tatters, to very rags, to split the ears of the groundlings, who, for the most part, are capable of nothing but inexplicable dumb-shows and noise: I would have such a fellow whipped for o'erdoing Termagant; it out-herods Herod: Pray you, avoid it.

First Player. I warrant your honour.

Hamlet. Be not too tame neither, but let your own discretion be your tutor: suit the action to the word, the word to the action; with this special observance, that you o'erstep not the modesty of nature: for anything so overdone is from the purpose of playing, whose end both at the first and now, was and is, to hold as t'were the mirror up to nature; to show virtue her own feature, scorn her own image, and the very age and body of the time his form and pressure. Now, this overdone, or come tardy off, though it make the unskilful laugh, cannot but make the judicious grieve; the censure of the which one must, in your allowance, o'erweigh a whole theatre of others. O, there be players that I have seen play—and heard others praise and that highly,—not to speak it profanely, that, neither having the accent of Christians, nor the gait of Christian, pagan, nor man, have so strutted and bellow'd that I have thought some of nature's journeymen had made them, and not made them well, they imitated humanity so abominably.

First Player. I hope we have reform'd that indifferently with us, Sir.

Hamlet. O, reform it altogether. And let those that play your clowns speak no more than is set down, for them: for there be of them that will themselves laugh, to set on some quantity of barren spectators to laugh too; though, in the mean time, some necessary question of the play, be then to be consider'd; that's villainous, and shows a most pitiful ambition in the fool that uses it. Go, make you ready.

The "strutting and bellowing" style is illustrated by the interlude performed by Bottom the Weaver and the rustics in *Midsummer Night's Dream*—

> O grim-look'd night! O night with hue so black!
> O night which ever art when day is not!
> O night, O night! alack, alack, alack,
> I fear my Thisbe's promise is forgot!

Reduced to general terms, it means that there was still in the air a certain vague respect for classical standards of decorum and moderation, but that the practical instincts of the Elizabethan dramatists were powerful enough to guide them, without help from tradition, through this unmapped territory of art. Lyly discovered for himself the comedy of dialogue, Shakespeare the comedy of romantic episode, and Ben Jonson the comedy of humours. Only Jonson was much concerned with keeping tragedy and comedy distinct. We may gather from Polonius's enumeration of the separate "kinds" more than a hint of Shakespeare's own impatience with such an analysis—

The best actors in the world, either for tragedy, comedy, history, pastoral, pastoral-comical, historical-pastoral, tragical-historical, tragical-comical-historical-pastoral, scene individable, or poem unlimited.

Any attempt to classify Shakespeare's plays by rule or system must lead to failure. It has to be remembered that he, like his fellow dramatists, was writing for the stage and not for the study, and that the pragmatic test was the only one he needed to consider.

SUGGESTIONS FOR FURTHER READING

GEORGE PUTTENHAM: *Arte of English Poesy* (Cambridge Univ. Press).
J. W. H. ATKINS: *English Literary Criticism: the Renascence* (Methuen).
R. P. COWL: *Theory of Poetry in England* (Macmillan).
G. SAINTSBURY: *History of English Criticism*, Vol. I (Blackwood).
SIR PHILIP SIDNEY: *Apologie for Poetrie* (Cambridge Univ. Press).
WORLD'S CLASSICS: *Shakespeare Criticism*, 2 vols (Oxford Univ. Press).

CHAPTER XXVI

MODERN LITERARY CRITICISM

W ITH the change in manners and modes which accompanied the restoration of the monarchy in England in 1660, there came also a change in the technique of criticism. During the seventeenth century, France had become the arbiter of artistic taste, displacing Italy, which had dictated the standards of the sixteenth century. "For some three-quarters of a century," says Saintsbury in his *History of Criticism*, "France was the head manufactory in which Italian, Classical and other ideas were torn up and remade into a sort of critical shoddy with which . . . Europe was rather too eager to clothe itself."

The exiles returning from France with Charles II swung England into line with continental criticism, which took its bearings from the *Poetics* of Aristotle and the *Ars Poetica* of Horace. French critics from Boileau to Bossuet had built up a system of abstract rules which claimed to be authoritative with respect to each several form of literary work, a poem or play being good or bad in virtue not of its intrinsic qualities, but of its fidelity to the nature of its "Kind." Examples of each "Kind" for guidance were to hand from classical literature.

> Learn hence for ancient rules a just esteem;
> To copy nature is to copy them.
>
> POPE: *Essay on Criticism*

Neo-classicism: Dryden

John Dryden was the first notable exponent of the neo-classical doctrine in England. His critical opinions are to be found in his *Prefaces*, his *Essays*, and his *Prologues*.

In his early play *The Rival Ladies*, acted at the Theatre Royal in 1663, Dryden decided to use rhymed verse. He thus cut himself adrift from the blank verse tradition of the Elizabethans and their followers, and brought our drama close to the French tradition established by Molière, Corneille and Racine. He defended his choice in a dedicatory essay, declaring that there is no substance in the argument that rhyming is unnatural, and asserting that rhyme, while stimulating the imagination, also puts a brake on discursiveness. Thus at the

outset of his career as a dramatist he found himself the centre of a
controversy. In the interval during the Great Plague, when the theatres
were closed, he worked out his views more fully in his *Essays of
Dramatick Poesie*. It is in the form of a discussion between four writers
of Dryden's circle, including Dryden himself, using the disguise of
Latin names. Seated in a barge on the Thames, they consider first the
literary scene in general, and more or less agree—

> how much our poesy is improved by the happiness of some writers yet
> living; who first taught us to mould our thoughts into easy and signi-
> ficant words; to retrench the superfluities of expression, and to make
> our rhyme so properly a part of the verse, that it should never mislead
> the sense, but itself be led and governed by it.

They then decide to confine their attention to the drama, and two
principal conflicts of opinion arise, firstly, regarding the value of the
classical "rules," which had been given new authority by the recent
French practice, and secondly, regarding the use of rhymed verse in
serious drama. With respect to the first, Neander (Dryden) defends
the English stage, and pays a warm tribute to "our" Shakespeare,
whom he sets "far above" Jonson—

> He was the man who of all modern, and perhaps ancient poets, had the
> largest and most comprehensive soul. All the images of nature were still
> present to him, and he drew them not laborously, but luckily; when he
> describes anything you more than see it, you feel it too. Those who
> accuse him to have wanted learning, give him the greater commendation:
> he was naturally learned; he needed not the spectacles of books to read
> Nature; he looked inwards, and found her there.

On the question of rhyme he repeats his earlier defence, and delivers
the astonishing judgment: "Blank verse is acknowledged to be too
low for a poem." This was said at the time when *Paradise Lost* was
being published.

Some pregnant remarks on poetry are to be found in the letter
introducing *Annus Mirabilis*, the poem describing "the year of wonder,"
1666. Declaring that "the composition of all poems is or ought to be
of wit," he goes on to define "wit," or "wit-writing," as "no other
than the faculty of imagination in the writer" . . . "Wit . . . is
some lively and apt description, dressed in such colours of speech,
that it sets before your eyes the absent object as perfectly and more
delightfully than nature. So then the first happiness of the poet's
imagination is properly invention, or finding of the thought; the
second is fancy, or the variation, driving or moulding of that thought

as the judgment represents it proper to the subject; the third elocution, or the art of clothing that thought so found and varied in apt, significant and sounding words. The quickness of the imagination is seen in the invention, the fertility in the fancy, and the accuracy in the expression."

Other important critical pronouncements of Dryden are *Grounds of Criticism in Tragedy* and the *Preface to Fables, Ancient and Modern,* containing the excellent appreciation of Chaucer.[1]

As a critic, Dryden towers above all his predecessors in England. His independence of judgment, his refusal to condemn our authors to lie on the Procrustean bed of categories, his insistence on the place of imagination, and his conception of poetry as existing for men's delight, saved our literature from too complete a subjection to a code. At the same time, he was so far a lover of order that he searched in the poets themselves for organic principles, and thus put criticism on the right path.

Addison

Addison, the next great figure in the development of literary criticism, was not an innovator. His achievement was to give expression in a clear, attractive style to the ideas which were forming in the best minds of the day regarding the "obvious things that every man may have use for." (*Tatler*, No. 18.) Among these was literature, now the main theme of good conversation in the coffee-houses.

The *Spectator*, in a series of critical papers, comments on three principal topics: wit and judgment, Milton and *Paradise Lost*, and the pleasures of the imagination. Addison's general outlook on these matters is that of one who, while loving correctness, yet recognizes that there must be scope for a free play of the mind. He considered that all good style in art has an element of spontaneity, and that criticism is something more than an account of "beauties" and "faults," measured by external standards. He was an apostle of Good Sense, applying to literature, and to the arts in general, the new rational spirit popularized by John Locke.

Pope

The apogee of eighteenth-century "correctness" is represented by Alexander Pope. He was a conscious artist: "I corrected because it was as pleasant to me to correct as to write" (Preface to *Works*, 1717).

[1] See p. 218.

His own question "Why did I write?" he answers in the *Epistle to Dr. Arbuthnot*, being the *Prologue to the Satires*. His views on the art of poetry are contained in two poems: the *Essay on Criticism* and the *Imitation of the Epistle of Horace to Augustus*.

An important part of Pope's argument in the *Essay on Criticism* is contained in the lines—

> Those Rules of old discovered, not devis'd,
> Are Nature still, but Nature methodis'd;
> Nature like liberty, is but restrain'd
> By the same laws which first herself ordain'd.

That is to say, the rules which the ancients followed were based on nature: and the poet who would follow nature,

> At once the source, and end, and test of Art,

can only proceed by imitating the ancients—

> Learn hence for ancient rules a just esteem;
> To copy nature is to copy them.

Although Pope puts the matter here so positively, he is forced to admit that the rules are not all-comprehensive—

> Some beauties yet no Precepts can declare,
> For there's a happiness as well as care.
> Music resembles Poetry; in each
> Are nameless graces which no methods teach.

It might be argued that Pope thus contradicts himself. The "happiness" which is produced by "nameless graces" comes near to summing up the romantic manner.

Dr. Johnson

Dr. Johnson, in *The Lives of the Poets* (1779–81), produced one of the greatest works of criticism in the language. The booksellers of London had asked him to write short biographical notes for a new edition of the English Poets then in preparation. The task was so congenial to him that the notes grew into eleven volumes. They show the limitations of Johnson as a critic, for though he had read widely (a fact of which the *Dictionary* gives evidence), his appreciation did not extend to all kinds of writing. He disliked anything archaic, had little taste for any writers, Shakespeare excepted, earlier than Dryden, and was capable of such dubious estimates as that on the Spenserian stanza, which he found "at once difficult and unpleasing; tiresome to the ear from its uniformity, and to the attention by its length." His judgment on the sonnet in general is equally dogmatic: "The fabric of a sonnet, however adapted to the Italian language, has never succeeded in ours." To the core of his being he was a creature of his own time. The *Lives* are concerned for the most part with the poets of the period beginning in the middle of the seventeenth century, and he is at his best when dealing with those who wrote in a style congenial to him, e.g. Dryden, Addison, and Pope. His comparative study of Dryden and Pope is a model of this kind of criticism. On the other hand, he allowed his pronounced Tory-Anglican principles to influence some of his literary judgments, as in the case of Milton and Gray.

Johnson is the master of the biographical-critical method. He had a retentive memory, and the literary gossip of the clubs and drawing-rooms he loved to frequent provided him with an abundance of the anecdotal material which makes the *Lives* such entertaining reading. With him ends the criticism which supported the Ancients in the great battle of Ancients *versus* Moderns, and allowed merit to the Moderns only occasionally, by way of a concession reluctantly granted. The exponents of this school urged the need for objective standards, and condemned the kind of literary criticism which rested only on the shifting base of subjective preferences.

New Directions in Criticism

Before the advent of Coleridge, one of the chief interpreters of Romanticism, there were at the end of the eighteenth century several movements afoot which tended to make criticism more catholic in outlook, and applied to it the transcendental philosophies which were then gaining popularity. Thomas Warton (1728–90), in his *Observations on the Faerie Queene of Spenser* and in his *History of English Poetry*, showed how since the Middle Ages there had been a continuous literary development, which made it impossible to dismiss the early centuries of our literature as if they offered nothing worth attention except the works of Chaucer and Spenser. By transcribing large passages of early poetry and prose, he furnished critics for the first time with material upon which judgments could be based. The few early writers whose works had been available before could now be studied in a wider setting, among a host of their contemporaries, and thus it became possible for the valuable historical method of criticism to be developed. In particular Warton was sympathetic towards the sixteenth century, a seedtime in our literature. He also made available for study parts of the wide field of Teutonic and Celtic romance. All this was of the greatest importance for the growth of the romantic spirit. Further material was provided by the publication of Hurd's *Letters of Chivalry and Romance* in 1762, which preceded the Gothic revival, and of Percy's *Reliques of Ancient Poetry*.

While the early centuries were thus being rescued by research from an obscurity which had excused the imputation of barbarism, there was a great development of aesthetic theory. The germ was already present in Addison's *Spectator* essays on the Imagination, which he subjected to a scientific analysis. Sir Joshua Reynolds, in his fifteen *Discourses*, which were delivered in the Royal Academy between 1769 and 1791, essayed a philosophy of art, and Edmund Burke, in his *Philosophical Enquiry into the Origin of our Ideas on the Sublime and the Beautiful*, was concerned with the psychological aspect of a similar subject. Although this work had little influence, its appearance is at least an indication that attention was turning from the ponderables of art to the imponderables, from what was demonstrable to what was intuitive. It was becoming recognized that aesthetic criticism should study not only the manifest qualities of a work of art, as, for instance, the formal properties of a poem, its subject and so forth, but also the creative process whereby it came into existence, and the creative response of the reader.

Wordsworth and Coleridge as Critics

The *Preface to the Lyrical Ballads*, containing Wordsworth's views on Poetic Diction, has been touched on elsewhere.[1] An exposition of "romantic" criticism may be found in Coleridge's *Lectures on Shakespeare* (1811–12), and in his *Biographia Literaria* (1817). In these works, which were strongly influenced by the new school of criticism which had grown up in Germany, under Lessing and Goethe, Coleridge maintains that poetry is an organic growth, and that the function of the imagination is to "unite opposites." The consummate dramatist, for example, recognizes and gives expression to the kind of experience in which laughter and tears are close associates—

> Our sincerest laughter
> With some pain is fraught.
> SHELLEY: *To a Skylark*

Comedy and Tragedy are not incongruous elements to be rigidly kept apart in drama. It is just because tragic plays like *Hamlet* and *Antony and Cleopatra* are streaked with humour that we accept them as

[1] See p. 126 *ff.*

valid transcripts of human life. According to this view the comic relief in romantic tragedy needs no defence, and there is no such thing in human life as unadulterated villainy, or folly unrelieved by pathos. Coleridge thus answers the detractors of Shakespeare by claiming for him an art which is superior to that based on the classical rules.

But the main part of Coleridge's criticism is concerned with Wordsworth. He tells us the story of the genesis of the *Lyrical Ballads*, and proceeds to a statement of his own views on the merits of Wordsworth's attempt to revolutionize the language of poetry. He rejects altogether the dictum that the language used by men in humble and rustic life is close to poetry, and points out that if we excluded the poems of Wordsworth which contradicted this dictum, "two-thirds at least of the marked beauties of his poetry must be erased." Coleridge also disagreed with the even more dogmatic assertion that "there neither is nor can be any essential difference between the language of prose and metrical composition." In another passage he admits that "poetry of the highest kind may exist without metre," and it is to him that we owe the pregnant statement that poetry is to be distinguished not from prose, but from science.

But although Coleridge thus controverts Wordsworth's critical attitudes, and points out defects, such as banality, prolixity, and incongruity of thought and subject, he considers that his friend's best work reveals an outstanding creative imagination.

Hazlitt and Lamb

Coleridge influenced English criticism for most of the nineteenth century. Hazlitt (1779–1830), who acknowledged his indebtedness in the most generous terms, lacked the brilliant and penetrating, if wayward, intellect of Coleridge, though his criticism was coherent and systematic. His output was considerable, and includes the *Characters of Shakespeare's Plays* (1817), *Lectures on the English Poets* (1818), the *Lectures on the English Comic Writers* (1819), and *Dramatic Literature in the Age of Elizabeth* (1821), the whole constituting a broader survey of our literature than any major critic had yet attempted.

Hazlitt is usually associated with his friend Charles Lamb (1774–1834), whose *Essays of Elia* touch on books and on the pleasures of reading from a hundred different angles, and this in an inimitable style which has made his critical essays some of the most familiar in our literature. It may, however, be objected that Lamb, since he does not offer us a coherent body of doctrine, is a commentator rather than a critic. He appears moreover to be deficient in some qualities necessary to criticism, particularly with regard to poetry. His interest is in the capacity of books to give delight, rather than in the manner in which this result is achieved. Nevertheless, Lamb did much to develop the understanding and appreciation of early, and especially Elizabethan, drama. His *Specimens of English Dramatic Poets who lived about the Time of Shakespeare* (1808) was valuable not only because it increased the range of English literature accessible to the general reader, but also for his notes and comments. Lamb considered that the greatness of the Elizabethans lay in their creative imagination, and he shared with Coleridge a strange opinion that "the plays of Shakespeare are less calculated for stage performance than those of almost any other dramatist whatever." His favourite reading was the work of the moralists of the seventeenth century; Burton, Fuller, Sir Thomas Browne, Donne, and Jeremy Taylor. From each he derived some particular quality of thought and style to add to his own gentle and frolic humour.

Shelley's "Defence of Poetry"

Shelley's *Defence of Poetry* (1821) recalls, in its title and its abstract method, the work of Sidney which it resembles also in spirit. There is a further parallel in the fact that Shelley's *Defence*, like Sidney's, was called forth by a violent attack on poetry. Thomas Love Peacock, in *The Four Ages of Poetry*, had argued that poetry belonged only to the heroic ages, and that in the conditions of the modern world it could not survive—

> A poet in our times is a semi-barbarian living in a civilized community. He lives in the days that are past. His ideas, thoughts, feelings, associations, are all with barbarous manners, obsolete customs, and exploded superstitions. The march of his intellect is like that of a crab, backwards. The brighter the light diffused around him by the progress of reason, the thicker is the darkness of antiquated barbarism, in which he buries himself like a mole, to throw up barren hillocks of his Cimmerian labours. . . . The highest inspirations of poetry are resolvable into three ingredients: the rant of unregulated passion, the whining of exaggerated feeling, and the cant of fictitious sentiment.

To this diatribe Shelley replied with a vindication of poets as "the unacknowledged legislators of mankind" and "the founders of civil society." Poetry was "the record of the best and happiest moments of the happiest and best minds," and among these he included such writers as Plato, Herodotus, Plutarch, and Bacon, notwithstanding that they did not employ the medium of verse, since they too used "a sweet and majestic rhythm" and kindled a harmony of thought. He claimed that in the infancy of society every author was necessarily a poet, because language itself was poetry, and a single word might be a spark of inextinguishable thought. It was therefore no academic apology which Shelley offered. He allowed that rhythm was a natural pleasure, but insisted more on the need for poetry to express the life of imagination.

Victorian Criticism: Arnold

Literary criticism in the Victorian Age is represented by Matthew Arnold, one of the greatest poet-critics in our literature. His first critical work was the Preface to his volume of *Poems*, published in 1853. Soon after, he became Professor of Poetry at Oxford, and wrote three major works: *On Translating Homer*, *The Study of Celtic Literature*, and *Essays in Criticism*.

Arnold was essentially classical in outlook, and he revived classical values in his criticism. He contrasted what he called the Grand Style of the ancients with the "incredible vagaries" of most of modern literature, which was "fantastic" and wanting "sanity." The Grand Style, he said, "arises in poetry when a noble nature, poetically gifted, treats with simplicity or severity a serious subject." Such a style he found in Homer, in Dante, and in Milton. Shakespeare did not uniformly manifest it. This insistence on "nobility" and "seriousness" points to the peculiar trend of Arnold's criticism, which demanded that poetry should have a moral purpose. Poetry is, in his view, "a criticism of life," and literature is "the best that has been thought and said in all ages." He was profoundly affected by the *malaise* of his time, and expresses it in his poetry again and again. He sought in noble poetry the means of recovering "the freshness of the early world" and applying it to the healing of

> this iron time
> Of doubts, disputes, distractions, fears.

For Arnold, therefore, the subject-matter of poetry and the spirit in which it was treated were of supreme importance. He claimed that a sensitive reader could, by holding in his mind a number of lines and expressions from acknowledged masters, use them as "an infallible touchstone for detecting the presence or absence of high poetic quality, and also the degree of this quality, in all other poetry which we may place beside them."

Twentieth-century Criticism

The outstanding literary critic in the present century is T. S. Eliot, whose volume *The Use of Poetry and the Use of Criticism* (1933) reviews the great English critics from Sidney to Arnold. Other critical works are *The Sacred Wood* (1920) and *After Strange Gods* (1933).

His own attitude is one of strong reaction against the moods and pre-occupations of the romantics, and he clings to such surviving rocks of the traditional order as have not been swept away by modern tides of thought and morality. He denies the romantic supposition that it is the principal business of poetry to express the unique personality, and individual experience, of the poet. On the contrary, Eliot urges that poetry should progress through "a continual extinction of personality." The poet should possess a historical sense, and should write from a far wider standpoint than that of his own experience of life, since it is only with reference to the timeless order of things that his own thought has any significance.

Faithfulness to tradition does not therefore mean for Eliot adherence to this or that form or diction: that would be mere imitation. The poet has perforce to use images ("the objective correlative") which in his own life since childhood have become charged with emotion for him. Thus, although Eliot's poetry is that of a traditionalist, he refuses to use conventional "poetic" imagery and situations which have become standardized. The "objective correlative" of Eliot is the dreariness and fecklessness of contemporary urban life, contrasted with a more gracious past. But the past is not invoked by direct description: it is rather summoned to the memory by means of literary allusions, sometimes obvious but often erudite, embedded in the text, and serving as points of orientation, by means of which the direction of current tendencies may be clarified and evalued.

SUGGESTIONS FOR FURTHER READING

I. A. RICHARDS: *Principles of Literary Criticism; Practical Criticism* (Routledge and Kegan Paul).

VIRGINIA WOOLF: *The Common Reader*, I and II (Hogarth Press).

T. S. ELIOT: *The Sacred Wood; The Use of Poetry and the Use of Criticism* (Faber & Faber).

VARIOUS AUTHORS: *Tradition and Experiment in Present Day Literature* (Oxford Univ. Press).

H. W. GARROD: *Poetry and the Criticism of Life; The Profession of Poetry, and Other Lectures* (Oxford Univ. Press).

A CHRONOLOGY OF ENGLISH CLASSICS
WITH CONTEMPORARY EVENTS

I. PRE-CONQUEST

Seventh Century (late)

CAEDMON

Eighth Century

THE VENERABLE BEDE
Beowulf, Widsith, Complaint of Deor, The Wanderer, The Seafarer.

Eighth Century (late)

CYNEWULF: *Crist, Juliana, Elene, Fates of the Apostles.*

Ninth Century

Anglo-Saxon Chronicle (800–1154).

Ninth Century (late)

KING ALFRED: Translations—*Orosius' History of the World, Bede's Ecclesiastical History, Boethius' Consolation of Philosophy, Pope Gregory's Pastoral Care, Homilies.*
Judith, Dream of the Rod, Riddles, Bestiaries.

Tenth Century

Brunanburh, The Battle of Maldon.

Tenth Century (late)

AELFRIC: Paraphrases of Scriptures and patristic homilies.

Eleventh Century (early)

WULFSTAN: Homilies and sermons.

II. ANGLO-NORMAN PERIOD (1066–1360)

Twelfth Century

Chanson de Roland and other *Chansons de Geste.*
CRESTIEN DE TROYES, author of Arthurian romances.
GEOFFREY OF MONMOUTH: *Historia Regum Britanniae.*
WALTER MAP: *Launcelot du Lac, Mort d' Arthur.*

Thirteenth Century

Roman de Renart, Roman de Troie, Roman de Brut, Ancrene Riwle.
LAYAMON: *Brut.*

Fourteenth Century

ROBERT MANNYNGE: *Handlynge Synne, Cursor Mundi.*
RICHARD ROLLE OF HAMPOLE
The Pricke of Conscience, The Owl and the Nightingale, Havelock the Dane, King Horn.
LAWRENCE MINOT: *Halidon Hill, Crecy, Siege of Calais.*
Miracle plays (Chester, York, Coventry, Towneley). *Sir Gawayn and the Green Knight, Pearl, Purity, Patience.*
SIR JOHN MANDEVILLE: *Travels.*

Contemporary Events

529 Benedictine Order founded.
597 St. Augustine landed in Thanet and introduced Christianity.
664 Synod of Whitby and adoption of the Roman ritual in England.
771 Invasion of Spain by the Moors.
800 Charles the Great crowned Emperor; foundation of Holy Roman
     Empire.
     German alliterative poem *Hildebrandslied* written.
900 Classic age of the Scandinavian (Icelandic) sagas.
     Rise of Feudalism in Western Europe.
     The Northmen established in France (Normandy).
1066 Norman Conquest of England.
1096 First Crusade against the Turks.
1098 Cistercian Order of Monks founded.
1099 Death of the Cid (Roderigo Diaz), national hero of Spain.
Eleventh Century: Rise of the Troubadours and Trouivères in France.
Twelfth Century: Beginnings of Gothic Architecture in France; Classic age
     of Spanish medieval ballads and romances.
1174 Building of Canterbury Cathedral begun.
1209 Franciscan Order of Friars founded.
1214 Roger Bacon, founder of English philosophy, born.
1225 St. Thomas Aquinas, author of *Summa Theologiae*, born.
1264 Marco Polo, medieval traveller in the East, born.
1265 Dante, author of the *Divina Commedia*, born.
1304 Petrarch, originator of the sonnet form, born.
1313 Boccaccio, author of the *Decameron*, born.
1337 Froissart, author of the *Chronicles*, born.
1348 Black Death in England.

19

III. MIDDLE ENGLISH PERIOD (1360–1500)

Fourteenth Century (Second half)

JOHN LANGLAND (1330–1400): *Piers the Plowman*.

JOHN GOWER (1330–1408): *Speculum Meditantis* (French), *Vox Clamantis* (Latin), *Confessio Amantis* (English).

GEOFFREY CHAUCER (1340–1400): *Romaunt of the Rose, Boke of the Duchesse, House of Fame, Troylus and Criseyde, Legend of Good Women, Parlement of Fowles, Canterbury Tales*; (prose): Translation of *Boethius, Treatise on the Astrolabe*.

JOHN WYCLIF (1320–84): translation (with collaboration) of the Bible, polemical pamphlets.

Fifteenth Century

THOMAS HOCCLEVE (1370–1450): *Regiment of Princes*.

JOHN LYDGATE (1370–1446): *Story of Thebes, Troy-Book, Fall of Princes, Temple of Glass, London Lickpenny, The Flower and the Leaf*.

KING JAMES I of Scotland (1394–1436): *The Kingis Quair*.

ROBERT HENRYSON (1425–1500): *The Testament of Cresseid*.

WILLIAM DUNBAR (1465–1530): *The Thissel and the Rois, Dance of the Sevin Deidly Synnis*.

GAVIN DOUGLAS (1475–1522): *The Palice of Honour*, translation of the *Aeneid*.

The Paston Letters (1422–1509).

SIR THOMAS MALORY (d. 1471): *Morte d'Arthur*.

WILLIAM CAXTON (1422–91): translations—*Recuyell of the Histories of Troy, Historye of Reynart the Foxe, The Aeneid*.

Contemporary Events

1373 John Huss, early Bohemian church reformer, born.
1381 Peasants' Revolt in England.
1396 Chrysoloras of Constantinople teaches Greek in Italy.
1405 Aneas Silvius (Pope Pius II), patron of letters, born.
1410 Gutenberg, inventor of printing, born.
1431 Villon, French writer of *ballades* and *rondeaux*, born.
Joan of Arc burned at Rouen.
1441 Thomas à Kempis wrote *The Imitation of Christ*.
1450 *Amadis de Gaula*, Spanish romance, written.
1452 Leonardo da Vinci, Italian artist and scholar, born.
1453 Capture of Constantinople by the Ottoman Turks.
1463 Pico della Mirandola, Italian humanist, born.
1469 Lorenzo de Medici (The Magnificent) became ruler of Florence.
1476 Bayard, last representative of medieval chivalry, born.
Caxton introduced printing into England.
1488 Raphael, Italian poet and painter, born.
1492 Columbus discovered America.
Moors driven from Spain.
1498 Discovery of the Cape Route to India by Vasco da Gama.
Savonarola, religious leader in Florence, executed as a heretic.
1500 Benvenutto Cellini, author of the *Autobiography*, born.

IV. THE RENAISSANCE IN ENGLAND (1500–1625)

SIR THOMAS MORE (1478–1535): *Utopia* (translated into English, 1551).

JOHN SKELTON (1460–1529): *The Boke of Colin Clout, Boke of Phillipp Sparrowe.*

JOHN TYNDALE (d. 1536): translations of *New Testament, Pentateuch, Jonah. The Book of Common Prayer* (Archbishop Cranmer and others).

LORD BERNERS (1467–1533): translations—*Chronicles of Froissart, Huon of Bordeaux.*

HUGH LATIMER (1485–1555): *Sermons.*

JOHN FOXE (1516–87): *Book of Martyrs.*

JOHN KNOX (1508–72): *The Monstrous Regiment of Women, History of the Reformation.*

SIR THOMAS ELYOT (1499–1546): *The Governour.*

MILES COVERDALE (1488–1568): translations—*The Bible, The Apocrypha.*

NICHOLAS UDALL (1505–56): *Ralph Roister Doister*, translations from Terence.

SIR THOMAS WYATT (1503–42): *Sonnets* and *Satires.*

HENRY HOWARD, EARL OF SURREY (1517–47): *Sonnets*, translations from the *Aeneid.*

THOMAS SACKVILLE (1536–1608): *Mirror for Magistrates.*

THOMAS SACKVILLE and THOMAS NORTON: *Gorboduc* (1561).

ROGER ASCHAM (1515–68): *Toxophilus, The Scholemaster.*

The Miscellanies (TOTTEL'S 1567; *Paradise of Dainty Devices*, 1576, *Gorgeous Gallery of Gallant Inventors,* 1578).

JOHN HEYWOOD (1506–65): Interludes—*The Four P's, A Play of Love.*

RAPHAEL HOLINSHED (d. 1580): *Chronicles.*

RICHARD HAKLUYT (1552–1616): *Navigations, Voyages and Discoveries.*

JOHN STOW (1525–1605): *Survey of London.*

SIR THOMAS NORTH (1535–1601): translation—*Plutarch's Lives.*

SIR PHILIP SIDNEY (1554–86): *Arcadia, Apologie for Poetrie, Astrophel and Stella.*

EDMUND SPENSER (1552–99): *Shepherd's Calendar, Faerie Queene, Amoretti, Epithalamion, Prothalamion, View of the Present State of Ireland.*

JOHN LYLY (1554–1606): *Euphues, Alexander and Campaspe, Endimion.*

SIR THOMAS OVERBURY (1581–1613): *Characters.*

THOMAS KYD (1557–95): *Spanish Tragedy, Hamlet.*

GEORGE PEELE (1552–97): *Arraignment of Paris, Chronicle of Edward I, Old Wives' Tale, David and Bethsabe.*

ROBERT GREENE (1560–92): *Orlando Furioso, Friar Bacon and Friar Bungay, James IV, George a-Greene.*

CHRISTOPHER MARLOWE (1564–93): *Tamberlaine the Great, Dr. Faustus, Jew of Malta, Edward II, Hero and Leander, Massacre at Paris.*

WILLIAM SHAKESPEARE (1564–1616): *Henry VI, Parts 2 and 3, Henry VI, Part 1, Richard III, Comedy of Errors, Love's Labour's Lost, Two Gentlemen of Verona, Taming of the Shrew, Richard II, Titus Andronicus, Romeo and Juliet, Midsummer Night's Dream, King John, Merchant of Venice, Henry IV, Parts 1 and 2, Henry V, Much Ado about Nothing, As You Like It, Twelfth Night, Julius Caesar, Merry Wives of Windsor, Hamlet, Troilus and Cressida, A'lls*

Contemporary Events

1504 Sannazaro published *Arcadia* (prose pastoral romance).
1506 First stone laid in erection of St. Peter's Cathedral, Rome.
1513 Machiavelli completed *Il Principi* (The Prince).
　　　Balboa discovered the Pacific Ocean.
1515 First regular drama (*Sophonisba*) acted in Europe presented at Rome.
1517 Luther published his theses at Wittenburg (the breach with Rome).
　　　Erasmus's *Greek Testament* published in Basle.
1519 Leonardo da Vinci, Italian scholar and artist, died.
1520 Raphael, Italian poet and painter, died.
1524 Camoëns, national epic poet of Portugal, born.
　　　Ronsard, French Renaissance poet, born.
1528 Albert Dürer, German Renaissance artist, died.
　　　Palestrina, father of Italian music, born.
　　　Publication of *Il Cortegiano* (The Courtier) by Castiglione.
1532 *Orlando Furioso* by Ariosto, greatest Italian romantic epic, published.
　　　Process of etching on copper invented in Italy.
　　　Pantagruel by Rabelais published.
1533 Montaigne, French essayist, born.
1535 Sir Thomas More beheaded.
　　　Calvin's *Institutes of the Christian Religion* published in Basle.
1536 Dissolution of the monasteries in England begins.
1540 The Academy in Florence established.
　　　The Society of Jesus (Jesuit Order) founded by Ignatius Loyola.
　　　Joseph Scaliger, the founder of historical criticism, born.
　　　William Gilbert, founder of the science of Magnetism, born.
1543 Hans Holbein, portrait painter, died.
　　　Copernicus published at Nuremberg his *Revolution of the Heavenly Bodies*.
1545 The *Pleiade* (for the reformation of the French language and literature on classical models) established.
1546 Tycho Brahe, founder of modern astronomy, born.
1547 Cervantes, author of *Don Quixote*, born.
1550 John Napier, inventor of logarithms, born.
1553 Chancellor, exploring the North-East Passage, penetrates into Russia.
1556 The first Oratorio introduced in Rome.
1557 The first *Index Purgatorius* (list of forbidden books) issued by Pope Paul IV.
1558 Calais, England's last possession in France, lost.
　　　Queen Elizabeth orders church services to be read in English.
　　　Westminster School founded.
1562 Lope de Vega (founder of Spanish drama) born.
　　　Outbreaks of religious wars in France against the Huguenots.
1564 Michelangelo, Florentine artist, died.
　　　Galileo, Italian astronomer and inventor of telescope, born.
1572 Massacre of St. Bartholomew in France.
1576 Death of Titian, Venetian painter.
　　　Frobisher sailed in search of the North-west Passage.

THE RENAISSANCE IN ENGLAND (Contd.)

Well that Ends Well, Measure for Measure, Othello, Macbeth, King Lear, Antony and Cleopatra, Coriolanus, Timon of Athens, Pericles, Cymbeline, The Winter's Tale, The Tempest, Henry VIII (Two Noble Kinsmen ?); Venus and Adonis, Rape of Lucrece, Sonnets.

SAMUEL DANIEL (1562–1619): *Delia* (sonnet-sequence), *Defence of Rhyme*.

HENRY CONSTABLE (1562–1613): *Diana* (sonnet-sequence).

THOMAS LODGE (1558–1625): *Phyllis* (sonnet-sequence), *Rosalynde*.

MICHAEL DRAYTON (1563–1631): *Idea* (sonnet-sequence), *Polyolbion*.

GILES FLETCHER (1585–1623): *Christ's Victory and Triumph*.

PHINEAS FLETCHER (1582–1650): *The Purple Island*.

WILLIAM BROWNE (1591–1643): *Britannia's Pastorals*.

WILLIAM DRUMMOND (1585–1649): *Flowers of Zion, The Cypresse Grove*.

BEN JONSON (1572–1637): *Every Man in His Humour, Every Man out of His Humour, Cynthia's Revels, The Poetaster, Sejanus, Volpone, Epicoene, The Alchemist, Catiline, Bartholomew Fair, The Staple of News, The Forest, Underwoods, Masque of Blackness, Masque of Hymen, Masque of Queens, Timber or Discoveries*.

GEORGE CHAPMAN (1559–1634): *All Fools, Monsieur d'Olive, The Gentleman Usher, Bussy d'Ambois, Revenge of Bussy d'Ambois, Caesar and Pompey,* translation of *Homer*.

FRANCIS BEAUMONT (1585–1616) and JOHN FLETCHER (1579–1625): *Philaster, The Maid's Tragedy, Knight of the Burning Pestle, The Scornful Lady,* (by FLETCHER alone) *The Faithful Shepherdess*.

THOMAS DEKKER (1570–1640): *Shoemaker's Holiday, Old Fortunatus, Satiro-Mastix, The Honest Whore*.

THOMAS HEYWOOD (1570–1650): *The Woman Killed with Kindness, Edward IV, The Four Prentices of London*.

THOMAS MIDDLETON (1570–1627): *A Mad World My Masters, A Trick to catch the Old One, A Game at Chesse*.

JOHN WEBSTER (1580–1625): *The White Devil, The Duchess of Malfi, Appius and Virginia*.

CYRIL TOURNEUR (1575–1626): *Revenger's Tragedy, Atheist's Tragedy*.

JOHN MARSTON (1575–1634): *The Malcontent, The Dutch Courtesan, Eastward Ho!*

JOHN FORD (1586–1639): *Perkin Warbeck, The Lover's Melancholy, The Broken Heart, Love's Sacrifice*.

JOHN DONNE (1572–1631): *Satires, Elegies, Divine Poems, Sermons*.

RICHARD HOOKER (1554–1600): *Laws of Ecclesiastical Polity*.

SIR FRANCIS BACON, LORD VERULAM (1561–1626): *Essays, Advancement of Learning, The New Atlantis, History of Henry VII*.

SIR WALTER RALEIGH (1552–1618): *History of the World*.

WILLIAM WEBBE (d. 1591): *Discourse of English Poesie*.

GEORGE PUTTENHAM: *Art of English Poesie* (1589).

THOMAS CAMPION (d. 1619): *Art of English Poesie*.

Authorized Version of the Bible (1611).

ROBERT BURTON (1577–1640): *Anatomy of Melancholy*.

Contemporary Events (Contd.)

1577 Drake started on his voyage round the world.

1578 William Harvey (discoverer of the circulation of the blood) born.
Death of Hans Sachs, German poet, dramatist, novelist.

1579 The United Netherlands formed after the revolt against Spain.

1581 Tasso, Italian epic poet, published *Gerusalemme Liberata* (Jerusalem
Delivered).

1582 Gregorian Calendar introduced.
Shakespeare married Anne Hathaway.

1583 Hugh Grotius, Dutch jurist and writer on international law, born.

1585 Raleigh led first colonizing expedition to the New World (Roanoke
Island)—withdrawn 1586.

1587 English actors perform at courts of Hesse and Brunswick.

1588 Defeat of the Spanish Armada.

1595 Raleigh sails up the Orinoco river (Guiana) in quest of El Dorado.

1596 Descartes, author of *Le Discours de la Méthode*, born.
Swan Theatre opened on Bankside, London.

1598 Building of the Globe Theatre, Southwark (first production *Henry V*,
1599).

1599 Oliver Cromwell born.

1600 East India Company chartered.

1600 Giordano Bruno, Italian philosopher, burned at Venice for heresy.
Calderon, Spanish dramatist, born.

1603 Union of Crowns of England and Scotland.

1604 Hampton Court Conference, leading to the preparation of the
Authorized Version of the Bible.

1606 Corneille, French dramatist, born.
Charter granted to the Colony of Virginia.

1607 First grand opera, Monteverdi's *Orfeo*.
Rembrandt, Dutch painter, born.

1612 Guarini, author of pastoral poem *Il Pastor Fido*, died in Italy.

1610 The Douai Bible (Roman Catholic version) appeared.

1611 Publication of Authorized Version of the Bible.

1616 Ben Jonson created *Poet Laureate*.

1617 James I issued *The Book of Sports* permissible on Sundays.

1618 Outbreak of the Thirty Years War in Germany.

1620 Sailing of the Pilgrim Fathers to New England in the *Mayflower*.

1621 John Donne became Dean of St. Paul's.
La Fontaine, author of the *Fables*, born.

1622 Molière, French dramatist, born.

1623 William Byrd, English musician, died.
Pascal, author of *Les Pensées*, born.

1624 Capt. John Smith published *General Historie of Virginia*.

1625 Charles I succeeded James I on throne of England.
Marino, Neapolitan poet noted for flamboyant diction, died.

V. CAROLINE AND COMMONWEALTH PERIOD (1625-1660)

POETRY

THOMAS CAREW (1598-1639): miscellaneous poems.
SIR JOHN SUCKLING (1609-42): miscellaneous poems.
RICHARD LOVELACE (1618-58): miscellaneous poems.
ROBERT HERRICK (1591-1674): *Hesperides* (1648).
GEORGE HERBERT (1593-1633: *The Temple* (1633).
RICHARD CRASHAW (1612-49): *Steps to the Temple* (1646), *Delights of the Muses*.
HENRY VAUGHAN (1622-95): *Silex Scintillans*.
FRANCIS QUARLES (1592-1644): *Emblems*.
ANDREW MARVELL (1621-78): *Poems*.
JOHN MILTON (1608-74): Early poems—*Hymn on the Nativity* (1629), *L'Allegro* and *Il Penseroso, Arcades, Comus, Lycidas*, sonnets; prose—*Tractate on Education, Areopagitica*, Pamphlet on *Divorce*; *Paradise Lost* (1667), *Paradise Regained, Samson Agonistes* (1671).
ABRAHAM COWLEY (1618-67): *Pindarique Odes, Davideis*, miscellaneous poems.
EDMUND WALLER (1606-87): *Poems*.
SIR JOHN DENHAM (1615-69): *Cooper's Hill*.

PROSE

JOHN EARLE (1601-65): *Microcosmographie*.
SIR THOMAS BROWNE (1605-82): *Religio Medici, Urn Burial, Garden of Cyrus*.
JEREMY TAYLOR (1613-67): *Liberty of Prophesying, Holy Living, Holy Dying*.
RICHARD BAXTER (1615-91): *Saint's Everlasting Rest*.
WILLIAM PRYNNE (1600-1669): *Histrio-Mastix*.
THOMAS HOBBES (1588-1679): *Leviathan*.
THOMAS FULLER (1608-61): *Worthies of England*.
IZAAK WALTON (1593-1683): *The Compleat Angler*.

Contemporary Events

1625 Grotius published *De Jure Belli et Pacis* (Of the Law of War and Peace).
1626 St. Peter's, Rome, consecrated.
1627 Gongora (Spanish "Euphuistic" poet) died.
1629 French Academy founded.
1632 Galileo summoned before the Inquisition.
    Gustavus Adolphus, King of Sweden, killed at Battle of Lützen.
1634 John Hampden refused to pay Ship-money.
    Struggle between Charles I and Parliament entered a more embittered
      phase.
1639 Racine, French dramatist, born.
1640 The Long Parliament met (finally dissolved 1660).
1642 Outbreak of the Civil War.
    Closure of the theatres.
    New Zealand and Tasmania discovered by Tasman.
    Death of Cardinal Richelieu, Minister of Louis XIII of France.
1648 George Fox founded the Society of Friends (Quakers).
1646 Leibniz, German scientist and philosopher, born.
1649 Trial and Execution of Charles I. Establishment of the Commonwealth.
1652 Dorothy Osborne's *Letters* to her husband, Sir William Temple.
1656 Opera introduced into England with d'Avenant's *Siege of Rhodes*.
1658 Death of Cromwell.
    Purcell, English musician, born.
1660 Restoration of the Monarchy in the United Kingdom.

VI. THE RESTORATION PERIOD (1660-1700)
POETRY

SAMUEL BUTLER (1612-80): *Hudibras.*
JOHN DRYDEN (1631-1700): *Heroic Stanzas* (1658), *Annus Mirabilis, Absalom and Achitophel, The Medal, McFlecknoe, Religio Laici, Hind and Panther;* translations—Satires of Juvenal, Virgil, Horace; paraphrases of Chaucer, Boccaccio, Ovid.
JOHN OLDHAM (1653-83): *Satires against the Jesuits.*

DRAMA

JOHN DRYDEN: *Wild Gallant, Tyrannic Love, Aureng-Zebe, All for Love, Conquest of Granada, Marriage à la Mode, Spanish Friar.*
THOMAS OTWAY (1651-85): *The Orphan, Venice Preserved.*
SIR GEORGE ETHEREGE (1634-81): *The Man of Mode.*
GEORGE VILLIERS, DUKE OF BUCKINGHAM (1627-88): *The Rehearsal.*
WILLIAM WYCHERLEY (1640-1715): *Love in a Wood, The Plain Dealer, The Country Wife.*
SIR JOHN VANBRUGH (1664-1726): *The Relapse, The Provoked Wife, The Confederacy* (1705).
GEORGE FARQUHAR (1678-1707): *The Constant Couple, Recruiting Officer, The Beaux' Stratagem.*
WILLIAM CONGREVE (1670-1729): *Old Bachelor, The Double Dealer, Love for Love, The Way of the World.*

PROSE

JOHN BUNYAN (1628-88): *Grace Abounding, Pilgrim's Progress, Life and Death of Mr. Badman, The Holy War.*
EDWARD HYDE, EARL OF CLARENDON (1609-74): *History of the Rebellion.*
JOHN LOCKE (1632-1704): *Essay concerning Human Understanding, On Civil Government, Letters on Toleration, Thoughts concerning Education.*
JOHN EVELYN (1620-1706): *Diary.*
SAMUEL PEPYS (1633-1703): *Diary.*
JOHN DRYDEN: *Essay of Dramatic Poesy, Preface to Fables.*
JEREMY COLLIER: *Short View of the Immorality of the Stage* (1698).

Contemporary Events

1661 Sir Christopher Wren became Surveyor-General to Charles II.
1662 Richard Bentley, English scholar, author of *Phalaris*, born.
      Royal Society incorporated.
1663 Licensing Act passed.
      Laws passed for the suppression of Dissent.
1665 Great Plague of London.
1666 Great Fire of London.
1667 Paris Observatory founded.
1670 Habeas Corpus Act passed.
      Hudson Bay Company chartered.
1673 Parliament passed the Test Act.
1675 Building of the new St. Paul's Cathedral begun.
1677 Spinoza, Jewish philosopher, author of *Ethics*, died.
1680 French National Theatre established in Paris.
      La Rochefoucauld, author of *Maxims*, died.
1682 Peter the Great of Russia succeeds to the throne.
1685 Revocation of Edict of Nantes leads to flight of Huguenots from France.
      James II succeeded Charles II on the throne.
1687 Sir Isaac Newton published the *Principia*.
1689 Montesquieu, author of *Esprit des Lois*, born.
      Constitutional revolution carried through in Great Britain; William III
          and Mary succeeded to the throne.
1690 Calcutta founded.
      Samuel Pepys published *Memoirs of the Navy*.
1692 Publication of *Memoirs* of Sir William Temple.
1694 Bank of England incorporated.
      Beginning of the National Debt.
      Voltaire born.
1696 Madame de Sévigné, famous letter-writer, died.

VII. THE EIGHTEENTH CENTURY

POETRY

ALEXANDER POPE (1688–1744): *Essay on Criticism, Pastorals, Rape of the Lock, Translation of Homer, Dunciad, Epistle and Satires, Essay on Man.*

JAMES THOMSON (1700–48): *The Seasons, The Castle of Indolence.*

JOHN DYER (1699–1758): *Grongar Hill.*

WILLIAM SHENSTONE (1714–63): *The Schoolmistress.*

EDWARD YOUNG (1683–1765): *Night Thoughts.*

THOMAS WARTON (1728–90): *The Pleasures of Melancholy.*

WILLIAM COLLINS (1721–59): *Persian Eclogues, Odes, Highland Superstitions.*

THOMAS GRAY (1716–71): *Eton College, Elegy in a Country Churchyard, Progress of Poesy, The Bard, Descent of Odin.*

OLIVER GOLDSMITH (1728–74): *The Deserted Village.*

JAMES MACPHERSON (1738–96): *Fragments of Ancient Poetry, Fingal.*

BISHOP PERCY (1728–1811): *Reliques of Ancient English Poetry.*

THOMAS CHATTERTON (1752–70): *The Rowley Poems.*

WILLIAM COWPER (1731–1800): *Olney Hymns, The Task.*

GEORGE CRABBE (1754–1832): *The Village, Parish Register, The Borough.*

ROBERT BURNS (1759–96): *Poems.*

WILLIAM BLAKE (1757–1827): *Songs of Innocence, Book of Thel, Songs of Experience, Marriage of Heaven and Hell, Book of Los.*

DRAMA

JOSEPH ADDISON (1672–1719): *Cato.*

RICHARD STEELE (1671–1729): *The Funeral, The Tender Husband, Conscious Lovers.*

HENRY FIELDING (1707–54): *Tom Thumb, The Mock Doctor.*

JAMES THOMSON: *Sophonisba, Agamemnon.*

DR. SAMUEL JOHNSON (1709–84): *Irene.*

OLIVER GOLDSMITH: *The Good-natured Man, She Stoops to Conquer.*

RICHARD BRINSLEY SHERIDAN (1751–1816): *The Rivals, School for Scandal, The Critic.*

DAVID GARRICK (1717–79): *The Lying Valet, The Clandestine Marriage.*

HANNAH MORE (1745–1833): *Percy, A Tragedy.*

THE NOVEL

SAMUEL RICHARDSON (1689–1761): *Pamela, Clarissa Harlowe, Sir Charles Grandison.*

HENRY FIELDING: *Joseph Andrews, Jonathan Wild, Tom Jones, Amelia.*

TOBIAS SMOLLETT (1721–71): *Roderick Random, Peregrine Pickle, Humphrey Clinker.*

LAURENCE STERNE (1713–68): *Tristram Shandy, Sentimental Journey.*

OLIVER GOLDSMITH: *The Vicar of Wakefield.*

FRANCES BURNEY (1752–1840): *Evelina, Cecilia.*

HORACE WALPOLE (1717–97): *Castle of Otranto.*

MRS. ANN RADCLIFFE (1764–1823): *Mysteries of Udolpho.*

Contemporary Events

1701 Outbreak of War of Spanish Succession.
1703 Charles Perrault died, author of *Histoires et Contes*.
     John Wesley born.
1704 First translation of Arabian and Turkish manuscripts of *Arabian Nights' Entertainments* (into French).
1707 Goldoni, Italian playwright, born.
     Union of Parliaments of England and Scotland.
     Death of Aureng-Zebe and collapse of Mogul Empire in India.
1709 Pianoforte invented by Cristofori.
1711 Boileau, French critic, author of *L'Art Poétique*, died.
1713 Diderot, French philosopher, born.
1714 Hanoverian dynasty established on the throne.
1715 *Gil Blas*, by Le Sage, published.
     Memoires of Madame de Maintenon published.
1718 Voltaire's *Oedipe* acted at the Théâtre Français.
1719 John Law's "Mississippi Scheme" for colonizing Louisiana, came to grief.
1720 Collapse of the South Sea Bubble.
1721 Watteau, French painter, died.
1722 John Churchill, Duke of Marlborough, English general and diplomatist, died.
1723 Sir Joshua Reynolds, English portrait painter and first President of the Royal Academy of Art, born.
1726 Fahrenheit thermometer invented.
1728 Gay's *Beggar's Opera* first performed.
     Thomas Gainsborough, English artist, born.
1731 *Manon Lescaut*, by L'Abbé Prévost, appeared.
1739 Methodist Revival begun by Charles Wesley and George Whitefield.
1740 Frederick the Great ascended the throne of Prussia.
1745 Jacobite Rising (The "Forty-five") suppressed.
1748 Klopstock, German poet, began publication of *Messias*, a religious epic inspired by Milton.
     Isaac Watts, hymn-writer, died.
1749 Goethe born at Frankfurt on Main.
     Alfieri, Italian playwright, born.
1751 First volume of the *Encyclopédie* published in France (contributors: Voltaire, Montesquieu, Rousseau, Buffon, Turgot, Diderot).
1753 Handel's *Messiah* first performed at Foundling Hospital.
     British Museum established by Act of Parliament.
1754 *Annual Register* began publication.
1755 Sarah Kemble (Mrs. Siddons), the actress, born.
1756 Outbreak of the Seven Years War.
     Physiocratic economic doctrines formulated in France.
1757 Benjamin Franklin came on a political mission to England.
1758 Blackstone lectured at Oxford: *Commentaries on the Laws of England*.
     Nelson born.

EIGHTEENTH CENTURY (Contd.)

MATTHEW GREGORY LEWIS (1775–1818): *The Monk, Castle Spectre.*
WILLIAM BECKFORD (1760–1844): *Vathek.*

ESSAYS, HISTORY, PHILOSOPHY, LETTERS

DANIEL DEFOE (1661–1731): *Shortest Way with the Dissenters, Robinson Crusoe, Journal of the Plague Year.*

JONATHAN SWIFT (1667–1745): *Battle of the Books, Tale of a Tub, The Examiner, Journal to Stella, Drapier's Letters, Gulliver's Travels.*

JOSEPH ADDISON: *The Campaign, The Spectator, The Guardian, The Freeholder.*

RICHARD STEELE: *The Christian Hero, The Tatler, The Englishman.*

OLIVER GOLDSMITH: *The Bee, Citizen of the World.*

DR. SAMUEL JOHNSON: *The Rambler, The Idler, Dictionary, Lives of the Poets, Journey to the Western Isles.*

BISHOP BERKELEY (1685–1753): *Principles of Human Knowledge.*

DAVID HUME (1711–76): *Treatise on Human Nature, Principles of Morals, History of England, History of Religion.*

WILLIAM ROBERTSON (1721–93): *History of Scotland, History of America.*

EDWARD GIBBON (1737–94): *Decline and Fall of the Roman Empire.*

HENRY ST. JOHN, VISCOUNT BOLINGBROKE (1678–1751): *Idea of a Patriot King.*

EDMUND BURKE (1729–97): *Vindication of Natural Society, The Sublime and Beautiful, Thoughts on Present Discontents, Conciliation with America, Reflections on the French Revolution, Letters on a Regicide Peace.*

JEREMY BENTHAM (1748–1833): *Fragment on Government, Principles of Morals and Legislation.*

SIR WILLIAM BLACKSTONE (1723–80): *Commentaries on the Laws of England.*

ADAM SMITH (1723–90): *Theory of Moral Sentiments, Wealth of Nations.*

THOMAS PAINE (1737–1809): *Rights of Man.*

WILLIAM GODWIN (1756–1836): *Political Justice.*

THOMAS MALTHUS (1766–1834): *Essay on Population.*

SIR JOSHUA REYNOLDS (1723–92): *Discourses on Painting.*

GILBERT WHITE (1720–93): *Natural History of Selborne.*

JAMES BOSWELL (1740–95): *Journal of a Tour to the Hebrides, Life of Dr. Johnson.*

EARL OF CHESTERFIELD (1694–1773): *Letters to his Son.*

HORACE WALPOLE: *Letters.*

FRANCES BURNEY: *Letters, Diary.*

WILLIAM COWPER: *Letters.*

Contemporary Events (Contd.)

1760   Rousseau published *La Nouvelle Héloise.*

1762   Rousseau published *Contrat Social* and *Emile.*
       John Wilkes founded *The North Briton.*
       Catherine II became Empress of Russia.

1764   Suppression of the Jesuits in France.
       Hogarth, English painter and engraver, died.
       Dr. Johnson's "Literary Club" founded.

1768   First circulating libraries founded.

1769   Napoleon Bonaparte born in Corsica.
       Letters of Junius began to appear in the *Public Advertiser.*
       Chardin, French painter, died.

1770   Beethoven, German musician, born.
       Hegel, German philosopher, born.
       James Watt invented the steam-engine.

1772   André Chénier, French romantic poet, born.
       Swedenborg, Swedish philosopher and theosophist, died.

1774   Oxygen identified by James Priestley.

1776   American Declaration of Independence signed.

1778   Voltaire and Rousseau died.

1781   Kant's *Critique of Pure Reason*, published.

1785   Daily Universal Register (renamed *The Times* 1788) began to appear.

1787   Wilberforce founded the "Association for the Abolition of Slavery."

1789   The French Revolution: Capture of the Bastille.

1791   Metric System adopted in France.

1793   "Festival of Reason" celebrated at Notre Dame, Paris.

1795   Goethe's *Wilhelm Meister* published.

1796   Napoleon set out on his Italian Campaign.

VIII. THE ROMANTIC PERIOD
POETRY

WILLIAM WORDSWORTH (1770–1850): *An Evening Walk, Lyrical Ballads, The Excursion, Ecclesiastical Sketches, The Prelude.*

SAMUEL TAYLOR COLERIDGE (1772–1834): *Ancient Mariner, Kubla Khan, Christabel.*

ROBERT SOUTHEY (1774–1843): *Thalaba, Curse of Kehama, Roderick.*

SIR WALTER SCOTT (1771–1832): *Border Minstrelsy, Lay of the Last Minstrel, Marmion, Lady of the Lake, Lord of the Isles.*

THOMAS MOORE (1779–1852): *Irish Melodies, Lalla Rookh.*

THOMAS CAMPBELL (1777–1844): *Pleasures of Hope, Gertrude of Wyoming.*

LORD BYRON (1788–1824): *English Bards and Scotch Reviewers, Childe Harold, The Giaour, Manfred, Beppo, Mazeppa, Cain, Don Juan.*

PERCY BYSSHE SHELLEY (1792–1822): *Queen Mab, Alastor, Revolt of Islam, Prometheus Unbound, The Cenci, Epipsychidion, Adonais, Hellas.*

JOHN KEATS (1795–1821): *Endymion, Lamia, Eve of St. Agnes, Isabella, Hyperion.*

WALTER SAVAGE LANDOR (1775–1864): *Gebir, Hellenics.*

THE NOVEL

JANE AUSTEN (1775–1817): *Sense and Sensibility, Pride and Prejudice, Mansfield Park, Emma, Northanger Abbey, Persuasion.*

MARIA EDGEWORTH (1767–1849): *Castle Rackrent, Popular Tales, Leonora, Ormond.*

SIR WALTER SCOTT: *Waverley* (1814), *Guy Mannering, Old Mortality, Rob Roy, Heart of Midlothian, Bride of Lammermoor, Ivanhoe, Kenilworth, Quentin Durward, Talisman, Fair Maid* of Perth.

MARY SHELLEY (1797–1851): *Frankenstein.*

THOMAS LOVE PEACOCK (1785–1866): *Headlong Hall, Nightmare Abbey, Crotchet Castle.*

CRITICISM AND THE ESSAY

CHARLES LAMB (1775–1834): *Specimens from the Dramatic Poets, Essays of Elia, Last Essays of Elia.*

THOMAS DE QUINCEY (1785–1859): *Confessions of an English Opium-eater, Suspiria de Profundis, Revolt of the Tartars.*

WILLIAM HAZLITT (1778–1830): *Characters of Shakespeare, The English Comic Writers, Table Talk.*

LEIGH HUNT (1784–1859): *Story of Rimini, The Indicator, The Liberal, The Tatler.*

S. T. COLERIDGE: *Biographia Literaria, Aids to Reflection.*

Contemporary Events

1801 Edmund Kean acted with Mrs. Siddons and John Kemble at Drury
      Lane.
1802 Victor Hugo, French playwright and novelist, born.
      Edinburgh Review established (Sidney Smith first Editor).
      Cobbett's *Political Register* established.
1803 Alexander Dumas, French novelist, born.
      Emerson, American poet and philosopher, born.
1804 Nathaniel Hawthorne, American novelist, born.
1805 Threat of invasion from France.
      Nelson killed on board the *Victory* at the Battle of Trafalgar.
      Mazzini, Italian patriot, born.
      Schiller, German poet, died.
1806 William Pitt died.
      Charles James Fox died.
1807 Longfellow, American poet, born.
      Pall Mall, London, lighted by gas.
      Abolition of the Slave trade.
1808 Peninsular War began with landing of Wellesley in Portugal.
1809 Charles Darwin born.
      Gogol, Russian novelist, born.
      Edgar Allan Poe, American writer, born.
1812 War between Great Britain and U.S.A.
1813 Richard Wagner, German musician and poet, born.
1814 Napoleon banished to Elba.
1815 "The Hundred Days" and the Battle of Waterloo.
1818 Turgenev, Russian novelist, born.
      Karl Marx, author of *Das Kapital*, born.
1819 Walt Whitman, American poet, born.
      Princess Victoria (afterwards Queen Victoria) born.
1820 Death of King George III.
      Trial of Queen Caroline.
1821 Dostoevski, Russian novelist, born.
      Baudelàire, French poet, born.
      Flaubert, French novelist, born.
      Greek War of Independence.
1822 Louis Pasteur, French chemist and biologist, born.
1824 First collection of pictures bought for the National Gallery.
1825 Stockton and Darlington Railway opened.
1828 Tolstoi, Russian novelist and philosopher, born.
      Ibsen, Norwegian dramatist, born.
1832 First Reform Bill passed.

20

IX. THE VICTORIAN AGE

POETRY

ALFRED, LORD TENNYSON (1809–92): *Poems* (1830, 1833, 1842), *The Princess, In Memoriam, Maud, Idylls of the King*; plays—*Harold, Becket, Queen Mary.*

ROBERT BROWNING (1812–89): *Pauline, Paracelsus, Sordello, Pippa Passes, Bells and Pomegranates, Ring and the Book, Dramatic Idyls*; plays—*Strafford, A Blot on the 'Scutcheon, Colombe's Birthday, Luria.*

ELIZABETH BARRETT BROWNING (1806–61): *Essay on Mind and Other Poems* (1826), *Prometheus Bound, Sonnets from the Portuguese, Casa Guidi Windows, Aurora Leigh.*

ARTHUR HUGH CLOUGH (1819–61): *Bothie of Tober-na-Vuolich.*

MATTHEW ARNOLD (1822–88): *Thyrsis, Scholar Gipsy, Obermann, Dover Beach, Rugby Chapel, The Forsaken Merman, Sohrab and Rustum, Balder Dead, Merope, Empedocles on Etna.*

DANTE GABRIEL ROSSETTI (1828–82): *Poems, Ballads and Sonnets, House of Life.*

CHRISTINA GEORGINA ROSSETTI (1830–94): *Goblin Market, The Prince's Progress, Sing-Song.*

COVENTRY PATMORE (1823–96): *The Angel in the House, The Unknown Eros.*

WILLIAM MORRIS (1834–96): *The Defence of Guinevere, Life and Death of Jason, The Earthly Paradise, Sigurd the Volsung.*

ALGERNON CHARLES SWINBURNE (1837–1909): *Atalanta in Calydon, Poems and Ballads, Songs Before Sunrise, Tristram of Lyonesse, A Channel Passage*; plays—*Chastelard, Bothwell, Mary Stuart* (forming a dramatic trilogy).

EDWARD FITZGERALD (1809–83): *The Rubaiyat of Omar Khayyám.*

GERARD MANLEY HOPKINS (1844–89): *Poems—Wreck of the Deutschland, Windhover.*

ROBERT BRIDGES (1844–1930): *Shorter Poems* (1896), *Testament of Beauty* (1929).

A. E. HOUSMAN (1859–1936): *A Shropshire Lad* (1896).

FRANCIS THOMPSON (1859–1907): *Poems, Sister Songs, New Poems.*

RUDYARD KIPLING (1865–1936): *Barrack-Room Ballads, The Seven Seas* (1896), *The Five Nations.*

OSCAR WILDE (1856–1900): *The Ballad of Reading Gaol.*

THOMAS HARDY (1840–1928): *Wessex Poems* (1898). Also *The Dynasts* (1904).

WILLIAM BUTLER YEATS (1865–1939): *Wanderings of Oisin, Wind Among the Reeds, The Countess Kathleen, Wild Swans at Coole* (1917).

THE NOVEL

BENJAMIN DISRAELI (1804–81): *Vivian Grey, Coningsby, Sybil, Tancred.*

CHARLES DICKENS (1812–70): *Pickwick, Barnaby Rudge, Tale of Two Cities, Oliver Twist, A Christmas Carol, David Copperfield, Bleak House, Great Expectations, Nicholas Nickleby.*

WILLIAM MAKEPEACE THACKERAY (1811–63): *Luck of Barry Lyndon, Vanity Fair, Pendennis, The Newcomes, Henry Esmond.*

Contemporary Events

1837 Accession of Queen Victoria.
Pushkin, Russian national poet, died.
Electric Telegraph invented by Samuel Morse.
Leopardi, Italian poet, died.
1838 "Great Western" steamship crossed the Atlantic.
1839 Chartist riots.
Gold discovered in Australia.
1840 Emile Zola, French novelist, born.
Penny Post established in England.
Marriage of Queen Victoria to Prince Albert.
1841 *Punch* first published.
1842 Stendhal, French novelist died.
Monster Chartist petition presented to Parliament.
1843 First Telegraph Offices opened.
The Rebecca Riots.
1845 Elizabeth Fry, prison reformer, died.
1846 Repeal of the Corn Laws and adoption of Free Trade.
1848 Widespread revolutionary movements in Europe.
Gold discovered in California, U.S.A.
Publication of *Mabinogion* by Lady Charlotte Guest.
Pre-Raphaelite Brotherhood formed in Rome.
Balzac: Comédie Humaine (100 volumes) finished.
First Public Health Act passed.
Marx and Engels issued the *Communist Manifesto*.
1849 Chopin, Polish composer, died.
1850 Tennyson succeeds Wordsworth as Poet Laureate.
1851 Great Exhibition in Crystal Palace, Hyde Park.
First submarine cable (Dover to Calais) laid.
1852 Publication of *Uncle Tom's Cabin* (Harriet Beecher Stowe) and *La Dame aux Camelias* (Dumas *fils*).
1853 Wagner's *Ring des Nibelungen* composed.
1856 Bessemer process for converting iron into steel invented.
Congress of Paris.
Heinrich Heine, German poet, died.
1857 National Portrait Gallery founded.
Publication of *Madame Bovary* (Flaubert) and *Les Fleurs du Mal* (Baudelaire).
Indian Mutiny broke out.
Atlantic Cable laid.
1858 Robert Owen, founder of Socialism, died.
1859 De Quincey, Henry Hallam and Lord Macaulay died.
Work on Suez Canal begun by De Lesseps.
First oil-well discovered in U.S.A.
Sinaitic Manuscript of New Testament discovered by Tischendorf.
1860 Abraham Lincoln elected President of U.S.A.
Unification of Italy.

THE VICTORIAN AGE (*Contd.*)

CHARLOTTE BRONTË (1816–55): *Villette, Jane Eyre, Shirley.*

EMILY BRONTË (1818–48): *Wuthering Heights.*

MRS. GASKELL (1810–65): *Mary Barton, North and South, Cranford.*

CHARLES KINGSLEY (1819–75): *Yeast, Alton Lodge, Westward Ho!*

CHARLES READE (1814–84): *It is Never too Late to Mend, Hard Cash, Cloister and the Hearth.*

WILKIE COLLINS (1824–89): *The Woman in White, The Moonstone.*

ANTHONY TROLLOPE (1815–88): *The Warden, Barchester Towers, The Last Chronicle of Barset.*

GEORGE BORROW (1803–81): *The Bible in Spain, Lavengro, Romany Rye, Wild Wales.*

GEORGE ELIOT (1819–80): *Adam Bede, Mill on the Floss, Silas Marner, Romola, Middlemarch.*

GEORGE MEREDITH (1828–1909): *The Ordeal of Richard Feverel, Vittoria, Beauchamp's Career, The Egoist, Diana of the Crossways.*

SAMUEL BUTLER (1835–1902): *Erewhon, The Way of All Flesh.*

THOMAS HARDY: *Desperate Remedies* (1871), *Far from the Madding Crowd, Return of the Native, Mayor of Casterbridge, Tess of the D'Urbervilles, Jude the Obscure* (1895).

HENRY JAMES (1843–1916): *Roderick Hudson, Portrait of a Lady, The Ambassadors.*

OSCAR WILDE: *Picture of Dorian Gray.*

GEORGE GISSING (1857–1903): *The Unclassed, Demos, Odd Women.*

ROBERT LOUIS STEVENSON (1850–94): *Treasure Island, Kidnapped, Dr. Jekyll and Mr. Hyde.*

RUDYARD KIPLING: *Jungle Books, Kim, Stalky and Co., Just So Stories* (1902).

H. G. WELLS (1866–1946): *The Time Machine, War of the Worlds* (1898), *Love and Mr. Lewisham.* Also *Kipps* (1905), *Tono-Bungay, The New Machiavelli, Joan and Peter, God the Invisible King* (1917).

GEORGE MOORE (1852–1933): *A Mummer's Wife, Esther Waters* (1894), *The Brook Kerith.*

DRAMA

TOM ROBERTSON (1829–71): *Society* (1865), *Ours, Caste, School.*

HENRY ARTHUR JONES (1851–1929): *The Silver King, Saints and Sinners.*

ARTHUR WING PINERO (1859–1934): *Sweet Lavender, The Profligate, The Second Mrs. Tanqueray* (1893), *Trelawny of the Wells* (1898).

OSCAR WILDE: *Lady Windermere's Fan, A Woman of No Importance, An Ideal Husband, The Importance of Being Earnest.*

GEORGE BERNARD SHAW (1856–1950): Dramatic Opinions and Essays (1894–8). (See also p. 302.)

HISTORY, PHILOSOPHY, ESSAYS, CRITICISM

DAVID RICARDO (1772–1823): *Political Economy.*

THOMAS CARLYLE (1795–1881): *Sartor Resartus, French Revolution, Heroes and Hero-Worship, Past and Present, Frederick the Great.*

Contemporary Events (Contd.)

1861 Emancipation of serfs in Russia.
Post Office Savings Bank opened.
Hans Andersen's *Fairy Tales* appeared.

1862 Bismarck proclaimed "blood and iron" policy in Germany.
Maeterlinck, Belgian poet and playwright, born.

1863 First underground railway opened in London (Metropolitan Line).
Battle of Gettysburg, U.S.A.; Confederates defeated.

1865 End of Civil War in U.S.A.: Lincoln assassinated.
Salvation Army founded by William Booth.
Lewis Carroll published *Alice in Wonderland*.
Publication of Tolstoi's *War and Peace*.
Japan opened to the world.

1866 Mary Baker Eddy founded Christian Science Church.
Benedetto Croce, Italian philosopher, born.
Publication of Dostoevsky's *Crime and Punishment*, and Ibsen's *Brand*.

1867 *L'Art pour l'Art* movement founded in France.
First University Extension courses held.
Reform Bill passed.
First ship passed through Suez Canal.

1869 Girton College founded (beginning of University education for women).

1870 Franco-Prussian War broke out.
Dogma of Papal Infallibility declared by Vatican Council.

1871 William I proclaimed German Emperor at Versailles.
First exhibition of Impressionist painting in Paris.

1872 Ballot Act passed.

1873 Publication of *Round the World in Eighty Days* (Jules Verne).
Dr. David Livingstone died.

1874 International Postal Union formed at Berne, Switzerland.

1875 Thomas Mann, German novelist, born.

1876 Graham Bell invented the telephone.

1877 Proclamation of Queen Victoria as Empress of India.
Edison invented the phonograph.

1878 Hughes invented the microphone.
Congress of Berlin.
London University granted degrees to women.

1879 Gladstone's Midlothian Campaign.
Edison invented the electric bulb.

1880 St. Gotthard Tunnel completed.

1881 Revised version of *New Testament* completed.
Boer War started: British defeat at Majuba Hill.

1882 Garibaldi, Italian soldier and patriot, died.
Society for Psychical Research founded.
Phoenix Park murders in Dublin.

1883 War in the Sudan.

1884 Oxford English Dictionary began to appear.
Third Reform Bill passed.

THE VICTORIAN AGE (*Contd.*)

JOHN STUART MILL (1806–73): *Utilitarianism, On Liberty.*

JOHN HENRY NEWMAN (1801–90): *Grammar of Assent, Idea of a University.*

CHARLES DARWIN (1809–82): *Voyage of the Beagle, The Origin of Species*

HERBERT SPENCER (1820–1903): *First Principles, Principles of Biology, of Psychology, of Sociology, of Ethics.*

THOMAS BABINGTON MACAULAY (1800–59): *Essays, History of England.*

WALTER BAGEHOT (1826–77): *Physics and Politics, The English Constitution, Literary Studies, Biographical Studies.*

JOHN RUSKIN (1819–1900):. *Seven Lamps of Architecture, Stones of Venice, Unto This Last, Crown of Wild Olive, Fors Clavigera.*

JOHN ADDINGTON SYMONDS (1840–93): *Renaissance in Italy, Appreciations, Greek Studies.*

ROBERT LOUIS STEVENSON: *Travels with a Donkey in the Cevennes, Virginibus Puerisque, Familiar Studies of Men and Books.*

MATTHEW ARNOLD: *Essays in Criticism, On Translating Homer, Study of Celtic Literature, Culture and Anarchy, Literature and Dogma.*

GEORGE MEREDITH: *Essay on Comedy and the Uses of the Comic Spirit.*

Contemporary Events (Contd.)

1885 Gold discovered in Transvaal.
Dictionary of National Biography begun.
Canadian Pacific Railway completed.
Victor Hugo died.
1887 First Daimler motor-car built.
Queen Victoria's Jubilee.
1888 Local Government Act established County Councils.
Crossing of Greenland by Nansen, Norwegian explorer.
1889 Great London Dock Strike.
Eiffel Tower in Paris constructed.
1891 Free elementary education established in England.
Section of Trans-Siberian railway opened.
1894 *History of Trade Unionism* by Sidney and Beatrice Webb published.
1895 X-rays discovered by Röntgen.
Jameson Raid into the Transvaal.
Publication of *Confessions* by Verlaine.
1896 National Portrait Gallery opened.
1897 Klondyke gold rush.
Publication of *Cyrano de Bergerac* (Rostand) and *Resurrection* (Tolstoi).
1899 Boer War started.
Permanent Court of Arbitration at the Hague established.
1900 Proclamation of Commonwealth of Australia.
Boxer War in China.
1901 Queen Victoria died.

X. EDWARDIAN AND GEORGIAN PERIOD
POETRY

THOMAS HARDY: *Wessex Poems* (1898), *The Dynasts* (1904), *Satires of Circumstance, Moments of Vision.*

WILLIAM HENRY DAVIES (1871–1940): *Collected Poems* (1916–1923).

ALFRED NOYES (1880–): *Collected Poems* (1910, 1920, 1927).

RUPERT BROOKE (1887–1915): *Collected Poems* (1927).

WALTER DE LA MARE (1873–): *Songs of Childhood, The Listeners and other Poems, Collected Poems* (1942).

WILFRED WILSON GIBSON (1878–): *Collected Poems* (1926).

DAVID HERBERT LAWRENCE (1885–1930): *Love Poems and Others, Amores, New Poems* (1918).

JOHN MASEFIELD (1878–): *Collected Poems* (1938).

HAROLD MONRO (1879–1932): *Before Dawn, Trees, Strange Meetings.*

WILFRED OWEN (1893–1918): *Poems* (1931).

EDMUND BLUNDEN (1896–): *The Waggoner and Other Poems, Master of Time.*

HERBERT READ (1893–): *Collected Poems* (1935).

W. H. AUDEN (1907–): *Selected Poems* (1938).

STEPHEN SPENDER (1909–): *Poems* (1935).

C. DAY LEWIS (1904–): *Collected Poems* (1935).

THOMAS STEARNS ELIOT (1888–): *The Waste Land, Poems* (1936), *The Four Quartets.*

LOUIS MACNIECE (1907–): *Poems.*

EDITH SITWELL (1887–): *Collected Poems* (1930).

DRAMA

GEORGE BERNARD SHAW: *Widowers' Houses, Mrs. Warren's Profession, Arms and the Man, Candida, Caesar and Cleopatra, Back to Methuselah, Major Barbara, Pygmalion, Saint Joan,* etc.

JOHN GALSWORTHY (1867–1933): *The Silver Box, Strife, Justice, The Skin Game, Loyalties.*

JOHN DRINKWATER (1882–1937): *Abraham Lincoln, Mary Stuart, Cromwell.*

W. SOMERSET MAUGHAM (1874–): *Lady Frederick* (1907), *The Circle, Our Betters, East of Suez, Sheppey* (1933).

NOEL COWARD (1899–): *The Vortex, Fallen Angels, Cavalcade.*

SIR JAMES BARRIE (1860–1937): *Quality Street, The Admirable Crichton, Peter Pan, Dear Brutus, Mary Rose.*

T. S. ELIOT: *Sweeney Agonistes, The Rock, Murder in the Cathedral* (1935), *The Family Reunion* (1939), *The Cocktail Party* (1950).

JOHN MASEFIELD: *Pompey the Great, The Tragedy of Nan, Philip the King, A King's Daughter, Good Friday.*

J. M. SYNGE: *The Tinker's Wedding, The Playboy of the Western World* (1907), *Riders to the Sea.*

SEAN O' CASEY (1884–): *Juno and the Paycock, The Plough and the Stars, The Silver Tassie.*

"JAMES BRIDIE": *The Anatomist, Tobias and the Angel, Mr. Bolfry.*

Contemporary Events

1901 First wireless message sent across the Atlantic.
1902 End of the Boer War.
Death of Cecil Rhodes.
1903 Orville Wright made first aeroplane flight.
1904 *Entente Cordiale* made with France.
Russo-Japanese War.
1905 Kingdoms of Norway and Sweden separated.
Einstein published his Theory of Relativity.
1907 Dr. Maria Montessori introduced her system of child education in Rome.
Bergson published *L'Evolution créatrice*.
1908 Boy Scout Movement founded by Baden Powell.
1909 Louis Blériot made first crossing of English Channel by air.
Peary discovered the North Pole.
1910 Tolstoi died.
Florence Nightingale died.
Union of South Africa established.
1911 National Insurance introduced.
Amundsen reached the South Pole shortly in advance of Captain Scott.
1912 China became a Republic.
Suffragette agitation in England.
Strindberg, Swedish novelist and dramatist, died.
1914 Panama Canal opened.
Outbreak of the First World War.
1917 Bolshevik Revolution in Russia.
1918 Reform Bill passed, granting parliamentary franchise to women.
Armistice with Germany signed (11th November).
1919 Alcock and Brown made first direct crossing of Atlantic by air.
Lady Astor, first woman to sit in Parliament, elected.
Treaty of Versailles.
1920 First meeting of the League of Nations.
Permanent Court of International Justice established.
1922 Irish Free State inaugurated.
Fascist march on Rome; Mussolini became Prime Minister of Italy.
1923 Republic of Turkey established under Kemal Ataturk.
1924 Death of Lenin, architect of Russian revolution.
1926 General Strike in Great Britain.
1927 *The Jazz Singer*, first full-length talking film, shown.
1930 Rise of Hitler and Nazi party in Germany.
1931 Financial crisis; abandonment of Gold Standard in Great Britain.
Spanish Republic proclaimed.
1933 Hitler became German Chancellor.
Franklin Roosevelt became President of U.S.A.
1935 Italian-Abyssinian War started.
1936 Outbreak of Civil War in Spain.
Death of King George V.
Abdication of King Edward VIII.

EDWARDIAN AND GEORGIAN PERIOD (*Contd.*)

J. B. PRIESTLEY (1894–   ): *Dangerous Corner, I Have Been Here Before, Time and the Conways, Johnson over Jordan.*

W. H. AUDEN (1907–   ): *The Dog Beneath the Skin* (1935), (with Christopher Isherwood) *Ascent of F.6, On the Frontier.*

H. GRANVILLE BARKER (1877–1946): *The Voysey Inheritance, Waste, The Madras House, The Secret Life.*

FICTION

EDWARD MORGAN FORSTER (1879–   ): *Where Angels Fear to Tread, A Room with a View, Howard's End, A Passage to India.*

JAMES JOYCE (1882–1941): *Portrait of the Artist as a Young Man, Ulysses, Finnegan's Wake.*

D. H. LAWRENCE (1885–1930): *Sons and Lovers, Kangaroo, The Rainbow, Lady Chatterley's Lover, The Man Who Died.*

ALDOUS HUXLEY (1894–   ): *Crome Yellow, Antic Hay, Those Barren Leaves, Point Counter Point* (1928), *Eyeless in Gaza.*

VIRGINIA WOOLF (1882–1941): *The Voyage Out, Night and Day, Jacob's Room, Mrs. Dalloway, To the Lighthouse, Orlando, Between the Acts.*

ARNOLD BENNETT (1867–1931): *The Old Wives' Tale, Clayhanger, Hilda Lessways, Grand Babylon Hotel, Riceyman Steps.*

JOSEPH CONRAD (1857–1924): *Nigger of the Narcissus* (1897), *Youth, Typhoon, Lord Jim.*

G. K. CHESTERTON (1874–1936): *The Napoleon of Notting Hill, The Man who was Thursday, Father Brown Stories.*

J. B. PRIESTLEY: *Good Companions.*

JOHN GALSWORTHY: *The Island Pharisee* (1904), *The Country House, The Patrician, The Forsyte Saga, A Modern Comedy* (1929).

KATHERINE MANSFIELD (1889–1923): short stories—*Bliss, The Garden Parties, The Dove's Nest, etc.*

HISTORY, CRITICISM, ESSAYS, BIOGRAPHY

LYTTON STRACHEY (1880–1932): *Eminent Victorians* (1918), *Books and Characters.*

G. M. TREVELYAN (1876–   ): *History of England, Social History of England* (1944).

T. S. ELIOT: *The Sacred Wood, The Use of Poetry and the Use of Criticism.*

MAX BEERBOHM (1872–   ): *Yet Again, Zuleika Dobson, Even Now.*

W. H. HUDSON (1841–1922): *Nature in Downland, Hampshire Days, A Shepherd's Life.*

ALDOUS HUXLEY: *Ends and Means.*

Contemporary Events (Contd.)

1937 Japanese onslaught on China.
1938 Annexation of Austria by Germany.
Munich agreement between Hitler and Chamberlain.
1939 Czechoslovakia annexed by Germany.
Albania occupied by Italy.
Russo–German pact of non-aggression.
Outbreak of Second World War.
1940 Air Battle of Britain.
1941 Germany invaded Russia.
Japanese air raid on Pearl Harbour; U.S.A. entered the war.
1942 Battles of El Alamein and Stalingrad.
1943 Italian armistice; fall of Mussolini.
1944 D-day; the landings in Normandy.
1945 Atomic bombs dropped on Hiroshima and Nagasaki, Japan.
Capitulation of Germany and Japan.
Potsdam Conference.
Labour Government established in Great Britain.
1946 League of Nations dissolved.
First meeting of United Nations Assembly in New York.
1947 Nationalization of coal mines.
1948 Assassination of Mahatma Gandhi in India.
State of Israel proclaimed.
United Europe movement launched.
Western Union Treaty signed.
National Health scheme inaugurated.
1950 Korean War.

GENERAL BIBLIOGRAPHY

EDWIN MUIR: *The Present Age, from* 1914 (Cresset Press).

W. H. HUDSON: *Introduction to the Study of Literature* (Harrap).

GEORGE SAMPSON: *Concise Cambridge History of English Literature* (Cambridge University Press).

H. V. ROUTH: *English Literature and Ideas in the Twentieth Century* (Methuen).

LEGOUIS AND CAZAMIAN: *History of English Literature* (Dent).

JOHN BUCHAN: *A History of English Literature* (Nelson).

B. IVOR EVANS: *English Literature between the Wars* (Methuen).

SIR A. QUILLER-COUCH: *Studies in Literature*, I and II (Cambridge University Press).

EDMUND WILSON: *Axel's Castle; A Study of the Imaginative Literature of* 1870–1930 (Scribner's).

A. C. BRADLEY: *Oxford Lectures on Poetry* (Macmillan).

CHARLES WILLIAMS: *The English Poetic Mind* (Oxford University Press).

H. J. C. GRIERSON AND J. C. SMITH: *A Critical History of English Poetry* (Chatto & Windus).

H. J. C. GRIERSON: *The Background of English Literature* (Chatto & Windus).

TOPIC INDEX

INDEX OF AUTHORS